395

# Wedding Days

# Wedding Days

## When and How Great Marriages Began

SUSAN J. GORDON

WILLIAM MORROW AND COMPANY, INC.
NEW YORK

It is the policy of William Morrow and Company, Inc., and its imprints and affiliates, recognizing the importance of preserving what has been written, to print the books we publish on acid-free paper, and we exert our best efforts to that end.

Library of Congress Cataloging-in-Publication Data

Gordon, Susan.
Wedding days : when and how great marriages began / Susan J. Gordon.
p. cm.
Includes bibliographical references and index.
ISBN 0-688-14860-3
1. Marriage.   2. Courtship.   3. Biographies.   4. Reference.      I. Title.
HQ503.G67      1998
306.81—dc21                                                              97-13405 CIP

Printed in the United States of America

First Edition

1   2   3   4   5   6   7   8   9   10

BOOK DESIGN BY LEAH LOCOCO

www.williammorrow.com

For my husband, Ken, and in memory of my grandmother
Etta Lambert Billow. His love never lets up; hers never let me down.

# ACKNOWLEDGMENTS

MOST MARRIAGES BEGIN WITH GIANT leaps of faith; I was blessed to wed an incredibly loving and devoted man. Ken participated in every facet of this book, fully sharing (and seeming to enjoy!) all the research and work. His extraordinary energy, enthusiasm, and encouragement never wavered—in spite of countless pressures from his own work and the major "distractions" of our two sons' weddings within a six months' span. Night after night, Ken met me at the library after work and spent hours helping me discover rich and valuable material. He is a gifted and indefatigable researcher and lover of history; I might have written this book without him, but I never could have accomplished it so well or so joyously.

Thanks and my unconditional love go also to my sons and daughters-in-law—Edward and Patrice, Peter and Melissa—helpmates and devoted partners whose relationships and love have led their (unbiased) mother to predict that great things will surely be achieved in their own marriages.

Special thanks also go to my very dear friend Gail Gitman, who often dropped everything to search meticulously for much needed and sometimes obscure information, to create complicated charts, and to lend a sympathetic ear to my occasional frustrations. The lifelong love and marriages of my aunts and uncles, Muriel and Maynard Petkun and Selma and Leo Berkowitz, have always been inspirations to me. Other close friends and relatives, including Carol and Mike Dyer, RoseMarie and Jeff Foster, Marcia, Philip, and Meredith Gethin-Jones, Paul Gitman, Barbara and Jeff Gullotta, Maury and Gerry Kaplan, Elaine and Bob Klein, Barbara and Ken Leish, Roberta Meyer, Georgia and Bill Pollak, Barbara and George Quint, Pat Tomassi and members of the Westchester writers' group, also contributed useful information and endless support.

I am deeply indebted to my agent, Henry Morrison, who fell in love with the project almost as quickly as I did and helped me structure it and define my goals. Thanks also to my talented editor, Toni Sciarra, and her assistant, Katharine Cluverius, for their boundless enthusiasm and tireless dedication. Deftly and thoughtfully, Toni edited the entire manuscript, putting it into the fine shape that has resulted in this book.

# S E E I N G   L O V E

## AN INTRODUCTION

THIS BOOK IS A CELEBRATION of marriage and a toast to 366 couples throughout 1,500 years of recorded history—husbands and wives who have achieved greatness and made a difference in our lives. It focuses on the courtships and marriages of artists, composers, writers, statesmen, explorers, athletes, scientists, inventors, performers, musicians, monarchs, and philanthropists and cites their major accomplishments. Wealthy or poor, royal or obscure, they all began their marriages with timeless dreams of hope for the future and heartfelt prayers for a joyful, productive, and satisfying life together.

My earliest memories of weddings and new marriages were not stories my parents told about how they fell in love and were married, but glimpses into other people's lives. When I was about five years old, I saw a young couple driving in a blue convertible trailing tin cans and old shoes. I was riding in my father's car, a rare event since my parents had already been separated for three years and were on the verge of a divorce.

The blue convertible sped by with its "Just Married" sign stretched across the trunk. As the young man turned the steering wheel deftly with one hand, he caressed the neck of his yellow-ponytailed bride with the other. In an era before seat belts, she snuggled right beside him and closed her eyes. This must be what love looks like, I remember thinking. I must be seeing love.

A few years later my aunt and I were driving on a country road outside of Boston. It was a gloriously bright springtime afternoon, and as we passed a steeple-topped church on a hillside, the doors flew open and a bride and groom rushed out in a whirl of white. The wedding guests followed, throwing rice at the happy couple. The bride tossed her bouquet to cheering girlfriends, waved to everybody, and then hopped into a car with her new husband and drove off.

I, who had no personal experience seeing love between a man and a woman in my own home, remembered the newlyweds in the car, saw the couple dashing out of the church, and could only conclude that surely, this was love. Because if it isn't love right then, on the very day you are married . . . when is it?

Fortunately, I grew up to celebrate my own marriage to a man I continue to fall in love with after thirty-two years. I first saw Ken when I was the new girl in high school. Eight years passed before we married, after going steady, breaking up, and getting back together again. But all along I knew that Ken was the smartest, funniest, and most passionate young man I ever dated—the one I knew I'd never get tired of seeing every single morning and the one I most definitely wanted to be the father of my kids.

Neither Ken nor I came from whole families; neither of us has seen our parents grow old together. Doing research on great marriages has been meaningful to both of us; it's also been heartwarming, eye-opening, and full of surprises.

Marriage was on my mind a lot several years ago, when my two sons became engaged to wonderful young women. I thought about famous people throughout history; what kinds of marriages had they had?

Thinking about George and Martha Washington, Pierre and Marie Curie, and Ozzie and Harriet was easy, but what about other well-known people? I knew about Daniel Boone; was there a Mrs. Boone? What role did she play in her husband's trailblazing expeditions? Was there a Mrs. Dostoyevsky? Mrs. Rembrandt? Did comedian Henny Youngman really mean it when he said, "Take my wife"? And what kind of wife inspired a seventeenth-century shah to commemorate her death by building the Taj Mahal?

I also thought about great women. Who did Annie Oakley marry? Who married Grandma Moses and Betsy Ross? What kinds of marriages did writers Agatha Christie and Laura Ingalls Wilder have?

I began reading lots of biographies and I uncovered great information: Charles Darwin married his first cousin; Marc Chagall's future in-laws told their daughter she would starve if she married that worthless painter; future president Andrew Johnson's wife taught him to read and write; the original Siamese twins married two sisters . . . and fathered twenty-one children!

I also learned about significant couples who were well known in their own time but are mostly forgotten now. Few people know about the nineteenth-century English circus performer Andrew Ducrow and his bareback-riding wife, Margaret, or African-American investigative journalist Ida B. Wells and her equally committed lawyer husband, Ferdinand Barnett, or Bertha Kinsky von Suttner, who founded European pacifist organizations with her husband, Artur, and in 1905 became the first woman to win the Nobel Peace Prize. I'm happy to bring their stories to life again.

From Pocahontas to Priscilla Presley, no woman ever forgets her courtship and wedding day. Even fifty-three years after Julia Dent married Ulysses S. Grant in 1848, the former first lady still smiled and said, "Never shall I forget . . . that hot August night. . . ."

Not much has changed throughout the centuries. Brides and grooms have always had last-minute jitters; parents have always felt no one is good enough for their "perfect" child; living together is nothing new; stepparenting has always been tricky; intermarriages have always taken place; and some people don't find their ideal mate until their second or third trip to the altar.

For the most part, first meetings were unremarkable. Future sweethearts met in grammar school, college, railway cars, and art classes, at lectures, dances, and church choir rehearsals, or after a messy divorce. Introductions were made by siblings, classmates, business associates, and rivals. Some couples fished each other out of lakes, nursed each other through illnesses, or spotted each other at garden parties or across proverbial crowded rooms.

I have been pleased to discover a good number of long-lasting Broadway and Hollywood marriages, belying the myth that actors are too self-absorbed to settle down and be happy with one other person. I also enjoyed learning that many well-known figures, such as Rembrandt, Bach, and Darwin, literally thrived in the married state.

Some marriages were relatively short; others lasted more than fifty years. While it's true in many cases that only one spouse—frequently the husband—achieved greatness, it probably wouldn't have happened if his wife hadn't taken care of the house, the kids, and him, creating a satisfying, secure environment conducive to the flowering of genius.

What actually went on between husbands and wives can only be conjectured as we study their autobiographies, letters, and journals, as well as historical analyses and "facts" provided by others. Difficulties in determining the accuracy of information about someone else's life are greatly compounded when studying a marriage. Now it's not just one life we are trying to understand, but two—in a deeply complicated, extremely private relationship. All we know is what we are told or can see for ourselves; what we understand best is the work they have done—what these people have achieved and left for us and future generations.

The information in this book was collected from more than 2,000 books and other sources. Wedding dates have been determined through efforts of serious scholarship and are as exact and reliable as possible. When no firm date exists, I've selected one based on the best evidence available, and this has been noted in the entry. Sometimes different source materials present conflicting information; they might refer to the date a marriage license was issued instead of the date of the actual wedding ceremony. Other times, researchers simply made mistakes. I welcome readers' help with new information for subsequent editions.

Most stories describe how these amazing couples' marriages began, but sometimes the spotlight shines on their accomplishments. In many cases, these people were young and ambitious when they married, but they had not yet found fame in their chosen careers. Their listed names are the ones they had at the time they were wed. Since this book is about husbands and wives, children are mentioned only to make a point about the parents.

This is not a complete list of great marriages throughout history, because there wasn't enough room to include all of them! Nor is this book the last word on marital happiness. Times weren't always good, and many of these couples had their share of sadnesses. Some had extramarital affairs and some eventually were divorced. But for a variety of reasons, in most cases they stayed together, and that unique combination of marital passion, support, happiness, and peace helped him, her, or them achieve something truly wonderful.

Everyone's here—reluctant bridegrooms, frazzled brides, interfering fathers, meddling mothers, helpful aunts, and rich, controlling relatives threatening to change their wills. And century after century, in the center of all these melodramatic maelstroms are young couples bent on matrimony, proving again and again that true love "conquers all." My unending fascination with "seeing love" has caused me to search for the couples' own words and to use them whenever possible. Virtually every quotation (including those beneath their names) comes from their letters, journals, recorded conversations or published work; their words can help us all see love.

I hope these stories will inspire you to read more about these celebrated two-somes' lives. Let their favorite phrases become your good-luck expressions. Name your kids after them, use the same colors for your wedding celebrations, eat the same foods, and honeymoon in the same places.

After everything is said and done, no one is luckier than those who are lovers. "Take any streetful of people buying clothes and groceries, cheering a hero or throwing confetti and blowing tin horns" wrote the poet Carl Sandburg ten years after marrying his beloved Paula. "Tell me if the lovers are losers . . . tell me if any get more than the lovers . . ."

More than 350 years ago, Sir Richard Fanshawe told his wife, Anne: "My life and fortune shall be thine, and every thought of my heart."

You, too, should be so lucky.

# Wedding Days

# JANUARY

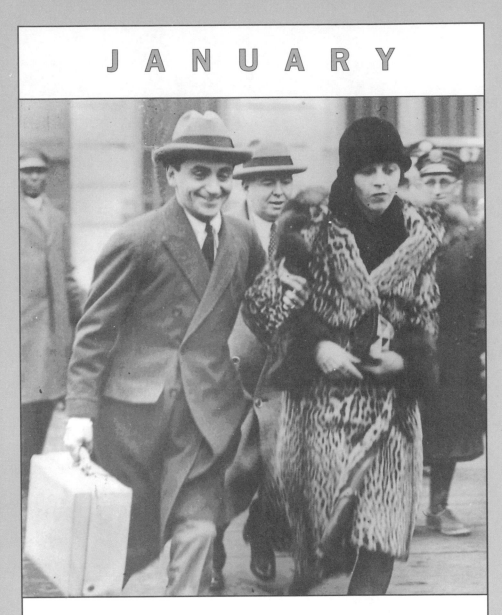

### IRVING BERLIN AND ELLIN MACKAY
*January 4, 1926*
Shortly after they eloped, the newlyweds fled reporters on an Atlantic City boardwalk.

## JAMES FENIMORE COOPER AND SUSAN DELANCEY

### *"My dearest Sue"*

"LIKE ALL THE REST OF the sons of Adam, I have bowed to the influence of the charms of a fair damsel of eighteen," James wrote shortly before he married Susan on New Year's Day in 1811. He also said his darling bride was congenial, merry, light-hearted, and well educated—"but hold a moment: it is enough she pleases *me* in the qualities of her *person* and *mind.*"

Years later, he wrote about youthful love in *The Crater.* The framed silhouette that the skipper keeps in his ship's cabin resembles a picture of Susan that has remained in the Cooper family ever since James himself probably took it with him to sea.

He had joined the navy at seventeen, after being expelled from Yale for pranks and misconduct. He met Susan on one of his furloughs, while visiting an old college friend. The well-to-do DeLanceys of Scarsdale would not have permitted just any sailor to court their lovely daughter, but they knew that the Coopers owned Otsego Hall and vast tracts of land in Cooperstown, New York.

After the wedding James became a gentleman farmer, colonel in the local militia, and part-owner of a whaling ship. He and Susan lived in Scarsdale and Cooperstown, and one night James threw down a mediocre English novel he'd been reading and told her that he could write just as well, if not better.

"You don't even like to write letters!" Susan laughed, challenging him to try. Six months later he finished his first novel, *Precaution.* Eventually James wrote thirty-two novels, including *The Deerslayer, The Last of the Mohicans,* and *The Pathfinder,* and more than a dozen other books.

He and Susan were rarely apart, and they never forgot their wedding day. Whenever they separated, even for just a short trip, they recited a brief prayer from their marriage service before they said goodbye.

## ANSEL ADAMS AND VIRGINIA ROSE BEST

*"Be yourself—I truly mean YOUR self"*

IT'S DIFFICULT TO KNOW WHAT Ansel fell in love with first at Yosemite National Park in California—the valley or Virginia Best. Her father was a landscape painter who kept an old Chickering piano in his art studio inside the park; Ansel was an accomplished pianist who gave concerts as well as lessons. He visited the Bests often, to practice his music and to photograph the scenery and the young woman who had captured his heart. By the time he was twenty-six, however, he and Virginia began to realize that photography, not music, would be his life's work.

"Know that I love you," he wrote her shortly before their wedding in 1928. Ansel also described the "acoustically correct" studio he wanted, with plenty of wall space for pictures and workrooms for him and Virginia, too. He wanted lots of friends around him, as well as "green things—and the air of the hills."

They married at Best's Studio, six years after they had met. Virginia wore her best dress, which was black. Ansel wore knickers and his "trusty basketball shoes," along with a coat and tie. The best man almost lost the wedding ring, dropping it into the snow while putting snow chains on the honeymoon car.

Both sets of parents approved wholeheartedly of the match and were delighted to attend the marriage ceremony. Their family had grown, wrote Ansel's father subsequently, having "taken into . . . our hearts one of the finest girls in the whole world."

It didn't take long for Ansel to become one of the best-known and most beloved photographers of the American West. Even today, many of his sharply focused pictures of majestic landscapes remain unparalleled and magnificent. From sunrises in the towering Sierra Nevada Mountains to moonrises over tiny western towns, his pictures are breathtaking and evocative. In 1940 Ansel helped establish the photography department at New York's Museum of Modern Art.

## JOHN MARSHALL AND MARY WILLIS AMBLER

*A lock of hair brought him back*

JOHN'S FATHER LIKED BOASTING ABOUT his son, an intrepid colonel fighting in the Revolutionary War. His Yorktown, Virginia, neighbors—especially the Ambler sisters—were impressed until John came home on a furlough and they saw he was only an unsophisticated frontiersman in buckskin, friendly and pleasant but definitely unpolished.

Fourteen-year-old "Polly" Ambler was dazzled, however, and vowed to seek him out at a society ball. She knew that her mother, Rebecca Burwell Ambler, had once been courted by the young law student Thomas Jefferson but had rejected him to marry Polly's father, an older and more established suitor, instead. Polly sensed that John also had a potential for greatness, and she hoped he'd wait for her until she grew up.

John was twenty-seven when he came home a few years later. As a war hero, lawyer, and member of the Virginia House of Delegates, he could have won one of many wealthy and eligible young widows. Instead he chose Polly.

He proposed to her shortly before her seventeenth birthday. She teased him and declined, thinking he would ask again. But John was too deeply hurt to speak, and Polly burst into tears as she watched him ride away on his horse. Fortunately, a cousin who witnessed the incident surreptitiously managed to snip off a small lock of Polly's light brown hair, race after John, and give it to him. He took it as a sign that Polly had changed her mind—which, of course, she had.

They married soon afterward in 1783, in an Ambler cousin's home in Hanover County. Polly wore an off-the-shoulder white brocaded dress with shirred sleeves. Around her neck was a fine gold locket containing that precious ringlet of her hair.

Eighteen years later, John became Chief Justice of the United States.

## IRVING BERLIN AND ELLIN MACKAY

### *"Always"*

*"Irving Berlin Weds Ellin Mackay—Elopers Speed Away, Rich Father Ignored for Composer by Society Bud . . . Broadway's King of Jazz . . . crossed labyrinths of social and religious difference and carried off the youngest daughter of Clarence H. Mackay, multimillionaire . . ."* headlines blared in 1926.

THE THIRTY-SEVEN-YEAR-OLD RUSSIAN-JEWISH IMMIGRANT proposed to twenty-one-year-old Ellin on New Year's Eve. Four days later, on a foggy, fairly mild Monday morning, she put on a gray suit and an orange hat, slipped out of her father's apartment, and took her first subway ride downtown to the marriage chapel at City Hall, where she married Irving. They spent a few days in Atlantic City after the wedding and then sailed to Europe for a two-month honeymoon.

"Don't think our marriage was sudden," Ellin told reporters. She'd been interested in Irving ever since she first heard his music. But love meant everything to her, she declared. "I'm happy because I've done exactly what my heart told me to do."

Ellin's father made no public statements, although he was hounded by the press. But he drew up a new will, cutting his daughter out of her share of his $10-million estate. After the stock market crash of 1929, the fortune was worthless.

Irving gave Ellin much more—the copyright to his new song, "Always," which he had dedicated to her for a wedding gift. Eventually it was worth hundreds of thousands of dollars, as were many other songs she inspired him to write, such as "Blue Skies," "Cheek to Cheek," and "Remember."

Clarence Mackay didn't speak to his son-in-law for years. Although he mellowed after he lost his wealth, he was never comfortable with his daughter's marriage to a Tin Pan Alley Jewish songwriter. Years later, Ellin liked to say, "Certainly, I married out of my social order. I married up."

## ETHELBERT NEVIN AND ANNE PAUL

*"My melodies are you"*

"THE HAPPIEST EVENT OF HIS life was his marriage, on the fifth of January, 1888, to Miss Anne Paul. . . . Their lives flow along . . . happily because of the love and devotion they bear to one another," wrote "Bert's" mother several years after the wedding at St. Peter's Episcopal Church in Pittsburgh. Guests were ushered into "a veritable Christmas forest" filled with holiday trees and overhanging boughs as a choir of children and adults marched in pairs down the center aisle, singing the bridal chorus from *Lohengrin.* Bert's wedding gift to Anne was his new song, "Oh! That We Two Were Maying!"

He had quit college eight years earlier and headed for Boston, the center of American music at that time. Although his father objected, his mother, also a musician, never doubted her son's choice of a career. One day he would become a concert pianist and composer. Bert's first collection of melodies was published within a year of his marriage, by Gustav Schirmer's Boston Music Company. Many of his best-loved pieces, including the poignant scores for Eugene Field's famous poems "Wynken, Blynken and Nod" and "Little Boy Blue" were inspired by his love for Anne and their two children.

In a contemporary newspaper article, novelist Willa Cather described visiting the Nevins and listening to Bert play. Anne, she believed, was a good deal like her husband's music, with the same "idealism and delicate sympathy and sweetness." Bert agreed with Cather. "My life is yours and yours alone," he wrote Anne afterwards. "My melodies are you; my harmony is you!" He was working on a piece called "Love Song," which began:

> *Thy presence brings to me sweet rest,*
> *Thy hands bring soothing to my brow,*
> *Thy words such sympathy avow,*
> *Thy going leaves me all unblest.*
> *Abide with me.*

## GEORGE WASHINGTON AND MARTHA DANDRIDGE CUSTIS

*His "agreeable consort"*

AMERICA'S MOST FAMOUS GEORGE AND Martha probably met at a dinner party in Williamsburg, Virginia, where the wealthy young widow lived with her son and daughter. George was twenty-six; Martha was a year older. Remarriage was not in her best interests, because it meant relinquishing control over her late husband's estate. But Martha wished for a loving and energetic partner and a good stepfather for her children.

When not away at war, George had been living alone at Mount Vernon. He was 6'2" tall and tended to be shy. Martha was quite short, and she enjoyed social gatherings. She also was intelligent, affable, and a good listener. George's size might intimidate others, but Martha thought nothing of pulling him down by his coat lapels when she had something important to say.

They were married in 1759 at St. Peter's Church, near Martha's home. She wore a white quilted silk and satin dress and was driven to the church in a coach drawn by six horses. George wore his regimental regalia and rode beside Martha on his horse.

Shortly before the wedding, George resigned his military commission and planned to settle down at Mount Vernon as a gentleman farmer. He wrote, "I am now . . . fixd at this seat with an agreeable consort . . . and hope to find more happiness in retirement than I ever experienc'd amidst a wide and bustling World." In time he would reenter that "world," however, as commander-in-chief of the Continental army and then as president of the world's first constitutional democracy when he was fifty-seven years old.

George had been a lucky man in battle; during the French and Indian War, two horses had been shot out from under him and at least four bullets had struck his coat, although he remained unharmed. Martha had been lucky, too. She had married "well" the first time. Now she had "done well" again, although she didn't know it. Yet.

## GEORGE BURNS AND GRACIE ALLEN

*"Say goodnight, Gracie"*

BEFORE GEORGE AND GRACIE BECAME a comedy team, they'd both been working in vaudeville—she as a dancer and he as a song-and-dance man. George had also been part of a roller-skating act. But in the 1920s, their humorous routine became their ticket to fame, with Gracie as the scatterbrained wife and George as the patient, reflective, and always somewhat amused straight man and husband. Earning five dollars a day on the well-known Orpheum circuit, they delighted audiences across the United States and eventually performed on radio and television and in motion pictures.

George proposed to Gracie in San Francisco on Christmas Eve, 1925. They were married two weeks later in Cleveland. For twenty dollars he bought his bride a ring, which surprised him by changing colors the longer it stayed in his pocket! Gracie became sentimentally attached to that ring and always wore it, even when she and George could afford more expensive jewelry.

Privately, he called her "Googie" and she called him "Nat" or "Nattie," because his real name was Nathan Birnbaum. George wrote many books about his life with Gracie. In *Gracie: A Love Story*, he noted, "In our marriage—I suspect in every marriage—the really important things become, 'How do you feel?' 'Is the soup hot?' 'Want to see a movie tonight?' Those are the things that keep a marriage together."

Gracie adored George and projected her characteristically zany, cockeyed confusion when she described him to Blanche, their friend and neighbor on *The George Burns and Gracie Allen Show* on television: "George has more sex appeal in his whole body than most men have in their little finger."

Every show ended the same way: He'd tell her "Say good night, Gracie," and she'd reply "Good night, Gracie."

## HENRI MATISSE AND AMELIE PARAYRE

*He always loved the way she looked*

AMELIE WAS A DRESSMAKER AND milliner in Paris when she met Henri, and she continued working after they married in 1898 so he could keep on painting. Right after the wedding they went to London to visit the art museums; then they traveled to Toulouse and Corsica to visit her family. They spent a year in the south of France, where Henri fell in love with the Mediterranean light and bright colors that he painted over and over again throughout his long career.

Returning to Paris, Amelie continued working at her shop. Henri painted in their small apartment and in nearby parks, and studied sculpture at night. Periodically, he found work painting theatrical scenery. One year he painted miles of laurel leaves along the cornices of the Grand Palais of Paris exhibition hall.

Amelie was "very lovely . . . erect, with a good carriage and the possessor of beautiful dark hair that grew charmingly, especially at the nape of the neck," Henri wrote years after they married. He also admired her "pretty throat and very handsome shoulders." She was his model for the bright pink-faced woman with red hair in "The Green Line," "The Woman with the Hat," "The Guitarist," and many other works.

Henri worked feverishly and slept restlessly; when he woke up in the middle of the night, Amelie would talk softly or read to him until he fell asleep again. "Despite the fact that she was timid and reserved, she was a person of great kindness, force and gentleness," he said.

Amelie never forgot one of Henri's gifts, which he gave her when they had little money. He bought her a mounted butterfly with iridescent blue wings, saying it was because the beautiful color reminded him of the intense and magnificent azure light of the Mediterranean and their first year of marriage, when they lived beside the sea.

## LOUISE DILWORTH BEATTY AND SIDNEY HOMER

*"Two musical waifs threw their fortunes together"*

TWENTY-TWO-YEAR-OLD MISS BEATTY WAS DETERMINED to learn "all about music" when she came to Sidney's studio for singing lessons in 1893. She thought he was extremely bright and handsome, and he was enchanted by her demeanor and voice. "It was not like the contralto voices I had heard. . . . It was low but it had the sparkle and the brilliance of a great dramatic soprano," he wrote years later in their autobiography. Eventually she became an internationally famous American contralto singer.

Sidney began taking meals at the boardinghouse where Louise lived, on Boylston Street in a Boston suburb. They talked incessantly about music and attended concerts and operas together. She inspired him to write music, and he encouraged her to sing.

Their wedding in January 1895 was followed by a reception at her sister's house in Arlington, Massachusetts. Driving to catch a train to "the snowy wilds" of the Baldpate Inn, they wondered why strangers on the streets waved and smiled at them, until they noticed a little shoe—announcing they were "just married"—that had been tied to their coach's roof by one of the wedding guests.

After their daughter was born in 1896, the Homers sailed for France, where they spent borrowed money and a small inheritance on advanced vocal training for the new mother. Louise deftly turned her wedding dress into an evening gown for concert performances in Paris. In 1898, she made her European operatic debut in *La Favorite*, while Sidney and their daughter listened and applauded.

Although Sidney continued to compose, he was primarily devoted to his wife's singing career. Louise rarely missed a performance—despite having six children! She sang Emilia in *Otello* at New York's Metropolitan Opera House in 1902, only five weeks after giving birth to a son. By 1909 she had made more than fifty recordings.

## JULES VERNE AND HONORINE DE VIANE MOREL

*Flying to the moon was less daunting
than getting married*

"THE MERE THOUGHT OF INVITING friends to the marriage service makes my hair stand on end in horror!" wrote the future author of books about fearless exploits under the sea and incredible trips to the moon. In 1857, Jules's farfetched fantasies seemed less frightening to him than being married before a crowd of people.

Honorine was a twenty-five-year-old widow with two small children when she and twenty-nine-year-old Jules met at her sister's wedding. They fell in love quickly, but Jules had not yet realized his creative genius as a writer. Although he'd sold some short stories and written a few plays, he worked primarily as a stockbroker.

They married at the Church of St. Eugene in Paris. The groom was somewhat dazed and later wrote, "I didn't know where I was, and I handed out money to everyone. . . . Someone shouted for the bridegroom! They meant me!"

A few days later he and Honorine stood before the statue of Venus de Milo in the Louvre, and he introduced his bride to "the only woman of whom you need ever be jealous."

Long before polar explorations, spaceships, airplanes, helicopters, escalators, automobiles, and motion pictures were realities, Jules was imagining them. Honorine didn't complain when he came home at night from the stock exchange and sat down to write. She enjoyed reading his manuscripts and sometimes rescued "failures" he had hurled into the fireplace.

After five years Jules sold *Five Weeks in a Balloon* to a publisher. He quit his job (which he hated) and continued writing more than sixty-five books, including *Journey to the Center of the Earth, 20,000 Leagues Under the Sea,* and *Around the World in 80 Days,* as well as essays, short stories, geographical works, plays, and librettos.

## DR. BENJAMIN RUSH AND JULIA STOCKTON

*"my Sweet Julia"*

BENJAMIN AND JULIA FIRST MET in 1763, when he was an eighteen-year-old student at Princeton and she was four years old, apparently lost in the college commencement crowd. He recognized the little Stockton girl immediately and carried her to her father's house, "listening with great pleasure to her prattling all the way." Benjamin and Julia didn't meet again for twelve years; by then, he had become a surgeon and physician and a delegate to the Continental Congress in Philadelphia.

Julia's father, also a congressional delegate, invited Dr. Rush home to dinner and reintroduced him to his daughter. That evening Julia charmed Benjamin by singing Scottish tunes. She was sixteen, he later reminisced, with "a complexion composed of white and red, a countenance at the same time soft and animated, a voice mild and musical." He visited the Stocktons' estate, Morven, every week and gently prodded his Philadelphia patients to please pay his bills; after all, he was planning to be married!

After a wedding at Morven in 1776, the Rushes settled down on Walnut Street in Philadelphia. A few months later Julia visited her family. Benjamin missed her terribly. "My loveliest girl," he wrote. "I think, write, talk, work, love—all, all—only for you."

That summer, Benjamin and other Continental Congress delegates signed the Declaration of Independence. The subsequent years were hard: there was a long, painful war and many illnesses, including a yellow fever epidemic that paralyzed Philadelphia in 1793. Julia and Benjamin corresponded constantly whenever they were apart. She was his most sincere and trusted friend, as well as "the dear right side of my heart."

Shortly before their wedding, Benjamin had asked the artist Charles Willson Peale to paint Julia's portrait. In it she is elegantly seated, plucking lute strings. Probably she is singing a simple Scottish tune to delight her beloved husband.

## CHARLES WILLSON PEALE AND RACHEL BREWER

*Her face was the kind "that painters love to imitate"*

WHEN CHARLES WAS THIRTEEN, HE quit school and became a saddler's apprentice in Annapolis, Maryland. He had already shown artistic talent, drawing complicated designs for his widowed mother's fine needlework and making pictures on glass with colored inks. The saddler taught him how to carve leather and wood, enabling Charles to set up his own shop soon after he and Rachel were married in 1762. Neither of them suspected that one day he would paint the portraits of virtually every famous citizen in the newly established United States of America.

Rachel was the fourteen-year-old sister of Charles's friend John Brewer, who lived by the South River. On the night Charles first met Rachel, he showed up unexpectedly after dark. "Go around the back, you impudent baggage!" Rachel called when Charles knocked on the front door. She thought he was an itinerant tradesman until her brother rushed out to greet him, but Charles quickly accepted her apologies when he looked into her dark brown eyes.

They struggled financially during the first years of their marriage because Charles owed money to creditors who had helped him set up his business. Besides saddlery, he learned how to upholster furniture and paint signs. Then Charles bought his first art book and supplies, after being inspired by the work of portrait painters he met in Philadelphia. Whenever he sold someone a saddle, he offered to paint the customer's portrait, too. Eventually a group of Maryland gentlemen were so impressed with Charles's self-taught skills that they sent him to London to study art. When he returned to Maryland, the years of struggle were over.

Charles never tired of painting pictures of his beautiful Rachel. They named their sons Raphael, Rembrandt, Titian, and Rubens—inspiring them to become painters, too.

## SIR KENELM DIGBY AND VENETIA STANLEY

*"Two hearts with mutual desire"*

TWO YEARS AFTER KENELM AND Venetia were secretly married in 1625, the future English naval commander, natural scientist, and diplomat began writing his *Private Memoirs*. He called himself "Theagenes" and his beloved Venetia "Stelliana." Their story, in the form of an allegorical romance, was first published 200 years later.

Childhood friends, they had played near the Digbys' Buckinghamshire estate, but Kenelm's mother disliked Venetia and encouraged her son to go abroad when he was seventeen. Before his departure, he and Venetia stole away from a hunting party and spent a passionate afternoon in a secluded wood. Her eyes were hazel, her cheeks rose pink, and her face framed by "heartbreaker" curls. There could be no other woman in Kenelm's life, he swore. Exclamations of love, rapturous kisses, locks of hair, and a diamond ring were exchanged.

At a masked ball in Angers, Marie de Médicis, the middle-aged queen mother of Louis XIII, took a liking to Kenelm and aggressively tried to seduce him. Escaping her clutches, he fled to Italy and circulated rumors of his death. He also wrote to Venetia, telling her the truth. Unfortunately, Kenelm's letter miscarried; others were either lost or intercepted by his mother.

For two years Venetia thought Kenelm was dead. Eventually she moved to London and became engaged to someone else. Kenelm howled when he found out and threw a bracelet made of Venetia's hair into the fire. Why didn't she wait? Had she doubted his love? He returned to England, vowing never to see her, but when their paths crossed accidentally, he was hooked again: "The sun seemed to grow pale at her appearance, as being dazzled by a greater light than its own."

Venetia was furious, believing he had tricked her. They fought and separated. A few weeks later Kenelm slipped into her bed and awakened her with love. Soon afterward they were married.

*Date approximate.

## JACK BENNY AND SADIE MARKS

*A great team*

THE FORMER BENJAMIN KUBELSKY MARRIED his beloved Sadie at a friend's apartment in the Clayton Hotel in Waukegan, Illinois, in 1927. Sadie fainted right after the rabbi pronounced them husband and wife, and it took an hour and a half to revive her. Then they called Sadie's folks in California, who wished the new couple luck but doubted the marriage would last.

After a quick celebration, the newlyweds raced to Chicago, where Jack had a part in *The Great Temptations*. Sadie spent the first part of their wedding night sitting in the audience watching Jack on stage. "But I was so tired from all the hectic running around during the week . . . I fell asleep long before the first curtain," she wrote in *Jack Benny: A Biography*.

The couple first met in Vancouver, British Columbia, where Jack was performing. His friend Zeppo Marx (of the famous Marx Brothers) invited him to a Passover seder at the Markses', Zeppo's distant relatives. Fourteen-year-old Sadie flipped for twenty-seven-year-old Jack right away, but he forgot about her until they went out on a blind date five years later. By then she was selling hosiery in a department store and was "exquisitely lovely," he recalled. Too shy to talk about romance, the lovesick entertainer bought silk stockings by the gross instead.

Eventually Jack achieved stardom on radio and television shows, with Sadie playing his devoted wife, "Mary Livingstone." Although Jack portrayed a violin-playing, self-deprecating skinflint, he actually was extremely generous, kind, and sentimental. Sadie was just like him.

Before their wedding, Jack's father had his late wife's wide gold wedding ring cut into two narrow bands—one for Jack's wife and the other for his sister, who was also getting married. Sadie wore that precious ring forever. "Until the day Jack died, he was . . . holding my hand," she wrote. "Jack thought I was everything; I thought he was everything."

## DANNY THOMAS AND ROSE MARIE CASSANITI

*Making room for Danny*

ROSE'S ITALIAN PARENTS DIDN'T LIKE the "Turk" their seventeen-year-old daughter had met in Detroit, where they both were entertainers on *The Happy Hour Club* radio show. Marry him, her father warned, and you'll find yourself living in a tent!

Danny (whose real, Lebanese name was Amos Jahoob) thought the petite dark-haired singer was a knockout, so he walked a mile out of his way each day just to hop on board her streetcar and ride with her. Rose knew he had very little money and burst into tears when he spent his last nickel buying her a candy bar.

They were married by an Italian priest in a Belgian church on Mack Avenue in Detroit in 1936. But joy was mitigated by sadness: Danny lost his job. Ready to quit show business, he got a chance to perform in Chicago after praying to Saint Jude, patron saint of lost causes. Danny became a nightclub emcee, USO performer, and movie actor, but being a comedian suited him best and brought him fame and financial success.

Danny often claimed that his three kids—including Margaret Julia, who grew up to be Marlo Thomas—created the title for his hit television show, *Make Room for Daddy,* which ran from 1953 to 1964. Just like the fictional character he portrayed, their own father was an entertainer on the road a lot. Whenever Danny was away, the kids slept with their mother in their parents' bedroom. When he came home, it was "make room for Daddy!"

Twenty-five years after Rose and Danny married, he stood outside his mansion with his family, watching celebrities and friends at the silver anniversary party he and Rose were hosting. Pointing to the very large, luxurious tent suspended over the swimming pool, Danny couldn't resist reminding his father-in-law of his dour prediction, made so long ago.

## LAFCADIO HEARN AND SETSU KOIZUMI

*Coming home, in a foreign land*

TWENTY-FIVE-YEAR-OLD SETSU, THE DAUGHTER OF a samurai, became Lafcadio's inspiration and constant source of love. When Lafcadio first arrived in Japan in 1890, he was a restless, shy, and insecure journalist, essayist, and novelist, born in Greece and educated in England and France. He had gone to the United States as a young man but never felt at home anywhere until he came to the Orient. Entranced by the beauty, solitude, and ancient customs of Japan, he was forty when he began teaching Western literature there in 1890.

As soon as Setsu met Lafcadio, she was deeply impressed by his sensitivity, kindness and honesty. He "was an extremely honest man," she wrote. "He did not have the least evil in his mind. . . . During his childhood he had always been teased by malicious people until he cried. The keening of his sensibility was astonishing."

They married some time in January, 1891, in a traditional Japanese ceremony that included an exchange of rice wine before witnesses. As a proper Japanese son-in-law, Lafcadio accepted the responsibility of caring for his wife's parents, as well as for his own wife and subsequent children. They lived in a traditional Japanese "birdcage house" on a lake in Matsue. "There is no such thing in Japan as privacy," he wrote. "There are no secrets. Every earthly thing a man does is known to everybody, and life is extravagantly, astoundingly frank." He began dressing and acting more and more like a native. Eventually he became a Japanese citizen, adopting the name Koizumi Yakumo.

Most literary biographers believe Lafcadio produced his best works in Japan because of his sympathetic observations of Asian life. He revived interest in Japanese folktales and was instrumental in bringing Japanese philosophy and art to Western audiences.

*Date approximate.

## ALEXANDER CALDER AND LOUISA JAMES

*Passionate about art, and Louisa*

THE NIGHT BEFORE THEIR 1931 wedding in Concord, Massachusetts, "Sandy" showed Louisa's relatives some of the wire sculptures he had made of circus animals that could oscillate, roll, hop, or twitch. Some people were shocked; others were amused and wondered just who was this young man Louisa was marrying? When the reverend arrived the next day, he apologized for missing the show. "But you are here for the circus, today," Sandy said wryly.

Although he was the son and grandson of artists, Sandy didn't intend to become one, too. After graduating from Stevens Tech in New Jersey, he tried a few "regular" jobs for a while, but when his parents offered to pay for drawing classes at New York's Art Students League, Sandy finally found his passion.

Inspired by Mondrian's shapes, Miró's forms, and other abstract art, Sandy began making stationary structures, called "stabiles," and sculptures that moved, called "mobiles."

He met Louisa on a transatlantic voyage. Her father was aloof and unimpressed with the young man who called himself a "wire sculptor," but back home, Louisa invited him to their Cape Cod summerhouse. Later she visited his Greenwich Village studio and was fascinated by his sculptures and drawings. One day she would create magnificent hooked rugs based on Sandy's designs.

They fell in love quickly but waited two years until Sandy—who traveled back and forth from Paris to see Louisa—was selling enough art to feel financially secure. Shortly before the wedding, he gave her a gold ring he had designed for her.

They sailed for Paris and lived in Sandy's small apartment at 7, Villa Brune. Louisa quickly got used to the contraptions Sandy hung around their home. All the door latches had been rigged with strings and wires; from the bathtub he could open the front door, just by moving his hand!

## WASHINGTON ROEBLING AND EMILY WARREN

*"A strong tower to lean upon"*

WASHINGTON AND EMILY MET AT a Union army officer's ball during the Civil War, ten years before he and his father designed and began building New York City's Brooklyn Bridge.

"Miss Emily Warren . . . has captured your brother Washy's heart," he wrote his sister back home in Troy, New York. To Emily he said, "I think we will be a pair of lovers all our lifetime."

They were both twenty-six when they married in Cold Spring, New York, soon after Washington's honorable discharge in 1865. For a while they lived in Ohio, where the Roeblings built the Cincinnati and Covington suspension bridge. Afterwards they studied steel mills and bridges in Europe, and Emily learned about engineering. Then the Roeblings won the contract to build what would be called "The Eighth Wonder of the World."

During the fourteen years it took to construct the Brooklyn Bridge over the East River, the elder Roebling died and Washington became chief engineer. Tragically, he contracted "the bends" in 1879, after staying underwater too long in one of the caisson chambers. Bedridden and weak, he could no longer supervise completion of this mammoth project.

"At first, I thought I would succumb," he later wrote. "But I had a strong tower to lean upon, my wife, a woman of infinite tact and wisest counsel."

Emily became her husband's spokesperson, inspector, and messenger, consulting with workmen and bringing them instructions. In an eloquent and impassioned plea, she convinced the board of trustees not to replace Washington with another chief engineer.

Washington supervised the construction process from the bay window of their home at 110 Columbia Heights in Brooklyn. On May 24, 1883, the bridge was completed. Crowds cheered, bands marched, and fireworks soared over the water. Dignitaries, including President Chester A. Arthur and Governor Grover Cleveland, congratulated the Roeblings personally. Their parlor was filled with refreshments and flowers; some people said the celebration resembled a wedding.

### FRANCIS SCOTT KEY AND MARY TAYLOE LLOYD

*The sweetest smile*

THE FUTURE AUTHOR OF "The Star-Spangled Banner" was a twenty-two-year-old Virginia lawyer in 1802 when he married Mary at Chase House, her family's mansion in Annapolis, Maryland. Always a poet at heart, Francis fell in love with Mary soon after his uncle Philip introduced them. Mary's golden hair, merry dark eyes, and sweet disposition inspired her beau to pen some sonnets. In "To Mary," Francis wished,

> *Perhaps she'll value more my love,*
> *Perhaps give more of hers to me,*
> *Perhaps may greet me with a smile*
> *More sweet, if smile more sweet can be.*

After their wedding they moved to Washington, D.C., where Francis joined Uncle Philip's law firm. They went home for Francis's sister's wedding to Roger B. Taney, who eventually became a Supreme Court justice.

The Keys remained with their children in their Georgetown home on Bridge Street throughout most of the War of 1812, even during an oppressively hot summer when the British attacked and burned the city. When a prominent doctor friend was imprisoned on a British ship anchored near Fort McHenry in Baltimore harbor, Francis and another volunteer went to negotiate Dr. Beane's release. Afterwards the British prevented the three Americans from departing until after the fort was bombarded.

The American flag waved all day over the fort, until darkness fell and it could be seen no longer. At "dawn's early light" in the smoke of battle, Francis stood on the deck of a ship and began jotting down the words of what would become America's most patriotic song. He continued writing at home, shaping his words to fit the melody of "Anacreon in Heaven." A few weeks later his poem appeared in a Baltimore newspaper. The editors accurately predicted that his song was "destined long to outlast the occasion" that had produced it.

## RICHARD E. BYRD AND MARIE AMES

*He named a new land after her*

WHEN RICHARD AND MARIE WERE growing up in Virginia, the future aviator and polar explorer often told her about famous adventurers who had "conquered" mountains, oceans, and faraway lands. Someday, Richard vowed, he would explore the North Pole. In 1900, when he was thirteen, he visited a family friend in the Philippines, becoming the youngest person to travel around the world alone.

He went to Virginia Military Institute and then to Annapolis, where his athletic career was ruined by serious leg injuries, but Marie's "TLC" helped heal his disappointments. Why not become a flyer? she suggested when they learned that Admiral Peary had reached the North Pole on foot. She told him he could explore far-off lands from the air, mapping out huge areas still unexplored.

Marie and Richard married in 1915, when he was a naval attaché stationed in Washington, D.C., during World War I. His brothers, Tom and Harry, were best men at the wedding. (Like Richard, they subsequently married their childhood sweethearts and were best men at each other's weddings, too.)

Richard's greatest achievements began in the 1920s, when he became the first man to fly over the regions of both the North and South Poles. He also piloted the first airmail flight across the Atlantic and organized the first full-scale exploration of Antarctica. Leading a group of scientists, reporters, and photographers across vast wastelands of ice and snow, the explorers established "Little America" as their base of future operations. Richard's expedition went on to discover and claim new regions in Antarctica under the flag of the United States.

When Richard established "Marie Byrd Land" in 1929, he named it for the woman "who has backed and helped me every foot of the way, who has shouldered much of the burden . . . and whose understanding has made my many expeditions possible."

## CASPAR DAVID FRIEDRICH AND CAROLINE BOMMER

*With Caroline, "more time is spent eating,
drinking, sleeping, joking, laughing"*

CASPAR WAS A RESPECTED FORTY-FOUR-YEAR-OLD German Romantic painter when he married Caroline, who was twenty-five. He'd always been a serious man whose early experiences with death and loneliness inspired much of his art. Caroline brought great joy into his life, but his works remained introspective and filled with allegory and symbolism.

They married in 1818 in Dresden, where Caspar was a member of the Academy of Art, and Caroline became her husband's primary model. He painted her standing on faraway fields and waving goodbye from a ship heading toward a distant port. Her figure dominates "Woman Before the Setting Sun"; we see her from the back, facing the sun which has dropped behind a mountain. Caroline's arms are spread out; both she and the sun are the givers of light and of life. Probably Caroline is already pregnant. In 1819 their first child, Emma, would be born.

"On the day Caspar is painting air, he may not be spoken to!" said Caroline, who became her husband's dearest friend and lover. She understood his great need for solitude and the long walks he often took in the moonlight. Caspar believed that God was everywhere and that Nature should be revered. At Christmastime they decorated their home with evergreen branches, rather than cut down a tree unnecessarily.

In the 1830s he painted "Evening Star." In the golden tones of late afternoon, Caroline crosses an open field with one of their daughters, and their son, Gustav Adolf, stretches his arms toward the sky.

"Close your physical eye," Caspar suggested, "so that you first see your picture with your spiritual eye. Then bring to light what you have seen in the dark so that it is passed on to others from the outside to the inside."

## SIR RICHARD BURTON AND ISABEL ARUNDELL

*"One soul in two bodies"*

AT THIRTY, RICHARD WAS TALL and broad, with thick dark hair and arched eyebrows. His head was leonine and his black eyes were piercing and magnetic. He was half-Irish, half-English, but he looked quite exotic.

He first met Isabel by chance, on the ramparts of the French city of Boulogne, when she was eighteen and traveling with her mother and sisters. The dashing and mysterious English officer's glance was mesmerizing. Hadn't a fortune-teller told her, "You will cross the sea and be in the same town with your Destiny and not know it?"

Neither one spoke, but Richard stared at Isabel with his dark, penetrating eyes. He did not know about the Gypsy's predictions, or that Isabel would always save the gloves and sash she wore a few nights later when they danced together at a society ball.

Soon afterwards Richard left for Mecca disguised as an Arab merchant. No white man had visited Mecca before, and he wrote about his travels in books that brought him fame. Future works would include translations of *The Arabian Nights* and *Kama Sutra,* in which he restored much of the passion and eroticism missing from other versions.

Isabel's conventional Victorian mother opposed her daughter's infatuation, but Isabel would not give up. "If Richard and I never marry," she wrote, "God will cause us to meet in the next world; we cannot be parted; we belong to each other." Years passed; Isabel rejected other suitors and promised Richard she would wait for him. On he went—from Mecca to Medina, to India and the American West— until at last he returned to her.

They married in 1861, eleven years after their first encounter. "My darling," Isabel said, "I have read every word you ever wrote, and I would rather have a crust and a tent with *you* than be queen of all the world!"

## EDWARD THE CONFESSOR AND EDITH GODWINE

### *aka Eadward and Eadgyth*

EDITH WOULD HAVE BEEN THE first to say it wasn't easy being married to someone who was "holier than thou." Still, clerics had given the chubby albino king of England his saintly nickname, and he tried his best to live up to it.

Everyone was glad when Edward ascended to the throne, replacing that wretched Dane Harthacanute who had treated England shabbily. Once England was back in the hands of a native-born king, Edward decided to seek a good wife.

Edith's father, Godwine, the pushy and powerful earl of Wessex, introduced Edward to his eldest daughter. Edward thought that the twenty-four-year-old maiden was bright and beautiful, as well as suitably God-fearing. She thought he was affable and gentle, although a bit pale.

They married on a Wednesday in 1045, and straightaway Edith was crowned. As part of her "morning gift," which brides customarily received after the wedding night, Edward gave her Winchester and Essex.

Most of the time their kingdom was at peace. Edward and Edith devoted themselves primarily to religion and supervised early construction of Westminster Abbey. Edith gave grammar lessons to local scholars and was also an accomplished spinner and embroiderer. She stitched elaborate robes for Edward. The king admired her work profusely but usually hung the garments in the back of his closet. A creature of habit, he preferred putting on his plain old robes over and over again, confessing softly that Edith's were a bit too showy.

When the monarchs didn't produce an heir, rumors and speculation arose. Some said that Edward and Edith were too pious to find time for sex, others said they didn't like sex, and some silly fools said they never had sex at all! But Edward and Edith, like every wise couple, kept their private life private.

## KING EDWARD III AND PHILIPPA OF HAINAULT

*"Hay, hay, the White Swan,*
*by God's soul—I am thy man!"*

AFTER PHILIPPA'S UNCLE AND HIS Dutch mercenaries fought with Edward's troops against the Scots in Northumberland, he invited the fourteen-year-old future king and his mother to drop by sometime for a visit.

Perfect timing, thought Queen Isabella, a forceful and bossy woman. She'd been considering possible brides for her son; why not the flaxen-haired thirteen-year-old daughter of the wealthy and powerful Count William of Hainault, Holland, and Zeeland? There were three other sisters, equally apple-cheeked and pretty, but Edward preferred Philippa. Like other Plantagenets, he was fair-haired, blue-eyed, and tall. Philippa thought he looked like an angel.

Back in England, Isabella coerced her husband, Edward II, to abdicate. Young Edward was crowned in January 1327, and that fall he and Philippa were married by proxy in her Flemish home. In December the bride sailed to England for a rousing reception in London and a ride across snow-covered country roads to York, where the archbishop formalized her marriage to Edward in 1328. Edward didn't remain under his mother's wicked thumb much longer. By the time he was eighteen, he had executed her paramour and forced her into retirement.

*"Honi soit qui mal y pense"* (Evil to him who evil thinks), said Edward, making it the motto of the Order of the Garter. He had so much confidence in Philippa, he made her regent whenever he went overseas. In 1346 she assembled her own army and drove back more invading Scots. She could be bellicose, and also just; after Edward laid siege to Calais in France, Philippa persuaded him to rescind the executions of six town leaders.

Edward would be the first English king to make women an integral part of court life. He and Philippa encouraged the arts, especially poetry, and like all happy parents, they encouraged their children to marry for love.

## JOSIAH WEDGWOOD AND SARAH WEDGWOOD

*"two married Lovers, happy as this
world can make them"*

"I YESTERDAY PREVAILED UPON MY dear Girl to name the day, the blissful day! when she will reward all my faithfull services, & take me to her arms! to her Nuptial bed!" Josiah wrote to his good friend and partner, Thomas Bentley, in 1764. Josiah and "Sally" were third cousins who had known each other since childhood, yet they did not marry until he was thirty-four and she was thirty years old.

Josiah, who had learned about pottery-making while apprenticed to his older brother Thomas, was a master potter by 1759. That year he opened his own small factory, Ivy House, in Burslem, England, and produced cream-colored "Useful" ware, decorated with simple designs. Many potteries existed in England then, but Josiah soon earned a reputation for perfection: His spouts poured evenly, his pot lids fit properly, and all his handles were easy to grip.

A year after he and Sally married, Josiah received his first royal order—a tea service for Queen Charlotte and King George III. Sally gave birth to their first child, Susannah, who would one day become Charles Darwin's mother. More children would be born to the Wedgwoods, but Sally also maintained an active role in her husband's business. Evenings, he showed her new designs and products, and she visited his factory and shops often. They were a liberal-minded couple, involved in community life and supportive of the American and French Revolutions.

Josiah's partnership with Bentley represented an ideal combination: Josiah was a perfectionist craftsman and Bentley had extensive knowledge of classical and Renaissance art. Their early black basalt vases painted with red classical figures led to the development of what would become the most famous Wedgwood pottery: neoclassical white clay patterns and cameos superimposed on the flat surfaces of vases, mugs, pitchers, bowls, platters, and teapots.

## MADELEINE L'ENGLE AND HUGH FRANKLIN

*Always "more than music"*

WHEN THE FUTURE NEWBERY AWARD–WINNING author of *A Wrinkle in Time* and other exceptional children's books first met the man who would one day become famous as Dr. Charles Tyler of TV's soap opera *All My Children,* he was a struggling actor and she had just gotten a bit part in the same play.

After graduating from Smith College, Madeleine moved to Greenwich Village in New York City and supported herself by selling stories and poems and appearing in theatrical productions. In 1944 she was thrilled to win even a small role in a touring company production of Chekhov's *The Cherry Orchard.* Hugh was cast as the student Trofimov; she was the maid and thought the handsome dark-haired actor would never notice her. But at the end of the first day, Hugh asked her out to dinner. They talked until almost 2:00 A.M. When Madeleine got home, she was sure she had met the man she wanted to marry.

The road company traveled across the United States, led by the stars Eva Le Gallienne and Joseph Schildkraut. Madeleine kept writing in her spare time and eventually completed her first novel. When the show's run was over, she and Hugh kept in touch and saw each other whenever he was in New York.

In her memoir, *Two-Part Invention,* written many years later, Madeleine described an evening when Hugh played music from *Swan Lake* on her phonograph and recited lines from a poem by Conrad Aiken:

> *Music I heard with you was more than music,*
> *And bread I broke with you was more than bread.*

And then he proposed. They were married in an Episcopal church in Chicago in 1946 during the run of *The Joyous Season,* in which they were performing. After the ceremony Hugh and Madeleine raced back to the theater in time for the next show.

## GEORGES ROUAULT AND MARTHE LE SIDANER

### *"Faithful Marthe"*

WHEN GEORGES AND MARTHE MARRIED in 1908, he was thirty-six and working on his series of paintings of judges and tribunals. He and Marthe met at the home of mutual friends in Paris. She was a witty and well-born pianist from Saint-Malo, who had been raised to appreciate art: Her mother was a musician, her father was a seafaring captain who also painted and sculpted, and her brother was a Pointillist painter.

Georges was born in Paris during the brutal Franco-Prussian War of 1871, and the bombings may have foreshadowed his dark, serious paintings. Most likely, his greatest influence was a devoted grandfather who taught him to appreciate the art of Rembrandt, Daumier, Monet, and other masters and gave him the courage to find his own style. Georges's teenage apprenticeship to a stained-glass maker also made an impact on his future work, especially those pictures in which bright colors are separated by thick black lines.

Marthe got along well with the Rouault family, which was fortunate, because during the first years of their marriage the young couple lived with Georges's parents in Versailles. His beloved grandfather died soon after the wedding, but his grandmother gladly watched over her great-grandchildren so Marthe could give piano lessons and supplement the family income.

Although Georges reproached himself for not earning enough money, Marthe didn't complain about having to work. She often played music at gatherings of friends and especially admired the works of Ravel and Debussy. Georges painted park scenes in Versailles as well as landscapes, religious subjects, clowns, and other performers. He also wrote poetry about "Faithful Marthe" and their four children—Genevieve, his "chiming bell," Isabelle, his "little dove," Agnes, a "little pigeon," and his son, Michel, "frail pillar of the house." Some of Georges's work was published in Apollinaire's new magazine, *Soirees de Paris*.

## KURT WEILL AND LOTTE LENYA

*With Lotte, life and music were never dull*

ALTHOUGH THE MARRIAGE OF KURT Weill, an introverted and brilliant German-Jewish composer and musician, and Lotte Lenya (born Karoline Blamauer), a street-smart, extroverted, and highly talented Viennese singer and dancer with freethinking attitudes towards sex, was rarely peaceful, their union—especially their early years together—inspired Kurt to produce seven works for the stage and more than a dozen concert pieces and scores within three years. In many cases he wrote his music for Lotte's gravelly voice, which he loved "like a very force of nature."

Kurt was twenty-four and writing *Der Protagonist,* a tragic opera, in Berlin in 1924 when he met twenty-six-year-old Lotte, who'd been asked to meet his train and accompany him to a well-known dramatist's home. Kurt had broken away from his conservative family, and here was Lotte—homely yet magnetic, a bohemian artist with an anti-bourgeois attitude. Soon after their 1926 marriage in a civil ceremony at Berlin's city hall, he wrote his parents, saying that living with Lotte made his music "more confident, much freer, lighter—and simpler." A year later he began collaborating with Bertoldt Brecht, who wrote the libretto while Kurt composed the music—including "Mack the Knife"—for *The Threepenny Opera,* one of their most famous works.

In the 1930's Kurt and Lotte lived apart at times, but emotionally and psychologically they were always attached. They left Berlin in 1933, divorced in Italy, and then sailed to America together. In 1936 they bought a pair of wedding rings in Woolworth's and remarried in New York. He wrote scores for Hollywood films, and Lotte performed in plays and in radio productions. In later years Lotte appeared in films, such as *From Russia With Love.* After Kurt's death in 1950, she dedicated herself to protecting and preserving his work and eventually donated everything to Yale University.

## CHARLES DARWIN AND EMMA WEDGWOOD

### *"My wonder Charley"*

THE FUTURE AUTHOR OF CLASSIC theories on evolution and natural selection saw no problems in marrying his first cousin. A few weeks before their wedding in 1839, other things worried him terribly. "I wish the awful day was over," Charles wrote Emma. "I am not very tranquil when I think of the procession; it is very awesome."

The ceremony was conducted by another cousin, John Allen Wedgwood, at St. Peter's Church in Shrewsbury, Charles's birthplace. Having a friendly relation guide him in repeating those hallowed vows of matrimony helped Charles get through the service and begin life with the woman he would call his "greatest blessing."

Charles had doubts about marriage in general and had composed a list of pros and cons. Not marrying meant "freedom to go where one liked" and "not forced to visit relatives, or bend to every trifle," but marriage could bring a "constant companion" and "object to be beloved & played with—better than a dog anyhow." "Only picture to yourself a nice soft wife on a sofa with good fire, & books & music perhaps," he concluded. "Marry—Marry—Marry Q. E. D!"

Charles and Emma were both twenty-nine when they married. She wore a gray-green silk dress and a white bonnet trimmed with feathers. Afterward they dashed off for a train to London, eating sandwiches and toasting their future with bottled water.

Their first home was Macaw Cottage at 12 Upper Gower Street in Bloomsbury, not far from Regent's Park. They often took long walks and looked at the animals (especially the apes!) in the Zoological Gardens nearby. Charles's father encouraged his son's research by giving the young couple financial help during their early years.

Although Charles never shared Emma's deep religious faith and she couldn't accept his views on evolution, it didn't stop her from helping out whenever possible and proofreading his *The Origin of Species* before its publication.

## SALVADOR DALI AND "GALA"

### *"Muse of the Surrealists"*

GALA AND DALI MET ON the beaches of Cadaques, Spain, in July 1929. She and her husband, French surrealist poet Paul Eluard, had been part of the circle of artists drawn to Paris in the rich, creative years after World War I. Now their marriage was virtually over, and Gala sought a new artist to cling to and inspire.

Dali was twenty-five, flamboyant, outrageous, eccentric, and extravagant. He pomaded his hair, painted in the nude, and often wore pearl necklaces and ribbons around his wrists. Gala was in her mid-thirties, with long black hair, piercing dark eyes, and a highly liberal attitude toward sex. She slithered when she walked and resembled a mysterious and exotic panther. No one knew her age or details from her past. "The secret of all my secrets," she said, "is that I do not tell them."

If Dali was bizarre, so was Gala. In Paris she had stirred the passions of many young artists, inspiring them to create radically new work. She believed Dali was a genius, but on the verge of madness. She would help him keep a grip on reality while he unleashed his wild visions on his canvases. Soon he began work on "The Accommodations of Desires," a haunting glimpse into the world of dreams.

Dali's fascination with Gala never ceased. "I fixed in my memory the value of every grain of her skin. . . . her back ravished me with the delicacy of the joints. . . . her hair, her intimate hair, her odors, intoxicated me," he later wrote in *The Secret Life of Salvador Dali.*

In 1934 "The Persistence of Memory" attracted worldwide attention, and he was offered his first one-man show in New York. But since Americans were too conventional to accept his exotic mistress, Dali and Gala were married in a civil ceremony in Paris shortly before they sailed. Witnesses included their landlord, landlady . . . and Paul Eluard.

## WILLIAM TEMPLE AND DOROTHY OSBORNE

*"Dear, shall we ever be happy, think you?"*

WILLIAM AND DOROTHY HAD A brief shipboard romance while crossing the English Channel on the way to Saint-Malo, France, in 1648. She was twenty-one, beautiful and spirited, and traveling with her adolescent brother Robin. William was twenty, good-looking, cultured, and charming, and on his way to the continent to continue his education. They had met shortly before embarkation, on the Isle of Wight. Civil war raged in England, and King Charles I was imprisoned by Cromwell's forces nearby. One night Robin scratched an anti-Cromwell message on a windowpane, and the next morning the three young travelers were arrested.

When Dorothy took the blame for her younger brother, William was deeply impressed and touched. She was set free after a scolding, and the three were soon on their way again. Voyaging together, Dorothy and William became inseparable, talking about literature, music, art . . . and love. He lingered with Dorothy and her family in St.-Malo for months until his father learned about the romance and wrote—Leave for Paris now, as planned!

The young lovers corresponded; would they ever meet again? A few years later the Osbornes returned to Chicksands, their ancestral home in England. Other men courted Dorothy, including Cromwell's son Henry, but no one could match her beloved William. She teased him about marriage, writing that the perfect husband should not be "a traveled monsieur whose head is all feather inside and out . . . He must not be a fool, nor peevish, ill natured, nor proud nor covetous, and to all this must be added, 'he must love me.'"

In 1651 they became secretly engaged in London. He sent her a gold ring, inscribed: "The love I owe/I cannot showe."

At last William's father softened, her father died, and they married in 1655. William became a great statesman and author, and Dorothy—Lady Temple—was his loving hostess and helpmate.

# FEBRUARY

## ARTHUR ASHE AND JEANNE MOUTOUSSAMY
### *February 20, 1977*

Heel surgery kept the groom on crutches but didn't mar the festivities
at the United Nations Chapel in New York City.

## JULIA MARGARET PATTLE AND CHARLES HAY CAMERON

*"his constant tenderness has sweetened every hour"*

JULIA MARRIED CHARLES IN 1838 in Calcutta, where her father served in the Bengal civil service. She was twenty-two, witty, and bright; Charles was forty-two and a member of the Indian Law Commission and Council for Education. Julia knew that their marriage would be passionate; at a time when few Victorians wrote or even spoke about sexuality, Charles had published his "Essay on the Sublime and Beautiful" about the power of sexual attraction. Rejecting most of the conventions of expatriate English society, they helped establish universities in India and admit Indians into the civil service.

The Camerons and their eleven natural and adopted children lived in India, Ceylon, London, and the Isle of Wight. Julia wrote poetry and translated famous German works into English, but when her children gave her a wooden camera and darkroom equipment, photography became her life's work. "From the first moment," she wrote, "I handled my lens with a tender ardour, and it has become to me as a living thing."

Soon Julia's photography took priority over household affairs. She invited—and sometimes summoned—servants, family members, houseguests, even strangers to sit before the camera, often for as long as five or seven minutes. The Camerons' chicken house became Julia's "glass house" or studio, and the coalhouse nearby served as a darkroom. She called her photographs "theophanies"—representations of God in human beings. She won medals for her work and photographed such notable Victorians as Browning, Darwin, and Tennyson.

Julia favored close-ups of the face, deliberately blurring the rest of the body, and often created symbolic scenes with religious or literary themes. Her friends dressed up and posed as people from the Bible, history, or great works of literature. Charles, with his long white beard, was a perfect Merlin in her series of illustrations for Tennyson's *Idylls of the King*.

## SAMUEL CLEMENS AND OLIVIA LANGDON

### *"Darling Livy"*

SAM AND "LIVY" PROBABLY WOULDN'T have met if he hadn't sailed with her brother Charles to Europe and the Holy Land in 1867. In Charles's stateroom was a picture of Livy; Sam saw it and claimed he fell in love on the spot. Six months later he greeted the entire Langdon family at New York City's St. Nicholas Hotel, while he was working on *The Innocents Abroad*. He showed them the sights, including Steinway Hall where Charles Dickens read from *David Copperfield*. At twenty-two, Livy was ten years younger than Sam. Her devoted father, a wealthy coal magnate, knew "Mark Twain" was a celebrated journalist and author, but was the "Wild Humorist" right for their Livy? She also had doubts; the first time Sam proposed, she turned him down.

The Langdons returned home to Elmira, New York, and Sam went off on the lecture circuit, writing to Livy and devouring every word she wrote back. Livy represented perfection to Sam. Like Tom Sawyer and other male characters he created, Sam believed such cultured and refined women were made to "sivilize" rough-edged men like himself. He also enjoyed her affectionate family; his had always been cold and reserved.

For the next two years he visited Livy whenever possible, until at last she confessed that she loved him, too. They married in 1870 in the Langdons' front parlor. The next day family and friends rode with them on a train to Buffalo, where they expected to settle into rented rooms. Instead, their sleigh pulled up in front of a private house, bought and furnished by the Langdon family.

Married life was blissful, and Sam wondered why on earth he had waited so long to marry. If he had the chance to do it over, he wrote, "I would marry in early infancy instead of wasting time cutting teeth and breaking crockery."

## SAMUEL RICHARDSON AND ELIZABETH LEAKE

*Riding "double" is better than "single"*

SAMUEL BEGAN WRITING HIS CLASSIC novels *Pamela* and *Clarissa* a few years after he married "Bett" in 1733. They had met ten years earlier, when he worked for her printer father in London before Samuel's first wife died. No children survived that marriage, but Samuel would have many daughters with Bett. Although he occasionally "complained" about being the only man in an all-female household, in truth he loved it.

Women had always liked Samuel. They confided in him, sharing some of their most private thoughts. "I was not more than thirteen," he later wrote, "when some . . . young women . . . having a high opinion of my taciturnity, revealed to me their love-secrets, in order to induce me to give them copies to write after, or correct, for answers to their lovers' letters." Their requests inspired his most significant literary achievement—*Pamela,* the first English-language novel, a story told in a series of letters written by Pamela Andrews, a young woman who successfully defends her virtue and honor.

Samuel and Bett lived at Blue Ball Court near Salisbury Square; she was a devoted and capable housekeeper, although he fretted that she "had a Love of bed on mornings." He rose early and often wrote during the quiet hours. He loved to eat but hated to exercise. When he gained a lot of weight, his doctor convinced him to buy a "chamber horse"—a large chair set on a wooden board, flexible in the middle, with braces for the arms and a footstool for the feet.

Samuel "worked out" on his "horse," reading, dictating, and writing some of his novels there. Sometimes Bett sat with him. The chamber horse "rides double better than single," he joyfully recounted to a friend.

Educated at an early age in the delights of love and passion, Samuel appreciated all the good things in life and encouraged others to feel the same way.

## SAMUEL CUNARD AND SUSAN DUFFUS

*Sail away with me . . .*

MRS. DUFFUS ENCOURAGED THE ROMANCE between her daughter and Sam Cunard, who courted Susan for a year before they married in 1815. He'd grown up in their Halifax, Nova Scotia, neighborhood and had always been bright, energetic, and resourceful. One day he would make a fine catch for her Susan. No one realized that he would also revolutionize ocean transportation.

Sleigh bells announced the arrival of wedding guests at the Duffuses' mansion on a cold, snowy day. The wedding in the grand drawing room was followed by a festive banquet. Sam and Susan set up housekeeping in a four-story house on Brunswick Street and filled it with furniture Sam had bought in London.

Mr. Duffus was a prosperous tailor of custom-made military and naval uniforms for the officers attached to the English forces based in Halifax. Sam's father owned a fleet of cargo ships carrying goods between England, New England, Bermuda, and Nova Scotia. Delivering mail to the military was a high priority for years, but after Wellington defeated Napoleon in the summer of 1815, service was cut drastically.

Sam was as enterprising as Susan's mother had predicted; within months he had set up S. Cunard & Company, a packet service of fast boats for the British Postal Service, delivering mail to Boston as well as Bermuda. Five years later passengers began traveling on Cunard ships. Under the blue flag with a white star in the center, Cunard's square-rigged cargo ships also carried New World lumber, food, sheep, and horses to Britain.

The shipping industry was booming, but other Halifax businesses suffered after Wellington's victory. Sam and Susan helped her parents financially after many English officers—who were her father's valued customers—were sent back to England. Susan also assisted the governor's wife in collecting food and clothing for needy families and persuading the local government to finance soup kitchens.

## JENNY LIND AND OTTO GOLDSCHMIDT

*"all my heart ever wanted"*

THE "SWEDISH NIGHTINGALE" WAS TWENTY-FIVE when she met Otto, a sixteen-year-old music student at Leipzig Conservatory. She had been singing professionally for seven years, and her powerful, vibrant soprano—with a range of 2¾ octaves extending to the G above high C—thrilled audiences everywhere.

The two musicians tried to suppress their passion for each other as Otto accompanied Jenny at local concerts. "Isn't it cruel?" she wrote a friend about Otto. "He is the first person that I could confidently . . . swear before God that I could make happy in every way and that I am really made for. But he is so young!"

Jenny left Germany and became engaged to a member of Sweden's Royal Opera Company. A few months later P. T. Barnum invited her to tour with his show in America. Everything she sang, from operatic solos to "Home Sweet Home" and "My Old Kentucky Home," had audiences cheering and begging for more.

After her ninety-third performance, Jenny was exhausted. She hated the circus atmosphere of Barnum's extravaganzas and persuaded him to terminate her contract. She began singing at small recitals and wrote to Otto, begging him to come to America and accompany her. Soon after he arrived, Jenny broke her engagement.

Jenny married Otto in 1852 in Boston at the Beacon Hill home of close friends. She wore a traditional Swedish wedding gown of white muslin, with a white veil secured by orange blossoms and myrtle. The silverware she had selected was engraved with the letter *J* encircled by an *O*, symbolizing her belief that with Otto she would be surrounded by happiness.

After a month-long honeymoon in the mountains of western Massachusetts, Jenny gave forty more concerts in America with Otto before they returned to Europe. Eventually, they made their home in England.

## MARGOT FONTEYN AND ROBERTO ARIAS

### *100 Red Roses*

THE 1955 MARRIAGE OF ONE of Britain's prima ballerinas and a Panamanian diplomat may have surprised some of Margot's fans, but it brought her more happiness than all her years on the stage. Margot and "Tito" had met eight years earlier at a party in Cambridge, England. They saw each other a few times. When they parted, he gave her a 1936 Panamanian coin honoring his father's second term as President of Panama, and she gave him an autographed photo of herself.

Six years later Margot was in New York performing in *The Sleeping Beauty* when Tito, now Panamanian delegate to the United Nations, reentered her life. He had married in Panama but was getting a divorce. "Will you marry me?" he asked her. She wondered . . . was he serious?

Tito wrote Margot long, passionate love letters, saying he'd never been able to forget her and had often consoled himself by believing that Margot's name was literally engraved on his heart. He sent her 100 red roses. A diamond bracelet. His chauffeur's services. Anything, if only she would marry him.

After dancing in *Daphnis and Chloe,* Margot flew to Paris with Tito, where they were married at the Panamanian consulate. The tiny room was meant for ten guests; more than fifty showed up! She forced her way through the crowd, searching for her parents. Swarms of newspaper photographers surrounded her, noisily clamoring for attention as their flashbulbs exploded and camera shutters banged. She could barely hear the consul general performing the ceremony. What should have been the loveliest and most meaningful day of Margot's life was "worse than a prize fight," she recalled in her autobiography.

After a honeymoon in the Bahamas, they lived in London. Margot continued to dance; he was ambassador to the Court of St. James's.

## AMELIA EARHART AND GEORGE PALMER PUTNAM

*For the fun of it*

ON THE DAY IN 1931 that Amelia married George at the Putnams' Noank, Connecticut, estate, the famous thirty-three-year-old aviatrix handed him a note stating, "I shall not hold you to any medieval code of faithfulness to me, nor shall I consider myself bound to you similarly." The woman who had soared above the clouds, free as a bird, could never endure "the confinements of even an attractive cage."

The forty-five-year-old heir to a publishing empire respected his bride's hard-won independence and freedom. He also accepted her decision to keep her maiden name. They had met in 1928, soon after Charles Lindbergh flew nonstop to Paris. The publisher G. P. Putnam's Sons was looking for a female flyer to accompany male pilots bound for Europe in a Fokker plane as part of a publicity campaign. Amelia grabbed the opportunity. After they took off in June, one of the pilots drank so excessively on a layover in Newfoundland that Amelia—dubbed "Lady Lindy" by the press—stepped in to fly part of the way.

Afterward, George invited Amelia to stay at his lavish home in Rye, New York, and write about her accomplishments. She also lectured about flying, tested new equipment, and became a magazine columnist. He divorced his first wife in 1929 and helped guide Amelia's career. The more time they spent together, the more they fell in love. Still, it took six proposals of marriage from George to win her, although she insisted on terminating the union after one year if either partner was unhappy.

That never happened. Instead, Amelia, one of the best-known feminists of her time, continued flying in air races and in award-winning nonstop and cross-country flights. Eventually she set records flying solo from Newfoundland to Ireland, Hawaii to the U.S. mainland, and Mexico City to Newark.

## RAPHAEL SOYER AND REBECCA LETZ

*"How autobiographical my art is"*

REBECCA'S FRIEND AND FELLOW TEACHER Fanny Soyer often spoke of her three talented brothers—Isaac and the twins, Raphael and Moses—but it was Raphael who captured the young teacher's heart. At thirty-two, he still lived at home with his family and would be the last brother to marry, in 1931. For inspiration Raphael roamed the streets of New York City. Frequently he painted scenes of people without hope—vagrants, men outside missions, people sleeping in parks or under bridges.

Rebecca was tall and slender, with red hair wrapped in braids around her head. She modeled for Raphael, as did dancers, actresses, other artists, and Lower East Side bohemians. Many of his paintings revealed a keen appreciation of female sensuousness. He liked painting women in intimate settings—sleeping, sitting, or conversing in small groups. He also made money illustrating books and painting portraits.

In 1929 Raphael brought "Dancing Lesson," a painting depicting his sister, brothers, mother, and grandmother, to a gallery in Manhattan. The director was impressed and told him, Bring back a dozen like this and I'll give you a show.

Raphael's paintings sold quickly, enabling him to rent studio space with other artists. Rebecca helped out by sewing curtains for the windows. After his third one-man show, Raphael was invited to teach at the Art Students League. At last, he and Rebecca could afford to marry.

In the early years Raphael and Rebecca had little money, but they managed to travel to Europe before their children were born. The Soyers always talked about political events and believed that art should never be censored. They supported the antifascists during the Spanish Civil War and spoke out against war and Naziism as members of the American Artists Congress.

"If Raphael isn't painting, he's sick," said Rebecca many times. Aside from his family, his art was his life.

## ETHAN ALLEN AND FRANCES MONTRESOR BUCHANAN

*"partner of my joys, my dearest self"*

THE FAMOUS REVOLUTIONARY WAR GENERAL and leader of the Green Mountain Boys was forty-six when he proposed to "Fanny," a twenty-four-year old war widow. She was bright, beautiful, and witty, and although she had a temper, she also had a passion for life. Ethan's first wife had died, but his second marriage would be as joyous as his first one had been disappointing and sad.

He met Fanny in Westminster, Vermont, in January 1784. Ten years earlier her late stepfather had sided with the British in New York and posted a reward for the capture of Ethan and other "Green Mountain outlaws, dead or alive." If Fanny remembered the incident, she quickly dismissed it now.

A month later she was standing on a chair in her mother's home, putting dishes into a china closet, when Ethan entered. "Fanny," he declared, "if we are to be married, now is the time, for I am on my way to Sunderland."

"Very well," Fanny answered, stepping down from the chair. Their engagement lasted only as long as it took them to walk into the dining room, where Vermont's Chief Justice Moses Robinson was having breakfast with some lawyers. They were lighting their pipes when Ethan asked Robinson to marry them then and there.

Are you sure? asked Robinson. Of course! Ethan said. He'd taken Fort Ticonderoga with less thought. After the ceremony Ethan and Fanny rode in a sleigh across the Green Mountains to the home he shared in Sunderland with his brother Ira. Ethan and Fanny later moved with their children to Burlington, where he concentrated on writing for the rest of his life. Besides philosophical treatises and histories, he penned sweet romantic verses:

> *Dear Fanny wise, the beautiful and young,*
> *The partner of my joys, my dearest self,*
> *My love, pride of my life . . .*

## QUEEN VICTORIA OF GREAT BRITAIN AND
## PRINCE ALBERT OF SAXE-COBURG

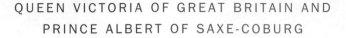

*"My dearest dearest dear"*

"MONDAY, FEBRUARY 10—THE LAST time I slept alone," wrote Victoria on the morning of her wedding in 1840. Three days before, she had sent carriages to fetch Prince Albert from Gotha, Germany. The Channel crossing had been rough, and when he arrived, onlookers said his face was the color of a wax candle.

He was tall; she was small and thought him "beautiful." He was motherless; she was fatherless. They both were eighteen and about to begin one of the most romantic marriages in royal history.

The Archbishops of Canterbury and York and the Bishop of London officiated at the wedding on a cold rainy day at the Chapel Royal of St. James's Palace. When someone asked why only three Tories were on the extensive guest list, Victoria replied, "This is *my* marriage and I will only have those who sympathize with me!"

The evening before the wedding she and Albert dined together, read the marriage service, and practiced putting on her ring. She thought a rehearsal was unnecessary but regretted it later. Her bridal train wasn't long enough for her twelve bridesmaids to carry, and they "all huddled together, and scrambled rather than walked along, kicking each other's heels and treading on each other's gowns." As for Albert, he never knew whether he was supposed to stand, sit, or kneel!

But Victoria looked appropriately regal in a white satin dress trimmed with orange blossoms and lace, a diamond necklace, and a sapphire brooch from Albert. Like other royal brides, she did not conceal her face behind a veil. One hundred wedding cakes made by various London confectioners were served at the reception. The grandest cake was 9 inches in its circumference and 16 inches high.

Honeymooning at Windsor Castle, Victoria wrote about the "happiest day of my life": "I *never never* spent such an evening! . . . He clasped me in his arms and we kissed each other again and again! His beauty, his sweetness and gentleness— really how can I ever be thankful enough to have such a *husband!*"

## RICHARD TUCKER AND SARA PERELMUTH

*"by my side all the way"*

SARA ALWAYS WAITED IN THE wings whenever "Ruby" left the stage of New York's Metropolitan Opera House, even if only for a quick wardrobe change. The internationally acclaimed Jewish tenor sang many roles, including Canio in *Pagliacci,* Rodolfo in *La Boheme,* and Don Alvaro in *La Forza del Destino.* After the rousing finale, Sara usually heard the audience's "bravos" and boisterous pleas for "encore!" before her dark-haired, smiling husband appeared backstage. Holding hands, they walked to Ruby's dressing room and welcomed adoring fans. Ruby autographed playbills as Sara jotted down the names and addresses of those who brought gifts or requested photographs.

Years later, Ruby's lifelong enthusiasm for opera continued through the Richard Tucker Foundation, established by Ruby's family to assist young opera singers.

"The American Caruso" began dating Sara in 1934, when her uncle gave him her phone number. The younger sister of tenor Jan Peerce, Sara was impressed by Ruby's magnificent voice, especially after he serenaded her in a Romanian restaurant on the Lower East Side. His clothes were shabby and his income low, but Ruby convinced Sara and her parents that he would become a *hazzan,* or cantor, and a great opera singer and make everyone proud of him.

He married his "dearest Kitten" on a Tuesday in 1936 at the Grand Mansion, a Ludlow Street banquet hall partially owned by the Perelmuths. After a storm-tossed honeymoon cruise to Bermuda, the newlyweds returned to Manhattan. Ruby worked in the fur district, sang at bar mitzvahs and weddings, and became a part-time cantor. Sara worked, too, enabling them to buy voice lessons for Ruby and occasional opera tickets. At last, the man who would become one of the twentieth century's greatest tenors could take his wife to the Metropolitan Opera. They sat in the audience, but both knew that one day Ruby would be singing center stage.

## FRANS HALS AND LYSBETH REYNIERS

*Her "jolly Hans"*

IN THE HALS FAMILY REGISTRY, baby Sara's birth was recorded nine days after Frans married Lysbeth in 1617. Maybe their wedding was held in a hurry, but they remained happily together for the next fifty-two years and had eight more children, including three who became painters.

Frans had been married before, but his wife had died after five years and he didn't seem to regret it. Now in his mid-thirties, he hoped to find a sweet, affectionate wife and raise a family. The most lucrative field for an artist was portrait-painting. Wealthy Dutch burghers wanted pictures of themselves and their growing families and also bought paintings to decorate their homes.

In Haarlem, the Netherlands, Frans became a member of the painters' guild, established an art school, and married Lysbeth in Spaarndam, a small city nearby. Frans was able to capture the fleeting expressions of his sitters—even the stolid merchants whom he painted so often. Some men belonged to shooting clubs, groups of volunteers who gathered together socially during peacetime and assembled posthaste for the national defense. Frans's "Banquet of the St. Joris Shooting Company," done in 1616, has long been considered a masterpiece, magnificently depicting thirteen men in high, stiff ruffled collars at a table.

Frans rarely spent much time sketching but got right to work with his paintbrush and colors. In most of his pictures, everything happens in the foreground. His figures look you straight in the eye. Frans painted for the viewer, as if he was saying, Here it all is, right up front.

Although Frans always enjoyed his schnapps, a close look at the details in his paintings shows that he never shortchanged his art. Lysbeth was spirited and strong-minded herself, happy to see Rubens, Van Dyck, and other painters who came to their home.

## PRINCESS ELIZABETH OF ENGLAND AND
## PRINCE FREDERICK OF BOHEMIA

*Father of the bride (almost) breaks the bank*

ON THE "CAN YOU TOP this?" list of elaborate wedding celebrations, Elizabeth and Frederick's nuptials surely rank among the highest.

They met in 1612 when Frederick visited England. The sixteen-year-old princess's beauty and charm had been celebrated by court poets, and the Elector Palatine of Bohemia wasn't disappointed. Although their marriage was "arranged," the young couple had truly fallen in love. Later on, Elizabeth was called "The Queen of Hearts" by her subjects.

Sadly, preparations were interrupted by the sudden death of Elizabeth's brother Henry, the Prince of Wales, but the wedding celebrations that followed softened the nation's grief. A mock naval battle involving thirty-six ships, five hundred sailors, and one thousand musketeers took place on the Thames River. Fireworks exploded above four floating castles, and giant puppets of Saint George, a beautiful maiden, and a fire-eating dragon hurled torches at each other until, one by one, they burst into flames. Masked balls, theatrical productions, and other spectacles also took place before the 1613 wedding.

Frederick's entrance at Whitehall Chapel was heralded by trumpets. Elizabeth followed, wearing a richly embroidered silver gown and a gold crown embellished with diamond and pearl pendants swinging gently against her waist-long hair. Her bridesmaids numbered sixteen, to match her age in years, and they walked behind her in white satin dresses. Someone likened the sight to a constellation of stars trailing behind a glorious moon.

Royal pockets were turned inside out to pay for all the merrymaking, but King James remained more than 50,000 pounds in the red. The royal exchequer was completely bankrupt, and his royal highness was forced to levy taxes to help make ends meet. Elizabeth was mortified when the new groom's household was temporarily dismissed, and her father left town for a while to avoid further embarrassments.

*Date approximate; the wedding pageant lasted more than a week.

## CHARLES BOYER AND PATRICIA PATERSON

*Lifelong love after a whirlwind courtship*

COUNTLESS LOVERS HAVE CHOSEN VALENTINE'S Day as the perfect wedding day—even some who've known each other only twenty-two days.

Charles Boyer, the thirty-four-year-old suave French actor with impeccable charm, thought he was past the age of falling in love when he met Pat at a Fox Studio lunch party on January 23, 1934. Already he'd become a success on the French stage and in silent films in America. When the talkies began, Charles learned English, and with his velvet voice and captivating dark eyes, he was soon playing leading roles.

That winter Charles was in Hollywood to film *Caravan*. He wasn't looking for romance, but he found it in Pat, a twenty-four-year-old vivacious blond English musical comedy actress. Her breakthrough role in the movie *Bitter Sweet* had brought her to California and the brink of stardom the previous year.

If Cupid ever shot his arrow into anyone, it was Charles. As soon as he saw Pat at the party, he couldn't think of anyone else. Other beautiful actresses were there, but Charles looked only at Pat. She was intrigued by his continental charm and French accent, and they began seeing each other right away. He had always avoided "affairs of the heart," but not being with Pat, even for a day, was more than he could bear.

They talked about getting married and all the reasons it was better not to do it—until they jumped into Charles's Plymouth roadster, drove to Yuma, Arizona, and were married by a justice of the peace. After a one-night honeymoon in a nearby motel, they went back to Hollywood. Charles's friend, singer Maurice Chevalier threw a party for them and their stunned but delighted friends.

Who says whirlwind courtships never work out? These two sweethearts were married more than forty years, and their love for each other never wavered.

## FYODOR DOSTOYEVSKY AND ANNA SNITKINA

### *"Fedya" and his "Golubchik"*

ANNA BEGAN WORKING FOR FYODOR in 1866 when the forty-five-year-old author needed a stenographer to help him meet the deadline for his new novel, *The Gambler.* Almost two years had passed since his first wife's death, and he still was visibly depressed. Anna arrived every weekday morning wearing her best—and only—dress, which was black. The color suited Fyodor's serious mood. He paced his study as he spoke and pulled on his long hair when stymied for a word or phrase.

After several hours of intense work, they'd take short breaks. Anna made *pastila,* Fyodor's favorite dessert of dried apricots, pears, and peaches, which they ate while drinking tea. He spoke about his hard life and five years of imprisonment as a political criminal. Creditors hounded him; he had been forced to pawn family valuables. But Anna had a soothing effect on Fyodor, and gradually he grew to care for her. He called her "Golubchik," an affectionate term meaning "little bird."

Her job ended when *The Gambler* was completed on time. A week later Fyodor asked her to come back so he could dictate *Crime and Punishment.* He also confessed that he missed her deeply. Many years later Anna wrote in her *Reminiscences,* "I won't try to convey the words full of tenderness and love that he said to me then; they are sacred to me. I was stunned, almost crushed by the immensity of my happiness and for a long time I couldn't believe it."

They married in 1867 in Ismailovsky's Cathedral in St. Petersburg. Fyodor's stepson, Paul, was the only one to protest, saying the "old man" should have asked him first!

With Anna, Fyodor finished *Crime and Punishment* and wrote *The Idiot, The Brothers Karamazov,* and other great works. She gave birth to three children but also continued to be Fyodor's secretary, stenographer, copyist, and financial manager.

## JAMES MONROE AND ELIZABETH KORTRIGHT

*"dear Eliza"*

THOMAS JEFFERSON WAS THE FIRST one to notice that James was in love, because his letters had become brighter and more optimistic. After three years in the Congress of the Confederation, James had come home to Virginia to hang up his lawyer's shingle in Fredericksburg. But he kept going back to New York City, where he had met Elizabeth at a party. Within a year they were engaged.

At nineteen, Elizabeth was the beautiful and aristocratic daughter of a well-regarded New York merchant who had been a British captain during the Revolutionary War. Her friends had always predicted that Elizabeth would marry well and were somewhat disappointed when she accepted James's proposal in 1786. (They changed their minds later, when he became the fifth president of the United States!)

Perhaps it was his energy and devotion to their new nation that attracted Elizabeth to James. He dressed poorly; once he came calling in a worn-out coat and shapeless breeches, and she said teasingly that he looked like a "woodman." He also refused to wear a powdered wig.

Jefferson was glad that the new couple would be settling not very far from his home at Monticello. Fredericksburg's solid population of merchants and businessmen needed good lawyers. Although practicing law never interested James very much, he knew it would bring financial security. He and Elizabeth found a house only a short walk from the office, which enabled him to come home quickly after work. Within a year, a daughter was born, "who tho' noisy, contributes greatly to our amusement," he wrote.

To strangers and people she barely knew, Elizabeth appeared reserved and at times too formal, but with James and her immediate family she was affectionate and loving. Their marriage became extremely close, and both hated parting from the other, even for a day.

## ALICE LEE ROOSEVELT AND NICHOLAS LONGWORTH

*"Princess Alice" and "Nick"*

"PRINCESS ALICE" WAS OUTSPOKEN, ARGUMENTATIVE, peevish, beautiful, demanding—and the favorite daughter of President Teddy Roosevelt. Fashion-conscious women wore "Alice blue," her favorite color, and everyone danced to the popular song "Alice Blue Gown." In 1904, when she turned eighteen, her name was linked with eligible monarchs, military officers, Harvard and Yale football players, and former Rough Riders.

Alice met Nick at a Washington dinner party. The Ohio congressman was a clever and self-confident man-about-town who would one day become speaker of the House. Fifteen years older than Alice, he most certainly attracted her attention. They saw each other often but kept their relationship light and fun-filled.

In 1905 Alice was invited to join the secretary of war and a large contingent of political figures—including Nick—on a four-month-long boat trip to visit heads of state in the Far East. When it ended, they were engaged, and she wrote in her diary, "I love you with everything that is in me Nick, Nick, my Nick." Then she told her parents that she wanted to be married in February 1906—only two months away—which didn't give her stepmother, Edith, much time to make the arrangements!

The weather was unseasonably warm that Saturday as one thousand invited guests arrived at the White House. Alice's wedding dress was white satin, trimmed with lace that had enhanced her late mother's wedding dress, with a long train of white and silver brocade. Not wanting to be upstaged by anyone, Alice refused to have any bridesmaids in her wedding party.

At noon the Marine Band began playing and TR escorted his daughter down the aisle. When the bishop asked, "Who gives the bride away?," the usually loquacious president was speechless.

## ALEXANDER PUSHKIN AND NATALYA GONCHAROV

### *Torment and bliss*

THE WEDDING OF THE FUTURE national poet of Russia was postponed many times before his bride's grasping, meddlesome mother finally relented and let him marry her precious daughter. Long ago the Goncharovs had been wealthy, but their riches had been squandered by their descendants. Now widowed, Mrs. Goncharov was determined that her daughter marry well. Who was this worthless poet? Just a scribbler with no steady income!

Natalya was sixteen, beautiful, and deeply attracted to Alexander's genius. He was twenty-nine and knew she wasn't brilliant, but he wanted a wife and a home.

> *My desires have been fulfilled.*
> *The creator has sent you to me, you my Madonna,*
> *The purest example of purest loveliness.*

But Mrs. Goncharov listed her demands. Natalya needed a large trousseau; could Alexander provide it? He struggled to get enough money together, but Mrs. G. postponed the wedding anyway and made more demands. Alexander sold poems and short stories. He mortgaged his property. But time and again the wedding was delayed. When he and Natalya did marry in Moscow in 1831, the bridegroom was so shaky and exhausted that as they exchanged rings, one slipped out of their hands. He bent down to pick it up, bumping into the lectern and knocking a crucifix and Bible to the floor. Then Alexander's candle went out. "All the bad omens," he muttered nervously.

Married life did not prove blissful until they packed their bags that May, leaving town—and Mrs. Goncharov—for a rented house in Tsarskoe Selo. Finally Alexander could enjoy Natalya and finish *Eugene Onegin,* his greatest work. He also wrote other poems, including one in which he tells his wife,

> *How sweeter far are you, my meek, my quiet one—*
> *By what tormenting bliss is my whole soul undone . . .*

## THOMAS HART BENTON AND RITA PIACENZA

*They "fooled them!"*

"MY HUSBAND IS A GENIUS," Rita often said, even when they had very little money and lived on the top floor of a walk-up apartment near Union Square in New York City. Tom eventually achieved greatness as a painter and muralist, focusing on themes from American history. But what kept them going in the early years was the money Rita earned designing hats and writing a sewing column for *Ladies' Home Journal* magazine. She also recognized the value of Tom's paintings more quickly than he did and sometimes sold works that he had discarded.

Rita was seventeen, dark-eyed, attractive, and wearing a red hat when she signed up for Tom's adult education class in drawing at a Manhattan public school in 1917. He was twenty-nine and loved looking at her. After class he often sketched her face from memory. Once they became friends, Rita took Tom home to meet her family, and he began dropping in for Sunday dinner.

The Piacenzas didn't think it was right that Tom didn't have a "real" job and would be relying financially on Rita. The Bentons said . . . well, she was *only* the daughter of Italian immigrants. After all, Tom's father had served in the Confederate army, and his great-uncle and namesake was *the* Thomas Hart Benton, United States senator and writer.

Fortunately, by the time Tom and Rita married at St. Francis Xavier Church in New York in 1922, everyone agreed that "family" was "family." Mr. Piacenza insisted on cooking the celebration dinner. That June, the newlyweds went to Martha's Vineyard in Massachusetts and summered with other artists, writers, and musicians.

In Tom's autobiography, he recalled that some of his friends were surprised to learn that he had married, thinking he'd never be content to live with one woman permanently. "I fooled them," he wrote. "Or it might be better to say, my wife fooled them."

## ARTHUR ASHE AND JEANNE MOUTOUSSAMY

*Remembering love*

ARTHUR WAS IMMEDIATELY ATTRACTED TO the beautiful photographer who asked to take his picture at a United Negro College Fund benefit in October 1976. Jeanne worked for NBC, and although she liked the tennis star, she didn't expect anything serious to develop with someone known as a "carefree bachelor."

His father couldn't believe how much Jeanne looked like Arthur's mother, who had died when he was six years old. Arthur hadn't realized it, and yet he felt somehow that memories of his mother played a part in his falling in love with Jeanne. He gave her a red rose (his mother's favorite flower) on their first date and married her four months later.

Arthur had hoped to marry someday, but he knew it would have to wait until he had fulfilled his dreams as a professional tennis player. Jeanne was bright, thoughtful, and independent, and she seemed to accept the fact that much of their dating would be on the telephone. Arthur called her often from Europe, Australia, and everywhere else he traveled on tours. She enjoyed his quiet sense of humor: Instead of proposing formally when he came home that winter, he slipped an engagement ring into an envelope and stuck it inside her medicine cabinet. Three days passed before she noticed it!

Arthur had surgery to remove bone chips from his heel shortly before he married Jeanne in 1977. Their friend, Reverend Andrew Young, who was the United States Ambassador to the United Nations, performed the ceremony at the U.N. Chapel in New York City. Jeanne hoped that her work would still be judged simply on its own merits, not praised because now she was Mrs. Arthur Ashe. She continued to succeed, eventually producing works such as *Daddy and Me,* the touching and poignant book Arthur wrote with their young daughter about losing a parent at an early age.

## MARTIN VAN BUREN AND HANNAH HOES

*Everything was "OK" between them*

ALTHOUGH MATTY STARTED OUT AS a lawyer, he was active in politics even before he married his Dutch sweetheart, "Jannetje," in 1807. In 1800, when he was eighteen, he campaigned for Thomas Jefferson and began associating with political groups in New York City.

Upstate in Kinderhook, New York, bridegrooms traditionally invited the entire town to their weddings and hosted elaborate celebrations. But Matty was frugal and somewhat shy, so he and Jannetje were married at her sister's home in Catskill across the Hudson River, with only their immediate families present.

Within a year they bought a house on Warren Street in the nearby town of Hudson. In March 1808, Matty was appointed surrogate judge of Columbia County. He attended court sessions in Albany and New York City, sometimes sleeping in poorly heated, dilapidated inns. He rode the circuits rain or shine but was always grateful to come home to his Jannetje, the four sons they eventually had, and their clean and comfortable house.

Matty and Jannetje never forgot that first summer after their marriage, when Robert Fulton's steamboat, the *Clermont,* completed its maiden round-trip voyage between Albany and New York City. Until then, few people sailed on rivers, but a new age of transportation and commerce had begun in America. In five years Matty was elected to the New York State Senate. Eventually he became the eighth president of the United States and the first one born in the new nation.

No one's sure when the American expression "OK" was first used, although many historians think it referred to "Old Kinderhook," Matty's nickname in political campaigns. But perhaps its original use was more personal—when Jannetje asked Matty to do something, his response was like that of countless husbands. He'd look at his sweet wife and say, "OK!"

## AARON MONTGOMERY WARD AND ELIZABETH COBB

### *A real family business*

"MONTY" MET ELIZABETH IN CHICAGO in the 1860s, when his childhood friend George married Elizabeth's sister. Although Monty was tempted to follow his future brother-in-law into retailing, he had ideas for something better. Growing up in Michigan, he had worked in a general store, where customers always complained about limited selections and high prices. Yet they had no choice but to shop there: It was the only store in town.

After he moved to Chicago, Monty wondered, Why not establish a mail-order business and sell goods to small-town people directly, with payment on delivery? He'd need a catalog, and a store located near a railroad station. He talked it over with Elizabeth, and they decided he would carry shoes, farm equipment, carpets, nails . . . everything. Elizabeth said she'd help out in any way she could.

Monty opened his first mail-order store in 1871, right before the Great Chicago Fire. Confronted by so much devastation, many businessmen gave up, but not Monty. He started raising capital again, despite George's dire predictions that he'd go broke within a year.

In 1872, five days after Monty's twenty-eighth birthday, he and Elizabeth were married. They rented a small shipping room on North Clark Street, assembled a one-page price list, and sent it to almost half a million midwestern farmers. Monty visited many towns, introducing himself and encouraging people to order from his catalog. Elizabeth's family pitched in, too. Her brother worked in the packing rooms, her father was the night watchman, and her mother put together samples to send to customers and helped with the bookkeeping. And pretty soon George swallowed his pride, gave Monty his life's savings, and was made a partner in the growing business.

By the end of the nineteenth century, the Montgomery Ward catalog was one of the most widely read publications in American history.

## HUGO BLACK AND JOSEPHINE FOSTER

*A "sweet" and "spiritual" nobility*

JOSEPHINE AND THE FUTURE SUPREME Court justice had both grown up in Birmingham, Alabama, but they didn't meet until Hugo came home after serving in World War I. That summer Josephine postponed her plans to study journalism in New York and joined the Yeomanettes, a women's branch of the navy. Hugo, a labor lawyer, was living in a bachelor apartment on a very steep hill. One day, he recalled in his autobiography, he saw a brown-haired, beautiful young lady walking up the hill in a close-fitting, eye-appealing dress.

Later he saw her at a dance and at the home of mutual friends. Her escort lost track of Josephine after Hugo got her attention, and they spent most of the evening "hiding" behind a potted palm. There was something about the way she walked, smiled, and listened, he remembered. "She just seemed to have a sweet nobility about her. She just seemed to reflect a spiritual nobility."

The Fosters were somewhat disappointed when Josephine announced that she wanted to marry Hugo. She was only twenty-two, but he was almost thirty-five and his family was not well connected socially. Other beaux pursued her, but Josephine remained steadfastly committed to Hugo. She'd never known a man who exuded so much confidence. "Everyone in that false society we lived in felt he was common," she said. But Hugo was so brilliant, she knew he would surpass them all.

She wore a blue suit and a gray hat when they married at her parents' Birmingham home in 1921. Three years later Hugo was elected senator from Alabama. In 1937 he was appointed to the Supreme Court and was Justice Black for the next thirty-four years. He believed that freedom of speech and religious liberty were absolute rights, and that the Fourteenth Amendment made the entire Bill of Rights applicable to everyone.

## THOMAS ALVA EDISON AND MINA MILLER

*A Morse code proposal*

TOM MET MINA NOT LONG after his first wife died. The famous inventor was lonely; his daughter was at boarding school, and his two young sons were living temporarily with their aunt. At thirty-eight, he was a millionaire, having invented the phonograph, the incandescent electric lamp, and the quadraplex telegraph which sent four messages at one time. Most people were awed in his presence, but Mina wasn't intimidated. She was only eighteen but looked him straight in the eye. The "Wizard of Menlo Park" was impressed!

"Got to thinking about Mina and came near being run over by a streetcar," he wrote in his journal after Mina returned home to Ohio and he headed for Florida. "If Mina interferes much more, will have to take out an accident policy." He wrote to her often and visited her the following summer. Her protective parents wouldn't let him spend time alone with their daughter, so he taught her Morse code, enabling them to communicate privately by tapping on each other's palms, even in a room full of people.

One day he tapped his marriage proposal on Mina's hand and she tapped back . . . yes!

The Millers rolled out a red carpet on their front lawn in Akron and decorated the parlor with huge bouquets of calla lilies and palm leaves for the 1886 wedding. In the library, dozens of pink carnations spelled out "E—M." Tom got the jitters and told Mina, "I'm getting pretty scared—I wonder if I will pull through. I know you will, women have more nerve than men."

She walked down the aisle wearing a white silk dress edged in lace, with a diamond pendant suspended from a pearl necklace. After the reception they boarded a train for their honeymoon and new home in Fort Myers, Florida. More revolutionary inventions would follow, but for now Tom devoted all his attentions to the bride he affectionately called "Billy."

## HEINRICH STEINWEG (STEINWAY)
## AND JULIANNE THIEMER

*Perfect harmony*

"HENRY" AND JULIANNE MET IN Seesen, Germany, at the foot of the Hartz Mountains where the blond-haired girl lived with her family. Julianne loved music and soon fell in love with the young stranger who played the organ in the village church on Sundays. It's said that she pumped the bellows and Henry played the organ at their own wedding in 1825, right before the ceremony began.

Henry had been born in Wolfshagen Germany, but by the time he was fifteen, he was orphaned and alone in the world. He joined the army and fought against Napoleon at the Battle of Waterloo. Years later, veterans remembered a soldier who sat around the campfire strumming soothing melodies on his handmade zither. Although no one knew his name, most probably it was Henry.

He had learned the trades of cabinetmaker and organ builder and had a natural fondness for music. He built a small two-stringed piano and gave it to Julianne as a wedding gift. After a fire destroyed many parts of Seesen, the craft guilds relaxed their restrictions against outsiders. Henry went into business building furniture and repairing organs, and he began making bigger and better musical instruments.

He and Julianne had seven children who played in their father's workshop as he hummed sweet tunes and crafted his pianos. In time he developed a piano with purer and more vibrant tones than the tinkling sounds made by harpsichords. In 1839 one of Henry's pianos was played at the State Fair of Brunswick and awarded a first-prize medal. Eventually the "Steinway tone" would become a standard to which all other piano manufacturers aspired.

Henry and Julianne's son Charles was the first to go to America. The rest of the family followed in 1851, and "Steinway and Sons" began producing their remarkable instruments.

*Date approximate.

## JEFFERSON DAVIS AND VARINA ANNE HOWELL

*"my own sweet Wife"*

POLITICS, NOT MATRIMONY, WAS ON Jeff's mind when he was introduced to Varina at Christmastime, 1843. His first wife had died three months after their wedding, and Jeff spent the next eight years in virtual solitude, cultivating his land and reading extensively. At seventeen, Varina was half Jeff's age. "I believe he is old," she wrote her mother, "for from what I hear he is only two years younger than you are . . . yet he is most agreeable and has a peculiarly sweet voice and a winning manner of asserting himself." With remarkable intuition, she pinpointed the future president of the Confederacy's strength of character: "The fact is, he is the kind of person I should expect to rescue one from a mad dog at any risk, but to insist upon a stoical indifference to the fright afterward."

Varina was tall, vivacious, intelligent, and shapely. Although Jeff was formal and reserved, she recognized his sensitivity and his lingering sadness over his first wife's death. The Christmas celebrations lasted for weeks. Amid rose gardens and pathways shaded by native oaks and walnut trees, Jeff and Varina took long walks and rides on horseback. They read the poetry of Byron and Robert Burns to each other. By the time they parted at the steamboat landing, Jeff had proposed. After he won her parents' consent, he gave Varina a ring with a large emerald surrounded by diamonds.

They married in 1845 at her parents' Natchez home, in a parlor filled with bouquets of white hyacinths. Varina wore antique jewelry her grandmother gave her, which would be worn thereafter by future Davis family brides.

After Jeff was elected to the 29th Congress of the United States, he and Varina moved to a boardinghouse in Washington, D.C. She attended House sessions and helped Jeff with research and correspondence.

## MARY MONTGOMERIE LAMB AND
## HENRY SYDENHAM SINGLETON

*"My soul seems to rise and rejoice to the chime of a marriage bell"*

WHEN HENRY MARRIED MARY IN 1864, he sensed from the beginning that his beautiful, bright, and charming young bride would become more than a typical English wife and mother. Mary had written poems and stories ever since she was a child, even though her parents had discouraged her. Henry gave her the best gift any husband can offer—the freedom to develop her talents. No wonder she described him as

> *Love of my Life! Dearest of my desires!—*
> *The one who kindled in my breast those fires*
> *Which neither time nor tide can dull or dim.*

They married three days after Mary's nineteenth birthday and settled at Hazely Heath, Hampshire. Mary began working on a series of poems focusing on love and nature. She also gave birth to two sons and two daughters, and within eight years *From Dawn to Noon,* her first poetry collection, was published under her nom de plume, "Violet Fane," which she took from a character in one of Disraeli's novels.

Mary and Henry made frequent trips to London and became well known in society. Besides poetry, she also wrote essays and novels. A good friend, W. H. Mallock, called her a "London Sappho." But Henry was her soulmate; as she wrote in "Song":

> *There is a lustre in thine eye*
> *Which only sheds its beams for me,*
> *There is a language in thy smile*
> *Which others may not see. . . .*
>
> *Thou hast a beauty of thine own*
> *Which others do not care to see—*
> *There is a secret in thy heart,*
> *'Tis only told to me.*

## FIORELLO LA GUARDIA AND MARIE FISHER

*"I lost a good secretary and got a bum cook!"*

IN A WELL-KNOWN SCENE IN the 1959 hit musical *Fiorello,* the main character sits at his office desk on a cold December night and barks orders at his faithful secretary, Marie. Suddenly he pauses; no one has ever been as loyal and trustworthy as she, and yet he has never really noticed she's a woman . . . until now. When Marie puts on her coat and leaves, Fiorello runs after her. You're fired, he tells her, since how could he propose marriage to someone who works for him?

Although the script may not be entirely accurate, it closely resembles Fiorello and Marie's brief courtship. They were married two months later at his Q Street apartment in Washington, D.C., and went right back to work on Capitol Hill after the wedding breakfast. Fiorello represented New York's 20th District and was touched when the Speaker of the House declared that congratulations were in order.

The marriage in 1929 was no surprise to most of Fiorello's friends. Marie was thirty-three and had been his private secretary for the past fifteen years. Ever since his first wife died in 1921, Marie had been the most important person in his life aside from his children.

He was forty-six, high-strung, talkative, and bursting with energy; she was soft-spoken, reliable, and reticent. Marie quit work right after the wedding but remained an active assistant in Fiorello's future campaigns and activities. Together they made an unbeatable team in their private lives and in politics.

Although Fiorello was technically a Republican, party allegiance meant little to him. He represented the "forgotten" people—immigrants, the aged, and others without political clout. "Who's Afraid of the Big Bad Wolf?" became his theme song, and five years after his marriage to Marie, he became the most beloved and hardworking mayor of the City of New York.

## ADAM AND EVE

*Really made for each other*

IT DIDN'T TAKE LONG FOR Adam to realize he had found the girl of his dreams. Eve was young, friendly, and eager to start a relationship, although she hadn't gone out with men before. Adam also had no dating experience, but like most guys, he didn't want Eve to know it. He slicked back his hair and tried to act suave and sophisticated. The garden was very nice, he said, with interesting walks, secluded spots to sit and chat, and any number of places for a quick bite of something to eat. . . .

Eve knew she had finally met Mr. Right and that Adam came from a good family. So what if it was an "arranged marriage?" There was nobody like Adam.

Their wedding was a simple affair. The bride kept her own name and didn't wear anything except a few white blossoms in her hair. She carried a magnificent bouquet of flowers, but there was no one to toss it to. The menu was strictly vegetarian and the very short guest list eliminated all troublesome seating arrangements. Every day was sunny, so weather was no problem. Since nobody worked, the ceremony did not have to be held on a weekend.

They wrote their own vows, after discussing and debating words like "obey" and whether or not a woman's "place" was only in the home. Walking down the aisle to their favorite tune, "If You Were the Only Girl in the World and I Were the Only Boy," Adam and Eve concluded that only one promise had to be made: they would love each other, no matter what.

Eventually the honeymoon period was over. It's hard to say just how long it took, since the passage of time hadn't been figured out yet. But Adam and Eve would look back to the early years of their marriage, when life was peaceful, beautiful, and simple . . . just like paradise on earth.

*Date approximate.

# MARCH

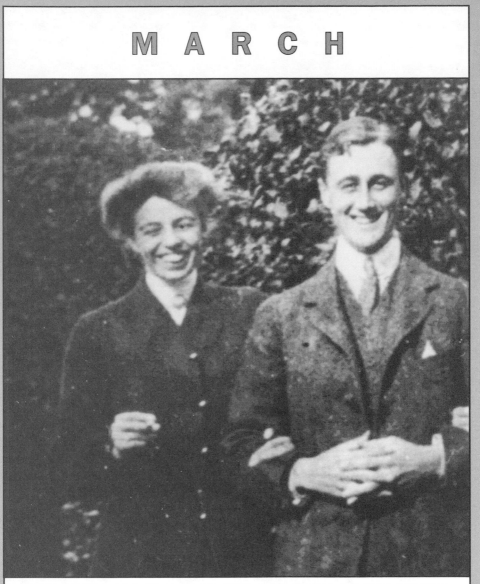

**FRANKLIN DELANO ROOSEVELT AND ELEANOR ROOSEVELT**

*March 17, 1905*

Honeymooning in Scotland that summer; later, Franklin bound all their
snapshots in an album as a Christmas gift for Eleanor.

## GEORGE BANCROFT AND SARAH DWIGHT

*"dearest Sally"*

GEORGE AND SARAH KNEW EACH other only a few months before he confessed his love in the spring of 1826. She was the daughter of a wealthy Springfield, Massachusetts, family, and he was a brilliant scholar teaching school at Round Hill Academy in nearby Northampton. When Sarah's father, Jonathan Dwight, learned about George's marriage proposal, he drove to the academy for a serious talk.

Eight years would pass before George published Volume One of his life's work—his monumental *History of the United States*. Writing it would take more than thirty years, while he held various jobs and government posts, including secretary of the navy under President James Polk. Now, at the age of twenty-six, George was still unsure about future plans but knew he could not live without his books, his research . . . and Sarah.

George told his future father-in-law about his experiences in Europe, where, after graduating from Harvard at the age of seventeen, he had studied with leading romantic poets and writers, including Goethe and Lord Byron. He had also been impressed by German historians, who taught him how to maintain objectivity and search for true historical sources. By the time he returned to America, George yearned for a satisfying academic life, solitude, and a loving wife.

Mr. Dwight was so impressed with George's intelligence and ambitions that he offered him the greatest gift: part-time employment in one of the family businesses, giving George time to work on his own.

The engagement would last almost ten months, a period filled with frustration and the fear that perhaps Sarah would change her mind. "Of all the human beings, on you my affections unite," he told her. At last they married at the Dwights' gracious home in Springfield in 1827. The wedding was followed by a reception and ball at George's house in Northampton.

## ROBERT MORRIS AND MARY WHITE

*"partner of my happy moments and sharer of my sorrowful hours"*

ALTHOUGH ROBERT WAS A PROSPEROUS Philadelphia businessman when he married "Molly" in 1769, neither could have predicted that within seven years he would be financing the American Revolution!

When they met, Robert was thirty-five—almost twice Molly's age. His partner, Thomas Willing, invited many socially prominent families, including the Whites, to a ball at the Assembly Hall. Other young men besides Robert asked brown-eyed, willowy Molly to place their names on her dance card, but he soon swept her off her feet. She was charming, gracious, and unaffected; Robert was confident, warm, and sincere. Their personalities never changed throughout the long years of their happy marriage. Their home on Front Street and their country estate, The Hills (which contained the first privately owned icehouse in America), were popular centers of gaiety, open for parties as well as political meetings.

Five years earlier Robert, who imported British products and exported American goods, had joined other frustrated colonists in resisting England's Stamp Act. When war broke out, he became a member of the Continental Congress. He also began financing munitions and naval armaments.

Robert's honesty was well known and respected, and by 1780 he was superintendent of finance for the new confederation, lending and borrowing money for the public cause. He also raised money by selling war bonds, even if it meant going from house to house to do it. Sometimes the only security Robert could offer was his own good name and reputation.

Hundreds of candles glittered in the crystal chandeliers of Philadelphia's Christ Church on the day Robert and Molly married. Church bells chimed as the bride and groom exited the chapel. They rang again for liberty in 1781, when the British surrendered at Yorktown.

## ELIAS HOWE AND ELIZABETH AMES

*Her "necessity" was the "mother" of his invention*

FOUR YEARS AFTER ELIAS MARRIED Elizabeth in 1841, he completed the first operating model of a sewing machine. He had met Elizabeth in Boston, where he was working in a machine shop. Three years earlier, at the age of sixteen, he had left his parents' farm for the textile mills of Lowell, Massachusetts. Elias had been born lame, which made farm work difficult, but he always liked tinkering with complicated machines. Soon he advanced from bobbin boy to making and repairing the cotton looms.

The Panic of 1837 closed down many mills and factories, so Elias and a few friends headed for Boston, where he fell in love with his dear Elizabeth and eventually made his fortune.

At that time all garments were sewn by hand, and workers were paid for each completed piece. Tailors and seamstresses spent hours hunched over worktables, but by the end of the day they had produced very little. Elizabeth always believed that Elias's own physical disability made him sensitive to the sadness in other people's lives. He also couldn't bear watching his wife take care of their house and family all day long and spend her evenings sewing garments to sell to neighbors, when he *knew* he could make a machine to do it faster, and better.

The problem was money. Elias needed his job at the machine shop and worked on his invention only late at night, when he was exhausted. Fortunately, his friends recognized his genius and provided financial support for the Howe family so Elias could concentrate on his sewing machine.

Like many inventors, Elias didn't become wealthy overnight. Crafty imitators began infringing on his patent, but after years of litigation, he won thousands of dollars in past royalties and guarantees for future royalties as they were accrued.

## RONALD REAGAN AND NANCY DAVIS

*"My life really began when I met Nancy"*

WHEN NANCY CAME TO HOLLYWOOD in 1949, her greatest ambition was not to be a famous film star. Instead, the future first lady hoped to have a successful, happy marriage. She met Ronnie a few months later. Already he was a president—of the Screen Actors Guild—and strongly opposed to Communist sympathizers. Nancy was very interested in political issues and admired every word Ronnie said. He also was attracted to her, but his eight-year marriage to actress Jane Wyman had just ended and he wanted to be single for a while. He did, however, give the name "Nancy D" to a new foal born at his ranch.

He was forty-one and she was thirty when they married in 1952 in a small ceremony at the Little Brown Church in the San Fernando Valley. Actor William Holden was best man, and his wife Ardis was matron of honor. Nancy wore a gray wool suit with a white collar and a small flowered hat with a veil. They spent their wedding night at the Mission Inn in Riverside and honeymooned in Phoenix, Arizona. On their way back to California, they drove through a sandstorm, which tore apart the canvas top of their convertible. Even then Nancy and Ronnie were a team; he drove the car as she held down the top!

For a while they lived in Nancy's Brentwood apartment and then settled into a comfortable but conventional home at 1258 Amalfi Drive in Pacific Palisades. Within fourteen years Ronnie would forgo Hollywood and the television career he had developed, switch from being a Democrat to being a Republican, and run for the governorship of California. He'd never been elected to public office before, but with Nancy at his side, he was unbeatable.

Eventually he dedicated his autobiography to her and wrote, "To Nancy: She will always be my First Lady. I cannot imagine life without her."

## JACOB RIIS AND ELIZABETH NIELSEN

*"Two, we would beat the world"*

SIXTEEN-YEAR-OLD ELIZABETH KEPT JACOB'S LOVE notes even when her parents insisted that she reject his marriage proposal. Wounded and impetuous, her twenty-one-year-old suitor sailed from Denmark to America, carrying the immigrant's classic dream that someday he would make his fortune and marry the girl back home. He struggled for several years, finding work as a coal miner, carpenter, brick-layer, and traveling salesman. Often he slept in five-cents-a-night flophouses and ate only when he earned enough money for a meal. But Jacob kept writing to Elizabeth. After he landed a job as a cub reporter for a New York news association, he knew that he had found his vocation.

Scraping together some money, Jacob proposed marriage to Elizabeth again. She didn't answer for months, but at last she agreed, having come to believe "that we were meant for one another." He sailed back home immediately.

They married in the Domkirke, the oldest church in Ribe, in 1876. Elizabeth wore flowers her friends had "loved up" and nurtured in their tiny winter gardens. As she and Jacob rode in a carriage toward the dock and the boat to New York, "her head was leaning trustfully on my shoulder and her hand was in mine; all was well," he later recollected.

They settled in Brooklyn, and Jacob got a job with the New York *Tribune.* Covering street life and local issues, he was so horrified by the bleak lives of hardworking poor families living in overcrowded, rat-infested tenements that he devoted himself to improving their situations. With articles, photographs, and books such as *How the Other Half Lives,* he stirred the social consciences of many New Yorkers, which led to vast improvements in child labor and sweatshop laws, as well as housing and school conditions.

# MARCH 6

## EDWARD JENNER AND CATHERINE KINGSCOTE

### *She rescued him . . . so he could save millions*

DR. JENNER WAS THIRTY-EIGHT WHEN he married the young woman who had saved his life. His older brother Stephen conducted the wedding ceremony in 1788 in a small country church in Berkeley, England, not far from the place where Catherine had found Edward two years earlier.

He had been riding to the village of Kingscote in a snowstorm to attend a pregnant woman in labor. As Edward pushed on through the blizzard, he knew that he would probably die if he lost his way or fell off his horse. Reaching the house, Edward knocked on the heavy front door and collapsed.

When he woke up, he was in a warm room, wrapped in a blanket. A sweet-faced twenty-three-year-old woman with large gray eyes was watching him. It was Catherine. Not only had she rescued Edward, but she had also helped his patient deliver a healthy child. Edward and Catherine talked about medicine, music, and poetry for hours until he fell asleep on the floor by the fire. When he recovered, she invited him to come back with his violin so he could accompany her while she played her spinet piano. With more time to talk, Edward told her he'd never wanted to be anything but a doctor. Even now, he would not have thought about marriage if Catherine hadn't entered his life.

He'd become obsessed by smallpox, the scourge of the eighteenth century. Even people who survived the disease suffered deeply and were disfigured by scars. Primitive inoculations required patients to be isolated for weeks, and the treatments produced great pain and suffering, and sometimes death.

After years of research and testing, including experimental inoculations on his own children, Edward confirmed that injecting people with cowpox vaccine immunized them from smallpox. By 1801 smallpox was virtually gone from Western civilization.

## ADOLPHUS BUSCH AND LILLY ANHEUSER

### *"Darby and Joan"*

IN 1911 LILLY AND ADOLPHUS celebrated their golden wedding anniversary by decorating their Pasadena, California, home with hundreds of golden flowers. Thirty-eight relatives sat on golden chairs and ate from golden plates. Adolphus placed a diamond, pearl, and gold tiara on Lilly's head and said his successful career would never have happened without her help and understanding. Then the man who created the "King of Beers" told her she would always be his queen. Other celebrations were held that night in thirty-five cities, including St. Louis, where 13,000 employees and business associates of the Anheuser-Busch company danced to a fifty-piece band, ate countless ham sandwiches, and drank more than 40,000 bottles of Budweiser at the Coliseum downtown.

Even before the joyful couple grew old, people called them "Darby and Joan," after the deeply happy elderly pair in an old English song. Adolphus met Lilly soon after he and his older brother, Ulrich, came to St. Louis from Germany and set up a brewer's supply store. One of their best customers was Eberhard Anheuser, whose daughters, Lilly and Anna, soon fell in love with the brothers. After a double wedding ceremony at St. Louis's church of the Holy Ghost Evangelical Lutheran, Eberhard hosted a lavish reception for the four newlyweds. That morning Adolphus had closed a major deal and made enough money to take Lilly to Europe for their honeymoon.

Soon Ulrich and Anna moved to Chicago, where he continued in the brewing supply business. Adolphus enlisted in the Union army but was discharged after three months. He and Lilly studied brewing techniques in Germany and Bavaria and learned about Louis Pasteur's achievements. Back in America, Adolphus was the first brewer to pasteurize beer.

In 1864 Eberhard invited him to help manage his brewery, and fifteen years later the Anheuser-Busch Brewing Association was established.

## CHARLES BEARD AND MARY RITTER

*"pure happenstance"*

WHEN CHARLES MET MARY, SHE was soaking wet. Years passed before the two scholars teamed up in "life-long partnership" and became internationally known historians, but that day marked the beginning. Mary and a few DePauw University friends had been paddling a small boat on an Indiana lake when suddenly they capsized. Within seconds, Charles was pulling Mary out of the water, helping her wring her skirts dry and gently brushing twigs out of her hair. In later years he looked back at that time of "pure happenstance" and knew he had been blessed with good fortune.

They married in 1900 and took a bicycling trip through Europe that spring. The next two years were spent at Oxford University in England, where Charles had helped establish a "free university" for working-class students. Among their friends was suffragist Emmeline Pankhurst, who lived nearby, as well as other socialists and labor sympathizers. Change was in the air as the new century began, and Mary hoped to see more women involved in work and politics.

Back in America, she and Charles enrolled in graduate programs at Columbia University, marched in suffrage parades, and expounded their views in progressive political journals. The Beards believed that a solid understanding of *past* history could positively affect the course of *future* history, a philosophy reflected in one of their major works, *The Rise of American Civilization,* written in the 1920s.

After many years Mary confessed to still being deeply in love with Charles and delighting in their "orgies of co-authorship." "I loved sitting at home with my darling every night and being at his side all the days," she wrote. No one could fully understand their "mutual happiness in working, jabbering and getting such exercise as we took in our simple ways. THIS IS AN ABSOLUTE TRUTH."

## NAPOLEON BONAPARTE AND
## JOSEPHINE TASCHER DE BEAUHARNAIS

*"To Destiny!"*

JOSEPHINE WASN'T IMPRESSED WHEN SHE met Napoleon. The French army officer was somewhat shy and inexperienced, six years younger and several inches shorter than she. Her late husband had been guillotined the year before, during the Reign of Terror. Josephine had been imprisoned, too, but was released days before her own scheduled execution. Virtually penniless, with two children to care for, she borrowed money from relatives, fixed herself up, and looked for a new and suitable protector.

When Napoleon was promoted to brigadier general, she focused all her attentions on him. At thirty-two, her body was still voluptuous. She flattered and teased him, beguiled and seduced him, making him half-mad with passion: "To live with Josephine is to live in Elysium," he wrote. "A kiss on your mouth, your eyes, your shoulder, your breasts, everywhere! everywhere!"

They married in Paris in 1796. Signing the wedding contract in the mayor's office, Napoleon added eighteen months to his age and Josephine subtracted four years, making them both—for the moment—twenty-eight. Afterward they walked back to her apartment; her children were with relatives, but her pet dog Fortuné was at home.

The tiny black-faced pug had a nasty disposition and snapped at everyone except his mistress. He snarled when Napoleon entered the house and barked ferociously when he climbed into Josephine's bed. Next he nipped at Napoleon's heels, sinking his teeth into his legs. Napoleon tried tossing the little monster out the door, but Josephine blocked the way, insisting that her sweet pet always slept beside her and getting married wasn't going to change that.

Two days later Napoleon and his troops departed for Italy and conquered it in record time. In eight years, he and Josephine were emperor and empress of France. She never parted with the wedding ring he gave her; inscribed inside were the words, "To Destiny!"

## GUSTAV MAHLER AND ALMA MARIA SCHINDLER

### *"Wonne über Wonne"*

GUSTAV COULDN'T TAKE HIS EYES off Alma at a dinner party in Vienna in 1901. He was forty-one and an internationally known composer and conductor. She was twenty-two, intelligent and incredibly beautiful. They began sharing stories, discussing music, and arguing about famous works. The next day Gustav wrote the first of many love poems for her. The great man was soon befuddled; he left his shoelaces untied and forgot his own phone number. All he could think about was Alma.

He wrote passionate letters to her, filled with longing for "the dearest and most sublime object of my life . . . my peace, my heaven in which I can constantly immerse myself."

"There was a magic circle round us which quickly encloses those who have found each other," Alma wrote almost fifty years later. A landscape painter's daughter, she understood the insecurities that plagued artists and the unpredictability of life in the public eye. No matter how famous Gustav became, much of his work was misunderstood because it was a departure from typical romantic nineteenth-century music. But Alma stayed by him, nurturing him through bouts of depression and inspiring him to compose magnificent symphonies.

"I want to become the sort of person you wish and need!" she wrote, reluctantly agreeing to give up her own musical ambitions. By Christmas they were engaged. The news leaked out. Audiences stared at Alma, not at the stage, when Gustav conducted operas.

"We're consumed with desire," she wrote in her diary. "It's sapping all our strength." A few days later— *"Wonne über Wonne!"* (Joy beyond all joy!). She was pregnant with their first child when they married at Vienna's Karlskirche in 1902 and honeymooned in St. Petersburg, where Gustav conducted three concerts.

Gustav's life was transformed. Soon he was composing his Fifth Symphony, generally considered his sunniest work. Alma's influence was magical.

\*March 9 has also been cited.

## RUSSELL BAKER AND MIRIAM NASH

*It wasn't "in the cards" but . . .*

RUSSELL WAS A TWENTY-FOUR-YEAR-OLD REPORTER for the *Baltimore Sun* when he married "Mimi" in 1950. Years later, in *Growing Up* and *The Good Times,* he described their relationship and all the times he had told her marriage wasn't "in the cards."

They first met one night in the parlor of a rooming house as he was dropping off his blind date. "This is Mimi," his date said. Those words changed Russell's life forever. But his mother wasn't happy when he brought Mimi home; after all, although she was only nineteen, she lived alone, wore makeup, and probably bleached her hair. Most women were considered either "good" or "bad" in those days, and Russell's mother implied that Mimi was the latter.

Russell didn't think he would marry Mimi, but he couldn't give her up. Exasperated by his stubbornness, after three years she moved to Washington to start a new job and hopefully a new life. A year later, after breakups, mix-ups, and passionate reunions—which Russell later described as "the routine stuff of Hollywood's romantic comedies on which we had both grown up"—he realized that he wanted to marry Mimi after all.

"What a lovely spectacle she was when I first saw her at the altar," he recalled. She wore a beige suit with a dark blue hat, and he felt rather spiffy in a blue suit with padded shoulders and wide lapels. They were married in a church near his mother's home on Marydell Road in Baltimore and took the train to New York for a short honeymoon at the Hotel Commodore. Within five years, he was writing for *The New York Times.* His columns are poignant, personal, universal, introspective, irreverent, and humorous—often all at the same time. In 1979 he became the first humorist to win the Pulitzer Prize for Commentary.

## PAUL MCCARTNEY AND LINDA EASTMAN

### *He saw her standing there*

LINDA, A ROCK BAND PHOTOGRAPHER, met Paul backstage at Shea Stadium in New York, where the Beatles were performing to sellout crowds in 1966. They crossed paths again at London clubs and at Brian Epstein's press party for the Sergeant Pepper album. Hordes of photographers vied for the attentions of the famous musicians, but blond-haired, attractive, miniskirted Linda was often the only one able to get close to them.

She'd always been comfortable around celebrities; her entertainment-lawyer father brought them home often when she was growing up. Linda was eighteen when her mother died; her feelings of devastation and loss were similar to those Paul felt at fourteen when his mother died.

Within two years he had fallen in love with Linda and her young daughter, Heather, and they began living together in Paul's house at 7 Cavendish Avenue in St. John's Wood, London, filling it with dogs and cats, as well as ducks, geese, and chickens in the yard.

In 1969 the band was on the verge of splitting up; no other Beatles attended Paul and Linda's brief wedding ceremony at the Marylebone registry office in London, but throngs of reporters and fans stood outside. Soon after Linda's baby was born, she and Paul moved to Scotland and withdrew from public life, inadvertently inspiring rumors that he had died.

How Paul and Linda met and married isn't, in the long run, half as interesting as the fact that they've managed to stay together through experiences that could easily cause less stellar couples to separate. More than twenty years later Paul was quoted as saying, "I twisted Linda's arm and she agreed to marry me. . . . Linda was afraid it wouldn't work out and I kept telling her, 'Aw, come on, it will be fine. Don't worry.' And I'm still telling her that."

## JAMES DALTON TRUMBO AND CLEO BETH FINCHER

*"under cloudier skies or sunnier"*

DALTON'S FIRST WORDS TO CLEO were an order: coffee and a hamburger. She worked at a popular drive-in restaurant near Hollywood, and he was a thirty-two-year-old up-and-coming novelist and screenwriter. Dalton was so transfixed by the adorable carhop that he asked her to marry him when he paid the bill.

Barely twenty years old, Cleo had enough self-confidence and good humor to think, This guy can't be serious. But Dalton persisted, dropping by the drive-in night after night. When she suddenly ran off with a boyfriend and got married in Reno, Dalton did some investigating and found out that Cleo's "husband" was already married! Although Cleo was crushed, she also was eternally grateful to Dalton. It took a year for her to officially disentangle herself from the cad she had "married" and marry Dalton in his mother's apartment in 1938.

She'd always been impressed by his energy, enthusiasm, and determination to win her. Those qualities helped them weather terrible times nine years later, when Dalton, now one of the highest-paid writers in filmdom, went to jail with other members of the "Hollywood Ten" after refusing to disclose his political views and testify before the House Un-American Activities Committee investigating Communists.

On their thirteenth wedding anniversary, he wrote to Cleo from a prison cell: "We shall have many good years together, under cloudier skies or sunnier, but our love for each other will make its own climate—the climate of springtime which surrounds me tonight as I think of you."

Blacklisted from Hollywood for years, he eked out a living by writing stories anonymously. In 1957 *The Brave Bulls* won an Academy Award; subsequently Dalton wrote the screenplays for *Spartacus, Exodus,* and other hit movies under his own name again.

## DON RICKLES AND BARBARA SKLAR

*"I married a Valium"*

THE WORLD-FAMOUS MASTER OF INSULT jokes didn't marry until he was thirty-eight. Barbara always knew that Don was a likable guy, in spite of his talent for hurling offensive remarks at everyone from the fat man sitting at a front row table in a Las Vegas nightclub to Frank Sinatra himself, in Hollywood.

"What do you eat for dinner? Furniture?" Don asked the overweight man. And just because he'd never met "Ol' Blue Eyes," he certainly grabbed his attention another time by politely suggesting, "Make yourself at home, Frank. Hit somebody."

No one escaped his barbs . . . except Barb. So what if he said "Marriage is a beautiful thing. It's better than laying in a dam watching a beaver eat your jacket or something . . ." Even his mother—"the Jewish Patton"—was a target, although Don loved her deeply too. In fact, after he and Barbara married in 1965, they remained in his old apartment, right next door to Etta Rickles. Barbara let her mother-in-law still be the boss about a lot of things, which convinced Don that his new wife was a "saint."

Barbara, who had been his film agent's secretary, saw Don whenever he dropped by. "I was searching for someone with beauty and simplicity," Don has said. "When I finally found her, I married her." A few months later he debuted on Johnny Carson's *Tonight Show* and had the chutzpah to greet his host with "Hello, dummy!" The audience—and Johnny—loved "Mr. Warmth," whose career picked up dramatically. Meanwhile, Barbara took care of their home and two kids; later on she traveled with Don more often. Just as private as he is offstage, she keeps him company, helps out in his dressing room, and is always his number-one fan.

## ELIZABETH TAYLOR AND RICHARD BURTON

### *"Le scandale"*

NEITHER RICHARD NOR ELIZABETH EVER forgot the first time they met, at a party in Los Angeles in 1953. She was twenty and he was twenty-eight. "She was unquestionably gorgeous . . . she was lavish," he wrote years later. "She was a dark unyielding largesse. She was, in short, too bloody much, and not only that, she was totally ignoring me." Elizabeth's first impression was that "he was rather full of himself."

They met again ten years later on the set of *Cleopatra,* a film remembered primarily for running millions of dollars over budget and for the real-life romance of "Antony" and "Cleopatra"—aka Dick and Liz. Although she teasingly called him "Gramps" and he addressed her as "Pudgy," their love scenes were passionately hot. She was not quite thirty and wed to her fourth husband, singer Eddie Fisher. That marriage, as well as Dick's to Sybil Burton, went on the rocks; by the time the film was released, Dick and Liz were an item in gossip columns everywhere.

One of Richard's first gifts to Elizabeth was a necklace of ancient Egyptian scarabs, probably made during the time of Cleopatra. When they married in 1964, she wore a low-cut yellow chiffon gown enhanced by another gift—a huge emerald brooch.

The ceremony was held in their hotel suite in Montreal's Ritz Carlton. The following day they flew to Toronto, where Richard was starring in a production of *Hamlet.* When the curtain came down that night, he invited Elizabeth to join him on the stage, where he introduced her to the audience. Then he quoted Hamlet's words to Ophelia in the nunnery scene—"I say we will have no more marriages!" The audience went wild. Within five years Elizabeth and Richard were probably the best-known and best-paid husband-and-wife acting team in the world.

### ROBERT MITCHUM AND DOROTHY SPENCE

*There never was anyone else . . .*

THE SEXY HOLLYWOOD STAR WITH sleepy eyelids found his perfect wife when he was in his teens and was married to her for more than fifty years.

Bob quit high school in New York at fourteen, left home, and worked at odd jobs as he hitchhiked around the country during the early 1930's. Bob's family moved, too, to Rising Sun, Delaware, where he met Dorothy on one of his visits. By then, he was sixteen and she was fourteen, already tall and slender with a serene disposition. Just being around her made Bob feel less lonely. At first she was put off by his wise-guy demeanor, but gradually she discovered gentleness underneath.

Dorothy's parents didn't like the brash and smart-alecky young man and forbade her to see him. He didn't admit that his limp was from gangrene he'd gotten while working on a chain gang, but they sensed his background had been unconventional. Bob hung around Dorothy for as long as possible and then headed for California, where he practically stumbled into acting in a local playhouse. He wrote to Dorothy often, warning her not to get serious with other men because someday he would be coming back to marry her.

They were twenty-two and twenty years old when he came east in 1940. On a Friday night they drove to Dover, Delaware, and knocked on the door of a Methodist minister, who married them amid the odors of cabbage his wife was cooking in the kitchen.

Bob and Dorothy's honeymoon trip was a bus ride to Los Angeles; years of financial struggle and the births of two children followed. His first acting break was playing bad guys in Hopalong Cassidy films. In 1945, his Academy Award nomination for best supporting actor in *The Story of G.I. Joe* put him on the road to stardom.

## FRANKLIN DELANO ROOSEVELT AND
## ELEANOR ROOSEVELT

*"Well, Franklin, there's nothing like keeping
the name in the family."*
—THEODORE ROOSEVELT

UNCLE TEDDY SAID HE'D BE delighted to give away the bride when she married his distant cousin Franklin in 1905. As president of the United States, Teddy also said they could have their wedding at the White House, but Eleanor preferred an aunt's Manhattan town house at Fifth Avenue and 76th Street. Okay, said Teddy, as long as they got married on St. Patrick's Day, when he'd be in New York marching in the parade. Onlookers swarmed around him and blocked nearby streets when he arrived at 3:30 P.M., preventing some guests from getting to the ceremony on time.

"Try and forget the crowd and only think of Franklin," Eleanor's aunt advised the nervous bride. "If you are wise, you will drink a cup of strong tea half an hour before you go downstairs. It will give you color and make you feel well. *No* sugar or cream in it!"

White lilacs, lilies, and roses decorated the townhouse. An orchestra played the wedding march as six bridesmaids wearing cream-colored taffeta dresses descended the circular staircase. Eleanor followed in a stiff white satin dress, carrying a bouquet of lilies of the valley. Her Brussels lace veil was secured to her hair by a diamond crescent comb. Around her neck was a "dog collar" of pearls with diamond bars, a gift from Franklin's mother. Under a bower of pink roses and palms, the couple recited their marriage vows loudly, so their voices could be heard over the din of bagpipes outside the windows.

The honeymooners spent a quiet week alone at the Roosevelt family's home in Hyde Park, postponing an extended trip to Europe until the summer, when Franklin would be on vacation from his studies at Columbia Law School. (He, too, had been under a lot of stress and failed two courses that semester!)

## JOHN LOCKWOOD KIPLING AND ALICE MACDONALD

*"Ruddy's" parents met at a lake*

ALICE HAD DARK RED HAIR and blue eyes and was witty and insightful. She often spoke in a rush, her sharp mind moving more quickly than her words. John, by contrast, was serene and smiling, somewhat forgetful but incredibly kind and gentle. Before he met Alice, he'd been working as a sculptor during construction of London's Victoria and Albert Museum in the 1860s and would be immortalized in a large group portrait there.

He then came to Staffordshire and was designing pottery in nearby Burslem when Alice's minister brother, Frederick, invited him to a gathering of local artists and scholars. The picnic was held by Lake Rudyard and that's where John met Alice. Later they commemorated that romantic spot by naming their first child after it.

They were determined not to marry until they could stand on their own feet financially. Both were twenty-seven when they decided boldly that John should accept the position of architectural sculptor at the Jeejeeboy School of Art in Bombay. They would leave for India as soon as they were wed.

Alice's younger sister Georgiana, who had already married the painter Edward Burne-Jones, handled all the arrangements for the wedding, held at St. Mary Abbot's church in London on a blustery day in 1865. Because Alice's father's health was poor, Frederick gave away the bride. Renowned writers and artists, including Charles Algernon Swinburne, the two Rosettis, and Ford Madox Ford attended the reception, though Alice and John had already slipped away and boarded a waiting ship.

For the next thirty years Alice wrote poems and articles for magazines and local newspapers in India and supported all of her husband's artistic endeavors. Later, she would also influence their dear son "Ruddy," who would be permanently inspired by life in that exotic land.

## JOHN CASSAVETES AND GENA ROWLANDS

*His leading lady*

GENA MET JOHN IN NEW York City in 1953, soon after she left the University of Wisconsin in her junior year and enrolled in the Academy of Dramatic Arts. He had graduated three years before but saw her performing in a student production. She was radiantly beautiful and determined to become an actress. He was bright, intense, and passionately in love with the theater, with acting . . . and with Gena. They were married in 1954 at the Little Church Around the Corner in Manhattan. She was nineteen and he was twenty-four.

At first they performed separately and together in television drama series, such as *Kraft Television Theatre* and *Lux Playhouse,* and acted in plays on and off Broadway. But by his late twenties John was eager to become an independent filmmaker and put a unique spin on his own productions.

The couple moved to Hollywood in 1958 and worked together on many of John's projects. He'd already produced *Shadows,* a grainy, poignant black-and-white film that grew out of a series of drama workshops he conducted. Many of John's other films featured Gena or close friends, such as Peter Falk and Ben Gazzara. Sometimes the scripts were only loosely written drafts, open to interpretation and improvisation by the cast, but he wrote *A Woman Under the Influence* in detail, tailoring it specifically for Gena. They promoted the film themselves until it was booked into theaters coast to coast. It won awards and citations and an Academy Award nomination for Gena.

Although some critics called their marriage tempestuous, providing John with rich material for his films, he and Gena remained devoted to each other. Next to John, "other people look squinched up," she said. Referring to his Greek ancestry, she added, "he's my Mediterranean madman and I wouldn't have it any other way."

## JOHN LENNON AND YOKO ONO

### *Life as Art, Art as Life*

A FEW DAYS AFTER BEATLE Paul McCartney married Linda Eastman in 1969, John and Yoko decided to do the same thing. As they drove around London in John's white Rolls-Royce, they considered various sites for their momentous event. Why not the Channel ferry between England and France? Or perhaps a very grand ceremony, performed by the Archbishop of Canterbury, no less. But that would take a lot of time to arrange, and besides, it was unlikely that the archbishop would agree.

Instead, John and Yoko flew to the island of Gibraltar and were married in a three-minute private ceremony. Both were dressed in white: John wore a sweater, jacket, and pants; Yoko wore a mini-dress, kneesocks, and a wide-brimmed hat. They held lit cigarettes and sported white tennis shoes. She was thirty-six and already had a daughter; he was twenty-eight and had a son.

Within the hour the newlyweds were on a plane to Paris, where the press surrounded them at Le Bourget airport. They stayed a few days, had lunch with painter Salvador Dali, and then were off to the Netherlands, where they staged a week-long "bed-in" for peace in the Amsterdam Hilton's Suite 902, pleading for the world to "Give peace a chance" and end the war in Vietnam. They produced a short documentary film called *Honeymoon,* as well as *Wedding Album,* a collection of recordings, photographs, and mementoes about their momentous day.

They had first met three years before, at a London art gallery where Yoko's avant-garde work was being exhibited. John was impressed with her bizarre conceptions and creations, and eventually he financed some of her shows. The other Beatles were never very comfortable with Yoko. But she and John became a powerful team, expressing themselves through musical and visual works of art.

## BENNY GOODMAN AND ALICE HAMMOND DUCKWORTH

*Let's dance!*

THE "KING OF SWING" WAS an internationally known clarinetist and band-leader when he and Alice married on the first day of spring in 1942. Benny was a thirty-two-year-old bachelor; Alice was thirty-five and had recently ended her marriage to a member of the British Parliament. She had three daughters and would have two more with Benny.

They'd met in England in 1934, when Alice's brother, music writer and producer John Hammond, brought Benny and other leading jazz musicians together to cut records. A year later, after a routine evening playing dance music at the Palomar Ballroom in Los Angeles, Benny and his new band broke loose with wild, improvisational sounds of pulse-pounding music—and the new era of "swing music" was born! In the late 1930's Benny was one of the first white bandleaders with an integrated band, featuring outstanding African-American musicians such as Lionel Hampton and Jess Stacy.

For a long time Benny had been focused on his career. People often joked that he was "married" to his music. By the early 1940s it had made him rich and famous. As the great-great-granddaughter of Cornelius Vanderbilt, Alice was wealthy, too, but her upper-crust background didn't stifle her interest in show business and in the personable and ambitious clarinet player. She helped Benny smooth out some of his rough edges, and although their families wondered sometimes what brought the society girl and jazz musician together, their relationship proved to be loving and long-lasting.

They married in Nevada and headed for California. Benny later said, "Hardly anyone thought the marriage would work. Alice had been married before to a rather staid Englishman and was used to a home life. We spent our first three months under seventy-three different roofs on the road."

## J.R.R. TOLKIEN AND EDITH MARY BRATT

### *His "Luthien"*

"RONALD" MARRIED EDITH IN WARWICK, England, in 1916, shortly before he left for military service in World War I. They had met eight years earlier in a boardinghouse in Cheltenham, when he was sixteen and she was nineteen. Bright, impressionable, but also lonely and orphaned teenagers, they became very close in the years they lived together.

Edith was a talented pianist whose family was distantly related to Sir George Grove, editor of the well-known dictionary of music. Ronald's guardian, Father Francis, discouraged his relationship with Edith because she wasn't Catholic, but by the time Ronald left to study at Oxford, he believed that Edith would wait for him and that they would marry one day.

Few people knew how he felt about Edith, but Ronald never stopped dreaming about her. In the meantime, however, she became engaged to another young man, having lost hope that Ronald would ever return. Soon after his twenty-first birthday, he hurried back to Cheltenham and convinced Edith that she should never have doubted his love.

Three years later there was time only for a short honeymoon in Somerset before Ronald left for France. While it's difficult to know where writers find their inspirations, it's likely that the darker parts of *The Lord of the Rings* were inspired by Ronald's experiences in trench warfare. Perhaps he created Middle Earth to escape the frightening realities of twentieth-century life.

After the war he and Edith lived on Northmore Road in Oxford, and eventually he became the Merton Professor of Linguistics and Literature at Oxford. He wrote *The Hobbit* and the *Rings* trilogy there and was known as a kind and generous teacher and man. As Edith's life brightened, she became a proper don's wife, keeping house and raising their four children. Ronald compared her to his character Luthien—"the fairest maiden that has ever been."

## LOUIS BRANDEIS AND ALICE GOLDMARK

*"we have found each other"*

LOUIS AND ALICE FELL IN love in the summer of 1890 at a family gathering in New York's Adirondack Mountains. The future Supreme Court justice was a brilliant and introspective thirty-three-year-old lawyer who had settled in Boston after graduating from Harvard Law School. His distant cousin Alice was twenty-three, brown-eyed and slender. Since Louis often worked seven days a week, his brief holiday in the mountains was a blissful time.

They took long walks, read together, and became inseparable. As moths fluttered against her window screen late at night, Alice opened her diary and wrote about Louis: "His eyes are always upon me. We go down to the river and he tells me his story—we have found each other."

By the time they parted, they were planning their engagement. Alice returned to New York City, and Louis began searching for a home for them in Boston. They corresponded constantly, and he admitted that ever since he had left for college seventeen years before, he had "stood alone—rarely asking—still less frequently caring, for the advice of others." Now everything had changed. Without Alice, Louis felt incomplete. "I feel myself . . . growing more into your soul," he confessed. "And I am very happy."

"If the 23rd were not fixed immutably, I should . . . break away and carry you off," he said one week before the wedding.

Alice's brother-in-law, Dr. Felix Adler, founder of the New York Society for Ethical Culture, conducted the ceremony at the Goldmarks' apartment in 1891. After honeymooning in the Berkshires, Alice and Louis moved to 114 Mt. Vernon Street, near Boston Common and Louis's office on Devonshire Street.

Louis often represented needy clients without charging them fees. Alice also was involved in social causes and set up night-school classes for working people.

## ANNE DUDLEY AND SIMON BRADSTREET

*"My head, my heart, mine eyes, my life, nay more"*

*If ever two were one, then surely we.*
*If ever man were lov'd by wife, then thee;*
*If ever wife was happy in a man,*
*Compare with me ye women if you can.*

So begins Anne's well-known poem, "To my dear and Loving Husband," written in Massachusetts Bay Colony about 1650. She would have been a writer, no matter where she lived—"I am obnoxious to each carping tongue/Who sayes my hand a needle better fits"—but her poems are the first known works of exceptional literary value to have been written in colonial New England.

Childhood sweethearts, Anne and Simon married in England two years before they sailed with her parents to America in March 1630, on John Winthrop's flagship, the *Arabella*. March is also the month of Anne's birth, as well as the beginning of springtime, and so it was chosen as the month of her wedding. She was sixteen and he was twenty-five years old. They were married for forty-four years, during which time they lived in various parts of the Massachusetts Bay area and raised eight children in an atmosphere of love and respect for education and literature. Future descendants would include nineteenth-century author and lawyer Richard Henry Dana and Supreme Court Justice Oliver Wendell Holmes, Jr.

The Puritans believed that marriages could end only with death. But Anne also hoped to be remembered on this earth. She wrote to her adored husband:

*Thy love is such I can no way repay,*
*The heavens reward thee manifold, I pray.*
*Then while we live, in love lets so persever,*
*That when we live no more, we may live ever.*

\*Date approximate.

## THOMAS MOORE AND ELIZABETH DYKE

*"those endearing young charms"*

TOM'S UPPER-CRUST FRIENDS WERE SURPRISED when he married "Bessy" in 1811. The thirty-one-year-old composer-poet was cultured and handsome enough to have married any number of wealthy women in London. He'd met Bessy, a poor but beautiful young actress, in Kilkenny, Ireland, three years before. Tom usually wrote the music for theatrical productions, but that season he and Bessy performed together in a play. Although she was not well educated, Bessy was talented, spirited, kindhearted, and adoring.

Tom had always been passionate about music and had also written rhymes since childhood. He'd left Ireland at the age of twenty and found patrons, including the Prince of Wales, in London. Soon the young Irishman was playing music, singing at social gatherings, and writing poetry.

After he married Bessy, Tom decided to give up depending on the precarious nature of patronage. For a while he and Bessy lived with friends. Then they moved to a small house he called "a nutshell of a thing" in the country, where he devoted himself to "the quiet pursuit of literature." A publisher advanced him money to write "Lalla Rookh," a long, lyrical poem about an oriental romance. It would become one of his most famous works and rank him alongside Lord Byron and Sir Walter Scott. But Tom's *Irish Melodies*—over one hundred pieces of lyrical beauty—became the crowning achievement of his life.

He was thinking of Bessy when he wrote:

> *Believe me, if all those endearing young charms*
> *Which I gaze on so fondly to-day,*
> *Were to change by to-morrow, and fleet in my arms,*
> *Like fairy-gifts fading away,*
> *Thou wouldst still be ador'd, as this moment thou art,*
> *Let thy loveliness fade as it will,*
> *And around the dear ruin each wish of my heart*
> *Would entwine itself verdantly still.*

## LESLIE STEPHEN AND JULIA PRINSEP DUCKWORTH

*"such a wife as no language can describe"*

"LORD, WHAT A CRANKY BRUTE I am!" Leslie wrote a friend in 1877. His first wife had died two years before, leaving him dejected and with a young child in their home near London's Kensington Gardens. A few months later Leslie's news was brighter: "Mrs. Duckworth is our neighbor almost, and I have been seeing her. . . . Her children have been the playmates of my poor little girl, who needed playmates very much. . . . We are to be married before very long . . . and if I am not happy . . . it will be my own fault."

Julia, too, had been widowed. "I was only 24 when life all seemed a shipwreck," she wrote Leslie after they became friends. She did not intend to marry again. It took a long time for her to accept his proposal, but one evening she suddenly looked up at Leslie and announced that she wanted to be his wife and would do her best to be a good one. Their marriage would be happy, and she would give birth to four more children, including future writers Virginia Woolf and Vanessa Bell.

On Sunday afternoons Leslie and Julia hosted salons for aspiring and well-established poets, artists, musicians, and novelists. Julia was particularly delighted to listen to her young guests talk about their romances and friendships.

As a respected Victorian man of letters, mountaineer, biographer, historian, and first editor of Britain's *Dictionary of National Biography,* Leslie encouraged many young writers, such as Robert Louis Stevenson, Thomas Hardy, and Henry James. Julia wrote, too, including *Notes For Sick Rooms,* a sympathetic and helpful book about how to care for ill people.

Many years after March 26, 1878, Leslie could still say, "Not a fibre in me but thrills at the thought of all the goodness lavished upon me since that day."

## PRINCE KHURRAM AND ARJUMAND BANU BEGAM

### *"Chosen One of the Palace"*

IN SEVENTEENTH-CENTURY INDIA, ROYAL WEDDING dates were determined by the emperor's astrologers. Khurram and Arjumand had to wait five years for an auspicious day to marry. During that time they were not permitted to meet or even see each other.

In 1607 the sixteen-year-old prince was walking through the Royal Meena Bazaar in Agra, near the palace harem. Vendors hawked jeweled silks, perfumes, and amulets, and young men flirted with innocent young women—until strict fathers chased them away. Outside one of the striped tents was the prime minister's lovely fifteen-year-old daughter. Arjumand's voice was soft as rain trickling down a gentle hillside. Her long eyelashes fluttered when she laughed, and Khurram was enchanted by her.

They married in 1612 in a glorious ceremony at the bride's home. Dancers swayed and dervishes whirled; dignitaries arrived in palanquins and on the backs of elephants. Everyone feasted until long after midnight. The emperor proclaimed that his daughter-in-law would be called Mumtaz Mahal—"Chosen One of the Palace."

Khurram, too, took a new name when he inherited his father's throne. As Shah Jahan, "King of the World," he ruled over a vast empire with Mumtaz, his closest companion and most trusted political advisor. She was wise and compassionate, encouraging him to sponsor new developments in music, architecture, and painting. Tragically, she died in 1631, after giving birth to their fourteenth child.

After a long period of mourning, Shah Jahan decreed that a mausoleum as perfectly formed and beautiful as his beloved wife be built beside the Yamuna river. It took 20,000 workers twenty-two years to create the exquisite Taj Mahal, which the poet Rabindranath Tagore called "a teardrop on the cheek of eternity." It still stands today, a tribute to undying love.

## FELIX MENDELSSOHN AND CÉCILE JEANRENAUD

*He composed his "Wedding March" <u>after</u> his wedding!*

"I HAVE JUST BECOME ENGAGED to Cécile Jeanrenaud," Felix wrote his mother six months before his wedding in 1837. "I feel quite dizzy . . . Oh, how wonderful and happy I feel!"

They had met in Frankfurt, Germany, when Cécile was nineteen and he was twenty-seven. Felix was already a famous composer, and she had imagined he would be a humorless and boring old man playing fugues on the piano. Instead, she found Felix elegant and good-looking, with dark curly hair and dark eyes.

Until then he had been living alone in Leipzig. Felix had been romantically involved before but had never thought seriously about marriage. One night his sister Fanny sat him down and said, Felix, it's time you got married. Of course, he told her, I will. Someday. When he directed a series of choral concerts that year, little did he know that the blue-eyed, blond soprano would become his wife.

He proposed to Cécile at the end of summer in a grove of beech trees outside of town. They were wed the following March at the Reformed French Church of Frankfurt, where her father was the pastor. Honeymooning in the Rhineland, Felix and Cécile filled a diary with stories and drawings of their first weeks together. The diary, which is now in Oxford's Bodleian Library, still contains a withered nosegay of violets that she had placed in his buttonhole, inspiring him to compose "a delightful allegretto."

"The weather this evening is magnificent and the whole landscape lies before us without a trace of fog," wrote Cécile. "We lie under the young trees which are planted around a church, we sing, dance on the thin grass, count the many islands in the Rhine . . . and love each other very much."

## CLARK GABLE AND CAROLE LOMBARD

*"Maw" and "Paw"*

IN 1939 CLARK WAS MGM'S "King of Hollywood" and Carole was one of the most glamorous and talented film stars and comediennes. Clark had been married twice before, and after Carole's untimely death he married twice again, but most film buffs agree that she was the love of his life.

They met on the set of *No Man of Her Own* in 1932. It was Clark's first comedy role, but his blond costar soon put him at ease. They called each other "Maw" and "Paw" and played practical jokes on each other. The day film work ended, Carole handed him a large ham.

She was almost thirty and he was thirty-eight when they got married in King-man, Arizona, on Clark's first day off while filming *Gone With the Wind*. MGM, squeamish about "Rhett Butler's" affair, had assisted Clark in getting his wife, Ria, to agree to a divorce.

Hollywood's latest lovebirds moved into a secluded white brick "farmhouse" on twenty acres in the San Fernando Valley. They planted citrus trees, rode, hunted, and fished. Carole wasn't thrilled about cooking over campfires or spending the night in a sleeping bag (once she was bitten by a rattlesnake), but she did it for Clark. No woman pleased him as much as she did, and throughout their marriage they adored each other.

During World War II Carole toured the United States selling war bonds. One night, when her plane was due back in Los Angeles, Clark tucked a blond depart-ment store mannequin into Carole's side of their bed as a gag. But Carole never made it back . . . and the "King" never got over it. He said he wanted to be buried beside her; eighteen years later, he was.

## LAURENCE STERNE AND ELIZABETH LUMLEY

### *"My dear Lawrey"*

"OUR COUSIN BETTY LUMLEY IS married to a Parson who once delighted in debauchery," wrote Matthew Robinson to his sister in 1741. Laurence may have been a high-spirited, rowdy student at Jesus College, Cambridge, but few pupils took their studies seriously. He became a clergyman after graduation, not because he was particularly devout but because he needed a career. Writing had always been Laurence's favorite occupation, and one day he would write the great novels *Tristam Shandy* and *A Sentimental Journey*.

Matthew's sister's reply was more favorable: "Mr. Sterne has a hundred a year living, with a good prospect of better preferment. He was a great rake, but . . . has varnished his character. . . . I wish they may live well together."

Laurence and Elizabeth had met in York, not far from Sutton-on-the-Forest where Elizabeth, who had inherited a tidy income from her late father, lived in a cottage on Little Alice Lane. She invited Laurence, the lively new vicar, for dinner often, and they spent evenings talking about music and song. He courted her for two years. When Elizabeth left town to visit relatives, she encouraged him to stay at her cottage.

"The hour you left," he wrote her, "I took to my bed. . . . One solitary plate, one knife, one fork, one glass!—I gave a thousand pensive, penetrating looks at the chair thou hadst so often graced . . . then . . . took out my handkerchief, and clapped it across my face, and wept like a child."

When Elizabeth returned, she became seriously ill. She told Laurence that if she died, all she owned would go to him, but he nursed her back to health. They married on Easter Monday, and Elizabeth saved "Lawrey's" love letters for the rest of her life.

## WILLIAM MICHAEL ROSSETTI AND LUCY BROWN

*"my dearly loved wife"*

THE ROSSETTI AND BROWN FAMILIES had been close for many years and were uncharacteristically surprised when William and Lucy announced their engagement. In Victorian London, Ford Madox Brown was a well-known painter and the Anglo-Italian Rossettis were known for their Pre-Raphaelite philosophy of art. As an art critic, biographer, and man of letters, William provided financial and emotional support to his family, which included the poets Dante Gabriel and Christina.

"For several years preceding 1873 I had had a warmly affectionate feeling for Lucy Brown," wrote forty-four-year-old William in his typically restrained fashion. An artist like her father, Lucy painted watercolors, such as "Romeo and Juliet in the Vault," and took care of their London home. It was there "that I first met my future wife," William wrote, "a quiet candid-looking little girl, aged less than seven, modestly self-possessed." Now she was thirty and happy to accept William's proposal shortly after she returned from a trip to Italy.

"I decided that I would not again part with Lucy, if I could help it," he wrote in his diary, and was relieved when she agreed to live with all the Rossettis in their house on Euston Square. This event may have prompted William's sister Maria to escape the embarrassment of spinsterhood by joining a convent, but Christina was delighted, saying he had brought "a fresh spring of happiness . . . into our family." Dante's gift would be a portrait of his new sister-in-law, painted the following summer.

Lucy and William were married as agnostics on a Tuesday in 1874, and they honeymooned in Italy and France. Lucy gave birth to seven children within seven years, but she continued to exhibit her art and became involved with feminist causes. She later wrote a life of Mary Shelley, and he wrote a life of Keats.

# A P R I L

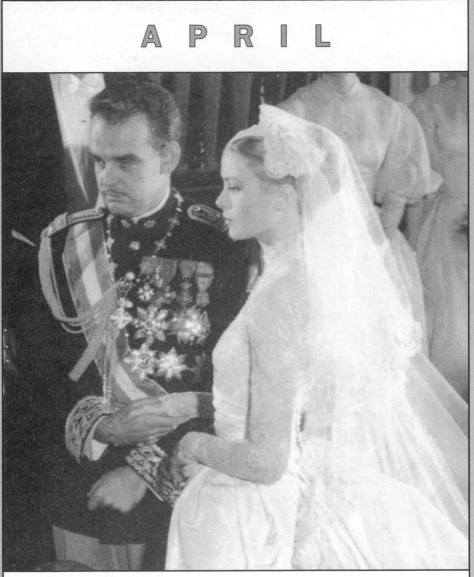

## GRACE KELLY AND PRINCE RAINIER III OF MONACO

*April 18–19, 1956*

The ceremony at Monaco's Cathedral of St. Nicholas
was part two of the dazzling nuptials.

## GENE AUTRY AND INA MAE SPIVEY

*No fooling!*

NOT UNTIL AFTER THEIR SPUR-OF-THE-MOMENT wedding did Ina realize that she had married the future singing cowboy on April Fools' Day. Gene was twenty-three and she was eighteen in 1932, and as they sat together in the corner booth of a St. Louis restaurant, he convinced his blue-eyed bride that he was as serious about marriage as she. She *had* wondered, since he proposed on their fourth date!

They'd been introduced by Ina's uncle Jimmy, who had worked with Gene before he began singing and playing his guitar on the *National Barn Dance* radio show. Like Gene, Ina had grown up in Oklahoma, but she lived with Jimmy and his family while studying music at a college in Springfield, Missouri. Gene said she had "skin like rose petals" and fell for her right away.

The well-known humorist Will Rogers had listened to Gene perform when he was an amateur and suggested he try singing professionally. By the time Gene married Ina, he was making $35 a week, which was a good salary during the Depression. Soon they were on their way to Hollywood, where he began appearing in cowboy pictures.

The 1935 movie *Tumbling Tumbleweeds* secured Gene's career. Two years later he was voted the top western-movie star, an accolade he won for the next six years. Wearing his spotless white ten-gallon hat, Gene appeared in more than one hundred western films and television shows. Later he founded the California Angels baseball team.

In 1938, Gene sang about the cowboy's declaration that no woman could ever hurt him "As Long as I've Got My Horse," although he always loved Ina more than his other famous "partner," Champion. If not for Ina, Gene might not have recorded "Rudolph, the Red-Nosed Reindeer," which reminded her of the story of the ugly duckling. More than 2.5 million records were sold the first year, and it's still a popular Christmas song.

## JACQUELINE SUSANN AND IRVING MANSFIELD

*Lovely them*

BEFORE JACKIE BECAME A WELL-KNOWN author, she was a Broadway actress appearing in such plays as Clare Boothe Luce's *The Women.* Jackie met Irving in 1937 at a party for theater people in New York City. She'd left home in Philadelphia after winning her parents' reluctant blessing for her to skip college and study acting instead. Two years later, at the age of eighteen, she married Irving in her parents' apartment. He was a press agent and theatrical producer, but he wrote "writer" as his profession on the marriage license, possibly to soothe his somewhat worried in-laws.

After the ceremony the rabbi said he hoped Jackie and Irving would establish a traditional home, but for the most part their "homes" would be hotel suites. "If I wanted a cook, I'd have married one," said Irving, pointing out that it took four years for Jackie to notice that their hotel apartment even had a kitchen!

The radio personalities Goodman and Jane Ace gave them a portable typewriter as a wedding present, and seven years later Jackie sat down to write. First she wrote the play *Lovely Me* with a friend; later came *Not Tonight, Josephine,* about being "owned" by a French poodle. Not until she was almost fifty did Jackie write *Valley of the Dolls.* The characters were modeled after recognizable Hollywood stars. Show-business lifestyles involving drug abuse, alcoholism, extramarital sex, and homosexuality quickly captured the public's attention.

Irving organized an elaborate publicity tour, and Jackie promoted her book, selling millions of copies. Another best-seller, *The Love Machine,* followed. Writing two number-one novels back to back quickly made Jackie rich and famous, despite reviewers' negative criticisms. "I'd like to have the critics like me," Jackie said. "I'd like to have everybody like what I write. But when my book sells, I know people like the book. That's the most important thing."

## F. SCOTT FITZGERALD AND ZELDA SAYRE

*his "darling heart"*

THEY MET AT A DANCE for soldiers on a summer night in Montgomery, Alabama, in 1917. "Scotty's" army uniform was Brooks Brothers' finest. If he looked a bit forlorn, it was because he had just learned that a former girlfriend had married someone else.

The incredibly beautiful daughter of a local judge was being whirled around the floor by one of Scotty's friends. Zelda smoked and drank liquor, shocking her parents and most people in the small southern town. But these young men at the dance were from faraway places, and Scotty was a writer, something Zelda desperately wanted to become. He pursued her intensively and proposed marriage as soon as he was discharged.

Zelda stalled him, wanting to be sure that Scotty could support her. He headed for New York City, got a job, and sold his first novel, *This Side of Paradise,* at the age of twenty-three. "I AM IN THE LAND OF AMBITION AND SUCCESS AND MY ONLY HOPE AND FAITH IS THAT MY DARLING HEART WILL BE WITH ME SOON," he wrote in a telegram.

Still, it took another year of mad dashes back to Montgomery, arguments, reconciliations, phone calls, and frantic letters before she told him yes.

The ceremony was held in 1920, in the rectory of St. Patrick's Cathedral in New York City the day before Easter Sunday. Zelda wore a dark blue suit and hat and carried a bouquet of orchids and white flowers. Their honeymoon began at the Biltmore Hotel, but they whooped it up so much that the management finally asked them to leave.

They were young, good-looking, rich, and successful, but with their nonstop parties, trips to Europe, and outrageous behavior, they became a tragic couple. Even so, they embodied the Jazz Age of the Roaring 20s, and Scotty wrote all about it.

## WILLIAM PENN AND GULIELMA MARIA SPRINGETT

### *"a match of Providence's making"*

WILLIAM AND "GULI" WERE MARRIED in 1672 in a Quaker ceremony at a fourteenth-century hunting lodge in Chorley Wood, England. Under the oak beams of a large white-plastered room, they sat beside each other, facing the Friends at meeting. As the silence deepened, the bride and groom stood, took each other's hands and, in the presence of God and the congregation, promised to love and be faithful to each other for as long as they lived.

Their words were simple and included no vows of obedience. No rings were exchanged, and no wedding attendants participated. Sunlight streamed through the casement windows, and when William and Guli sat down, the other Friends approached them, giving blessings and encouragement. Forty-six witnesses signed the wedding contract, along with the bride and groom.

Two years earlier, when William and Guli met, he was twenty-five and she was a few months older—a "spinster" who was beautiful as well as intelligent. From her mother she had learned a great deal about medicine and surgery, and she used her skills to help the sick. Their courtship had been interrupted by William's arrests and imprisonments for preaching Quakerism and writing religious treatises, but now there was time to spend five months alone at a honeymoon cottage called Basing House.

Ten years later King Charles II gave William a huge tract of land, which would become Pennsylvania. In his "Holy Experiment," William brought Quakerism and the concept of free public education to the American colonies.

William often sent loving notes to Guli, especially on his voyages to the new world. Fearing he might never see her again, he wrote: "My love—that neither sea nor land nor death itself can extinguish or lessen toward you—most endearedly visits you with eternal embraces, and will abide with you forever."

## POCAHONTAS AND JOHN ROLFE

*Native American Princess Marries Future Tobacco King*

IN 1614 THE YOUNG INDIAN princess whose story still fascinates people today stepped into a small Jamestown, Virginia, church decorated with wildflowers and became the wife of an English settler. She wore a muslin dress and tunic, a white veil, and a string of freshwater pearls given to her by her father, Chief Powhatan.

Pocahontas was probably seventeen and John was in his late twenties when they married. He'd been married before, but his first wife died soon after they arrived at the Virginia colony. By the time of the wedding Pocahontas had been living with the English settlers for almost a year, after she was captured during feuds with her father. But she was treated respectfully, more like a guest than a prisoner, and was considered resourceful and intelligent. Interested in learning English ways, Pocahontas accepted Christian instruction and was baptized as Rebecca.

Make peace with the English settlers, she encouraged her father. When she was ten years old, she had convinced him to spare the life of John Smith. Now John Rolfe, who had been experimenting with tobacco seeds brought from the West Indies, became friendly with Pocahontas and they began to care for each other. He wrote to Governor Sir Thomas Gates for permission to marry her.

With Pocahontas, John said, "My hartie and best thoughts are, and have a long time bin so intangled and inthralled in so intricate a laborinth, that I was even awearied to unwinde myselfe thereout." Wisely, the Governor agreed to the union, believing that it would bring the Indians and English together and end the bloodshed. It took a while for Powhatan to acquiesce, but he finally recognized that the settlers were here to stay and for the time being, anyway, there would be peace.

### JOHN GLENN AND ANNA MARGARET CASTOR

*Childhood sweethearts from way back*

"ANNA" AND "BUD" GLENN GREW up and went to high school together in New Concord, Ohio, in the 1930s. She was dark-haired and beautiful; he had red hair and freckles. Although Annie was outgoing, she had a serious stutter that wasn't corrected until many years later. Bud adored her, and throughout much of their life together he was her "voice" in public.

When Bud was sixteen, his father gave him a 1929 roadster. Bud painted "The Cruiser" red and drove Annie everywhere. Their friends knew how much Bud liked going at top speeds, so they weren't surprised in 1962 when he circled the earth three times in less than five hours on *Friendship 7* in the first manned American orbital space flight.

World War II had begun while Bud and Annie were students at Muskingum College, and he enlisted in the Navy Air Corps. Patriotism ran high in their hometown, which John later described as "a real-life version of *The Music Man*." In 1943, after his basic training, Bud and Annie were married in a small ceremony attended by their family and friends. After a short honeymoon they lived on an air base in Cherry Point, North Carolina.

John flew fifty-nine missions in the Pacific. Later, when he became a Marine test pilot, he and Annie lived in El Centro, California. When John was elected to the United States Senate in 1974, he won by the largest margin in Ohio's history.

John has always called Annie "the real rock of the family" and has never left her without feeling the pain of separation. Whenever he was ready to leave on a dangerous mission, they'd make light of it. He'd say, "Well, I'm going to the corner drugstore to buy some chewing gum," and Annie would smile and answer, "Don't take too long."

## CHARLES DE GAULLE AND YVONNE VENDROUX

*He changed her mind about soldiers*

CAPTAIN DE GAULLE WAS INTRODUCED to the Vendroux family and their twenty-year-old daughter, Yvonne, at an art exhibition in Paris in 1920. She was dark-eyed and petite, with masses of black hair swept up and away from her oval face. Yvonne had already rejected another military man because she didn't want to spend her life traipsing from one garrison town to another. But thirty-year-old Charles was intelligent, well-mannered, impeccably dressed, and very tall. She took his arm, which he had gallantly extended, and they walked off to look at the paintings.

Her family was from Calais, where her father owned a biscuit factory. Charles was originally from Lille but had grown up in Paris, where his father was a professor of philosophy and literature. He and Yvonne talked about art and poetry. He also described his wartime service and how he'd been wounded several times and made a prisoner of war by the Germans.

Two weeks later they met again at a ball at the Palace of Versailles. After Charles cut in for a waltz, he and Yvonne danced continuously in the glittering ballroom. By the end of the sixth waltz they were engaged.

Standing between statues of Saint Louis and Charlemagne, they were married at the church of Notre-Dame de Calais the following spring, shortly after Charles's military service ended. Arm in arm, they exited the church under the drawn sabers of fellow officers. The reception included an eleven-course dinner, music, and more waltzes.

After honeymooning at Lake Maggiore in northern Italy, the de Gaulles settled in an apartment on the Left Bank in Paris. Charles taught and wrote on military history and tactics. After the fall of France in 1940, he became commander of the Free French Army; by 1959 he was president of the Fifth Republic.

## MARIA MONTOYA AND JULIAN MARTINEZ

*Working together, with the clay*

MARIA AND JULIAN GREW UP in the 1890s in the pueblo of San Ildefonso, near Santa Fe, New Mexico. By the time they married in 1904, Maria's perfectly round, hand-built clay pots were already considered exceptional. Julian had various jobs but had not yet discovered his true calling as a painter. Many years later Maria remembered that her uncle couldn't understand why she wanted to marry Julian. He wasn't a farmer and he had no trade. But that didn't matter to Maria. To put it simply, she just loved him.

They married twice—in an all-day Pueblo ceremony during which Maria ground corn into a fine meal and brought it to her future mother-in-law, and then in a religious ceremony at the Catholic church. Afterward Maria and Julian boarded a train for the St. Louis World's Fair, where they spent the next four months demonstrating pottery-making and traditional dances with other Pueblo Indians. The trip exposed them to new art forms and the ways of the outside world.

Back at San Ildefonso, Julian worked as a maintenance man at a Santa Fe museum and helped out at a nearby archeological dig. Some days he brought home unusual pieces of black pottery he had found. With the curator's encouragement, Maria began reproducing the pots and Julian painted designs on them. They experimented with firing techniques and discovered how to carbonize the pottery, giving it a lustrous, metallic black finish that, when juxtaposed with Julian's matte painting, produced unique black-on-black ware.

Eventually Julian became governor of the pueblo, and Maria became a world-famous potter. "He helped me with everything," Maria said. "Oh, we had a nice life. . . . We were working together."

*Date approximate.

## SOPHIA LOREN AND CARLO PONTI

*I do, I do . . . I do, I do!*

SHE WAS TALL, GODDESSLIKE, AND Neapolitan; he was pint-sized, balding, Milanese, and married . . . but their relationship became a lifelong love affair and romance.

Sophia Scicolone first met Carlo at a beauty contest in Italy when she was fifteen and the Italian film producer was thirty-eight. She won second prize, but he had something better—the chance for a career in the movies. She and her mother had been extras in *Quo Vadis* that year. Photos of Sophia were also appearing in the *fumetti*, which were soap-operalike strips in daily newspapers. Still, she and her family were very poor. But Carlo, in his partnership with Dino de Laurentiis, had discovered other stars, and now he was offering Sophia a real contract.

At first the cameramen disliked her imperfect looks: Her mouth was too wide, her nose too long, and her hips too broad. Sophia changed her last name to Loren but she refused to change her features, and Carlo began to realize they would become part of her fame.

They married twice—first in September 1957, after Carlo's Mexican divorce. But five years later that marriage was annulled when the Italian government refused to recognize it and charged Sophia and Carlo with bigamy. In 1966, with the help of Carlo's ex-wife, they remarried in Sèvres, a Paris suburb.

Sophia had been filming *The Countess from Hong Kong* in London when she slipped into Paris and managed to evade the press long enough to marry Carlo in a small, simple ceremony. She wore a yellow dress and carried lilies of the valley. Later she remarked, "To be finally married after eight years of struggle and abuse, certainly had importance, but . . . I couldn't help but feel that Carlo and I had really been married for a long time."

## LUCRETIA COFFIN AND JAMES MOTT

*Equal and abiding respect*

THE GIRL WHO BECAME AN outspoken Quaker abolitionist and advocate for women's rights met her future husband in French class in 1809. Usually boys and girls were separated, but those in training to be teachers took some special classes together at the Nine Partners Boarding School in Dutchess County, New York. Lucretia was from Nantucket, Massachusetts, and James came from Mamaroneck, New York.

Often called a "spitfire," Lucretia was tiny, outspoken, and somewhat impulsive; James was tall, serious, and contemplative. They were a deeply loving couple throughout their long marriage, always sharing a double bed and bemoaning the nights when one was away traveling and they had to sleep apart.

They married in a Quaker ceremony at Philadelphia's Pine Street meeting house in 1811, where 175 witnesses signed the marriage certificate. Lucretia's family had moved to the city a year earlier, and now her father invited James to work with him in his retail business, changing its name to "Coffin and Mott—Merchants."

Lucretia became a Quaker preacher after the tragic death of their three-year-old son. While raising their five other children, she formed a women's antislavery society in Philadelphia with James's encouragement and support. He stopped selling cotton goods because they were made with slave labor, and their home became a stop on the Underground Railroad. Although angry protestors occasionally threw rotten eggs and rocks at the Motts' house, they persisted in advancing their principles. In 1840 they were delegates at the World's American Anti-Slavery Convention in London. When they returned, they met with President John Tyler and futilely tried to convince him to support emancipation.

After many years of happy marriage to James, Lucretia wrote down her philosophy of matrimony and often gave it to newly engaged couples: "In the true marriage . . . the independence of the husband and wife is equal, their dependence mutual and their obligations reciprocal."

## GILBERT DE LAFAYETTE AND ADRIENNE DE NOAILLES

*"My dear heart"*

GILBERT WAS ORPHANED BY THE time he was thirteen, but he inherited a great fortune, making him a very eligible bachelor. Marriages between aristocratic French families were often arranged in the eighteenth century, and the Duc d'Ayen de Noailles had five daughters. He and Gilbert's great-grandfather signed their agreement before they told Gilbert or Adrienne about it. The young couple was lucky, for they also fell in love.

In 1774, four hundred guests attended the ceremony of the sixteen-year-old marquis and his fourteen-year-old bride in the candlelit chapel of the Hotel de Noailles, her family's home near rue St. Honoré in Paris today. After a lavish reception, friends and relatives escorted the newlyweds to a bedroom. Everyone lingered for a while around the four-poster bed until the duke mercifully closed the curtains and ushered the teasing guests outside.

Gilbert and Adrienne were old enough to marry but too young to live independently, so they stayed with her family for several years. Gilbert became a captain at a garrison in Metz. Three years later he sailed to America and, at the age of twenty, became a volunteer major general in Washington's Continental Army, fighting bravely in the Revolutionary War. He played a major part in the American colonists' victory at Yorktown, and subsequently hung a copy of the United States Constitution on the wall of his study.

Although Gilbert was a wealthy aristocrat, when he returned to France he became a lifelong supporter of freedom. When the Reign of Terror began, Gilbert fled but was captured by right-wing emigrés. He spent the next five years in an Austrian prison, out of touch with his family, who were in danger also.

Adrienne was imprisoned for a year in Paris; then she and two daughters managed to get to Austria, where they joined Gilbert voluntarily for his last two years in prison. Someday, they fervently believed, their good name would be restored.

## ANTOINE DE SAINT-EXUPÉRY AND
## CONSUELO SUNCIN DE SANDOVAL

### *"Saint-Ex" and "Poussin"*

IN THE 1930s "SAINT-EX" WAS part of a bunch of foolhardy flyers who often flew without instruments through windstorms and bad weather. Although he is best remembered for his 1943 classic, *The Little Prince,* his writings also include *Night Flight* and *Wind, Sand and Stars.*

He met Consuelo in Buenos Aires, one of his mail delivery stops, when he was thirty. She was a very attractive twenty-eight-year-old widow from San Salvador, with large, expressive dark eyes and a rich imagination. Stories of their courtship varied, but Consuelo usually said they became involved after Saint-Ex took her and a small group of people up in the air for a ride. He asked her for a kiss. When she refused, he threatened to crash the plane if she didn't . . . so she did.

She was petite, extravagant, passionate, and unpredictable, and she liked to say her family was descended from Spanish royalty. Saint-Ex was tall and bearlike and was attracted to Consuelo's wildness and lack of inhibitions. Within a year he brought her to Paris, causing his mother to say, Marry Consuelo; this living-together business is very embarrassing! His writer friend André Gide noted that Saint-Ex had written a new book and brought home a fiancée: "Read one, seen the other. Congratulated him heartily, but more for the book; I hope the fiancée is as satisfactory."

They married in 1931 in a small chapel in southern France. Consuelo wore a black lace dress and mantilla and red roses in her black hair. Her Pekingese dog was one of the attendants. After honeymooning on the Riviera, Saint-Ex resumed flying and Consuelo, whom he called "mon poussin"—my chick—awaited him either in Paris or their Casablanca apartment.

## CHANG AND ENG BUNKER AND
## ADELAIDE AND SALLIE YATES

*The ultimate double wedding*

WHEN CHANG AND ENG WERE born in Siam in 1811, their parents never expected that their sons, who were attached at the waist, would become world-famous celebrities, loving husbands, and the fathers of twenty-one children.

For a while, curiosity seekers flocked to the village of Meklong, where the "Siamese twins" lived, but generally their childhood was uneventful and calm. At first they walked like tipsy drunks, but later they ran, swam, and even mastered complicated dances. What was difficult was deciding where to go, but Chang was more assertive and usually got his way because Eng was easygoing and placid.

When they were eighteen, the twins joined a traveling exhibit and sailed for Europe and America. They toured for years, making enough money to support their family and purchase a farm in Wilkesboro, North Carolina. They were thirty-one when they adopted the last name Bunker (after the famous hill) upon becoming naturalized American citizens. Around that time they also met the Yates family and their daughters, Adelaide, eighteen, and nineteen-year-old Sallie.

Adelaide and Chang were quickly attracted, but it took months for Sallie to fall for Eng. Certainly the prospect of being married to two men and never being alone with either one would have given most women pause. But once the sisters agreed to the twins' marriage proposals in 1843, they never wavered. After their parents overcame their initial shock, they hired the local parson and made all the arrangements. A lively dinner-dance celebration followed the wedding ceremony. Then the four Bunkers retired to a very large bed in their new home, where the phrase "alone together" was given new meaning. Years later they moved into two farmhouses within walking distance of each other in Mount Airy. Chang and Eng alternated houses, spending three days in each place with each wife and family.

## PIERRE-AUGUSTE RENOIR AND ALINE CHARIGOT

*Madame Renoir . . . at last*

IN PIERRE'S 1883 PAINTING "Beside the Sea," Aline wears a lace-trimmed blue dress and bonnet and sits in a yellow wicker chair by the Guernsey cliffs. She holds a pair of knitting needles, and a soft pile of wool rests on her lap. Aline stares directly at the painter, and it is clear that he adores her.

Four years before, she was a nineteen-year-old dressmaker working with her mother on rue St. George in Paris, not far from Pierre's studio. When Aline began modeling for him, she didn't understand anything about art, but she loved to watch him paint. Pierre was thirty-eight, with strong feelings about the physical proportions of a face. "Never marry a woman with a large chin. She'd rather be torn to pieces than admit she was in the wrong," he advised his son Jean, who became a film director. But Pierre liked Aline's looks, especially her almond-shaped eyes and well-balanced head. She also had a light step, and he said she "could walk on grass without hurting it."

Aline lived with Pierre for years as his common-law wife, partly because his wealthy patrons—on whom he depended—would not have approved of his marriage to a "peasant." The Renoirs were always hard-pressed for money. When their first child was born in 1885, Pierre gave the doctor "Roses and Gladioli" instead of cash.

By 1890 Pierre was more optimistic about his financial future and married Aline before old friends and family members in the town hall of the ninth Arrondissement. They stayed in Paris until July and then went to the country for the summer. Relaxed and at peace, Pierre immortalized his new bride and their child in "The Apple Seller" series of paintings.

## LORD RANDOLPH CHURCHILL AND JENNIE JEROME

*"the sky is bluer than I have ever seen*
*it since I first met you"*

THE NIGHT BEFORE JENNIE MARRIED Randolph in 1874, her thoughts resembled those of countless brides: "This is the last time I shall wind this clock . . . this is the last time I shall look in this old mirror. Soon nothing will be the same for me anymore: Miss Jennie Jerome will be gone forever."

A maid brought her a breakfast tray in the morning, but Jennie barely touched it. Then her corset was pulled in as tightly as possible—without causing her to faint during the ceremony. Her wedding dress was white satin, trimmed with yards of Alençon lace. A tulle veil covered her from head to foot. At twenty, she was marrying twenty-five-year-old Lord Randolph Churchill, third son of the seventh duke of Marlborough, at the British Embassy in Paris. He had proposed to her three days after they met.

His parents disapproved of the Brooklyn-born daughter of "flashy" self-made Americans and only consented to the union on the condition that Randolph run for Parliament and *win*. He'd never worked hard before, but his announcement that he would earn a living "in England or out of it," if that's what it took to marry Jennie, convinced them that he was serious.

"This was a love match if ever there was one," wrote their son Winston, born later that year. Fortunately, Jennie's father provided her with a generous dowry, although he balked at the British custom of giving husbands control of the money and insisted that Jennie receive part of it regularly.

The marriage was not ideal in every way, but it produced young Winston, whom his mother recognized as an exceptional child. She assisted in launching his career in literature and politics and helped him become one of the twentieth century's most outstanding politician-statesmen.

## NEWELL CONYERS WYETH AND CAROLYN BOCKIUS

*"she's just the girl I want"*

"N.C." AND CAROLYN MET AT a sleighing party one wintry evening in 1904, in a scene as magical and evocative as his book illustrations. Twenty-two years old, he was studying art at the Wilmington, Delaware, art school run by the famous illustrator Howard Pyle. That fateful night, snow was falling heavily, causing the young couple to huddle close together. For N.C., it was bliss.

He first mentioned Carolyn to his parents in a letter he wrote a few days later. Like most young men embarrassed to share their romantic feelings, N.C. simply said that a "Miss Bockius" had invited him to church on Sunday. Soon he was visiting the Bockius house regularly. By spring he and Carolyn were packing picnic baskets and taking long walks in the Brandywine countryside.

He kept talking about Carolyn in his letters but couldn't admit his growing love. Back home in Needham, Massachusetts, Mrs. Wyeth sensed that her son had more on his mind than art and wrote back, asking if he was concentrating enough on his work. "Mama," he replied, "*please* have faith in me. . . . Do you think I would do anything rash?"

He didn't marry Carolyn until more than a year later—after she'd won his parents' approval. N.C. and Carolyn spent the weeks before their 1906 wedding painting, papering, and fixing up their future home at 1331 Shawcross Avenue in Wilmington. That spring he worked on his "Solitude Series" of paintings, which were very well received. Commissions for book illustrations began coming regularly. When *McClure's* magazine offered N.C. $4,000 a year for magazine covers and story illustrations, his financial future was secured.

In 1908 he and Carolyn moved to a farm in Chadds Ford, Pennsylvania, the future home of their five children, including the artists Henriette and Andrew. A few years later N.C. began a series of illustrations for children's classics, starting with *Treasure Island*.

## NORMAN ROCKWELL AND MARY BARSTOW

*She read to him while he painted*

SOON AFTER NORMAN'S FIRST MARRIAGE ended, he left New York for a California vacation and met Mary, a twenty-two-year-old schoolteacher. Still depressed, Norman was in no mood to think about romance. Anyway, he wondered, who would want him? He was divorced and "thirty-six years toward the grave," he wrote in his autobiography. But Mary liked Norman right away. They decided to marry within weeks but waited a few months to please her parents, who hosted the wedding in the garden of their Alhambra home in 1930.

A recent Stanford University graduate, Mary knew a lot about art. Norman was a high school dropout who already was a fairly successful illustrator, with work on the covers of *Boy's Life* and other magazines. For many years his pictures were on every front cover of the *Saturday Evening Post.*

Unlike Norman's first wife, Mary was sincerely interested in his work. They raised three children in their New Rochelle, New York, home on Lord Kitchener Road, and she often kept Norman company while he painted. First he made preliminary sketches, followed by a full-size charcoal drawing made from life, using friends and neighbors dressed in appropriate costumes as models. Next, another sketch was made in color. The final stages of a painting were reached in anywhere from two weeks to two months. During those long days, Mary often read to Norman; they enjoyed the works of Tolstoy, Dickens, Jane Austen, and Voltaire, as well as contemporary best-sellers.

Norman had the remarkable ability to create thoughtful, detailed pictures of American life, focusing on family relationships, romance, and age and youth. People were deeply touched by his heartwarming scenes during the Depression. Those who couldn't afford to buy art taped his magazine covers on the walls. Norman's most memorable series was "The Four Freedoms," painted during World War II and used to promote the sale of war bonds.

## GRACE KELLY AND PRINCE RAINIER III OF MONACO

*Hollywood Princess Weds Real-Life Prince*

SHE WAS EXTREMELY BEAUTIFUL, MORE regal in bearing than most blue-blooded women. Grace was filming *To Catch a Thief* on the French Riviera in 1955 when she met Prince Rainier, one of the world's most eligible bachelors. He gave her a private tour of Monaco's Palace Gardens and came to see her in Philadelphia several months later. Right after Christmas he gave her the engagement ring she wore in her last film, *High Society*.

Gossip columnists called Grace a bricklayer's daughter, but by now her father, Jack Kelly, was extremely wealthy. What he didn't like was the old European tradition of paying a dowry for his daughter. At first Jack refused, saying Monaco must be in financial trouble and he didn't want Grace marrying some "broken-down prince." Finally he came to accept the arrangement and probably paid about $2 million.

The civil wedding ceremony was held first, on April 18, 1956, in the throne room of Rainier's palace. Immediate families and close friends attended, and Europeans watched it on television. A religious ceremony followed the next morning at Monaco's Cathedral of St. Nicholas. Grace wore an ivory taffeta dress trimmed in Valenciennes lace. Tiny lace lovebirds were appliquéd to the back of her veil, dotted with thousands of seed pearls. Since Rainier was royalty, his bride was expected to precede him to the altar. Jack Kelly escorted Grace down the aisle and was directed to a nearby pew. But the upstart American dad wouldn't leave his daughter alone at the altar and insisted, in a quiet, dignified way, on standing beside her until Rainier arrived.

The wedding was followed by parades and receptions for hundreds of guests, until the newlyweds sailed off for a seven-week Mediterranean cruise.

"We both understood what marriage meant," Rainier said years later. "We fell in love. . . . A lot of people never thought it would last. I guess we fooled them."

## LAWRENCE WELK AND FERN RENNER

*Wunnerful, Wunnerful!*

THE BOYS IN LAWRENCE'S BAND slept through his 1931 wedding to Fern. But since it took place at 5:30 A.M., it's no wonder that some well-wishers weren't awake for the ceremony!

Fern and the future leader of television's Champagne Musicmakers were married in Sioux City, Iowa's Sacred Heart Cathedral. Fern had just arrived from Dallas on the early morning train. By 10:00 A.M., they all would be heading for a gig in Wisconsin that night. The bride and groom weren't the only jumpy participants; it was the priest's first wedding, too, and he forgot to bless Fern's ring until after the ceremony was over.

Fern and Lawrence had met in Yankton, South Dakota, a few years before, when she was a student nurse attending his radio concert. As he played the accordion and led his band through waltzes, polkas, and other tunes, Lawrence couldn't take his eyes off the "prettiest girl I had ever seen in my life. She had great big brown eyes . . . fair skin and dark hair . . . and she looked very unimpressed by everything that was going on around her," he wrote later.

He asked her out repeatedly until she accepted, providing she was home early enough to study. "I promised," he said. "I would have promised almost anything to get to know her better." "Anything" included having elective surgery, because it meant spending a few days in the hospital where Fern was training.

By the time they married, Lawrence's band had become well known in midwestern dance halls and on the radio, but as the Depression worsened, bookings became harder to get. Fern traveled with Lawrence as much as possible, and quickly learned to keep a mop and pail in their car so she could clean the dismal rooms they sometimes occupied. Later he achieved fame as a big-name orchestra leader and TV host.

## EDMOND HALLEY AND MARY TOOKE

*"beloved wife"*

FANCIFUL BIOGRAPHERS HAVE SAID THAT Edmond first saw "his" comet on his honeymoon in 1682, but it's probably not true. However, the blazing ball of light with a fiery tail, which was eventually called "Halley's comet," did appear over England that same year.

When Edmond met Mary two years before, he was twenty-four and she was the amiable and attractive daughter of a London bank official. He and Mary often watched the night sky, and he jotted down notes about everything they saw. He probably also saw stars in Mary's beautiful eyes, because when he left for Italy, he wrote to her often. They were married at St. James's Church in London three months after his return and moved to a house in the suburb of Islington, where Edmond set up his first observatory.

Edmond was cheerful, well-liked, and extremely happy at home. Mary adored him and even tolerated his pranks; when the young Czar Peter (who became Peter the Great of Russia) visited London, he and Edmond spent a lot of time talking and drinking together. Late one night they got drunk. Peter jumped into a nearby wheelbarrow, and Edmond pushed him until he rolled down a hill and crashed into a row of topiary hedges.

Edmond was very supportive of his friends. When Isaac Newton needed financial help to publish his discourse on gravity and the laws of motion, Edmond solicited contributions to help Newton defray the costs.

As Edmond charted the frequencies and paths of comets, he noted that the comet he and Mary saw in 1682 had the same orbital characteristics as others that had been observed seventy-six years earlier . . . and seventy-six years before that. Eventually he developed theories for predicting the motions and movements of comets and their counterclockwise orbits. True to his predictions, "Halley's comet" returns to our world every seventy-six years and was last seen in 1986.

## OWEN WISTER AND MARY CHANNING

*His "Molly"*

FOUR YEARS AFTER "DAN" MARRIED "Molly" in 1898, he wrote *The Virginian*, a best-selling, highly acclaimed western novel whose central character is a handsome but nameless cowpunch who overcomes dangers and hardships and wins the heart of a pretty schoolteacher. It didn't take long before his words "When you call me that, *smile!*" became part of American folklore, as did the image of the noble and lonely cowboy.

The first time Dan saw Molly, he was ten and she was a newborn baby and daughter of his mother's second cousin. Molly was a descendant of a signer of the Declaration of Independence and of the noted abolitionist and preacher William Ellery Channing. Throughout her life Molly was involved in social causes and reforms. She became a member of Philadelphia's Board of Education at the age of twenty-six, a rare position for a young single woman to hold.

Dan's great-great-grandfather, Pierce Butler, had signed the U.S. Constitution for South Carolina, and his grandmother was the famous Shakespearean actress Fanny Kemble. A Harvard-educated lawyer, Dan had camped and hunted in Wyoming and Arizona for years. He gladly gave up his law practice soon after he sold his first western short story, "Hank's Woman," to *Harper's* magazine. The editors were willing to send him out west again to soak up the atmosphere and write more great tales. His friend Teddy Roosevelt said that Dan had "the power of the born story-teller" and read everything he wrote with great enthusiasm.

Dan and Molly were married at her parents' Germantown, Pennsylvania, home on the day the Spanish-American War began. For the next six months they traveled across the country, visiting relatives and historical sites, before settling down at 913 Pine Street in Philadelphia. They hung Fanny Kemble's portrait in the parlor and also displayed a few pictures by Frederic Remington, who illustrated some of Dan's western stories.

## ANDREW CARNEGIE AND LOUISE WHITFIELD

*"our cup runneth over"*

LOUISE WAS THIRTY WHEN SHE married the fifty-one-year-old millionaire in 1887. They had met seven years earlier, but Andrew was too focused on work to think about marriage. Besides, he had promised his widowed mother that he wouldn't marry as long as she lived, and Mama Carnegie held her "Andra" to his word. However, he did enjoy taking Louise to concerts and the opera and for carriage rides through New York's Central Park. "Other young ladies were on my list," he wrote in his autobiography, but they "all faded into ordinary beings. Miss Whitfield remained alone as the perfect one beyond any I had met." Secretly engaged in 1886, he told no one—including Mama.

The powerful steel magnate had started out as a bobbin boy in a Pennsylvania cotton factory. After Andrew made his fortune, he began giving it away to worthy causes, such as public libraries, colleges, art foundations, and the magnificent Carnegie Music Hall. Louise fully supported Andrew's plans to use his "surplus wealth" for the common good. Before they were married, she renounced most claims to his vast estate.

After their wedding in New York City, they honeymooned in Britain's Isle of Wight and at a castle Andrew had rented in Scotland. " 'Happily married,' " wrote Louise, "two words fraught with the deepest meaning in the world." Andrew said, "She seems to have been made to turn the earth into a heaven for me." He often described her by quoting these lines from Shakespeare's *The Tempest*:

> *Full many a lady*
> *I've eyed with best regard: for several virtues*
> *Have I liked several women, never any*
> *With so full soul, but some defect in her*
> *Did quarrel with the noblest grace she owed,*
> *And put it to the foil; but you, O you,*
> *So perfect and so peerless are created*
> *Of every creature's best.*

## DIEGO RODRÍGUEZ DE SILVA Y VELÁZQUEZ
## AND JUANA PACHECO

*Mi corazón (my heart)*

JUANA WAS A LITTLE GIRL when young Diego came to her father's house in Seville in 1610. The boy's parents had told Don Francisco Pacheco, a painter, that Diego was always sketching and that he seemed to have a strong understanding of light and shade—something that would later be called "chiaroscuro." The don studied Diego's pictures and invited him to be his apprentice; one day Diego would become the preeminent Spanish painter of the seventeenth century.

For the next six years Diego lived with the Pacheco family while he assisted the don in painting religious pictures for churches. Juana brought trays of food to the artists and lingered in the studio to watch them work. Diego did not intend to paint religious subjects all his life, he whispered to her. He wanted to portray living subjects—the people he saw in the streets, in shops, and inside taverns. His paintings were extraordinarily realistic; later he worked exclusively from life.

In 1618, after Diego's apprenticeship concluded, he passed the examinations of the painters' guild of Seville and won the don's permission to marry Juana. Pleased and proud, the don gave the young couple several houses in the city, including one with sufficient room for Diego's own studio.

Diego was eighteen and Juana was sixteen when they married at the church of San Miguel de Sevilla. Poets and artists joined family and friends at a lavish wedding banquet hosted by the don, who subsequently arranged for his son-in-law to be presented to King Philip IV in Madrid. After the king appointed him court painter, Diego painted the royal family many times; in "The Maids of Honor," he included himself at work before an easel. In the king's service, he also traveled to Italy, where he bought paintings for the royal court and was inspired by the works of Michelangelo, Raphael, and Titian. But Diego never grew tired of painting his beloved Juana, who is immortalized exquisitely in his "Lady with Fan."

## EMPEROR FRANZ JOSEPH OF AUSTRIA
## AND ELIZABETH OF BAVARIA

*"Franzi" and "Sisi"*

NOT ONLY WAS THE 1854 marriage between the twenty-three-year-old emperor and sixteen-year-old princess witnessed by hundreds of guests and more than fifty mitered bishops but the royal wedding night began in the presence of their mothers!

The bride was so nervous, she barely touched her food at the reception at Vienna's Hofburg Palace. When it ended after midnight, her mother, Ludovika, and mother-in-law, Sophia, escorted her down a candelabra-lit corridor to the bridal chamber. Sophia fetched Franz and brought him to his bride. By now the new empress was cowering in the bed, and Sophia noted unpleasantly, "She hid her natural loveliness, for only a wealth of beautiful free-flowing hair buried in her bolster caught my eye, like a frightened bird lying low in its nest."

Like most sheltered nineteenth-century young women, "Sisi" knew virtually nothing about sex. Mothers prided themselves on *concealing* the facts of life from their daughters, and new husbands expected them to shriek and carry on. Sisi and Franz barely endured the early days of their marriage but eventually became deeply attached.

Sophia had expected Franz to marry Sisi's sophisticated older sister. But at his most recent birthday party, he had kept dancing with Sisi, waltzing her around the floor in her peach-colored gown. "She is as fresh as a newly peeled almond, and what a splendid crown of hair frames such a vision! How can anyone help loving such tender eyes and lips like strawberries!" he wrote afterwards. "I will marry Sisi!"

Whether or not their marriage fulfilled all of the young girl's fantasies, from the moment Franz took Sisi's hand as she stepped out of the flower-bedecked ship that brought her down the Danube to Vienna, he had found someone who would influence and love him for their entire married life.

## JEAN LOUIS AGASSIZ AND ELIZABETH CABOT CARY

*A brilliant and loving couple*

"LIZZIE'S" MOTHER SAW LOUIS FIRST. The Swiss naturalist was attending church with the Lowells in Boston when he attracted Mrs. Cary's eye. Her matchmaking plans for her daughter dissolved when she found out Louis had a wife and family in Europe. But within three years, his wife died . . . and Louis became terribly lonely.

He met Lizzie at a Cambridge dinner party in 1848, soon after he became a professor of natural history at Harvard. She was twenty-six, well educated, wealthy, and good-natured. Although Louis was fifteen years older, his enthusiasm for life and his scientific work attracted her. He showed her his collection of fossils, crustaceans, mollusks, and coral and talked incessantly about it. Natural history fascinated Lizzie. "You will see that I have eyes for its beauty, ears for its melody, and a heart to understand its teaching," she told him soon after they became engaged.

She also had a heart for Louis's thirteen-year-old son, Alexander, who soon arrived by ship. "She learned to know me through and through and placed in me the most unbounded confidence," he would remember. His two sisters also became very close to their new "mother."

"Lizzie looked lovely," wrote her sister after the wedding at King's Chapel in 1850. "She was dressed in green silk, with a white camel's hair shawl and a straw bonnet trimmed with white feathers on each side." After a gala reception at her parents' home, she and Louis walked to his house in Cambridge.

Eventually Louis's collection would be kept at the Harvard museum he established, but now his materials were all over the house. Nothing perturbed Lizzie, not even live snakes in Louis's closet! Besides raising her three stepchildren and accompanying him on scientific expeditions, Lizzie was a pioneer of women's higher education and founded Radcliffe College at Harvard.

## ALBERT, DUKE OF YORK, AND
## LADY ELIZABETH BOWES-LYON

### *"The sun seemed always to be shining"*

"YOU'LL BE A LUCKY FELLOW if she accepts you," England's King George V told his son "Bertie" after he proposed to Elizabeth in 1923. Long ago they had met at a children's party; five-year-old Elizabeth had eyes like sapphires that brimmed with excitement. Bertie was ten, but his shyness and stammer made him dread royal get-togethers. He sat beside Elizabeth at teatime and was deeply touched by her calm acceptance of his handicap. She also gave him the cherries from her sugar cake.

Fifteen years later they met again at his sister's wedding. Elizabeth was very fond of Bertie, but she knew that marrying into the royal family meant a life governed by rules and restrictions. When she finally accepted his proposal, she expected that they would simply be the duke and duchess of York.

No one anticipated that thirteen years later Bertie's older brother, Edward, would give up his kingdom for the woman he loved and that Bertie would become King George VI and Elizabeth his queen consort. Nor could anyone predict that Elizabeth, with her warmth, sincerity, and strong sense of duty, would help restore the monarchy to public favor after the shocking abdication.

The wedding was held at Westminster Abbey but was not broadcast on the radio because the archbishop of Canterbury feared that disrespectful Englishmen might listen in pubs and forget to remove their hats! Many British hearts were deeply touched, however, when the young bride placed her wedding bouquet on the Tomb of the Unknown Soldier, remembering those lost so recently in the Great War.

Elizabeth would always be her father-in-law's favorite. April 26, he wrote, "was rather gray and inclined to rain, but as soon as the bride arrived at the Abbey the sun shone as it always does in her presence."

## MALCOLM CANMORE, KING OF SCOTLAND, AND PRINCESS MARGARET

*His saintly wife*

SEVERAL YEARS AFTER THE BATTLE of Hastings, Malcolm stood on the beach of the Firth of Forth and watched a storm-tossed ship with tattered sails steer into the harbor near Dunfermline. Two Saxon princesses and their mother stepped onto the shore, assisted by Prince Edgar the Atheling.

Some say it was love at first sight for the king of Scotland, a widower in his late thirties with plenty of passion deep inside. On that fateful autumn day, when the wind was snapping tree branches and playing havoc with small boat moorings, Malcolm watched Margaret's winsome body shudder as she covered her shoulders with a shawl. It took all his strength to resist rushing to her instead of ordering his servants to bring the four voyagers to his stone fortress up on the hillside.

They had sailed for the Continent to escape William the Conqueror, but their ship had veered off course and gone north. They spent the winter in Malcolm's castle, eating dried meats and vegetables and drinking mead while listening to stories about how Malcolm had defeated the murderous usurper Macbeth and reclaimed the throne of his father, Duncan.

Although Malcolm's nickname was "Bighead," he could neither read nor write. But he was a brave and honest man, with a gentle heart in his warrior's breast. For months he yearned for the twenty-two-year-old tall and stately princess, the niece of the late (great) Edward the Confessor. Marry me, Malcolm implored her. The long winter gave her plenty of time to appreciate his sincere affections, valor, and fierce loyalties. By spring she gave him her answer.

In 1070 the bishop of St. Andrew's united the glorious couple in marriage. Margaret, who would be declared a saint one day, helped to develop Christianity, culture, commerce, and art in her adopted land.

*Date approximate.

## ED SULLIVAN AND SYLVIA WEINSTEIN

*A really wonderful marriage*

IN 1926 SYLVIA WAS CELEBRATING her high school graduation with friends at a New York City nightclub when she noticed a handsome young man with wavy hair and a wide smile. Ed was a sports reporter who frequented the clubs, looking for athletes to interview. He also was friendly with lots of entertainers, whom he still knew years later when his Sunday-night variety show, *The Toast of the Town,* became one of television's most popular programs.

Ed asked the club's public relations man to introduce him to the attractive young woman. When he found out that Sylvia liked sports, he quickly invited her to upcoming tennis matches and a prize fight at Brooklyn's Ebbets Field. They dated for over three years, although Ed's Roman Catholic parents weren't happy he was seeing a Jewish girl. Sylvia's family was more comfortable with the prospect of an interfaith marriage, especially because they realized how happy Sylvia and Ed were.

They married secretly at Manhattan's City Hall in 1930, intending to slip away to Atlantic City for two days before their "officially scheduled" wedding at a Catholic church. The news leaked out, however, so they told their parents before someone else beat them to it.

Two years later Ed began writing "Little Old New York," a *Daily News* column that was soon syndicated nationally. He also hosted a radio variety show, introducing such stars as Irving Berlin and Jack Benny. *The Toast of the Town* (later *The Ed Sullivan Show*) began in 1948 and debuted such performers as Jackie Gleason, Carol Burnett, the Supremes, and Elvis Presley.

Sylvia and Ed went nightclubbing almost every night and never tired of living in hotel suites. Years later he remarked that without Sylvia, he probably wouldn't have accomplished so much. "Hers has been the grim and the lonely job of waiting and watching," he told a biographer. "No matter what I've done, she's been there."

## JOHANNES VERMEER AND CATHERINA BOLNES

### *Sweet Vrou Vermeer*

CATHERINA WAS FROM THE DUTCH town of Gouda, about fifteen miles east of Delft, a picturesque town of canals, tidy houses, and tree-lined streets where Johannes lived for his entire life. His paintings are small in scale, just like his hometown; household interiors are often the settings for his work. He focused on details: a woman pouring milk, handling jewelry, sitting before a mirror, writing a letter.

Johannes was twenty and Catherina one year older when they married at the town hall of Schipluy in 1653. Later that year, after he joined the Guild of St. Luke as a master painter, Johannes could paint, teach art, and sell his work in Delft, just as his father, an art dealer and weaver, had done before him.

At first he and Catherina lived with her mother, Maria Thins, who was legally separated from her husband but received an income from him. She had not been delighted when Catherina chose Johannes—probably because he was Protestant and they were Catholics—but she proved to be a financially supportive and loving mother for many years to come. Even so, the Vermeer family was fairly poor and occasionally was forced to sell his paintings to satisfy creditors.

Eventually the couple established a home and studio for themselves and their eight children. Johannes's remarkable paintings covered the walls. He captured light in incredible ways: Vases, pitchers, casement windows, maps, and other objects of daily life are bathed in luminosity. A sense of stillness permeates his pictures. Ordinary events and objects are imbued with universal meanings.

Family belongings often appear in Johannes's pictures. Catherina's yellow silk jacket is in "Woman with a Pearl Necklace" and "Lady with a Maidservant Holding a Letter." Most probably Catherina also posed for "Young Lady in Blue Reading a Letter."

*Date approximate.

## FRANK STOCKTON AND MARIAN TUTTLE

*Better to be killed . . . or get married?*

EVEN WHEN HE WAS A kid, Frank could create an entire story in his head before committing it to paper. He wrote many tales throughout his life but is best remembered for "The Lady or the Tiger?," which he dictated to Marian in 1872.

Thirteen years before, she had been teaching literature at the West Philadelphia School for Young Ladies, which Frank's mother had established. He showed up one day and soon became interested in sweet Miss Tuttle from South Carolina. She noticed that twenty-six-year-old Frank was small-boned and limped from a congenital defect, but that his eyes were merry and his humor was boundless. They were married the following year, in 1860.

At first they lived in Nutley, New Jersey. As Frank commuted to his engraving shop on Fulton Street in New York City, he thought about new stories, which Marian recorded when he came home. She later collaborated with him on *The Home: Where It Should Be and What to Put in It,* a guide for young married couples with moderate incomes. Originally Frank wrote "The Lady or the Tiger?" not for publication but to entertain friends at a party. Time ran out before he could tell his story, which was just as well because Frank hadn't finished it . . . and never did!

Eventually *Century* magazine printed it, and readers were fascinated right away. The story was widely discussed at literary clubs and in newspaper editorials, primarily because of its unanswered—possibly unanswerable—question: When the king refused to let his beautiful but strong-willed, impulsive daughter marry the noble young man, did she send him to his doom or into the arms of another woman?

Frank always admitted that he didn't know what happened, but he gave his readers a thought-provoking clue: "If you decide which it was—the lady, or the tiger—you find out what kind of person you are yourself."

# MAY

## ANTON CHEKHOV AND OLGA KNIPPER
*May 25, 1901*

The playwright and his "precious . . . divine treasure"—his radiant actress-bride.

## ELVIS PRESLEY AND PRISCILLA ANN BEAULIEU

*"Love Me Tender"*

ELVIS'S ROMANCE WITH A TEENAGE girl grabbed everyone's attention in the 1960s. "The King of Rock 'n' Roll," who could have had countless women, was stuck on "Cilla," whom he first met in West Germany when she was fourteen years old.

Cilla's stepfather was in the air force and so was Elvis, but unlike other GIs, he lived in his own home at 14 Goethestrasse, near the Bad Neuheim base. He met Cilla at a party. After his military discharge, she transferred to a school near Graceland, Elvis's Memphis mansion. Cilla also dyed her hair black, teased it to great heights, applied thick makeup, and did everything else Elvis wanted, turning herself into his perfect dream.

Some people think Elvis's manager, Colonel Parker, had decided it was time for his boy to marry. After all, the colonel decided most things, and he certainly orchestrated the wedding as well. By 1967 Elvis was thirty-two and Cilla was twenty years old. The "king" was ready to take a "queen."

A Nevada Supreme Court justice performed the double-ring ceremony at the Aladdin Hotel in Las Vegas. Elvis wore a black brocaded jacket, vest, and dark trousers; Cilla wore a white organza wedding dress with a six-foot train and a tulle veil. The bride and groom promised to love, honor, and "comfort"—not obey—each other. Their six-tiered wedding cake was covered with pearl-studded red and pink hearts.

At their honeymoon getaway in Palm Springs, California, Elvis sang "The Hawaiian Wedding Song" as he carried his new bride across the threshold.

The colonel had disappointed many people—including the bride and groom, who couldn't invite everyone they wanted to be at their wedding. So a few weeks later they put on their bridal clothes again and held a second celebration at Graceland for everyone who'd missed the main event.

## BENJAMIN HENRY LATROBE AND
## MARY ELIZABETH HAZLEHURST

*"a woman of honor"*

THE FUTURE ARCHITECT OF THE United States Capitol and Supreme Court buildings and numerous colleges, libraries, and churches came to America in the late 1790s after his first wife's death in England. The shock had left Ben despondent, but he found happiness in Philadelphia—in the architectural commissions he received and in Mary, who became his adoring wife.

They met when Ben was drawing up plans for a new Bank of Pennsylvania. Inspired by the Erechtheum of ancient Greece, he designed a splendid white marble edifice with porticos and columns and began the American trend of Greek revivalism. Mary's father was a Philadelphia merchant much impressed with Ben's ideas and intelligence. Soon Ben was courting Mary, taking her on carriage rides to look at new sites and showing her already completed buildings.

They married in her family's town house in Philadelphia in 1800. Mary was twenty-nine and Ben was thirty-six. His friend Thomas Jefferson sent congratulations—and subsequently enlisted Ben's advice about building the University of Virginia.

Mary insisted that Ben's young son and daughter, who had remained with relatives in England after their mother's death, come and live with them now in Pennsylvania. If anything, she would always be more forgiving and understanding of her two step-children than of the five she and Ben had together.

"The great feature," he wrote his sister-in-law, "next to her benevolence, of my wife's character is an undaunted firmness in the practice of what she deems right. She is in the highest sense of the word, *a woman of honor.*"

Ben was tall and muscular, but his health suffered when he overworked. Mary was the ideal artist's wife, respectful of his needs for solitude and inspiration and wondrously proud of all that he created.

## ALBAN BERG AND HELENE NAHOWSKI

*"my faith is built on you"*

ALBAN FIRST SPOTTED HIS WIFE-TO-BE in the standing-room sections of the Vienna Musikverein and Opera Houses in 1906. Like most students, they loved hearing concerts but could rarely afford seats. They both were twenty-one years old. Helene was a gifted singer and pianist, although not as talented as Alban, whose operas and atonal compositions attracted worldwide acclaim before he was thirty-five. But her looks certainly were glorious: She was tall and slender, with long ash-blond hair. If she noticed him first, she didn't show it. But Alban kept popping up at the musical performances she attended. At last they started talking and their lifelong passion began.

He begged her to stop seeing former beaux, but Helene needed time to sort out her feelings. Besides, her father, a practical civil servant, didn't like his daughter getting serious with an asthmatic musician and composer who lacked a financially secure profession. She met Alban secretly at train stations, museums, and cafés, and they sent each other lots of notes, which her sympathetic sister helped deliver.

"Well, I really *am* in love," he told Helene in 1907. He wrote her father heartfelt letters of entreaty, and after four years Herr Nahowski finally consented to their union on the condition that they convert from Catholicism to Protestantism, so that a divorce—if necessary—would be easier to obtain!

Alban dedicated many works to his beloved Helene, including his operatic masterpiece, *Wozzeck:* "I owe it to you and *you alone. You composed* it and I only wrote it down."

Tirelessly she championed his work, especially his unfinished opera, *Lulu.* "For twenty-eight years I lived in the Paradise of his love," Helene said later. "Our souls were long ago joined together in . . . a union through all eternity."

## HENNY YOUNGMAN AND SADIE COHEN

*"Take my wife . . . please!"*

THE STAND-UP COMEDIAN WHO MADE this line famous was actually a very happily married man. He met Sadie in Kresge's, a five-and-ten-cent store in Brooklyn where they both worked in the 1920s. Henny printed business cards and letterheads when he wasn't making music with his newly formed band, "The Swanee Syncopators." Right across the aisle was Sadie, selling sheet music and phonograph records.

It took months before Henny found courage to talk to her or even learn her name. Sadie was red-haired, freckle-faced, adorable . . . and most likely Irish—certainly not someone Henny could bring home to his Jewish mother. But one day when the band had been hired to play in Coney Island, he threw caution to the winds and invited Sadie to come and listen. That's when she told him she only dated Jewish boys!

They married in Brooklyn in 1928. Although Sadie's mother wasn't too impressed with her son-in-law's career, she gave the newlyweds space in her Chauncey Street apartment until they could afford their own. Henny's band kept performing, but he was also having fun making wisecracks to the audience. One night he filled in for an absent emcee and decided that comedy was better than music. Soon he became the "king of one-liners," which he delivered with rat-tat-tat speed, using his violin as a prop.

Henny's career really took off eight years later when he began appearing regularly on singer Kate Smith's popular radio show. He first uttered his famous words about Sadie when she and some friends came to the studio shortly before showtime. They were gabbing so loudly, Henny couldn't concentrate on his script. Hoping someone could help them find seats in the audience, he approached a stagehand and said, "Take my wife . . . please."

## MARY MARTIN AND RICHARD HALLIDAY

*Her heart belonged to . . . Richard*

ALTHOUGH MARY WAS ONLY TWENTY-FIVE when she met Richard in 1939, she already was the divorced mother of a seven-year-old son (future actor Larry Hagman) and a Broadway performer. Her big break had come in 1938, when she stole the show singing a blazing rendition of Cole Porter's "My Heart Belongs to Daddy" in the hit musical *Leave It to Me.*

Richard had seen the play, but he was feeling poorly and slept through most of Mary's performance. A story editor for Paramount Studios, he didn't notice her until a year later when she arrived on Paramount's Hollywood lot to appear in *The Great Victor Herbert.*

Richard was tall and thin with dark eyes and hair; Mary was petite and fair and thought he was "the most handsome, divine man I had ever seen." They dated on and off, drawn to each other but ambivalent about getting married. That didn't stop Richard from sending Mary cases of soap and cologne and cryptic notes telling her to "keep it clean" whenever one of her former beaux came to town.

A few months before they married, he gave Mary a gold ring with a man's hand clasping a woman's; hidden in the man's palm was a ruby heart. "To MM from RH with      ?" was inscribed inside. Soon after their spur-of-the-moment wedding in Las Vegas, he added, "Love!! May 5, 1940."

As Mary's producer and manager, Richard arranged for her to ride a real horse galloping on a concealed treadmill in *Annie Get Your Gun,* which toured for over a year, and encouraged her to wash her hair on stage eight times a week while singing "I'm Gonna Wash That Man Right Out of My Hair" in *South Pacific.* She dedicated her autobiography to him—"the one who taught me the meaning of the words *heart* and *belongs.*"

## LEW WALLACE AND SUSAN ARNOLD ELSTON

*She was "a composite of genius, common-sense
and all best womanly qualities"*

SUSAN AND LEW WERE BOTH avid readers, although he confessed that he never liked school very much, preferring to draw pictures or read books of his own choosing. When they married in 1852, they settled in Crawfordsville, Indiana, where Lew became a prosecuting attorney who wrote in his spare time. His fame as a writer was ensured with the publication of *Ben-Hur*, his epic novel about the life of Jesus Christ. Susan wrote poems and magazine articles, as well as popular "tearjerkers," such as *Ginerva: or the Old Oaken Chest,* and *Land of the Pueblos,* a collection of stories about life in New Mexico.

They'd moved out west from Indiana after the Civil War, when Lew gallantly assumed command of thousands of Indian soldiers and became a major general. He had begun writing *Ben-Hur* in Indiana, sitting beneath the trees beside their house. He continued working on the book while he was the territorial governor of New Mexico. The remainder was written at night on an old pine desk in a back room of the governor's palace on the Plaza in Santa Fe. Lew completed the book in 1880, dedicating it to Susan: "the Wife of my Youth who Still Abides with Me."

He wrote his first draft of *Ben-Hur* on slate, then copied it onto paper page by page. Never having visited the Holy Land, Lew learned about it from maps, journals, other books, and people he met who'd been there. Later, President Garfield appointed Lew as U.S. minister to Turkey, and he and Susan visited some of the sites he had described. They were astonished to see how accurate his depictions were.

When the Wallaces moved back to Indiana, Lew lectured about their experiences and continued to write. Avid fans of *Ben-Hur* often stopped by their house, hoping to meet the author of such a compelling novel.

## ALEXANDER SMITH AND FLORA MACDONALD

*"This happy bridegroom!"*

ALEX WROTE *A LIFE-DRAMA AND* Other Poems in 1853, when he was twenty-three. He had not yet met Flora, the Scottish lass from the Isle of Skye, but love and marriage were already on his mind when he wrote,

> *The lark is singing with the blinding sky.*
> *Hedges are white with May. The bridegroom sea*
> *Is toying with the shore, his wedded bride,*
> *And, in the fulness of his marriage joy,*
> *He decorates her tawny brow with shells,*
> *Retires a space, to see how fair she looks,*
> *Then proud, runs up to kiss her.*

Born in the Scottish Highlands, Alex became a lace designer like his father. But he also appreciated beauty that could be woven with words. Someday Alex would visit the Hebrides, and when he did, he fell in love with Flora and brought her to Edinburgh. The rich images of Alex's poetry are as evocative and dreamlike as the intricate designs of fine lace. His *Life Poems* went through four editions in three years, providing him with a comfortable income and enabling him to quit the lace profession and concentrate on writing full-time.

He and Flora married in the spring of 1857 and settled at Wardie, near Granton. Alex wrote *City Poems* and *Dreamthorp* before beginning *A Summer in Skye,* a novel containing many poems inspired by their life on the "misty isle":

> *. . . ring in the wind, my wedding chimes;*
> *Smile, villagers, at every door;*
> *Old churchyard, stuff'd with buried crimes,*
> *Be clad in sunshine o'er and o'er;*
> *And youthful maidens, white and sweet,*
> *Scatter your blossoms far and wide;*
> *And with a bridal chorus greet*
> *This happy bridegroom and his bride.*

*Date approximate.

## JOHN OPIE AND AMELIA ALDERSON

*"my heart springs forward at the thought of thy near approach"*

"ALMOST FROM MY FIRST ARRIVAL Mr. Opie became my avowed lover," Amelia wrote in her memoirs. The blue-eyed, auburn-haired neophyte writer was high-spirited and accomplished when she met the portrait painter at a London party in the autumn of 1797. He was thirty-five and recently divorced. Amelia was twenty-eight, somewhat old for an attractive single woman, but she had been raising younger siblings since her mother's death and had just begun to attend social gatherings.

If other artists painted to live, John lived to paint. He'd been at it since his childhood in Truro, Cornwall, and by the age of fifteen he had become a traveling portrait painter. One day the "Cornish wonder" would be a professor of art at London's Royal Academy. He lacked a formal education and was somewhat un-polished, but his feelings for Amelia were unabashed: He was in love! She adored him, too, although other men pursued her. None held a candle to John.

They married at Marylebone Church in London in 1798 and settled at John's home at 8 Berners Street. Wedlock suited the Opies beautifully, as each inspired the other to excel in their arts. John's paintings of women seemed more graceful and sympathetic now, and although he was not as comfortable as Amelia with the soirees held in their home, his career benefited from the exposure.

"Fear makes you overrate others and underrate yourself," he said, encouraging her to become what she described as "a candidate for the pleasures, the pangs, the rewards and the penalties of authorship." *Father and Daughter,* a "moral tale," was one of many books she wrote. It was very well received in 1801 and continued selling for the next fifty years.

John painted more than 500 significant portraits in his lifetime, including those of Dr. Johnson and Mary Wollstonecraft Godwin. He painted Amelia's portrait many times and illustrated some of her novels. Shortly before their wedding, he had written, "To love thee much better than I . . . is, I think, impossible."

## SAM HOUSTON AND MARGARET LEA

*The eyes of Texas were upon her*

SAM WAS FORTY-SIX WHEN HE met twenty-year-old Margaret in Alabama in 1839. His first two marriages had been short-lived and over before he defeated General Santa Anna at the Battle of San Jacinto in 1836 and helped establish the Republic of Texas.

When Sam's term as the republic's first president ended, he returned to the practice of law. He was in Mobile, Alabama, promoting interest among speculators in new Texas town sites when he noticed a soft-spoken young woman with dark brown hair and magnificent violet eyes. Margaret was with her mother, a wealthy widow looking for profitable investments; but Mrs. Lea was wary of Sam, whose reputation included heavy drinking and a questionable financial situation.

Margaret, however, was thrilled to meet the famous Texan, who began courting her immediately. A few weeks later he headed for Nashville and a visit with his old friend Andrew Jackson, but he wrote to her constantly, inviting her to come to Texas with her nay-saying mother. Mrs. Lea brought one of her sons instead. Not only did Sam convince her that he loved her daughter, he also got her to buy tracts of land near Galveston! Back in Alabama, Margaret studied Spanish and stitched her trousseau. She carried a tiny picture of Sam with her all the time, inspiring her to write,

> *Dear gentle shade of him I love,*
> *I've gazed upon Thee till thine eye,*
> *in liquid light doth seem to move,*
> *and look on me in sympathy.*

They married at her mother's gracious home in 1840. Although many people thought the union wouldn't last any longer than Sam's other marriages had, Margaret brought him joy, comfort, and eight children. They were together for the rest of his life.

## GILBERT STUART AND CHARLOTTE COATES

*Always together*

GILBERT HAD BEEN STUDYING ART in London for five years when he became friendly with William Coates, a medical student who sat beside him at anatomy lectures. One weekend William invited Gilbert to his parents' country home for Sunday dinner and introduced him to Charlotte, his younger sister.

Shortly before the American Revolution, Gilbert had left his home in Rhode Island and voyaged to London—the best place for a talented portrait painter to be in the late eighteenth century. He needed a regular income, as well as the guidance of a more experienced painter. Benjamin West, another expatriate American artist, took Gilbert into his studio and helped him get established.

Charlotte fell madly in love with Gilbert, but her parents thought he was somewhat irresponsible. They tried to discourage Charlotte from marrying him in 1786, not realizing, of course, that he would become the "Father of American Portraiture." Eventually countless schoolchildren would gaze at copies of his famous paintings of George Washington whenever they saluted the American flag.

Gilbert, Charlotte, and their children sailed for America in 1794, and the following year John Jay introduced him to the president. Washington was a restless man who disliked posing for portraits. His new false teeth bothered him a lot, but Gilbert was so congenial that Washington sat for three life portraits and Gilbert made many copies from them. His daughter Jane Stuart later recounted her mother's memories of George Washington: "She saw him as he entered the hall door, when she was passing from the entry to the parlour, and she thought him the most superb looking person she had ever seen."

Gilbert liked his "Athenaeum" portrait of Washington so much, he left it unfinished because he couldn't bear to part with it. (Mrs. Washington asked for it repeatedly, but he kept saying it wasn't ready yet!)

## ELIZABETH CADY AND HENRY BREWSTER STANTON

*Obey? No way!*

RECITING THEIR MARRIAGE VOWS, HENRY was somewhat startled when "Lizzie," who had been promising to "love and honor," refused to say "obey." In 1840 no one had ever heard of a bride omitting what every husband considered his rightful due. The wedding guests gasped. There was a short silence. The minister looked at Henry, who gestured—Go on with the ceremony. Henry wasn't surprised. Ever since he'd fallen in love with Lizzie, he'd known that life with her would not be conventional.

The future reformer had received a fine education at Emma Willard's seminary in Troy, New York. Listening to women clients share sorrowful tales with her lawyer father, Lizzie had also learned firsthand about injustices. Most girls were educated only to become useful wives and mothers; after marriage their husbands controlled their property, as well as their behavior.

Not Henry and Lizzie; they'd manage just fine. That's what he told her parents, who had been steadfastly opposed to the union, saying Henry had no steady means of employment. (He already was an abolitionist and would later become a lawyer and journalist.) Lizzie was twenty-five and knew her own mind. She and Henry slipped away from her home in upstate New York and were married in New York City. Soon afterwards they sailed for London to participate in an antislavery convention. Not much happened on the conference floor, where "strong-minded women" were shunned, but back at the boardinghouse Lizzie met Lucretia Mott and became firmly committed to the cause of women's rights.

Henry was the only man who had protested the rejection of women delegates. When he and Lizzie returned to America, she campaigned effectively for passage of the married woman's property bill of New York State, and they devoted their lives to women's suffrage and other issues of discrimination—while raising seven children.

*May 10 and 12 have also been cited.

## SHOLOM (ALEICHEM) RABINOWITZ AND HUDL LOYEFF

*"he enchanted me"*

"OLGA'S" MARRIAGE CEREMONY TO THE world's most beloved Yiddish storyteller was performed in secret in 1883. She had been the thirteen-year-old daughter of a wealthy Jewish landowner in Sofievka, Russia, when Sholom was hired as her tutor. He was eighteen, with wavy blond hair and blue-green eyes. In exchange for tutoring and handling secretarial affairs for Olga's father, Sholom received lodging, food, and time to write. He perfected his craft, creating stories such as the "Tevye" tales, adapted in *Fiddler on the Roof* many years later.

Sholom tutored Olga for three years. They read the classics and popular literature, took long walks in the woods . . . and fell in love. No day passed that they didn't see each other or yearn to do so. He recalled in his autobiography: "The word 'romance' was too clichéd, the word 'love' too banal for what the young couple felt. . . . Not a cloud specked their blue sky."

But "Aunt Toibe," a spinster busybody, noticed that they had become inseparable. Toibe didn't mean to make trouble . . . but wasn't it her duty to ask Olga's father, Where was it written that a teacher and pupil must be so close all the time?

Olga's father fired Sholom. He had liked the tutor, but if the young man was courting Olga, he should have asked for permission first! With her eyes full of tears, Olga watched Sholom depart down the road to Kiev. He sent Olga passionate love letters, which reached her father instead.

After two years she begged a sympathetic cousin to locate Sholom and arrange a marriage. Afterward her father accepted their decision and insisted that the newlyweds come home. Sholom adopted his pen name, which means "Peace among you," and began selling stories to a new Yiddish magazine.

## ROBIN HOOD AND MAID MARIAN

*"in solid content, together they liv'd"*
—FROM AN OLD ENGLISH BALLAD

THE LEGENDARY ENGLISH OUTLAW MARRIED his "bonny fyne mayde" in the late twelfth century under a canopy of trees in Sherwood Forest, away from their peaceful homes in the north Midlands but safely out of the clutches of the treacherous sheriff of Nottingham.

Robin and Marian's romance began before that fateful day when he fled into hiding after killing one of the king's foresters in self-defense. Until then he'd been a nobleman—Robert Fitzooth, Earl of Huntington—and she the fair lady Matilda Fitzwater. Now he was an outlaw, condemned to death for treason. He changed his name, changed his appearance and, with Friar Tuck, Little John, and other members of his band of "merry men," started robbing the rich and helping those in trouble.

Matilda pined for her sweetheart, knowing only that he lived somewhere in the dark forest. Robert was good-hearted, fair, and honorable to all. Could he be the one they were calling "Prince of Thieves"?

Sometime in the joyous month of May, when lovers' hearts will surely break if they are not united, Matilda put on men's clothes and stole into the forest. If marrying Robert meant giving up her cozy life back home, so be it.

In a small clearing stood a handsome man dressed in green, with a peaked cap on his head and a quiver of arrows slung over one shoulder. Robin stuck an arrow into his bowstring, pulled . . . and heard the faint sound of footsteps behind him. Instantly he turned and grabbed the intruder. They tussled silently in the shadows, not even groaning lest they attract the sheriff's men. Finally they quit and fell on the ground. "You're quite a fighter," Robin said. "Want to join me and my merry men?"

"Robert?" asked Matilda breathlessly. "Is that you?"

*Date approximate.

## OSCAR HAMMERSTEIN II AND
## DOROTHY BLANCHARD JACOBSON

*He missed the boat . . . and found true love*

OSCAR AND DOROTHY WERE MARRIED in 1929 in the bridal suite of the Belvedere Hotel in Baltimore, Maryland. They both had been married once before, but this time it was for keeps. Wearing a gray dress with a fur-trimmed cape, Dorothy looked at "Ockie" and beamed. He looked at his auburn-haired, blue-eyed bride and knew he had found contentment at last.

Two years earlier they had met on board the S.S. *Olympic* en route to London, when she was twenty-seven and he was thirty-one. Oscar was limping after spraining both ankles in a touch football game with friends. His injuries had delayed his departure, causing him to cancel reservations on another ocean liner and take the same one as Dorothy. Aboard ship their attraction was mutual, immediate, and intense. Soon after they reached England, Oscar wished he could ask Dorothy to marry him right then.

When Oscar got back to New York, he and composer Jerome Kern adapted Edna Ferber's novel *Show Boat* for the stage. Their musical production dealt with serious topics, such as racial prejudice, gambling addictions, and unhappy marriages, and contained memorable songs, including "Can't Help Lovin' That Man," "Make Believe," and "Ol' Man River." Oscar usually stood up while writing his lyrics, saying it saved him time when he needed to pace the floor. He had collaborated earlier with Sigmund Romberg in *Desert Song* and would spend twenty-seven years with Richard Rodgers after Kern's death.

Two years passed before Oscar and Dorothy could divorce their spouses and get married. After a wedding breakfast celebration, they sailed for a honeymoon in Europe on their favorite ship, S.S. *Olympic*, and promised each other they'd never part again. Oscar dedicated a new song, "Don't Ever Leave Me," to Dorothy.

She never did.

## OSA LEIGHTY AND MARTIN JOHNSON

*"Home" would be schooners, rafts, and tents*

FEW COUPLES CAN CLAIM BEING captured by cannibals and escaping their clutches, but Osa wrote all about it in *I Married Adventure,* describing expeditions she and Martin took soon after their marriage in 1910. Osa had been fifteen the year before, when she and her girlfriends attended Martin's film show and lecture near her home in Chanute, Kansas. He was a twenty-four-year-old photographer and adventurer who recounted tales of sailing the South Seas on board the *Snark* with writer Jack London. To a small-town girl from Kansas, Martin's stories were enthralling.

They married suddenly, on one of her visits to see him and his parents in Independence. She heard him tell his business partner about it on the phone: "Big brown eyes, taffy hair . . . Yes, that's her. . . . What? Sure, marriage is a serious thing, I know that. . . . What? . . . Young? Well, maybe so, but she's got spirit and spunk!"

When Osa brought Martin home, her father declared, "You've got her, now take care of her!" But Martin's plans did not include settling down. "We're going around the world!" he told Osa. She gulped and replied, "Well—all right, dear."

They sold their wedding gifts, gave film shows and lectures to raise money, and set off from San Francisco. They learned to sail, fly small planes, and photograph and film vanishing wildlife and native populations in Africa and the South Pacific. Whenever they'd gathered lots of material (and run out of money), they'd return to the United States and put on shows until they raised enough money to head off again.

Over the next twenty-seven years Martin and Osa made documentary films for the American Museum of Natural History in New York City and published eighteen books about their experiences. Osa also designed animal toys for the National Wildlife Federation.

## EDGAR ALLAN POE AND VIRGINIA CLEMM

### *"beautiful Annabel Lee"*

AFTER EDGAR'S MOTHER DIED, HE was raised by a merchant and his wife, who paid his tuition to the University of Virginia but insisted he support himself otherwise. Gambling debts destroyed Edgar's finances, however, and he finally burned the furniture in his room for heat. At age twenty-two he left college and moved in with his aunt, Maria Clemm, and her young daughter in Baltimore, after a brief stint in the army.

He was a sad-eyed, lonely young man, but Aunt Maria and cousin Virginia were loving and supportive. At last "Eddy" felt as if he belonged to a real family. He sold some poems and stories, but his earnings were meager. For a while he edited a literary magazine, but his book reviews were so scathing that he soon was nicknamed "The Comanche of Literature."

As time passed, Eddy and Virginia grew closer. They played the piano, took walks in the garden, fixed dinners together, and became inseparable. When they married in 1836, he was twenty-seven and she was thirteen, although the deputy clerk at the Richmond, Virginia, marriage office kindly wrote down, "21 years old."

To Eddy, she would always be "my own sweetest Sissy, my darling little wifey." Although biographers know relatively little about their private life, they agree that these two were a loving and devoted couple.

"You know I love Virginia passionately, devotedly," he wrote his aunt. "I cannot express the fervent devotion I feel towards my dear little cousin—my own darling."

Eddy worked hard, editing various magazines and writing frightening tales such as "The Fall of the House of Usher" and "The Murders in the Rue Morgue," one of the first modern detective stories. By 1846 his poem "The Raven" was published in a New York newspaper, and his fame increased dramatically.

## ANDREW JOHNSON AND ELIZA MCCARDLE

*Always on his side*

ANDY COULDN'T SIGN HIS OWN name on the wedding certificate when he married Eliza in 1827. Without her help, he might never have learned how to read and write. And he certainly wouldn't have become the seventeenth president of the United States.

Eliza was a twelve-year-old girl with soft hazel eyes and brown hair when Andy first saw her. He was thirteen and had recently moved to Greeneville, Tennessee, with his mother and brother. Andy worked as a tailor's assistant, and Eliza helped her mother sew quilts. She noticed Andy on Main Street and told her girlfriends that one day she would marry that good-looking fellow; five years later, she did. It would be many years before the Johnsons ever heard of Abraham Lincoln, yet the name of the justice of the peace was Mordecai Lincoln—a cousin of Abe's father, Thomas.

Their first home was the back room of the tailor shop, where Eliza read to Andy as he stitched. At night she taught him reading, writing, and arithmetic. When his boss retired, Andy took over the shop, which became a meeting place for townspeople to discuss political matters. Soon Andy discovered he was a persuasive speaker. Within a year he was elected town alderman and then mayor. He also became a great reader, but he never learned to spell very well. "It is a man of small imagination who cannot spell his name more than one way," he told his secretaries.

Eliza was a calm, down-to-earth woman who never questioned her husband's integrity, even when Congress considered impeaching him as president. An old friend said, "Their union was fortunate and, by her aid, he was better prepared for the long encounter which fate held in reserve."

## ANNE HARRISON AND SIR RICHARD FANSHAWE

*"my life and fortune shall be thine,*
*and every thought of my heart"*

RICHARD WAS A THIRTY-FIVE-YEAR-OLD STATESMAN and poet when he married Anne in 1644. She was nineteen and a boisterous tomboy, or "hoyting girl," she wrote in her memoirs. "I thought myself a queen," she said, "and my husband so glorious a crown that I more valued myself to be called by his name than born a princess."

They were married at Wolvercote Church, an ivy-covered stone edifice outside of Oxford, soon after King Charles I appointed Richard secretary of war to the Prince of Wales. After Charles was beheaded in 1649, the Fanshawes sided with the Royalists and lived for many years in poverty and danger. They fled to Bristol with the king's court, but plague drove them to Truro and Penzance. Sailing to the Scilly Isles, they were robbed. Later they were nearly shipwrecked en route to France, and Anne was almost taken into slavery by Turkish sailors.

In 1651 Richard was captured at the Battle of Worcester and imprisoned at Whitehall. For three months, until she was able to secure his release, Anne "visited" him every morning at four by standing under his prison window.

Following the Restoration, the Fanshawes regained much of their wealth. Richard became ambassador to Portugal and Spain, and he and Anne sailed to Madrid with their five children. He also had time to write some poems and translate the writings of Horace and other ancient texts.

The times were tumultuous, but Anne and Richard were happy. "Glory be to God," she wrote. "We never had but one mind throughout our lives. Our souls were wrapped up in each other's, our aims and designs one, our loves one, and our resentments one. We so studied one the other, that we knew each other's mind by our looks. Whatever was real happiness, God gave it me in him."

## ROBERT LOUIS STEVENSON AND
## FANNY VANDERGRIFT OSBOURNE

*"Tusitala" and his "Tiger Lily"*

ROBERT'S PARENTS REFUSED TO GIVE him money for a trip to California in 1879, hoping that their twenty-eight-year-old son would forget about Fanny Osbourne. She was eleven years older than he, married and the mother of two.

They had become involved two years before at an artists' colony in France. Robert was writing stories, and Fanny had come to study art. But now she was deeply depressed; her youngest child had just died and her marriage was a failure. Back home in Edinburgh, Robert's parents were distressed to look at him. His health problems were chronic; now he was particularly thin and sickly.

Nothing could deter him from winning Fanny. He crossed the Atlantic soon after her divorce and married her in San Francisco in 1880. Silver wedding bands were all he could afford, but he gave her some of his verses as a wedding gift. They spent two nights at the Palace Hotel, then headed north to Silverado and camped in a dilapidated cabin. They thought it all was an adventure.

In August they returned to Europe for a conciliatory meeting with his parents. Robert began writing something grand to please his new stepson, Lloyd. *Treasure Island* would be "about a map, a treasure, a mutiny and a derelict ship. . . . No women in the story, Lloyd orders." Robert read chapters aloud to Fanny and the children. The book became his first major literary success.

He wrote more classics for children, including *A Child's Garden of Verses* and *Kidnapped.* It took him only three days to write the first draft of *The Strange Case of Dr. Jekyll and Mr. Hyde.* By 1888 wanderlust drove him and Fanny to take his widowed mother and Lloyd on a sailing adventure. They visited Australia and many islands and settled down on four hundred acres in Samoa.

## JOHN GUTZON BORGLUM AND
## MARY WILLIAMS MONTGOMERY

*Mount Rushmore, here we come!*

MARY WAS A PETITE WELLESLEY College graduate who had just earned her Ph.D. at the University of Berlin when she met Gutzon on board a ship to New York in 1901. He was thirty-five, fairly short, and balding, but she was impressed by the American artist's boundless energy and ambition.

When Gutzon was twenty-two, he had married a forty-two-year-old art teacher in California. Although Liza helped him start his career, eventually they drifted apart. She'd gone with him to Paris, where he studied with Auguste Rodin, but when Gutzon sailed back to America, he was alone.

He set up a studio at 166 East 38th Street in New York City and worked on sculptures for the 1904 St. Louis World's Fair. He also made angels and the Twelve Apostles for Manhattan's Cathedral of St. John the Divine, many statues of political and historical figures, and the colossal marble head of Abraham Lincoln for the rotunda of the capital in Washington, D.C.

Gutzon married Mary in 1909, and they moved to Borgland, an estate in Stamford, Connecticut. Friends said she stabilized his life and helped the excitable but brilliant man become less hotheaded. Still, he championed the causes of labor and always defended freedom of speech. In the late 1920s Gutzon began his most ambitious work in the Black Hills of South Dakota.

Born in Idaho Territory, Gutzon always had a keen interest in western landscapes and American history. He jumped at the chance to sculpt massive busts of Washington, Jefferson, Lincoln, and Teddy Roosevelt into Mount Rushmore and determined the ideal locations of the sixty-foot-high heads after years of drilling and blasting. A small village was erected for his work crew, alongside a home and studio for Mary and their children. The project took fourteen years to complete and became one of the grandest man-made sculptures.

### HUMPHREY BOGART AND LAUREN BACALL

*She loved being "Mrs. Bogart"*

HORDES OF REPORTERS HAD DESCENDED on the small town of Mansfield, Ohio, by the time "Bogie" and "Betty" arrived on the Superchief train from California in 1945. A few days later they were married at high noon at Malabar, the farm belonging to Bogie's novelist friend Louis Bromfield. Bogie cried throughout the entire three-minute ceremony.

He and Betty had met on the movie set of *To Have and Have Not*. He was forty-four and a major star whose gruff exterior masked a polished and gentle man. She was a stunning nineteen-year-old model making her Hollywood debut.

"Have you got a match?" she asks him in the film. They are in a hotel corridor outside their respective rooms. Bogie searches through a table drawer while she leans against the door frame. "Here you are," he says, tossing her a box. It's a very short—but passionate—scene. Their real-life romance began just as quickly. By the time filming was completed, Bogie had left his third wife. Eleven days after his divorce was final, he married Betty and began his happiest years.

She wore a pale pink suit with a brown chiffon scarf, brown shoes and belt, and she carried white orchids. Bogie wore a gray tweed suit, a wine-colored tie, and a white carnation in his lapel. He kidded that he was "something old"; "something new" was Betty's outfit; "something borrowed" was her mother's handkerchief, and "something blue" was Betty's slip.

"I felt as though I owned the world," she recalled in *By Myself*. "How had I lived before him? . . . It seemed that everything that had ever happened to me had led to this day with him." Looking at Bogie, she began crying too, and "had no doubt that this happiness would last forever."

## AMOS BRONSON ALCOTT AND ABIGAIL MAY

*"My husband, hallowed be the name, is all I expected,*
*[and] this is saying a good deal."*

BRONSON WAS A PROGRESSIVE NEW England educator who observed his students carefully, much as he later kept detailed diaries about the three daughters he and Abby would have, including Louisa May, the famous author.

At twenty-eight, Bronson had started a private school on Salem Street in Boston and hired twenty-six-year-old Abby as an assistant teacher. Like her boss, she thought children learned best by "doing," and she favored a relaxed, permissive atmosphere in the classroom.

It didn't take long before Bronson confided in his journal, "I do love this good woman, and I love her because she is good." He was tall and blond, with intense blue eyes. She had dark eyes and hair and was outspoken and spirited. Too shy to admit his feelings, he won her affection by showing her his writings.

Her parents were opposed to their marriage until Bronson's income was sufficient to support a family. Still, they became engaged. Abby described Bronson to her brother: "He is moderate. I am impetuous—He is prudent and humble—I am forward and arbitrary. He is poor—but we are both industrious—why may we not be happy?"

By 1830 Bronson could wait no more and wrote, "Providence bestows her bounties equally upon all, and it will be our folly alone if we do not obtain our share." He and Abby would manage. He was sure of it. Together they won her parents' consent. They married in Boston, at King's Chapel on Tremont Street, and afterwards walked to their first home, a boarding-house at 12 Franklin Street. Later they received $2,000 from anonymous well-wishers. They never were told who sent it but just knew it was from Abby's parents.

## FRANCES MILTON AND
## THOMAS ANTHONY TROLLOPE

*"My future happiness on earth is at your disposal"*

"FANNY" MARRIED THOMAS ON HIS thirty-fifth birthday in 1809, a time when all that was expected of an English lawyer's wife was that she manage the household affairs and bear his children. She gave birth to five, including Anthony, one of the most prolific and well-regarded English writers of the nineteenth century.

Fanny and Thomas had been neighbors on Keppel Street in London, a few doors away from each other. She and her sister had moved there from the country to keep house for their older brother. It was a bold move for young women to take at that time; usually they only left home to be married. Thomas lived at number 16, which became the model for some of his son's future books.

She was twenty-seven, bright and lively, and thrilled by the cultural life of London. Thomas was a moderately successful barrister with good prospects, and she found him attractive, though somewhat reserved and quiet. In fact, he proposed to Fanny in a letter, saying he enjoyed her "society and conversation." Stiffly outlining the economics of his situation, he admitted that he didn't know how to express "the flippant nonsense . . . commonly used on occasions of this nature." Fanny wasn't worried by his unromantic tone, however. Deep feelings, she believed, were often difficult to express.

Life was good in the beginning, and all their children were born in the first ten years. Fanny and Thomas loved each other deeply, but as time passed he mismanaged the family finances repeatedly, investing in foolish schemes and undesirable real estate. But Fanny was not the kind of wife to sit back and bemoan the family's misfortunes. She began writing books, beginning with *The Domestic Manners of the Americans*, to help support everyone and for the next twenty years produced a continual stream of well-received popular novels.

## ANDREW DUCROW AND MARGARET GRIFFITH

*Ladies and gentlemen, in the center ring . . . !*

NO ONE KNOWS FOR SURE what first attracted Margaret to Andrew. Was it his grand leaps over seven horses? The way he juggled balls as he walked across the tightrope?

Andrew's father had been the "Flemish Hercules," a circus "strong man" able to lift and hold between his teeth a table with his five children on it. By the age of three Andrew was tumbling and balancing on ropes, fencing, and riding horseback. At fifteen he was chief equestrian and ropes dancer at Astley's Amphitheatre in London. Critics marveled at his discipline and courage. One said if Andrew were given the chance, he "would have danced on a rope stretched across the crater of Vesuvius during an eruption."

Margaret, too, came from a circus family. She met Andrew when he was appearing in a Liverpool circus with his "poses plastiques"—elaborate impersonations of antique statues in classical settings. Margaret watched all of Andrew's performances and soon was participating as an extra in many scenes. Charles Dickens described her as "a lady rider of rare accomplishments and remarkable beauty."

She was saucy, delightful, and twenty; he was twenty-five, blond-haired, good-looking, and ambitious. They married in Holland in 1818 at the beginning of Andrew's five-year tour of the Continent, which included a long stay with Franconi's circus in Paris.

When they came back to England, they had perfected amazing new "hippo-dramatic" acts such as "Cupid and Zephyr," "Cortez's Conquest of Mexico," and "Saint George and the Dragon." Margaret often rode in Andrew's spectacular processions as he performed incredible feats of daring, such as standing up and riding six horses at one time or leaping through hoops made of fire on his favorite trick horse, Jack.

\*Date approximate.

## ANTON CHEKHOV AND OLGA KNIPPER

*"Dear, marvelous actress"*

"THE MOST IMPORTANT THING IN family life is love, sexual desire, one flesh; everything else is unimportant and boring," Anton told a friend two years before he met Olga.

Although the Russian writer's health was poor, his life was satisfying; his plays *The Seagull* and *Uncle Vanya* were being performed and praised, and he was the author of numerous short stories. He was working on *The Three Sisters* when he became romantically involved with Olga, an auburn-haired Hungarian actress who often performed in his plays. At the age of thirty-nine, Anton had fallen in love.

He also was panic-stricken. A month before their 1901 wedding, he wrote to her from Yalta, promising to marry her as soon as he returned to Moscow if she swore to tell no one in advance. "I don't know why, but I am simply terrified of the wedding ceremony, and the congratulations and the glass of champagne you have to hold in your hand at the same time smiling vaguely."

*The Three Sisters*, starring Olga as Masha, had recently been presented by the Moscow Art Theater. The play was superb! Members of the audience were weeping when the final curtain came down. But the playwright couldn't deal with a wedding!

He married Olga on a Friday in a small church in Moscow. Anton also had arranged a special luncheon elsewhere for his friends. By the time they figured out what had happened, the newlyweds had left the church, visited Olga's mother, and boarded a train to see the writer Gorky, under house arrest in Nizhny-Novgorod. From there they continued to Axenovo for their honeymoon. "We were so close to each other then," Olga reminded Anton in a letter one year later. And their six-week honeymoon in the country had restored his fragile health, at least for a while.

## ALFRED LUNT AND LYNN FONTANNE

*Married to the theater, and each other*

IN THEIR HASTE TO GET married in 1922, after delays caused by the runs of their respective plays, Alfred and Lynn raced downtown to the marriage bureau in Manhattan with only ninety-five cents in their pockets. "Two dollars, please," said the clerk, after conducting the ceremony.

The bride and groom were forced to borrow money from their witnesses—two strangers they had corralled in the lobby. Then they kissed each other madly, kissed the witnesses, and kissed the clerk! After celebrating with chocolate sodas, they went home, got their wallets, packed some clothes, and headed for a short honeymoon in Atlantic City.

Although Alfred had been eagerly awaiting his wedding day, it unnerved him so that he forgot all his lines at his next performance. The stage manager had to hide behind props and recite everything for him while Alfred moved his lips silently.

His love for Lynn had left him "unbalanced" before. He had stumbled down the steps when they first met in 1919, while auditioning for parts in summer stock. The roles they won led to Alfred's breakthrough part as the title character in Booth Tarkington's play *Clarence,* and Lynn soon landed the lead in the comedy *Dulcy,* which established her career.

In 1924 they performed together in Molnar's romantic comedy *The Guardsman.* From that time on they were a great acting team. One critic wrote, "Those who saw them on opening night, bowing hand in hand for the first time, may well have been witnessing a moment in theatrical history."

For the next thirty years Lunt and Fontanne appeared on stage together in more than eighteen plays in America and abroad. Their performance in the 1931 screen version of *The Guardsman* still gives theater lovers a glimpse of their undeniable magic.

## CHARLES LINDBERGH AND ANNE MORROW

### *A secret wedding*

IN 1929, TWO YEARS AND one week after "Lucky Lindy" flew *The Spirit of St. Louis* solo from New York to Paris, he slipped into his future in-laws' Englewood, New Jersey, home to marry Anne without attracting throngs of fans and reporters. The newlyweds escaped from their reception in a borrowed car, with the bride hiding on the floor. But the press caught up with them on their honeymoon yacht off the coast of Maine. Life with Charles, Anne realized, would always be in the spotlight.

They had met in 1927 in Mexico City, where Anne's father, the United States ambassador, held a reception in Charles's honor. It had taken the twenty-five-year-old aviator twenty-seven hours to fly from Washington, DC, and meeting Anne was an unexpected delight. He took the Morrows for a plane ride over Aztec ruins.

The twenty-year-old Smith College student adored flying right away and subsequently realized that airplanes were one of the few places where she and Charles could be alone. Although goggles, helmets, and loud engine noises impeded conversations aloft, there was "a kind of bright golden 'bloom' over everything," Anne wrote. Eventually, "C." taught her how to fly, operate the radio, and read charts and Morse code. She became an excellent navigator and radio operator and helped Charles break his record for a transcontinental flight. She also became a well-respected poet, novelist, and essayist, writing about their adventures and her philosophical reflections.

Anne's well-connected, wealthy parents knew that Charles was considered a national hero, but all he'd ever been before was a barnstormer and stunt flyer, walking on plane wings and doing other tricks in the air. Was this "glorified mechanic" right for their daughter? Because they loved her, they accepted Anne's decision and made her a small but beautiful wedding.

## VERNON CASTLE AND IRENE FOOTE

*"Castles in the air"*

"I BELIEVE OUR LIVES ARE planned in detail before we are born," Irene wrote, describing her fateful first meeting with Vernon. The future team of world-famous exhibition ballroom dancers met on a float in Long Island Sound in 1910. She was eighteen and he was twenty-four. They probably wouldn't have spoken to each other if a mutual friend hadn't swum over and introduced them.

Vernon was a British comedian performing on Broadway. He managed to get Irene a bit part in the play—but her scene was stolen by an unknown child actress named Helen Hayes, who later admitted that she had a crush on Vernon, too. The following spring Vernon and Irene married at her parents' New Rochelle, New York, home on their anniversary day. After honeymooning in England, where they met Vernon's family, the Castles were back in New York in *The Hen-Pecks,* a slapstick comedy.

A year later they were in Paris, where "necessity made us dancers," said Irene, after promised roles in a play evaporated. Temporarily out of work, they danced so well in a supper club one night, the owner hired them to put on shows for the audience. Soon crowds of expatriates were coming to see and hear the latest American dances and tunes.

Ballroom dancing, especially to the tunes of Irving Berlin, became a popular pastime before World War I. Irene and Vernon created the "Castle Walk" by stepping up on the beat, rather than down, and also popularized the one-step, turkey trot, bunny hug, tango, and foxtrot. They toured cities across America and gave dancing lessons. When Irene cut her hair and put a band across her forehead, her devoted fans followed, calling their new look the "Castle bob" with a "Castle band."

## LOUIS PASTEUR AND MARIE LAURENT

*All for science*

IN FEBRUARY 1849, LOUIS—THE French chemist whose name would become linked to his process of destroying dangerous microorganisms in foods— wrote to the University of Strasbourg's rector, asking permission to marry his daughter Marie. Explaining his modest background, Louis said he also supported his three sisters. "I have therefore absolutely no fortune," he stated. "My only means are good health, some courage and my position at the University."

He had arrived in Strasbourg two months before as acting professor of chemistry. Soon afterwards he met Marie, and shortly after that, he proposed. Without her love, he confessed, "My work no longer means anything to me."

When they married three months later, at the Church of Sainte Madeleine, he was twenty-six and she was twenty-two, a cheerful, blue-eyed girl who loved to sing and understood the fate of a scientist's wife: a limited income; acceptance that Louis's work always came first; knowing that even when Louis was home, he often was preoccupied.

Marie assisted Louis as much as possible, copying his notes and writing down his dictations, and he tried his best to explain things to her. But science was Marie's only rival. Louis had no other interests besides his work and family, even when they moved to the Sorbonne in Paris. On their wedding anniversary many years later, she told their children, "Your father is absorbed in his thoughts, talks little, sleeps little, rises at dawn—in a word continues the life I began with him this day thirty-five years ago."

"The nights seem to me too long, yet I do not complain," Louis wrote a friend. "I am often scolded by Madame Pasteur, whom I console by telling her that I shall lead her to posterity."

## FREDRIC MARCH AND FLORENCE ELDRIDGE

*Favorite costars*

FREDRIC AND FLORENCE MARRIED IN Mexico in 1927 and then toured 132 American cities with the Theater Guild Repertory Company. They'd been acting together since the previous year, when they met in the dining car of a train bound for summer stock productions in Denver. Unfortunately, Florence's springtime wedding tossed her out of the leading lady spotlight for a while, because the management said that a husband-and-wife team was unromantic and not good for business.

They never forgot that "brutal tour" across the United States, performing in "barns, gyms and saloons" and sleeping in seedy hotels, but Fredric also said, "It was fun for Florence and me, this working together constantly." It also improved their acting skills, enabling him to win a five-year Hollywood contract. Although Florence was happier on Broadway, she gladly accepted film roles, especially when Fredric had a part, too.

She came from Brooklyn, was twenty-five, and had always wanted to act. He was twenty-nine, from Racine, Wisconsin, and tried acting after giving up a humdrum career in banking. By 1937 Fredric was earning more than $450,000 a year and was one of Hollywood's highest-paid actors. But he never gave up his love for the stage, returning often to costar with Florence. Even when a play flopped, the Marches were upbeat about it. In 1938 they apologized for *Yr. Obedient Husband* by publishing a cartoon of two trapeze artists missing each other in midair and saying, "Oops, sorry!"

They were Bothwell and Queen Elizabeth in *Mary of Scotland*, Fantine and Jean Valjean in *Les Misérables,* and Mr. and Mrs. Matthew Brady in *Inherit the Wind.* Always loyal to Florence, Fredric became so enraged at actress Tallulah Bankhead for deliberately upstaging Florence's performance in *The Skin of Our Teeth* that he gargled loudly backstage during one of Tallulah's soliloquies.

## ANNE KINGSMILL AND HENEAGE FINCH

*Her "much lov'd husband"*

ANNE AND HENEAGE MET AT King Charles II's court and were married in 1684, when she was twenty-two years old. The orphaned young woman had been appointed maid of honor to Mary of Modena, the duchess of York. Heneage was the duke of York's gentleman of the bedchamber. When the king died one year later, the duke became King James II. In three years he fled to France after unsuccessfully trying to convert England to Roman Catholicism.

Heneage and Anne refused to swear allegiance to the new monarchs, William and Mary, and swiftly lost their positions. Anne was deeply saddened to give up the "glorious show" of court life, but leaving it was the best thing for her as a future author. She and Heneage retired to his family seat in Kent, where the sweet countryside was highly conducive to contemplation and writing. They became count and countess of Winchilsea when Heneage succeeded to the title.

"They err, who say that husbands can't be lovers," Anne wrote, inspired by Heneage's boundless affection and support for her writing. Whenever he returned home from journeys, Anne shared new poems, fables, and religious meditations with him. Through poetry, she conveyed her passion for Heneage—at a time when few women revealed their amorous feelings in print. In "Mr. F, Now Earl of Winchilsea," she calls him "Dafnis" and herself "Ardelia" and concludes that when true love exists, a poet doesn't need the muses for inspiration.

Although Anne's work was respected by such writers as Alexander Pope, the world of seventeenth-century literature still belonged to men. More than one hundred years later her talents were rediscovered by the great poet William Wordsworth, who said she had been "a wood lark among the town sparrows."

*Date approximate.

# JUNE

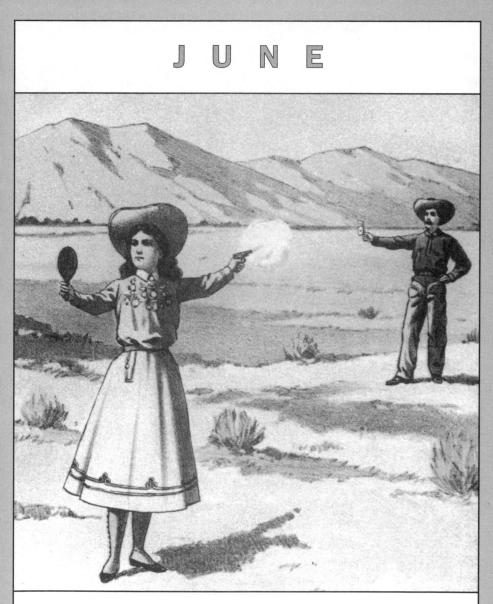

## ANNIE OAKLEY AND FRANK BUTLER
*June 22, 1876*

Frank's steady hand and faith in "Little Sure Shot" helps Annie
split a card with her revolver.

## JUDITH LEYSTAR AND JAN MIENSE MOLENAER

*True "lodestars" in art and matrimony*

EVEN BEFORE JUDITH AND JAN married in Holland in 1636, it was difficult to tell which paintings were hers and which had been made by him. The two artists probably met in Frans Hals's workshop and subsequently influenced and supported each other's work throughout their lives.

A few years before the wedding, Judith painted her self-portrait of a proud-looking, well-dressed woman holding a violin and smiling. Her lips are parted, and she might be saying, "I am Judith Leystar, a twenty-three-year-old painter, and I do not intend to marry until I have established my own workshop and studio, and have been accepted into the Haarlem Artists' Guild of St. Luke." (She became the first woman to do so.)

In Jan's "Self-Portrait in Studio," he holds a paintbrush and sits before an easel, and an old woman sits beside him. A gold coin rests in her lap; she is beseeching him. He looks us in the eye. Does the old woman represent the fleeting nature of life? Do her coins symbolize the emptiness of wealth?

Jan often painted pictures with double or hidden meanings, such as "Allegory of Marital Fidelity," which depicts good and bad qualities inherent in marriages. Judith's paintings focused on moral issues, too, which was typical of Dutch painting at that time. She also painted flowers, still lifes, and portraits, such as "Boy Playing a Flute" and "Jolly Topper." Usually she signed her work with the symbol of a "leystar," or lodestar.

She and Jan were both twenty-five when they married at a church in Haarlem. They moved to Amsterdam and set up a studio together. Following the births of their five children, Judith painted less often, concentrating instead on the family's business affairs. Her husband gave her power of attorney, enabling her to buy and sell properties for them.

## PRESIDENT GROVER CLEVELAND AND FRANCES FOLSOM

*"She'll do! She'll do!"*

MOST PEOPLE THOUGHT GROVER WAS kidding when the forty-something bachelor said he had waited for his future bride to grow up. "Frank" was the dark-eyed daughter of Grover's former law partner, who had died when she was eleven. That's when "Uncle Cleve" became her legal guardian.

By 1886, Frank was twenty-two, slender, intelligent, and imbued with "down-right loveliness," said a White House aide years later. Grover was stodgy and middle-aged, but Frank adored him. Theirs would be the first White House wedding of a president in office. Soon after Frank graduated from Wells College, she became the youngest first lady, and the most beloved since Dolley Madison.

The Blue Room was festooned with flowers as Grover escorted Frank down a wide staircase into the hall. Her white satin dress was enhanced by real orange blossoms bordering a white India silk overskirt. Around her neck was Grover's wedding gift—a magnificent diamond necklace.

After a twenty-one-gun salute on the White House lawn and a buffet celebration, guests were given slices of wedding cake in white satin boxes autographed by the bride and groom. Reporters lurked in the shrubbery and spied on the newlyweds outside their honeymoon cottage in Deer Park, Maryland. Grover railed futilely against "keyhole journalism" and tried staying out of sight.

Nothing fazed Frank, who was soon hosting banquets, balls, and receptions for the general public, including special ones held on Saturdays to accommodate working women. The press admired Frank, as did the public, and "Baby Ruth" candy bars were named after the Clevelands' eldest daughter.

When opponents vilified Grover during his reelection campaign, Frank defended him by saying she wished "the women of our country no better blessing than that their homes and their lives be as happy, and that their husbands may be as kind and attentive, as considerate and affectionate as mine."

## EDWARD, DUKE OF WINDSOR AND
## WALLIS WARFIELD SIMPSON

*The woman he loved*

ONLY SIXTEEN GUESTS ATTENDED THE wedding of the ex-ruler of 500 million people in the British empire—the man who gave up the throne of England to marry "the woman I love" in 1937. Edward was forty-two and Wallis was forty-one when the small ceremony took place in the music room of the Chateau de Cande, a sixteenth-century fifty-room estate belonging to friends in the Loire Valley of France. Edward had desperately wanted a religious wedding, but no English bishop would perform it. At last a vicar from Darlington, England, offered his services.

Wallis's two-piece silk crepe wedding dress was created by Mainbocher in "Wallis blue," and Schiaparelli designed her trousseau. Her wedding ring was made of Welsh gold, the same kind worn by British queens.

Once the poor relation from an old Baltimore family, Wallis had been married twice before, which is why Edward couldn't marry her and still be king. Even so, she was a stickler for tradition. They needed an altar; a large chest was placed near the front of the room. "Something old" was a piece of antique lace stitched to the bride's lingerie. "Something new" was a gold coin recently minted for Edward's coronation, which Wallis placed in the heel of her shoe. "Something borrowed" was her aunt Bessie's handkerchief (Bessie was the only relative from either family to attend), and "something blue" was sapphire and diamond jewelry—and Wallis's dress, of course. Edward was his usual elegant self in a morning coat and striped trousers.

After a wedding buffet celebration, they left in Edward's private railroad car on the *Orient Express* with 266 pieces of luggage. After a brief stopover in Venice, the honeymooners headed for a castle in Austria. Edward gave Wallis a diamond tiara as a wedding gift; at least she would always live like a queen.

## A. A. MILNE AND DOROTHY DE SELINCOURT

### *"my Collaborator"*

ALAN MET "DAPHNE" AT HER twenty-first birthday party in London. She laughed at all his jokes and had "the most perfect sense of humour in the world," he wrote in his autobiography. After graduating from Cambridge, he sold freelance stories and poems to *Punch* until the famous humor magazine hired him as an assistant editor.

With a dependable, although modest, income, Alan and Daphne married in 1913 at St. Margaret's Church, Westminster, and took a three-week honeymoon in Dartmoor. Soon after they settled in a flat in Embankment Gardens, Chelsea, Alan published his first book of essays and then served in France during World War I. When their only child—a son—was born, Alan chose his first name, "Christopher," and Daphne suggested "Robin." On his first birthday they gave him a large teddy bear that was promptly named Winnie the Pooh.

Soon the little boy had many stuffed animals, and his father was writing whimsical stories and poems about them—*When We Were Very Young* in 1924 and *Winnie-the-Pooh* three years later, introducing the now immortal characters Eeyore, Piglet, Kanga, and Roo. Although Alan also wrote plays and essays for adults, his biggest successes always were his books for children.

Many years later Christopher Robin would remember his father kidding his mother, saying he married her only to avoid having to deal with plumbers and other petty household details. Daphne, however, could do little more than light a fire if someone else had built it!

That didn't stop Alan from dedicating his first book, *Once a Week,* to her: "To my Collaborator—Who buys the ink and paper, laughs and, in fact, does all the really difficult part of the business."

## JOSEPH PENNELL AND ELIZABETH ROBINS

*On a bicycle built for two*

SHORTLY BEFORE ELIZABETH AND JOSEPH married in 1884, they resolved that they would "not allow anything to interfere with his drawing and my writing."

They had met three years earlier in a New York City magazine office. Joseph's assignment was to draw architectural etchings of historical buildings in Philadelphia, and Elizabeth was hired to write the text. Their first joint effort, "A Ramble in Old Philadelphia," appeared in the March, 1882, issue of *Century* magazine. Later Joseph left for Europe to illustrate William Dean Howells's book *Tuscan Cities.* He and Elizabeth corresponded often, and by the time he returned, they had decided to marry.

Elizabeth finished writing her *Life of Mary Wollstonecraft* shortly before the wedding. Joseph was twenty-six and she was twenty-nine years old. They sailed for Europe in August and rode a tandem bicycle from London to Canterbury, stopping along the way so he could sketch and she could take notes. The following year *A Canterbury Pilgrimage* was published, the first of many travel books they would produce together.

They settled in London, sending articles and drawings to American publishers and joining a circle of writers and artists including Henry James, Shaw, and Whistler, who asked them to write his biography, *The Life of James McNeill Whistler.* Eventually they visited most of Europe, and Elizabeth traveled by bicycle more than any other woman of her time.

The Pennells' work philosophy might have been summed up by Joseph in the introduction he wrote for a book about etchings: "Be yourselves, if you have anything in you, having studied . . . the great workmen of the past. . . . Do not copy them, but carry on their work . . . remembering they were known and hated, most of them in their day, because they did their work better than their fellows."

*Date approximate.

## OGDEN NASH AND FRANCES LEONARD

*Love never let up*

OGDEN FIRST SAW FRANCES AT a dinner dance in Baltimore in November, 1928. He was so impressed by the attractive dark-haired young woman's delightful sense of humor during the cocktail hour that he surreptitiously rearranged the place cards at their table, so they would sit next to each other at dinner.

By the end of the evening Frances's date was drunk and unfit to drive. Ogden suppressed his secret glee and gallantly offered to escort her home. He would become the famous author of humorous and satirical verses about marriage, children, family pets, politicians, and other matters of everyday life. But nothing ever mattered as much to Ogden as winning Frances, who always encouraged and supported his work.

He lived in New York City, where he was a book editor and writer of poems and prose for *The New Yorker.* Soon began a three-year courtship filled with hundreds of letters, phone calls, and mad dashes by train back to Baltimore to see Frances. Frequently Ogden's dispatches contained wildly optimistic and humorous rhymes; by August he declared he was a "silly lout, fumbling over phrases" and that "The more I see you the more I love you, and the more I don't see you the more I love you."

They married in 1931 at Baltimore's Church of the Redeemer. Frances carried lilies and wore a long white satin gown with a veil that fitted snugly against her head and sailed down to the floor, encircling her. As Ogden predicted in one of the many poems she inspired, someday she might meet a better poet, but Frances would never know a "truer lover."

After a honeymoon in Canada, Frances and Ogden settled in New York City. Within a few years, he became a full-time freelance writer working at home, never far from Frances.

## EDWIN MUIR AND WILHELMINA ANDERSON

*"This single song of two,
this is A wonder."*

"MY MARRIAGE WAS THE MOST fortunate event in my life," Edwin wrote in his autobiography thirty-five years after he married "Willa" in 1919. Although Edwin's childhood on a Scottish farm had been idyllic, all was shattered after his family moved to Glasgow, where his parents and two brothers died before he was twenty.

He had resigned himself to a lonely life when he met Willa at a dance in Glasgow in the early spring of 1919. She was a writer and a linguist, as well as vice-principal of a London teachers' college. Willa quickly became attracted to Edwin's brilliance and sincerity and to the "blue flash in his eyes whenever he laughed." Edwin sensed that with her, life could be joyous again:

> *Yes, yours, my love, is the right human face.*
> *I in my mind had waited for this long. . . .*

They were married at a registry office in London and honeymooned by the North Sea. Afterward they took a flat near the British Museum. It was Edwin's first real home since his parents died. For the next few years it was Willa, primarily, who saved Edwin from a nervous breakdown, helping him recover by writing beautiful poetry. Through psychoanalysis, Edwin became a great believer in dream analysis and discovered that tapping into childhood memories and dreams was an effective way to reach his deeper self.

He and Willa often conversed in their own particular Scottish dialect or read the classics aloud to each other in the evenings. He worked as an editor and began writing essays, fiction, and criticism. Willa wrote, too, and eventually they translated many novels by European authors, such as Franz Kafka's *The Trial* and *The Castle* and the novels of Sholem Asch.

## DON MARQUIS AND REINA MELCHER

*His "favorite copy reader"*

DON WAS A MAGAZINE EDITOR in Atlanta, Georgia, when Reina, a free-lance writer, literally walked into his life. He'd just published her latest story, and the slender blonde appealed to him right away. He took her for an ice cream soda—an event his friends joked about afterwards, saying, Good grief, what won't men do for women? . . . Don's much more at home in a tavern, so what was he doing in such an "unwholesome" environment?

Falling in love, he admitted later. Pretty soon he and Reina were getting together regularly, talking about everything from "peach ice cream to speculation about the hereafter" and giving each other nicknames like "Tommy" and "Queenie."

Don had not yet created his famous twosome—archy, the philosophical cockroach, and mehitabel, the amoral cat. But the talented young man who would be compared to Mark Twain was warming up nicely, writing parodies, satires, witty poems, and tall tales.

He and Reina married in 1909 and headed for New York the following winter. She wrote stories for magazines, and he got a job on a newspaper.

Then he was fired.

Reina persuaded Don to stick it out in New York, where they subsisted on "starvation diets" in a cold-water flat. Finally, one Saturday afternoon, another editor offered Don a job if he could write four humorous articles—five thousand words each—in two days. Don worked all day and night until Monday morning, when he passed out in front of the typewriter. Reina finished the job, tapping out the last three thousand words so well, "I can't tell to this day where my work stops . . . and hers begins," Don recalled years later. She delivered the manuscript to the newspaper office and came home with a generous check.

## EDDIE CANTOR AND IDA TOBIAS

*"sweet as apple cider"*

EDDIE STOOD OUTSIDE IDA'S HOME in Manhattan the night her older sister got married in 1909. He was almost seventeen and mad about Ida, but her parents had convinced her he'd never amount to anything.

Orphaned when he was a baby, Eddie had been raised in a Lower East Side tenement by his grandmother, Esther. But poverty didn't inspire the boy with bulging eyes and boundless energy to go into a good solid business. He was going to be a vaudeville star—hardly an impressive occupation to a girl whose mother had warned her about all the ne'er-do-wells looking for romance instead of sensible jobs.

"Either forget about acting or Ida will forget about you!" her father barked, but all Eddie really wanted was to perform. He sang, danced, and told jokes, and even worked as a singing waiter in Coney Island while another unknown named Jimmy Durante played the piano.

Somehow Eddie had to make enough money to convince the Tobiases and Ida that he could be a worthy husband. He spent the next few years traveling with vaudeville troupes, doing comical skits and song-and-dance routines—and saving every penny he earned. Then he returned to Henry Street and married Ida, who had refused to marry anyone else.

Eddie would become a major radio, stage, and film star who ended each show with his favorite song, "Ida." But right now "it was June, the 9th of June in 1914, and really, even if nobody else smiled, June smiled and Ida smiled and I just grinned," he recalled in his autobiography. They spent $700 on a trip to Europe. Eddie said he didn't care that they traveled second class, "for I traveled with a first class wife."

## REMBRANDT VAN RIJN AND SASKIA DE UYLENBURGH

### *His goddess*

REMBRANDT PROBABLY MET SASKIA IN Amsterdam while she was visiting her brother Hendrick. Like Rembrandt, she came from a small Dutch town and a family of many children, but her father was a wealthy lawyer and his was only a miller.

With the eyes of a true genius, Rembrandt began sketching Saskia. In the earliest picture she looks at us wistfully, her face partly shaded by a wide-brimmed straw hat adorned with flowers. Her head rests on one hand, and she holds a few flowers in the other. Rembrandt rarely painted flowers, except when he painted Saskia.

In another early painting, probably made shortly before their wedding in 1634, Saskia is costumed as Bellona, the Roman goddess of war. Although she is encumbered by heavy armor and her pose is somewhat stiff, modern X rays reveal that Saskia was first painted in the nude . . . and "dressed" afterwards.

They married in a small church not far from Saskia's hometown of Leenwarden. Rembrandt was thirty-three and she was twenty-one. For a few months they lived with Hendrick, who occasionally represented his brother-in-law as an art dealer. Later they rented rooms overlooking the Amstel River. Over the years Rembrandt painted Saskia many times, often in costumes of goddesses such as Flora, the goddess of love and prostitutes. Frequently Saskia appears boisterous and flirtatious, as if she enjoys posing for her husband.

Not long after the wedding, Rembrandt painted them together in a tavern. She sits on his lap, and they look over their shoulders and smile suggestively at the viewer. Like the peacock feathers in his hat, their faces imply a sensually satisfying relationship. Although some think this picture is a typical Dutch allegory, representing the evils of too much drink and wantonness, others who believe in love say it represents Rembrandt and Saskia's rich private life.

*June 22 has also been cited.

## EDMUND SPENSER AND ELIZABETH BOYLE

*"all her body like a palace fair"*

EDMUND MARRIED ELIZABETH IN IRELAND on St. Barnabas' Day, 1594, "so joyful a day, the joyfullest day that ever sun did see," he wrote. It was also the longest day of the year, according to the calendar then in use. Elizabeth was twenty-five and he was forty-two. She was beautiful, well educated, and blond, and inspired her remarkable husband—known as "the Prince of Poets of His Tyme"—to write some of the finest Elizabethan love poems.

Two major works, "Amoretti" and "Epithalamion," are believed to represent stories of their courtship and wedding. Wooing Elizabeth was one reason why Edmund stopped writing his "Faerie Queene" for a while; he returned to it after their marriage and mentions her in the fourth book. They met in County Cork, Ireland, where Elizabeth, an Englishwoman, had been living with distant relatives. Edmund wooed her for many months and remarked that the year it took to win her seemed much longer than all the forty years he had lived before!

He describes her in "Epithalamion":

> *Her goodly eyes like sapphires shining bright,*
> *Her forehead ivory white,*
> *Her cheeks like apples which the sun hath rudded,*
> *Her lips like cherries charming men to bite.*

Their wedding and a sumptuous feast followed, until, at last . . .

> *Now bring the bride into the bridal bowers.*
> *The night is come, now soon her disarray, . . .*
> *Lay her in lilies and in violets,*
> *And silken curtains over her display,*
> *And odoured sheets, and arras coverlets.*
> *Behold how goodly my fair love does lie. . . .*

## BERTHA KINSKY AND ARTUR VON SUTTNER

*"schätzchen (my treasure)"*

THE DAUGHTER OF A HIGHLY decorated Austrian field marshal, Bertha was Countess Kinsky, raised in an aristocratic world but helpless as her widowed mother squandered the family fortune at spas and casinos throughout Europe. In spite of her loss of income and social status, Bertha became an internationally respected writer, outspoken pacifist, and the first woman to win the Nobel Peace Prize, in 1905.

By the age of thirty, she had resigned herself to spinsterhood after her fiancé died in an accident. Forced to seek employment, Bertha was hired as a governess to Baron and Baroness von Suttner's four daughters in Vienna. Within a year she was amorously involved with Artur, her pupils' handsome twenty-three-year-old brother, known as the "Sunshine Boy." "When he entered a room, it immediately became twice as bright and warm as it was before," Bertha recalled in her memoirs.

Artur's parents were appalled and demanded that Bertha find work elsewhere. Reluctantly, she accepted a secretarial position in Paris with Alfred Nobel, the inventor of dynamite. The Swedish millionaire was quite taken with Bertha's beauty and intelligence and might have proposed to her himself, if she had not been so in love with Artur.

In 1876 Bertha sold her last piece of good jewelry for a train ticket back to Vienna, where the lovers were tearfully reunited at the Hotel Canova and ran off to be married secretly. They spent the next nine years in the Caucasus, barely supporting themselves by giving language and music lessons, writing books, and covering the Russian-Turkish war for European newspapers.

Returning to Austria, Artur founded the League Against Anti-Semitism, and they both joined organizations advocating world peace. Bertha's 1885 antiwar novel, *Lay Down Your Arms,* became an international best-seller, praised by pacifists including Tolstoy, and established her as a major spokeswoman for peace.

## KÄTHE SCHMIDT AND KARL KOLLWITZ

*"life's comrade"*

"MY HUSBAND AND I DID everything possible so that I would have time to work," Käthe wrote in her memoirs. In late nineteenth-century Berlin, such husbands were extremely rare. But Karl, a doctor, willingly helped care for their home and children and encouraged Käthe to become an artist.

They met when Käthe was seventeen and Karl was a twenty-year-old medical student, becoming engaged within the year. Marriage was delayed, however, until Karl established a practice, and Käthe pursued her graphic art studies in Munich and Berlin.

They married on Karl's twenty-eighth birthday in 1891 and moved into a third-floor apartment at 25 Weissenburgerstrasse in North Berlin. (They would live there for the next fifty years, until the Nazis banned Käthe's work and their home was destroyed in World War II.) Käthe's art studio was on the ground floor next to Karl's medical office. Committed to the values of socialism, he worked for a workers' health insurance fund and took care of tailors and their families. He also treated elderly people and others with little money for medical care.

Käthe was particularly touched by the hunger and despair she saw in many of Karl's weary patients and their children. She began sketching them and making etchings, using the rolling pin from her kitchen to apply sufficient pressure. She also sketched herself—her most reliable model—as well as her two sons. Hans was born after she completed "Greeting," a joyful welcome to him, in 1892. The lines of the etching are unusually dark because the artist went into labor soon after she put the plate into its acid bath . . . and it stayed there for a long time!

She and Karl had been blessed to find each other; if Käthe wasn't a typical "hausfrau," neither was Karl an ordinary husband.

## CAMILLE PISSARRO AND JULIE VELLAY

*A family of artists*

BY THE TIME CAMILLE AND Julie married in 1871, they'd been living together for ten years. They met near Paris, where she worked as a cook's helper for his parents, who strongly opposed their son's relationship with a servant. But the thirty-year-old Impressionist painter found Julie's energy and directness refreshing, compared to the "proper" behavior of the girls he knew, and very soon they were romantically involved.

Throughout the 1860s they lived in flats in Paris and in the countryside, where life was more relaxed and studio space was less costly. Camille came to Paris to visit galleries and spend time with other artists, such as Cézanne and Degas. Like Monet, Camille preferred painting directly from nature, bathing his scenes in glorious light and rich atmosphere. Julie worked for a florist and often posed for Camille, still a struggling artist. Although his parents weren't happy with the situation, they sent him money regularly.

Camille sold more and more paintings until the Franco-Prussian War began. He and Julie fled with their two children to a friend's farm in Louveciennes, Brittany, in 1870. Then they went to Norwood, England, where he painted many scenes and the influential art dealer Durand-Ruel agreed to exhibit his work abroad.

By now Camille was forty-one, his father had died, and Julie was thirty-two and pregnant with their third child. At last his mother gave them her blessing, and they married at the city hall in Croydon. They returned to Louveciennes, which had been decimated by the war. Many of Camille's unframed paintings had been ripped and dirtied by soldiers butchering poultry. Village washerwomen wore his tattered canvases as "aprons." A claims lawyer hired by Camille's mother helped Julie and Camille collect money for damages. Within a year he was producing magnificent work again, such as "Orchard at Louveciennes." Eventually five of their children would become artists, too.

## CARL SANDBURG AND LILIAN STEICHEN

*"Your hands are sweeter than nut-brown*
*bread when you touch me"*

BY THE TIME THE FUTURE Pulitzer Prize-winning poet and biographer of Abraham Lincoln was twenty-nine, he'd ridden freight trains, washed dishes, tilled fields, painted houses, fought in the Spanish-American War, and worked his way through college. In December 1907, he met Lilian, whom he subsequently renamed "Paula," at the Social-Democratic party headquarters in Milwaukee, Wisconsin. She was six years younger and noticed that Carl rarely went anywhere without a book—often by Whitman, Shakespeare, or Emerson.

When he left on a business trip for the party, he wrote to her about socialism and sent her some of his poems. The sister of photographer Edward Steichen, Paula recognized Carl's incredible talents and wrote back, telling her "dear Poet-of-Our-World-Today" that he was a far better poet than a socialist organizer.

Paula was Carl's "Ideal Woman" and "Dream-Girl," "tender as dew, impetuous as rain." Within six months they decided to marry. They didn't need much—just a small home with a coffeepot, hat rack, a few chairs, and a flower vase. So what if Carl wasn't handy around the house? She'd take care of all the mundane chores; his only task was writing!

They married at a friend's home in Milwaukee and set up housekeeping in Appleton, Wisconsin. Paula considered wedding rings "barbaric" and reluctantly agreed to buy one (insisting on paying for it herself) to wear only when they traveled—although friends couldn't recall ever seeing it on her finger. She wouldn't promise to "obey," and they made a pact that if either partner ever wanted to end the marriage, that's all it would take to dissolve it. During a heated argument years later, Paula reminded Carl of their arrangement, but he declared he'd never go through all that wooing again!

## CHARLIE CHAPLIN AND OONA O'NEILL

*She had "a luminous beauty"*

THE BRILLIANT FILM ACTOR, DIRECTOR, screenwriter, and producer, the screen clown and "little tramp" who poked fun at fascism, moral hypocrisies, and human foibles didn't marry Oona until he was fifty-four years old. She was eighteen and was his fourth wife. In many ways, she also was the best thing that ever happened to him.

They met at a film agent's home soon after the 1940 release of Charlie's motion picture *The Great Dictator,* in which he played the roles of a Jewish barber and a caricature of Hitler. The daughter of playwright Eugene O'Neill (who disapproved of the relationship), Oona was a radiantly beautiful aspiring actress who understood and respected Charlie's intelligence and artistry.

Early in 1943 Charlie was embroiled in a nasty lawsuit and a paternity case. Oona provided him with a safe haven of love and sympathy. They married that year in the small village of Carpinteria, California, after successfully evading newspaper reporters. Incognito, the Chaplins honeymooned for two months in Santa Barbara, anxiously awaiting verdicts in Charlie's court cases. He was found not guilty of federal charges, and blood tests proved he was not the father of the plaintiff's child, but the adverse publicity saddened Charlie and Oona a great deal.

For the next few years they lived quietly. Oona decided not to pursue an acting career and gave birth to Geraldine, the first of their six children. Charlie concentrated on *Limelight,* the touching (and somewhat autobiographical) story of a down-and-out middle-aged comedian who falls in love with a beautiful young dancer. Later the Chaplins settled in Switzerland, and Charlie continued to make films. At last, said a friend, the comedian Stan Laurel, Charlie "got his fairy princess and they sure as hell lived happily ever after."

## JEAN-HONORÉ FRAGONARD AND MARIE-ANNE GERARD

*"The Pursuit of Love"*

SHORTLY BEFORE JEAN-HONORÉ MARRIED MARIE-ANNE in 1768, he painted "The Swing," one of his most famous pictures. It was commissioned by a French baron who wanted a fanciful garden scene depicting his golden-haired mistress sailing on a swing pushed by a dutiful but foolish husband. The happy baron reclines on the grass beneath her; from his ideal vantage point he sees one tiny pink shoe kicked into the air and his mistress's white-stockinged legs under her billowing skirts. Overlooking the charming dalliance is a statue of Cupid, with a finger against his lips.

Unlike the baron, Jean-Honoré married his mistress, but it's pretty apparent that he seduced her first. Marie-Anne came to Paris in 1767 when she was twenty-two. One of her relatives had arranged for her to consult with M. Fragonard, an established, thirty-seven-year-old painter, about painting watercolors and miniatures.

She was charming, impressionable, and adorable, prompting him to offer very practical advice: Move in with me and I will teach you everything! In less than a year they were married at the Church of St. Lambert at Vaugirard, Paris. Marie-Anne gave birth to a daughter seven months later.

They lived in an apartment at the Louvre, home to King Louis XVI and Marie Antoinette. Jean-Honoré's happy family life inspired him to paint scenes depicting the joys of domesticity, such as "The Cradle" and "The Schoolmistress." Although some art critics have called his work frivolous, representing prerevolutionary life in France, Jean-Honoré was hardly a superficial man or painter. He cared for his elderly father, supported his family, and donated funds to the revolutionary cause. Marie-Anne and her sister Marguerite also helped the family financially by painting and selling miniatures.

## MARTIN LUTHER KING, JR., AND CORETTA SCOTT

*"M.L." and Miss Scott*

MARTIN WAS A MINISTER DOING graduate work in philosophy at Boston University in 1952 when he met Coretta on a blind date. She was studying voice at the New England Conservatory of Music nearby. Since her fellowship only covered her tuition expenses, Coretta worked as a mail-order clerk and also cleaned house for a family in exchange for room and board.

Martin was broad-shouldered and muscular, with almond-shaped eyes and a rich baritone voice. He looked at Coretta steadily as they ate lunch in a cafeteria near her school and talked about politics and philosophy. Each was impressed by the other's self-confidence and intelligence. "You're everything I'm looking for in a wife," he told her, proposing marriage right away. Coretta put off answering him, since it probably meant giving up her plans for a singing career. Finally she realized that things might work out differently from the way she'd imagined, and she agreed to marry Martin.

Coretta's family was impressed by Martin's seriousness and determination, and while no one knew that within ten years he would be the youngest person ever to win the Nobel Peace Prize, they all sensed that he wasn't going to be just an ordinary minister.

In 1953 Martin's father performed the wedding ceremony in the Scotts' garden. Coretta was twenty-six and Martin was twenty-four years old. Within a few months he became pastor of the Dexter Avenue Baptist Church in Montgomery, Alabama. A year later, when Rosa Parks refused to give her seat to a white bus passenger, Martin spearheaded a citywide boycott of buses by blacks that lasted for over a year and resulted in desegregated bus transportation. With Coretta beside him, Martin campaigned for voter registration and the end of racial discrimination in America.

## WILLIAM HOWARD TAFT AND HELEN HERRON

*"the dearest sweetest boy that ever lived"*
*and his "guardian angel"*

"OH, NELLIE," WILL WROTE IN 1885, "I believe you can be happy with me." He was twenty-eight and in love with the gray-eyed young woman who had brains as well as beauty. Although some men found Nellie a bit too outspoken, Will loved her energy and spirit. "Her capacity for work is wonderful," he told his father. But Nellie was cautious, believing "a woman is happier who marries exactly right—but how many do?"

Marrying each other *was* "exactly right." They were best friends and confidants in the years ahead, when Will became governor of the Philippines, Teddy Roosevelt's secretary of war, and president of the United States. Will would be the only president to become Chief Justice of the Supreme Court after his term in office. Through it all, Nellie encouraged him and spurred him on.

They met at a bobsled party in Cincinnati, and Will began attending Nellie's salons for young intellectuals in town. He had graduated second in his class at Yale and was studying law. Nellie was literary and musical and had attended Miami University of Ohio. Her father, a close friend of President Rutherford B. Hayes, had taken her to Washington when she was seventeen, and she fantasized about becoming a first lady someday.

Like most well-bred women of that era, Nellie rejected Will's first two proposals, making him pine for her all the more. But at last she yielded to his fervent pleas, and they were married at her parents' home in 1886. Nellie wore a white satin gown with an embroidered bodice and carried a bouquet of sweet peas and lilies. After a honeymoon tour of France, England, and Scotland, they settled down in Walnut Hills in Cincinnati.

## ALEC GUINNESS AND MERULA SALAMAN

*Lifetime roles as husband and wife*

ALEC WAS PERFORMING AS A wolf and Merula was a tiger in a children's play called *Noah* when they met on the English stage in 1935. Three years later the still-aspiring young players became engaged during a dress rehearsal for Shakespeare's *The Merchant of Venice.*

Although Alec's boarding school headmaster had declared that he wasn't the "acting type," by the time he married his auburn-haired fiancée he was twenty-four and on his way to achieving greatness as a stage and film actor for roles including Hamlet, Richard III, and Obi Ben-Kenobi in *Star Wars.* He would also win an Academy Award and be given a knighthood.

In 1938, en route to the marriage registry office in Reigate, south of London, Alec bloodied his hand on a rosebush while shaking hands with a well-known French actor. The wedding day was marred by first aid treatments, but it also marked the start of a long and happy married life.

After a short honeymoon in Dublin, he and Merula took a walking tour of Donegal. They visited the director Tyrone (Tony) Guthrie and his wife, Judith, at their family's run-down but atmospheric Victorian country estate. On warm lazy mornings Merula and Alec went rowing on a lake nearby, and she listened to him rehearse his lines for his upcoming role as Hamlet, which Tony would soon be directing for the Old Vic.

The actor John Gielgud also directed Alec that year—as Lorenzo in *The Merchant of Venice.* Critics said Alec performed splendidly, bringing new romance and passion to his role. It's not surprising; after all, he had just married Merula!

## RICHARD MILHOUS NIXON AND THELMA RYAN

*"dearest heart"*

WHILE IT'S UNLIKELY THAT "DICK" had his eyes on the White House back in 1940 when he married "Pat," it's worth noting that their wedding was held in the presidential suite of a California hotel, where Presidents McKinley, Roosevelt, Taft, and Hoover had stayed. It also happened to be the same day another former president—Zachary Taylor—was married, 130 years before.

Dick and Pat dated for two and a half years after they met as players in a Whittier community theater production, *The Dark Tower.* "It was a case of love at first sight," Dick said later. The young lawyer was entranced by the "beautiful and vivacious young woman with titian hair" who taught typing, and he told her someday he would marry her.

They went dancing and ice-skating—until he fell down too many times. He sent her poems and flowers. Some of their best evenings were spent grading papers together. He proposed to Pat at Dana Point, on a bluff overlooking the Pacific Ocean not far from San Clemente. During their engagement Dick wrote to her, saying she was "destined to be a great lady" and a great inspiration to him. "It is our job to go forth together and accomplish great ends and we shall do it too."

He was twenty-seven and she was twenty-eight when they married. Pat wore a rose-colored hat and an orchid from Dick pinned to her French blue lace suit. Afterward they drove to Mexico in her car, stocked with cans of food from his parents' grocery store so they could save money on meals. Friends played a trick on them, however, by peeling off all the labels, so they never knew what they were going to eat!

On Dick's birthday the following January, Pat gave him a ceramic knight riding a dark horse, the symbol of a candidate who is unexpectedly nominated for political office.

## ANNIE OAKLEY AND FRANK BUTLER

### *"Little Sure Shot" and Mr. Butler*

FRANK WAS MIGHTY SURPRISED TO meet a fifteen-year-old girl when he was introduced to a "crack shot from upcountry" challenging him to a shooting match on Shooter's Hill in Cincinnati. Phoebe Anne Oakley Mozee didn't doubt her abilities. Maybe the ruddy-faced Irish marksman was ten years older and had won competitions. She'd been shooting quail in the woods for years; hitting clay targets fired from a mechanical trap would be a breeze.

Onlookers placed bets on Frank and Annie; many doubted she would beat him and were sorely disappointed when she did. Frank was intrigued, however, and began courting Annie at her sister's house. A year later, in 1876, he married the pint-sized sharp-shooter he would always call "little girl." They teamed up as "Butler and Oakley," performing in variety shows and circuses throughout the United States.

Annie had quit school by the age of nine, so Frank taught her to read as well as develop trick-shooting skills. By the time Buffalo Bill hired her for his Wild West Show, Frank had quit performing to become Annie's manager and coach. She could hit dimes, shatter glass balls tossed in the air, and slice the thin side of playing cards in half at thirty paces, often while doing cartwheels or riding horseback. She also perforated playing cards with five or six holes before they fell to the ground. It didn't take long before theater stubs and other punch-marked tickets were nicknamed "Annie Oakleys."

Frank and Annie didn't have children, but they supported and educated eighteen orphan girls. They also toured Europe many times. On one trip, Crown Prince Wilhelm of Germany insisted that Annie shoot a cigarette from his lips. She'd been performing that trick with Frank for years, and no one was prouder than he when she did it again . . . perfectly.

## RUTH BADER AND MARTIN GINSBURG

*"my life's partner"*

IT DIDN'T TAKE MARTY LONG to realize that Ruth did many things well ... but cooking wasn't one of them. Shortly after their 1954 wedding, he began studying recipes as well as law books and assuming the role of family cook. More important, he became Ruth's "best friend and biggest booster," which is how she described him almost forty years later after her appointment as justice of the United States Supreme Court.

A Cornell sophomore in 1950, Marty wasn't intimidated by the brilliant freshman who lived down the hall from his roommate's girlfriend. By Marty's senior year, he and Ruth decided to attend law school together. He began at Harvard the following fall, while she finished up at Cornell—as class valedictorian.

They married in Marty's parents' home in Rockville Centre, New York, and went to Europe at a time when you really could manage on five dollars a day. Marty was drafted when they returned, and the future lawyers spent the next two years at Fort Sill, Oklahoma.

Ruth faced gender discrimination—an issue she eventually fought in lawsuits in the 1970's—while working in a Social Security office. After informing her supervisor that she was pregnant, Ruth was demoted to a lower-paying job.

She entered Harvard Law School in 1956 as one of nine women among five hundred students. The Ginsburgs hired a part-time baby-sitter for their young daughter and handled household chores along with their schoolwork. The next year, however, Marty became seriously ill. "Ruth was stuck with the care and feeding of one well-behaved small child and one not very well-behaved large child, obtaining and transcribing class notes for me, her own class schedule, and her work on the *Harvard Law Review*," he recalled later. "She persevered," however, "with grace and astounding stamina."

## THOMAS WOODROW WILSON AND ELLEN AXSON

### *"My own darling"*

"THE FIRST TIME I SAW your face . . . was in church one morning," Woodrow wrote Ellen soon after their 1883 engagement. He'd been visiting relatives in Rome, Georgia, and was attracted to the young woman sitting with four children. She was soft-spoken and beautiful, but her auburn hair was covered by a mourning veil. Woodrow thought she was a widow, but Ellen was really the minister's daughter. She'd taken over all the housekeeping responsibilities after her mother died and had resigned herself to a spinster's life. Meeting Woodrow would change all that and give Ellen a life beyond her dreams.

Woodrow was doing graduate work at Johns Hopkins University in Baltimore. Becoming governor of New Jersey and president of the United States was far from his mind when he courted Ellen. They went on picnics, searched for four-leaf clovers, and talked about poetry and art. After he left, they corresponded but were too shy to mention love.

Serendipity united them a few months later at the Eagle Hotel in Asheville, North Carolina. Both were waiting for train connections when Woodrow saw Ellen's face in the window of a restaurant and rushed inside to find her. They lingered for several days, enjoying the magic of being away from home and what Ellen would describe as "the joy of a sudden meeting and the pain of an imminent parting." By the time they said good-bye, they were engaged.

Two years later the "shy little maid" who once "found it hard . . . even to whisper, 'I love you' " married the reserved young man who was at last free from "all the dreariness of loneliness." The 1885 ceremony in Savannah was conducted by Ellen's grandfather and Woodrow's father. Afterwards Ellen's nine-year-old brother got into a fistfight with one of Woodrow's young cousins. Although the bride was horrified, the groom thought it was highly amusing!

## JAMES THURBER AND HELEN WISMER

*No one was ever like Helen*

"JAMIE'S" LINE DRAWINGS AND STORIES often poked fun at overbearing, nagging wives, but Helen was not a "Thurber woman." Nor was Jamie a henpecked "Thurber man." He'd been unhappily married before, but in 1935 the "second time around" brought him great happiness.

Helen was a pulp magazine editor when she met Jamie at a party in Greenwich Village, New York. "Is sex really necessary, Mr. Thurber?" she asked the tall man with thick glasses, echoing words from his latest book. That caught his attention and he laughed, but a year passed before they ran into each other again. They became better acquainted over the next five years, usually at gatherings with other writers and illustrators.

Jamie proposed to Helen at the Algonquin Hotel bar the day after his divorce became final. Somewhat shocked, Helen got up, went to the ladies' room, came back, and said yes. A month later they were married by her father, a Congregational minister, and honeymooned in Menemsha on Martha's Vineyard, Massachusetts. Low on funds, Jamie wrote "The Departure of Emma Inch" in one day and promptly sold it to *The New Yorker*.

Fans had worried that "wedded bliss" might dull Jamie's sharp-edged work, but it only got better. The human condition hadn't changed one bit, but Jamie's women had; *Let Your Mind Alone* contained fewer bad marriages, and wives often represented reason and common sense. When Helen objected to a particular scene in "The Secret Life of Walter Mitty," Jamie grudgingly accepted her opinion and rewrote it. Love and humor were vital in a happy marriage, Jamie believed. "Remember laughter," he wrote in *The Thirteen Clocks* in 1950. "You'll need it even in the blessed isles of Ever After."

## CLAUDE MONET AND CAMILLE DONCIEUX

*Camille, always Camille*

CLAUDE PAINTED "WOMAN IN A Green Dress" in four days in 1866, when he was twenty-six years old. He hurried for two reasons—because he had to submit it in time for the next Paris Salon exhibition and because he was enchanted with his new model, Camille.

The painting is not a conventional portrait. The young woman is seen from the back and turns her head toward the artist. Her face is lovely, but the focus of the picture is the sweep of her long striped silk dress and short black velvet jacket. "Look at the dress," said Emile Zola, the writer. "It is both supple and solid, it trails softly, it lives . . . !"

Claude's bourgeois family was not impressed; so what if he was a "promising young painter"? He was practically destitute. Grudgingly, they sent him small sums of money. Even that would stop when Claude began living with Camille, whom they never liked. Then Claude would have to choose between having enough food and having enough painting materials. Camille bore their dislike stoically.

They moved to the country, where she posed for all four figures in his next painting, "Women in the Garden," and he began working outdoors all the time, concentrating on the effects of natural light. When "The River," in which Camille sits on a riverbank, was exhibited in 1868, viewers said the light reflecting off the water was so intense, so "real," that it made their eyes tear.

Claude married Camille in 1870, and two years later they settled down in a cottage at Argenteuil with their young son, Jean. Camille continued to pose—holding a parasol, at the beach, in fields of poppies, anywhere Claude asked her to be. He painted her delicate features again and again, immortalizing his love and her beauty.

## IDA BELL WELLS AND FERDINAND LEE BARNETT

### *"Call Me Thine Own"*

ALTHOUGH IDA AND FERDINAND'S 1895 wedding in Chicago was a typical affair, their marriage would not be conventional. Many years later, the poet Langston Hughes wrote, "Ida B. Wells married another crusader . . . and together they continued their campaign for equal rights for Negro Americans."

She was an African-American writer and he was an African-American lawyer and widower with two sons. At thirty-two, Ida was tall and elegant, with wide-set eyes and dark hair piled gracefully on her head. Ferdinand was also tall and good-looking, and a few years older than Ida. After a three-day honeymoon they went right back to work.

They believed in racial equality but harbored no racist hatreds. Instead, they focused on specific issues of prejudice and discrimination, which Ida exposed as an investigative journalist. Before coming to the Windy City, she wrote bravely about lynchings in Memphis, Tennessee, and kept statistics on their frequency.

In 1893, the year she met Ferdinand, he helped her and Frederick Douglass write and circulate an 81-page booklet lamenting the fact that black people were not represented at the Columbian Exposition being held in Chicago.

Months before their wedding, Ida went on antilynching crusades in British and American cities. Returning home in June, she found that faithful friends and Ferdinand had made all the preparations: "The large double parlor had been turned into a bower of beauty, filled with ferns and palms and roses," she wrote afterward. They'd even gotten her a wedding dress!

As Ida Wells-Barnett, she became editor and publisher of the *Conservator*, the first newspaper for African-Americans in Chicago. Her campaigns never stopped, even with the births of four children. Eventually Ida met with Presidents McKinley and Wilson and with members of Congress in her fight for racial equality.

## HARRY S. TRUMAN AND ELIZABETH WALLACE

### *"Dearest Bess"*

HARRY AND BESS'S 1919 WEDDING was held at Trinity Episcopal Church in Independence, Missouri, six weeks after his army discharge, nine years after their courtship began, and six years after Bess said yes!

They'd grown up together in Independence. Bess was athletic, pretty, and popular and had lots of beaux besides Harry. But he never wanted anyone but Bess. "Please get ready to march down the aisle with me as soon as you decently can," he wrote from Europe. "I'm busted financially, but I love you as madly as a man can and I'll find other things." He also mentioned that he'd like to invite a few army friends to the wedding, if possible.

Bess wrote back and confessed that she, too, was eager to get married. Like Harry, she was thirty-five years old. "You may invite the entire 35th Division . . . if you want," she said. "I guess we might as well have the church full while we are at it."

The day was a scorcher. The flowers and wedding guests were wilting by the time bridesmaids wearing pastel-colored dresses came down the church aisle at 4:00 P.M., followed by the groom in a three-piece gray suit. In Harry's pocket was Bess's gold wedding ring, which he'd purchased at Tiffany's in New York City on his way home. She wore a white georgette crepe dress and picture hat, carried roses, and was escorted by her brother. After the ceremony everyone celebrated with ice cream and punch. One of Harry's former army buddies wished him luck in a letter, saying he hoped that Harry's "new war" brought him as much success as the "old" one.

The newlyweds drove away in Harry's roadster for a trip to Chicago, Detroit, and the beaches along Lake Huron. Their stay must have been pure bliss because "Port Huron" became Harry's special phrase to Bess from then on, referring to their happiness on their honeymoon.

## CHARLOTTE BRONTË AND ARTHUR BELL NICHOLLS

*"As to my husband—my heart is knit to him"*

"WOULD THAT CHARLOTTE'S LITERARY FRIENDS could have seen her," wrote her good friend Ellen after the wedding in 1854. "A halo of happiness seemed to surround her." Even before Charlotte and Arthur became engaged that March, her father, Reverend Brontë, had opposed their relationship. He didn't think that Arthur, a mere curate of Haworth Parish in Yorkshire, was worthy of Charlotte, already the well-known author of *Jane Eyre* and other works.

But Charlotte would not be swayed. Hadn't she dealt with sexual longings and the passion to be "absolutely bone of his bone, flesh of his flesh" in her novels? She was thirty-eight years old and would marry for love. "Providence offers me this destiny," she said. Arthur adored her and would be a deeply devoted husband.

"Reader, I married him," she had written in *Jane Eyre*. Seven years after she completed it, she and Arthur married before breakfast at the Haworth Church. When her father refused to give Charlotte away, her friend Miss Wooler stepped in and took his place. Only a few friends attended the ceremony, but news leaked out quickly and a crowd of villagers gathered outside the church to greet the newlywedded couple. Charlotte wore a white embroidered muslin dress with a white lace veil and a bonnet trimmed with green leaves; some people said she resembled a "snow-drop."

Her life had changed remarkably. Now she would be wanted all the time, and that was a "marvelously good thing," she wrote afterwards. She had been writing since the age of eleven, and yet she stopped soon after her marriage. She and Arthur honeymooned in Ireland, touring the countryside and meeting his relatives, who said that she had married one of the "best gentlemen in the country."

"No kinder, better husband than mine, it seems to me, can there be in the world," she concluded.

## ROBERT E. LEE AND MARY ANNE RANDOLPH CUSTIS

*His southern belle*

IT RAINED HEAVILY ON THE day Lieutenant Lee married Mary in 1831. The Reverend Keith arrived soaking wet, having traveled on horseback to the Custis mansion in Arlington, Virginia. The tall, thin minister stood in the grand foyer, puddles forming at his feet. Could anyone lend him dry clothing? The groomsmen, who were army friends of Robert's, had only their uniforms. Just one man had spare civilian trousers and a coat—the short, chubby father of the bride. Nothing fit well, causing some guests to titter.

At last the drawing room doors were opened, and under a large beribboned floral bell suspended from the ceiling, the bridal party of six groomsmen and six bridesmaids filed in, followed by Mary and her father.

The future general of the Confederate army and his new wife shared a common heritage. Robert's father, "Light-Horse Harry," had fought with George Washington in the Revolutionary War, and Mary was the great-granddaughter of Martha Washington. They would name their first child George Washington Custis Lee.

Robert was twenty-four and had proposed to Mary by the dining room sideboard as she served him a piece of fruitcake. He'd been reading a new novel by Sir Walter Scott to Mary and her mother all afternoon. When he left the room for something to eat, mother encouraged daughter to follow him. It was Robert's only chance to be alone with Mary that day, and he surely made the most of it!

She was twenty-three and would always be one of the brightest lights in Robert's life. On their wedding anniversary years later, he wrote to her from a Civil War battlefield, "Do you remember what a happy day thirty-three years ago this was? How many hopes and pleasures it gave birth to!"

# JULY

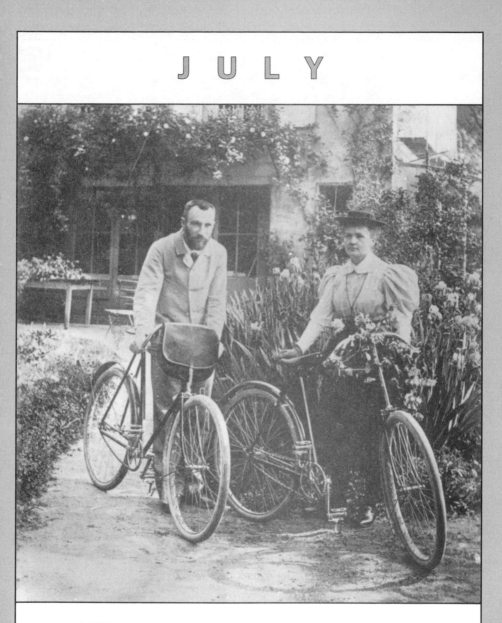

## PIERRE CURIE AND MARIE SKLODOVSKA

*July 26, 1895*

Honeymooning on bicycles through tiny French villages and the picturesque countryside.

## DWIGHT DAVID EISENHOWER AND MARY GENEVA DOUD

*She really liked Ike!*

LIKE MANY YOUNG COUPLES FACING wartime separations, "Ike" and "Mamie" moved up their wedding day in 1916. They'd known each other less than a year, having met at a Texas army base where he was stationed. Ike was twenty-six years old and immediately taken with the "saucy" brown-haired girl with bright blue eyes. She was nineteen and thought the junior officer was "just about the handsomest man" she had ever seen.

Ike telephoned the next day and asked Mamie for a date. She said she was booked for weeks, but he persisted. When she added that she usually was home each day by five o'clock, he said he'd be there tomorrow. It didn't take long to convince her to cancel all future plans not involving him.

Both the bride and the groom wore white when they married in her parents' home in Denver. Ike wouldn't sit down in his tropical dress uniform until after the ceremony, keeping the creases in his trousers razor-sharp. Mamie wore a dress of white Chantilly lace. As usual, her hair was in bangs over her forehead. They honeymooned at Eldorado Springs for two days and then went to Abilene, Kansas, where she met Ike's family.

Mamie hung up a "Bless This House" plaque in their tiny apartment on the base and brought it to all their future homes. She rented a piano and encouraged Ike's buddies to drop in for beer and food, prompting them to nickname the place "Club Eisenhower."

Ike and Mamie moved thirty-five times in the first thirty-five years of their marriage and finally "settled down" for eight years in the White House. She'd get upset when people said that as an army wife, she should be used to Ike's being away. "I never got used to his being gone," she explained. "He was my husband. He was my whole life."

## KING CAMP GILLETTE AND ATLANTA ELLA GAINES

*Look sharp!*

KING WAS A CLEAN-SHAVEN TRAVELING hardware salesman when he married "Lantie" in Ohio in 1890. Her father, a wealthy oilman, listened to King's stories about life on the road and was impressed by his determination to succeed.

King's mother, Fanny Camp Gillette, had written the *White House Cook Book*, and his father and brothers were always tinkering with one invention or another. So it's not surprising that when King started representing the Baltimore Seal Company, he accepted the advice of his boss, William Painter: "Think up something useful, like my 'Crown cork' bottle stopper." Painter had invented a non-reusable cork-lined tin cap that sealed in carbonation so well, it revolutionized the bottling industry.

One morning in a hotel room in Boston, King realized that the blade of his straight razor was particularly dull. Stropping it on a strap wouldn't be enough; it would have to be sharpened professionally by a barber or a cutler. On his way downtown, King impulsively purchased a small vise, pieces of brass, filing tools, and some very thin steel ribbon. Then he sent a wire to Atlanta, who was visiting relatives in Ohio, and said, "I HAVE GOT IT . . . OUR FUTURE IS MADE!"

No significant improvements had been made to razor blades in a long time, but as America moved toward the twentieth century, efficiency experts were talking about ways to save time and money. King envisioned fashioning a two-edged paper-thin razor blade so inexpensive to produce and purchase, it could be thrown away when it became dull. In 1903, he sold 51 razors and 168 blades. A year later— 90,000 razors and 12,400,000 blades. Lantie was thrilled, as was their son, baby "Kingie," who hated Daddy's scratchy face and no longer yelped when Daddy kissed him!

## LUCY APSLEY AND JOHN HUTCHINSON

*He could "beget love in anyone at the first"*

JOHN WAS ATTRACTED TO LUCY even before they met in 1637. He had come from London that spring for the social "season" at Richmond. Impressed by all the scholarly books at the Apsleys' house, he was doubly awed to learn that they belonged to Lucy, who was out for the day. He called on the Apsleys several times, but Lucy never seemed to be at home. There's magic in that house, a friend warned him; men who got involved with the Apsley daughters usually ended up marrying them. But the more Lucy avoided John, the more he longed to see her.

She thought he would be conventional and superficial, like most young men she knew, and even told her footman to show him a pair of bridal shoelaces she'd worn to a wedding, implying that she herself was married. But John's intelligence and sincerity surprised Lucy when they met. He also had the "most amiable countenance, which carried in it something of magnanimity and majesty mixed with sweetness," she wrote later. They became inseparable, taking walks and discussing philosophy—and exasperating friends who envied the closed circle of love they quickly built around themselves.

After they married at St. Andrew's Church in Holborn in 1638, John began studying for the ministry. Lucy gave birth to two sons and also translated six works of Lucretius into verse. Years later she wrote *Memoirs of Colonel Hutchinson,* in which she described seventeenth-century England during the civil war—a time when some Puritans sailed to the New World and others, such as John and Lucy, chose to stay, becoming caught up in those turbulent times.

Although Lucy was a Puritan, living an outward life of restraint and self-control, she wrote of John, ". . . never was there a passion more ardent and less idolatrous; he loved her better than his life, with inexpressible tenderness and kindnesses. . . ."

## JAMES JOYCE AND NORA BARNACLE

*"yes I said yes I will Yes."*

JAMES AND NORA WERE MARRIED in London on his father's birthday in 1931, twenty-seven years after they eloped, fleeing the religiously repressive world of Ireland for the Continent.

They met on June 10, 1904, on Nassau Street in Dublin. James was twenty-two, writing and sometimes selling poems and stories. He was immediately taken with the red-haired twenty-year-old chambermaid from Finn's Hotel down the block. Six months before, Nora had run away from her family's home in Galway. James asked her to meet him four days later. When she didn't show up, he sent a note, beseeching her for another "appointment"—". . . if you have not forgotten me!—James A. Joyce."

She hadn't forgotten. They went walking on June 16, a day James later immortalized as *the* day on which the events of his famous novel, *Ulysses*, take place. By July his letters were passionate: "Your glove lay beside me all night—unbuttoned—but otherwise conducted itself very properly—like Nora. . . . A twenty-five minute kiss upon thy neck. Jim."

On October 8, barely four months after they'd met, they left for Switzerland, where he believed a job was waiting at a Berlitz school. When they arrived, however, no job was available. James and Nora continued on to Pola, on the Adriatic Sea, and then Trieste, where he gave language lessons and wrote most of the stories for *The Dubliners*. The following year he worked at a bank in Rome and spent his spare time planning *The Dead* and a story called *Ulysses*.

When Nora ran off with James, he hadn't even said that he loved her, although she had admitted that she loved him. But she knew she was the woman he had chosen to take with him and that he was deeply happy she had agreed to go.

## HORACE GREELEY AND MARY CHENEY

*Love for "Hod" brought her back*

MR. SYLVESTER GRAHAM WAS TALKING about his healthy crackers and encouraging his audience to taste them when "Hod" glanced at the young woman sitting nearby. It was 1835, and he had been in New York City for four years. He started out as a printer but soon was writing articles and editorials for small newspapers. His new weekly magazine, *The New Yorker,* contained plenty of local news, as well as poetry and stories. Hod came to Graham's lecture as an interested journalist but was distracted by Mary's astute questions and charm. She was twenty-two years old and had masses of dark hair he was sorely tempted to touch. . . .

"Have a Graham cracker?" she asked him.

Mary lived at Dr. Graham's boardinghouse. Hod moved in, too. The doctor's prescription for good health seemed sensible: vegetarian meals made with plenty of brown Graham flour; no coffee, tea, or alcohol; cold baths; loose clothing; sleeping with the windows open. It also enabled Hod to see a lot of Mary.

She was a teacher who'd grown up in Cornwall, Connecticut. Hod was twenty-four and came from New Hampshire. He was enterprising, intelligent, and on his way to becoming a well-known journalist, firebrand, and conscience of the people, inspiring or infuriating many factions. During the Panic of 1837, he'd be telling unemployed workers in crowded eastern cities to "Go west, young man!"

Mary was bright, well read, and very knowledgeable about current events. But after a few months she accepted a teaching position in North Carolina and left town. Hod missed her terribly and wrote constantly. In spring, 1836, he described a house he'd rented at 124 Greenwich Street, large enough for a literary salon on Friday nights. They could live there quite happily, if only she would marry him.

Mary wrote back immediately, saying there was nothing she wanted more.

## GEORGE, DUKE OF YORK, AND PRINCESS MARY OF TECK

*"my sweet little May"*

GROWING UP WITH AN OLDER brother, "Georgie" never expected to become king of England. He also never thought he would marry his brother's fiancée, but that's exactly what happened. When Prince Eddy died suddenly in 1892, royal plans changed with remarkable speed, and Princess Mary received a second marriage proposal—from Eddy's brother, Prince George. His grandmother, Queen Victoria, pushed him to do it; she gave him a dukedom, an income, and two houses. The next thing he needed was a wife. Write to "May," Victoria suggested gently.

Georgie and May were both painfully shy, but they spent time together on the French Riviera where their families had gone to assuage their grief. In 1893 the two were married in the Chapel Royal at St. James's Palace. His parents gave her a spectacular diamond necklace—which is what they had intended to give her in the first place.

Georgie's mother, the Princess of Wales, faced a double sadness; her eldest son had died, and now she had "lost" her beloved second son, too. She turned to her three daughters for comfort, and the four women banded together, excluding May from informal get-togethers and even barging in unannounced at the newlyweds' home.

May bore their treatment stoically, and Georgie was deeply grateful. Although he was still too shy to talk openly about love, he conveyed his growing feelings for May in a letter: "When I asked you to marry me, I was very fond of you, but not very much in love with you," he confessed, "but . . . I know now that . . . *I adore you sweet May*, I can't say more than that."

After King Edward VII died in 1901, Georgie became King George V and May became his queen. They reigned for twenty-six years.

## JIMMY CARTER AND ROSALYNN SMITH

*Best friends*

ENSIGN CARTER PICKED UP ROSALYNN at her home on the day they married in 1946 and drove her to the Methodist church in town. They arrived a few minutes late, Rosalynn remembered years after. The wedding march was being played as "Jimmy grabbed my hand and literally pulled me up the church steps."

The place was packed. No invitations had been sent, but it seemed as if everyone in Plains, Georgia, knew about the nuptials and wanted to be there. What no one knew was that these "small-town kids" would eventually become president and first lady of the United States.

Rosalynn had fallen in love with Jimmy's picture before she met him. Her best friend, Ruth, was his kid sister, and the two girls imagined ways to bring them together. He was twenty and Rosalynn was seventeen when he came home from Annapolis one summer and finally asked her out. As Rosalynn recalled in *First Lady from Plains,* "The moon was full in the sky, conversation came easy and I was in love with a real person now, not just a photograph." She let Jimmy kiss her on the way home.

The following Christmas, he gave her a silver compact engraved with "ILYTG"—for "I Love You the Goodest," a phrase that became especially dear to them.

Their early married years were spent in the navy, moving from one base to another. Later Jimmy described this time as "one of constant separations interspersed with ecstatic reunions." At first Rosalynn deferred to Jimmy's needs and career, as most women did in postwar America, but later she asserted herself more and played an active role in family plans and decision-making. She and Jimmy became true partners—managing the family business, serving in the governor's mansion and in the White House, too.

## GUSTAVE EIFFEL AND MARIE GAUDELET

*His plans were extraordinaire!*

ALTHOUGH GUSTAVE DIDN'T DESIGN HIS amazing tower until many years after he married Marie in 1862, he was already an up-and-coming French engineer. He hadn't intended to become one, but a few years earlier his parents and his uncle, who owned a successful vinegar factory in Dijon, had severed family ties after foolishly quarreling over politics. Realizing that he no longer was welcome in his uncle's business, Gustave joined a civil engineering company specializing in steam engines and other railway equipment.

Unlike those families in town with more aristocratic lineages, the Eiffels were considered nouveau riche. Being on the road to financial success didn't make Gustave socially acceptable to many parents with marriageable daughters. "I shall be satisfied with a girl with a medium-sized dowry and passable looks," as well as "a good disposition and simplicity of taste," he wrote his mother. Marie, whose grandfather was his father's business associate, was all of that and more.

Gustave was twenty-nine and Marie was eighteen when they married in Dijon and moved to an apartment in Paris. A year later their first child, Claire, was born, to be followed by two more daughters and two sons. Marie was sweet-tempered, loving, and unpretentious, accepting her husband's long hours and frequent trips to oversee projects.

Within five years he was designing iron arch girders for the Palace of Machines at the upcoming Paris Universal Exposition, held in 1867. By 1884 Gustave was known as France's master builder in metal, having planned and built many bridges and viaducts, as well as the steel interior structure supporting Frederic Bartholdi's Statue of Liberty. Next would come Gustave's most incredible achievement, celebrating the centenary of the French Revolution. The Eiffel tower was intended to be a temporary structure, but it has remained the crowning glory of Paris.

## NATHANIEL HAWTHORNE AND SOPHIA AMELIA PEABODY

*"My beloved, you make a Heaven roundabout you"*

NATHANIEL AND SOPHIE FELL IN love in 1838 but delayed their marriage for four years because of her fragile health and his reluctance to share his joy with his widowed, sorrowful mother.

Sophie and her sisters had read Nathaniel's *Twice-Told Tales* and invited him to visit them in Salem, Massachusetts. He lived nearby and often took long walks through town, passing Gallows Hill and other sites of the seventeenth-century witch trials. His family was descended from one of the "hanging judges," and thoughts about that dark time in history would always influence his work.

Nathaniel enjoyed spending time with the Peabodys and was particularly drawn to Sophie's artistic talents, soft femininity, and gentleness. Within a year they were secretly engaged and exchanging long, romantic letters, calling each other "dearest Wife" and "lovingest Husband."

"How happy were Adam and Eve," Nathaniel wrote, for they had no other people—such as his withdrawn, moody mother and Sophie's overbearing, protective family—coming between them. "All the infinity around them only served to press their hearts closer together."

Sophie was thirty-three when they married in the Peabodys' parlor on West Street, five days after Nathaniel's thirty-eighth birthday. After a brief celebration they drove to Concord. "Every step the horses took, I felt better and not in the least tired," Sophie wrote her mother. "It seemed miraculous that I was so well."

Her good health continued at The Manse, rented from Nathaniel's friend Ralph Waldo Emerson and decorated as a surprise by Louisa May Alcott's mother. Another unexpected wedding gift was a vegetable garden, dug and planted by Henry David Thoreau.

"Say what you will," wrote Sophie, "there never was such a husband to enrich the world since it sprang out of chaos. I feel precisely like an Eve in Paradise."

## ISABELLA MAYSON AND SAMUEL BEETON

*"Bella figlia con amore"*

IN 1861 MOST ENGLISH WOMEN who read *Mrs Beeton's Book of Household Management* probably imagined the author was a kindly, white-haired old lady—not a bright, spirited young woman. But Isabella was only twenty-one when she sat down to write her domestic encyclopedia, a year after she married Sam in 1856.

He had already made a name for himself in publishing, and Isabella's parents were pleased with the match. Four years before, Sam had arranged for a British edition of *Uncle Tom's Cabin* and invested his earnings in new publications such as *The Englishwoman's Domestic Magazine,* filled with articles about hobbies, crafts, and the latest fashions. Victorian women began buying it regularly.

Sam and Isabella corresponded daily from her home in Epsom to his London office. He was ardent, enthusiastic, and charming. She was romantic, energetic, and brimming with self-confidence. They courted for a year, and shortly before their wedding, she closed her last letter by saying, "Trusting you are perfectly serene and happy as your humble servant, and that I shall see you jolly on Thursday morning, believe me, my loved one, yours eternally, Bella."

After a three-week honeymoon in France, Isabella set up their small house in Pinner, Middlesex, and joined Sam's staff. She wrote articles and collected information on countless household topics, such as handling domestic help, keeping accounts, planning menus, solving legal problems, overseeing nursery care, hosting dinner parties, caring for invalids, polishing furniture, and getting out stains. When she and Sam realized that she had enough material for a book, she concentrated on it full-time. It was published in 1861, and more than 60,000 copies were sold in the first year.

"A place for everything and everything in its place," Isabella wrote. Although few people know who first penned those oft-repeated words, all of us know it's good advice.

## ALEXANDER GRAHAM BELL AND MABEL HUBBARD

*Read my lips—I love you*

"I HAVE DISCOVERED THAT MY interest in my dear pupil has ripened into a far deeper feeling. . . . I have learned to love her," Alec wrote Mabel's mother in 1875. He'd been teaching her daughter visible speech, also called lipreading, at her Cambridge, Massachusetts, home. The twenty-seven-year-old Scotsman had been too preoccupied by his scientific inventions to think about romance, but Mabel had changed all that. Deafened by scarlet fever when she was five years old, she was now seventeen and lovely to behold. On evening strolls they'd pause under lampposts while Alec spoke and Mabel read his lips. Continuing their walk, she'd talk to him in the darkness until they reached the next lamppost, where Alec could reply.

His income was small and she was still fairly young, so her parents asked Alec to wait at least a year before proposing. "You can't support her on magnetism and electric wires," Mr. Hubbard declared. "That, sir, is precisely how I intend to support her," Alec answered. He hoped to devise a way to enable deaf people to hear. Attempts to transmit sounds from one place to another by means of electric current led Alec, indirectly, to invent the telephone.

Eager to marry Mabel, he tried selling some of his patents to Western Union Telegraph Company, but they weren't interested. So Alec kept on working and taking financial aid from supporters—including Mr. Hubbard, who wasn't skeptical any more. Alec's telephone was still a novelty, and some called him "Crazy Bell," when he married Mabel in 1877 in the Hubbards' parlor. The newlyweds honeymooned at Niagara Falls and visited Alec's family in Canada, where his cousins followed an old Scottish custom by breaking oatcakes over Mabel's head.

She didn't know it, but financially she was set for life: Alec's wedding gifts to Mabel were jewelry . . . and all but 10 of his 1,507 shares of Bell Telephone Company stock!

## NICOLAI RIMSKY-KORSAKOV AND NADYEZHDA PURGOLD

*"The rainy day has died away"*

IN THE LATE 1860S NICOLAI and his composer-friends Borodin, Balakirev, Cui, and Moussorgsky—a group known as "The Russian Five"—spent "exceedingly interesting" evenings in St. Petersburg with "Nadya" and her family. The Purgolds were very musical, and their daughter was quite beautiful. She also sang, played the piano, composed, and arranged music.

Soon everyone realized that Nicolai and Nadya were attracted to each other. Like his friends, Nicolai was, primarily, a self-taught musician. Nadya's musical education was far superior to his, and in future years she always provided him with useful assistance and advice. Although Nicolai was very shy, he shared some of his feelings about Nadya in a letter he sent from Italy: "I left Petersburg with an extremely painful feeling. . . . I thought about you a great deal on the way . . . and when I happened to see something nice, I always wanted you to look at it with me."

He was twenty-eight and she was twenty-four when they married at a little church outside St. Petersburg in 1872. They honeymooned in Switzerland, northern Italy, Vienna, and Warsaw. Previously Nadya had helped Nicolai develop his first major success, the opera *The Maid of Pskov.* With it, his musical career was launched, enabling him to quit full-time service in the Russian navy and accept an appointment as a professor of composition at the St. Petersburg Conservatory.

Later Nicolai's fame would be insured with orchestral music such as *Capriccio Espagnol* and *Scheherazade,* choral works, church music, and piano pieces. His music was rich with vitality and charm and with what Rachmaninoff would call "orchestral sound-painting."

For their twenty-fifth wedding anniversary, Nicolai composed five songs dedicated to Nadya. Set to poems by Pushkin and Tolstoy, the compositions were played at a celebration held at their lakeside estate in the country.

## WALT DISNEY AND LILLIAN BOUNDS

*Mickey's parents*

WHEN WALT'S OLDER BROTHER ROY got married in April 1925, Walt started thinking about matrimony, too. Until then, the twenty-three-year-old cartoonist had been too busy making animated films and setting up their new company in a small studio over a garage in Los Angeles.

Lillian had come from Idaho to visit her sister, found a job at the Disney studio, and decided to stay in California. She worked in the inking and painting department, copying cartoon drawings onto celluloid. Although Lillian's work was tedious, she liked the office, where everyone dressed informally and was on a first-name basis. Sometimes, on rainy late nights, Walt gave Lillian and another young woman rides home in his jalopy. Soon he was hanging around Lillian's work station all the time and even bought a suit to impress her.

Three months after Roy's wedding, Walt and Lillian were married in her brother's home in Idaho. They spent their wedding night on a train bound for Seattle, where Roy paid an emergency visit to a dentist for an infected tooth before he and Lillian embarked on a steamer to Long Beach, California. Walt relaxed aboard ship, enjoying the sea air and his new wife. He was wonderfully sweet, Lillian wrote her mother, and she was "divinely happy."

Walt assumed more responsibilities at work and promptly changed the company's name to the Walt Disney Studio. He and Lillian settled into a $40-a-month one-room apartment with "kitchen privileges," within walking distance of his Hyperion Avenue offices.

Before they became the parents of two daughters, Walt and Lillian celebrated the "birth" of another "child" in their family in 1928. Walt considered naming the little mouse Mortimer, but Lillian had a better idea—Mickey.

## WILLIAM OF NORMANDY AND MATILDA OF FLANDERS

### *A new dynasty begins*

WILLIAM'S "CONQUEST" OF MATILDA HAPPENED long before he conquered England. He'd been a fearless fighter in Normandy, overthrowing power-hungry nobles in his own duchy several times before his twenty-first birthday. Then he met Matilda, the petite blond daughter of the count of Flanders and niece of King Henry I of France. But she was not impressed with the "lowborn" young man who usually slept on stable floors and announced that she would rather be a "veiled nun" than marry him. Her opposition only inspired William to woo her more forcefully.

Some say that one day in the town of Bruges, William dismounted from his horse, grabbed Matilda, and pulled her down into the mud, where the two "lovers" rolled around for a few minutes. That done, William got up and rode off again, and soon afterward Matilda agreed to marry him.

In another version, William stormed into her father's palace one night and tramped upstairs to Matilda's apartments. He seized her by the hair and dragged her about the floor. Then he leaped onto his trusty steed and rode off again. In either case, Matilda knew she was marrying a strong-willed man.

They probably married in 1053 in a church at Eu, by the Norman and Flemish border. Matilda was twenty-one; she wore a fur-trimmed wool mantle and rode on a white mule. At twenty-five, William was decked out in a red cape, purple boots, and a crown decorated with gold oak leaves.

Unlike many monarchs, William never took a mistress after his marriage. He and Matilda were devoted to each other. He made her regent, a rare distinction at that time. They built monasteries in Normandy and hospitals for the blind and aged.

In 1066, after William's cousin King Edward the Confessor died, William won the Battle of Hastings and claimed England's throne. Matilda wasn't the least bit surprised!

*Date approximate.

## THOMAS GAINSBOROUGH AND MARGARET BURR

*She loved posing for him*

IN 1745, MARGARET VISITED HER older brother, who worked in the wool business in Sudbury. She'd already heard of his boss's artistic son, Tom, who'd been living in London for several years, struggling to establish himself as a portrait painter. But Tom's income was too unpredictable. Dejected and unable to support himself, he had moved back home recently.

Tom probably saw Margaret first in the woods of Suffolk County, where he took long walks and painted pastoral scenes of cows grazing in fields or birds taking wing. He offered to paint Margaret's portrait and was delighted when she accepted. The sittings were frequent and protracted until at last a beautiful likeness was achieved. Margaret, it has been suggested, then smiled and hinted subtly that perhaps someday Tom might "own" the original! Margaret's family history was somewhat mysterious; she never knew who her father was, but it's likely that he was an aristocrat because he had established a handsome lifetime annuity for her.

The following summer, when Tom was nineteen and Margaret was eighteen, they traveled by coach to London and were married in Mayfair Chapel. No public art galleries existed at the time, so they were thrilled when Tom was commissioned to paint a scene of London on a Foundling Hospital wall, one of the few places for artists to display their work.

Soon he was longing for the countryside again, and they moved to the seaport town of Ipswich. Fortunately, Margaret's income enabled Tom to paint only those portraits or scenes that inspired him. His paintings were filled with the lyrical charm and wistfulness for which he became known. On the rare occasions when Tom and Margaret argued, he apologized by writing a note and signing it "Fox," his dog's name. Fox delivered the message to Margaret, and her dog Tristram brought back her reply.

## CLARENCE DARROW AND RUBY HAMERSTROM

*"We both love Darrow"*

"NEWS OF MR. DARROW'S MARRIAGE was a complete surprise to most of his friends and . . . relatives," reported the Chicago *Evening Press* in 1903. Everyone knew how much Clarence cared for Ruby, but they never expected that the renowned trial lawyer who advocated free love would actually want to settle down.

Ruby was engaged to a New York stockbroker when she met Clarence four years earlier. He'd just given a lecture when his friend John Gregg (the creator of shorthand) introduced him to a pretty, red-haired, twenty-four-year-old journalist wearing a wine-colored suit and hat. Clarence was forty-two and divorced. He enjoyed the company of bright, good-looking women. Using his legendary powers of persuasion, Clarence pursued Ruby steadily, until even her foolish fiancé said he didn't see any harm in her going out—just once—with the famous man.

That ended that engagement. From then on Ruby and Clarence were together constantly. In his black frock coat, white shirt, and black bow tie, Clarence was admired and respected even by his adversaries. Two of his most famous cases would be immortalized in *Compulsion* and *Inherit the Wind.*

Clarence and Ruby married in the Greggs' home soon after he successfully defended the new United Mine Workers union in Pennsylvania. After a European honeymoon, he and Ruby lived on Sheridan Road in Chicago. Always a "meat and potatoes man," Clarence often said, "I don't like spinach, and I'm glad I don't, because if I liked it I'd eat it and I'd just hate it!"

Ruby was feisty and spirited, just like Clarence. Their arguments could be heated and boisterous, but their love never wavered. A close friend called Ruby "a solicitous and loving wife. . . . She watches over Clarence day and night, like a baby, and Clarence delights in it. . . . Without Ruby, he would be completely lost—and he knows it."

## SID CAESAR AND FLORENCE LEVY

*"the most beautiful girl . . ."*

"OY VEY!" SAID FLORENCE'S FATHER.

"What's the hurry?" said Sid's mother before the wedding in 1943. Sid and Florence were only twenty years old, and he was on active duty in the Coast Guard. Would Mr. Levy's son-in-law ever amount to anything? Within ten years, the kid from Yonkers was one of the funniest men on television, starring in *Your Show of Shows* and *Caesar's Hour.*

Sid and Florence met at the Avon Lodge, her uncle's Catskill Mountains hotel, in 1942. She was a Hunter College student working for the summer, and Sid had just been hired as a comedian and saxophone player. "I saw her near the office and thought, 'Wow! That's the most beautiful girl I've ever seen,' " Sid wrote years later in *Where Have I Been?* Florence was tall, blue-eyed, blond, intelligent, and classy. Expecting no more than a summer romance, Sid promptly told her he was in love. Florence usually preferred more serious boys, but she was willing to go steady with Sid for a while.

In the evenings they danced together whenever Sid wasn't performing, until her uncle told him to go dance with some of the "ugly girls." Soon Florence began to realize how bright Sid was. He knew a lot about classical music and loved to read history, explaining that understanding the habits, opinions, and daily routines of people throughout the centuries often inspired great comedy routines.

That October Sid was sent to a navy base in Brooklyn and got the chance to produce and perform in skits, shows, and musical revues for servicemen, including a ludicrous conversation between Donald Duck and Adolf Hitler—with Sid playing both parts. Off duty, he always saw Florence; the following summer they were married in a restaurant on Manhattan's Lower East Side. She still is Sid's most devoted audience and friend.

## EDNA ST. VINCENT MILLAY AND EUGEN BOISSEVAIN

### *She burned her candle "at both ends"*

"DO YOU REMEMBER MEETING EUGEN Boissevain one day in Waverly Place?" Edna wrote to her mother in May 1923. When the red-haired, green-eyed poet drafted her letter, she was confident that her mother had liked Eugen. It mattered a lot, for Edna had decided to marry him.

After living on her own for ten years in Greenwich Village, thirty-one-year-old Edna had fallen in love fast. She had already won fame for "Renascence" and other poems published when she was a student at Vassar. Now friends had introduced her to Eugen, at forty-three a genial, spirited, and sensitive Dutch-Irish coffee importer. Although he was not artistically talented, he loved being around creative people.

One evening they participated in an impromptu skit by turning around the conventional plot of country bumpkins corrupted by life in the big city. Instead, Edna and Eugen played an innocent young couple from the city who fall prey to sinister and corrupt country folks. By the end of act three, Edna and Eugen wouldn't part from each other.

She won the Pulitzer Prize for Poetry shortly before they married, but poor health dampened the celebrations. After the wedding in Croton-on-Hudson, Edna underwent intestinal surgery and Eugen nursed her tirelessly. The following year they took a leisurely trip to the Orient, inspiring her to write poems including "For Pao-Chin" about the Chinese boatman who played his flute as they sailed along in his junk.

Eventually Eugen would quit his business to manage "Vincie's" affairs. He took care of her and Steepletop, their home in Austerlitz, New York, handling all the chores and petty details of everyday life so Edna could work undisturbed. "Anybody can buy and sell coffee," he said, "but not anyone can write poetry."

## DAPHNE DU MAURIER AND
## SIR FREDERICK A. M. BROWNING

*Her book and "Ygdrasil" brought them together*

IN THE LATE SUMMER OF 1931, DAPHNE fixed her field glasses on a motorboat cruising Fowey harbor in Cornwall, England, and caught sight of Grenadier Guard Major Browning. She couldn't hear his voice, but the handsome thirty-five-year-old helmsman was telling his fellow officers that he'd recently read her novel *The Loving Spirit* and wished he could meet the author.

"Tommy" came back the following spring and sent Daphne a note, saying he was pretty sure their fathers used to know each other and would she come for a ride on his boat the next day? She wrote back that she would be "delighted."

Friday, April 8, was a "fine bright day with a cold wind," she recounted in *Daphne du Maurier: Enchanted Cornwall,* her pictorial memoir. He told her that everyone called him Tommy, and that his boat was named *Ygdrasil* after the Tree of Fate in Norse mythology. He came back to see Daphne again and again, "hatless, brown-leather jerkin, grey flannel trousers thrust into sea-boots . . . green eyes, and a smile that curled at one corner. Yes, no doubt about it, he was good."

The twenty-five-year-old storyteller who would continue to write award-winning tales about Cornwall had found a soul mate almost as passionately in love with the region as he was with her.

Daphne married Tommy in 1932 and began writing *Frenchman's Creek.* Five years later she completed *Rebecca*, her gothic novel about a woman's obsession. It won the National Book Award and was made into a film directed by Alfred Hitchcock. *Rebecca* also provided Daphne and Tommy with enough compensation to purchase and move into Menabilly, the seventy-room, supposedly haunted mansion that had inspired her to write the book.

## PETE SEEGER AND TOSHI-ALINE OHTA

*Ballad of a long and happy marriage*

AFTER PETE CAME TO NEW York City in 1939, the future songwriter and folksinger lived on the Lower East Side, studying painting and looking for work as a journalist. Sometimes he made money playing his banjo for a folk dance troupe; Toshi was at one of the get-togethers.

Her name meant "beginning of a new era." The daughter of a Japanese father and a Virginia-born mother, Toshi's American roots went back to Jim Bowie, the nineteenth-century Texan who fought at the Alamo. Pete's family had been in America for three hundred years, but he and Toshi always felt connected to outsiders and "protest" movements in America.

Pete was twenty-four and Toshi was a few years younger when they married in a Greenwich Village church in 1943. He'd been performing with Woody Guthrie and the Almanacs until he was drafted in 1942. During World War II, Pete served in the army's Special Services, singing and performing for troops. After his discharge, Pete, Toshi, and other singers set up People's Songs, a union of songwriters and a clearinghouse for folk songs. A few years later he sang with a new group called the Weavers, performing old favorites such as "On Top of Old Smoky" and new tunes including "Kisses Sweeter Than Wine." Pete sang ballads, spirituals, lullabies, and work songs in tents, concert halls, churches, meetinghouses—anyplace people would listen to him.

In 1949 Pete and Toshi built a home overlooking the Hudson River near Beacon, New York. Songs such as "Where Have All the Flowers Gone?" and "If I Had a Hammer" would follow, as would Pete and Toshi's efforts to clean up the Hudson by raising funds to build the *Clearwater*, a replica of a nineteenth-century sloop that sails up and down the river, promoting conservation.

## EDWARD MACDOWELL AND MARIAN NEVINS

### *"Thy Beaming Eyes"*

EDWARD AND MARIAN WERE YOUNG Americans in Germany when they met at Frankfurt's Conservatory of Music in 1881. He was nineteen, with bright blue eyes, black hair, and a reddish mustache; she was a country-bred twenty-three-year-old from New England who hoped to become a concert pianist. Edward had already been noticed by such composers as the great Franz Liszt during his two years at the Conservatory and would become America's first internationally known composer. Recently Edward had been hired as head piano teacher at a conservatory in the nearby town of Darmstadt. He found it a dreary place with dull, uninspiring students, and he went back to Frankfurt regularly. There Marian's aptitude and talent impressed him, and he offered her private lessons.

At first the gifted teacher and his promising pupil only talked about music, but as the time approached for her return to America, they confessed their love. They married in 1884 in Waterbury, Connecticut. On their honeymoon in London, they saw Shakespeare's *Much Ado About Nothing* and particularly enjoyed the gentle sparring between Beatrice and Benedick, a couple also powerfully drawn to each other.

For a few years Edward and Marian lived in Germany, where he composed concertos, symphonic poems, and pieces for pianoforte, including *Opus 19: Forest Idyls,* which he dedicated to Marian. Eventually Edward became the first professor of music at Columbia University. He and Marian built a log cabin in the pines—"a house of dreams untold"—in Peterborough, New Hampshire, providing him with all the peace and solitude he needed for work. Kneeling before the newly finished fireplace hearth, he wrote "*Edward—Marian—1899*" in the damp cement. Many years later Marian established the MacDowell Colony for artists in Peterborough; it has been a home and inspiration for countless artists ever since.

## HARRY HOUDINI AND BESS RAYMOND

*"The Master Monarchs of Modern Mysteries"*

THE 1894 MARRIAGE OF EIGHTEEN-YEAR-OLD "La Petite Bessie" (Beatrice Rahner) and "Mysterious Harry" (Ehrich Weiss)—the legendary twenty-year-old magician who walked through walls and escaped from straitjackets, leg irons, locked trunks, and Scotland Yard—was sudden, but not surprising.

He was five feet five inches tall, with a winning smile and mesmerizing eyes. Bess had wavy brown hair, was curvaceous and slim, and looked terrific in tights. She was one of the Floral Sisters, a song-and-dance act at Coney Island on the same bill with the Houdini Brothers.

One evening the brothers made a date with the sisters after the show. As they walked along the beach, Harry and Bess fell in love fast. They disappeared two weeks later and came back . . . married! The exact date of this event is debatable: although they celebrated it on June 22, the *Coney Island Clipper* reported that Harry married "Miss Bessie Raymond, the petite soubrette" on July 22. They were married in a civil ceremony near Coney Island and subsequently exchanged vows in two religious ceremonies to appease their Catholic and Jewish families. "I'm the most married woman I know," Bess used to say. "I've been married three times and all to the same man."

Bess joined Harry's show as his assistant, replacing his brother Theodore. Within a year they received their first major booking at Tony Pastor's Theater in Manhattan. They traveled extensively, and by 1904 they lived at 278 West 113th Street whenever they were in New York.

Some women joked that they envied Bess: how many wives spent their lives blindfolding, handcuffing, and padlocking their husbands inside watertight containers? Of course, Bess had other duties—she fell into trances, let Harry read her mind, and climbed into boxes so he could "saw her in half!"

## PADRAIC COLUM AND MARY MAGUIRE

*"Marry me," he suggested*

IN 1912 MARY WAS IN no hurry to marry. "I did not have any taste for exchanging the independent and interesting life I was leading for pottering around in a kitchen, planning meals, hanging curtains and so on," she explained in her autobiography. A twenty-four-year-old university graduate, her circle of young talented Irish writer-friends in Dublin included the poet William Butler Yeats as well as the playwright and poet Padraic Colum.

One young man who wouldn't take no for an answer showed up at Mary's flat one evening with an engagement ring, telling her "that I had better accept my destiny." Mary had thought a great deal about the inferior position of women in the world and was offended at the concept of someone else determining her "destiny." She threw the young man out and collapsed on the sofa.

A few minutes later Padraic stopped by. They had met frequently at literary gatherings, and Mary wrote literary criticism for his journal, *The Irish Review*. Padraic was thirty, soft-spoken and sensitive. He never felt threatened by competent, bright women. After Mary told him what had happened, he came up with a way to get all the other fellows to stop bothering her: "I think that to save yourself trouble, you should marry me," he advised. Padraic's suggestion made perfect sense to Mary.

They were married by "an old scholarly bearded priest" in Dublin in a church called Star of the Sea and traveled to London for a few days. Two years later they sailed for the United States, where Mary wrote literary criticism for well-regarded publications such as the *Saturday Review* and Padraic wrote plays, poetry, and children's books. He later taught comparative literature, she gave special lectures at Columbia University, and they collaborated on a biography of their friend James Joyce.

## MARIAN ANDERSON AND ORPHEUS FISHER

*Amazing grace*

"KING" WAITED TWENTY YEARS TO marry Marian. He first heard her sing at a benefit concert in Delaware when she was a high school student from south Philadelphia. They chatted afterwards at a reception held in the Fisher home. It didn't take long for the tall, African-American architectural student to propose marriage, but he accepted Marian's decision to fulfill her dream of becoming a great concert singer before she settled down.

Eventually her extraordinary voice, combined with her quiet dignity and firm resolution to sing even under the most stressful conditions, brought Marian accolades and the title "The World's Greatest Contralto." Her correspondence with King and their relationship during those years provided her with immeasurable support through glorious as well as appalling experiences. After Marian became famous, she refused to sing in segregated southern concert halls unless "vertical" seating arrangements were made, giving African-American ticket purchasers their own sections in every part of the auditorium.

In 1939 the Daughters of the American Revolution denied Marian the use of Washington's Constitution Hall, so she sang outdoors for more than 75,000 cheering Americans in front of the Lincoln Memorial. She would become the first African-American singer to perform in the White House and in New York City's Metropolitan Opera House; she also performed at the inaugurations of Presidents Eisenhower and Kennedy.

She and King were married at last at the Bethel Methodist Church in Bethel, Connecticut, in 1943. They bought 105 acres of land in nearby Danbury, and he built a dream house for them called Marianna Farms. There was room for horses, cows, chickens, a pond, and an apple orchard, as well as a separate music studio where Marian and her accompanist practiced freely—and loudly. "Marriage to King was worth waiting for," she said after their wedding.

## MARC CHAGALL AND BELLA ROSENFELD

*"blue air, love and flowers entered with her"*

"WHO IS THIS CHAGALL?" BELLA'S parents asked her in 1915. "An artist? He'll never earn a good living! You'll starve with him," they warned. They knew she had been seeing Marc in his studio in Vitebsk, their tiny Russian village. She brought him sweet cakes, milk, and fish to eat, and boards to use as easels. What they didn't know was that sometimes she also posed in the nude for him.

The Rosenfelds were well-to-do merchants who owned three jewelry stores. Marc's father was poor and worked in a herring warehouse. "What will people say?" Mrs. Rosenfeld fretted. But that summer she acquiesced and stood proudly beside her husband when Bella married Marc under a bright red wedding canopy.

Five years earlier Marc had gone to Paris to study art and had met many painters, including Picasso, Braque, Modigliani, de Chirico, and Leger. Everyone inspired everyone else. They painted in riotous colors, shattering old conventions by breaking down images and reassembling them into unbelievably new combinations. It was a glorious time to be an artist! Still, Marc missed Bella deeply. She sent him letters from college, saying she loved his enthusiasm, his laughter, and his sense of color, which inspired him to continue his studies. On one of his many trips home, he painted "Portrait of My Fiancée in Black Gloves," in which Bella poses confidently in a formfitting white dress.

Shortly before their wedding Marc painted "Happy Birthday," commemorating one of Bella's visits to his studio. In the picture, he leaps into the air to kiss her. She, too, is on the verge of flying; the young lovers will remain blissfully entwined all their lives.

Bella was every bride Marc ever painted. "Her . . . eyes. How large, round, black they are!" he wrote. "They are my eyes, my soul."

## MARIE SKLODOVSKA AND PIERRE CURIE

*"no better life companion"*

NEITHER MARIE NOR PIERRE BELIEVED that a life of scientific research could be combined with marriage . . . until they met at the Sorbonne in Paris in 1894. She was twenty-seven and considered herself a spinster. He was a thirty-five-year-old professor and laboratory chief who had written, "women of genius are rare." But Pierre fell in love quickly with the physics and mathematics graduate student from Warsaw. He sent her a copy of his latest publication, "On Symmetry in Physical Phenomena." Not only did Marie understand it—she enjoyed it! They spent hours in her garret apartment in the Latin Quarter, sipping tea and discussing complicated theories.

Marie, whose family was extremely poor, had intended to work in Poland after completing her studies. Marriage to Pierre would mean settling in France instead. She went home that summer, but he begged her to come back. If she wouldn't marry, perhaps they could share an apartment, he suggested, "divided into two independent parts." The following winter Marie relented, telling a friend, "Fate has made us deeply attached to each other and we cannot endure the idea of separating."

Freethinkers, she and Pierre were married in a civil ceremony in Sceaux, his parents' village, in 1895. A relative offered to buy Marie a wedding dress, but she chose a practical navy blue suit "so that I can put it on afterwards and go to the laboratory."

The newlyweds purchased two bicycles with their wedding money and set off the following day on a month-long "wedding tramp" across the French countryside. Years later, after they made their Nobel Prize–winning discoveries in chemistry and physics, their daughter, Eve, wrote about their marriage and described their honeymoon, when "two hearts beat together, two bodies were united, and two minds of genius learned to think together."

## HENRY MOORE AND IRINA RADETZKY

*"with love and kisses"*

IRINA WAS STUDYING PAINTING AT London's Royal College of Art when she met Henry. In the autumn of 1928, she was twenty-two years old, slim and graceful, with limpid dark eyes and rich long hair. She passed by the sculptor's studio one day, and Henry looked up and thought, That woman is incredibly beautiful. Later he would say that he married her because of her magnificent shoulders.

An English miner's son, Henry was thirty and already a well-known British sculptor who based much of his work on organic shapes found in natural rock formations and the landscape. A Royal College graduate, he taught students on a part-time basis, frequently declaring that "really serious artists shouldn't get married" and should remain devoted to their art, as did Michelangelo and Beethoven. But after Henry fell in love with Irina, he began talking about Rembrandt, who adored his wife, and Johann Sebastian Bach, who fathered twenty children!

Irina had emigrated to England with her mother and stepfather after her family lost everything during the Russian Revolution. Henry found her imperfect English charming. They parted at the end of the school semester, and he wrote her many long letters. His first salutations were "Dear Irina," then "My dear," then "Dearest," she recalled. He closed with "my best wishes," then "with love," and then "with love and kisses." "By the time the holiday was over, we were thick."

He courted her for nine months while he worked on "West Wind," a commissioned sculpture, followed by "Reclining Figure" for the city of Leeds, a piece that has been called his finest stone carving.

They married in 1929, three days before Henry's thirty-first birthday, and spent their honeymoon near Tintagel by the Cornish coast, at a boardinghouse that could be reached only by boat.

## PRINCESS ANNE OF ENGLAND AND
## PRINCE GEORGE OF DENMARK

*Good friends*

SOON AFTER KING CHARLES II of England began thinking about a husband for his eighteen-year-old niece, George's marriage proposal arrived from Denmark and was promptly accepted. Although the 1683 match had been arranged, the dark-haired, gentle-mannered princess who would become known as Good Queen Anne, the last and most beloved of the Stuarts, really did fall in love with the thirty-year-old, tall, blond, sweet-natured prince.

Anne's childhood had been subdued and lonely. What she wanted most in a husband was constancy and companionship. At first George spoke only a little English, making their conversations brief, but the betrothed couple seemed happy just spending time together, strolling in the gardens, playing cards, horseback riding, and visiting the zoo at the Tower of London. Evenings, they watched theatrical performances in the Cockpit, a small playhouse inside Whitehall Palace, overlooking St. James's Park.

Anne wore George's gift, a magnificent pearl necklace, when they married at ten o'clock in the evening in the Chapel Royal at St. James's Palace. The bishop of London officiated and read from the Book of Common Prayer, reminding everyone that matrimony should be taken "reverently, discreetly, advisedly, soberly, and in the fear of God." When the ceremony ended, church bells rang all over London and bonfires were lit in celebration.

Anne and George spent their first summer at Windsor Castle, which Samuel Pepys described as "the most romantique castle that is in the world." The newlyweds often sat in a sheltered seat at the far end of a stone terrace built a century before by Queen Elizabeth. There Anne helped George with his English and encouraged him to say as little as possible to members of the court . . . until he knew just what he was saying!

## POTTER PALMER AND BERTHA HONORÉ

*Worth waiting for*

POTTER WAS A MIDDLE-AGED SELF-MADE millionaire when he married Bertha in 1870. She was the twenty-one-year-old daughter of a Chicago real estate developer who often invited Potter to their home. He'd made his fortune in retailing with the "Palmer system," which pampered customers and permitted them to try out merchandise before purchasing it. In 1867 Potter sold his store to his partners and constructed the Palmer House Hotel and other buildings on State Street. Bertha was only thirteen when they first met, but he quickly sensed her intelligence and self-confidence and silently decided to marry her when she grew up.

Some people thought the Honorés had wheedled Potter into marriage because he was so wealthy. Others said the older man had to "buy" his wife. The Chicago *Tribune* defended everyone's motives, declaring, "It is stated that the bridegroom . . . offered to settle a million dollars on his intended bride but she nobly and persistently refused."

At 6:00 P.M, they married in the Honorés' Michigan Avenue home. Forty friends and relatives attended the ceremony, but seven hundred came to the reception. Potter and Bertha slipped away on a train to New York, heading for an ocean voyage and honeymoon in Europe. In Italy, Bertha purchased two wedding chests, which she always kept in her boudoir.

Fourteen months later the Great Chicago Fire destroyed most of downtown. Hundreds of people died and 17,000 buildings were destroyed. Only five percent of Potter's buildings remained, and he probably wouldn't have had the strength to rebuild if Bertha hadn't encouraged him. She participated in all facets of reconstruction, including the acquisition of new building materials, which were difficult to locate.

Bertha became a legendary hostess and collected early Impressionist paintings, which were displayed three rows high on the walls of their Lake Shore Drive mansion. She and Potter promoted many worthy causes, including educational and business opportunities for women.

## KING CANUTE OF ENGLAND AND EMMA OF NORMANDY

### *He fell for the "Gem of the Normans"*

EMMA WAS THE BEAUTIFUL WIDOW of Ethelred the Unready when she married Canute in 1017, eight months after he became king of England. Soon he would also be king of Norway and Denmark, where his father had ruled. Canute had been a bellicose warrior, but now he humbly refused to wear a gold crown, asserting that kings were merely human and only God was perfect.

Emma liked this bright new monarch and welcomed the chance to share the throne a second time. She didn't miss Ethelred, who'd been an unfaithful brute most of the time. She even encouraged her chroniclers to call her "virgo," although she was the mother of two sons. Canute also had a few children by a previous marriage, but he agreed to Emma's one stipulation when he proposed—that the throne should pass eventually only to Canute's children by her.

She'd gone back to Normandy when Ethelred died, and here she was crossing the English Channel as a bride-to-be again. The last time Emma had been much younger. Now she was a mature woman tying the knot with a twenty-two-year-old. Canute wore his hair and beard untrimmed, Danish style, and had definitely won her heart. He also hoped that their union would help him win the affection of his English subjects . . . and it did.

In a gesture of hope for the future, Canute dispensed earldoms to worthy constituents, including Leofric of Mercia, whose wife was Lady Godiva, another strong-willed woman. Canute also brought security to England's borders. With Emma behind him, he became a great statesman and munificent ruler who established a code of laws for England. Some people balked at his abolition of tree worship, but for the most part, they accepted it!

*Date approximate.

## STEVE ALLEN AND JAYNE MEADOWS

*A highly entertaining team*

WHEN JAYNE MET STEVE IN 1952, he already was a television host and was two years away from becoming the first emcee of the *Tonight Show*. Steve had been a writer, composer, and disc jockey, but his radio monologues were often more entertaining than the music he played. Eventually he began ad-libbing, playing the piano, and inviting celebrities to join him on the air. When a guest star didn't show up one night, Steve left the stage and began chatting with members of the audience.

One night he sat beside a beautiful red-haired actress at a dinner party in New York City but never said one word to her. Later Jayne recalled saying, " 'Mr. Allen, you're either the rudest man I ever met or the shyest.' His face turned beet red and his head slumped. I had my answer."

In his autobiography, *Mark It and Strike It*, Steve said that meeting Jayne "was like being exposed to the Statue of Liberty or the Grand Canyon for the first time; one is apt to just stand and look." They were married in Waterford, Connecticut, in 1954, shortly before the *Tonight Show* permanently changed late-night television.

The show was "live" every night from 11:30 P.M. to 1:00 A.M. Steve introduced routines that have since become staples of the talk show format: conversing with the band; strolling into the audience; and sitting behind a desk while gabbing with his guests. He also took chances with zany routines, such as trying out new and complicated recipes and jumping into a giant bowl of Jell-O. Occasionally Jayne came up with ideas for Steve's shows and performed with him. Only later did she tell him what she'd been thinking when they first met: "If he's not married, he's going to be someday, to me."

# AUGUST

## LAURA INGALLS AND ALMANZO WILDER
### *August 25, 1885*

Their wedding picture wasn't taken until winter, when the itinerant
photographer finally came to town.

## CHARLES FRANKLIN KETTERING AND OLIVE WILLIAMS

*"Ket" and "Ollie"*

IN 1900 THE FUTURE INVENTOR of "Delco" automobile products "test called" an Ohio telephone customer while installing a new exchange. Miss Williams had a delightful sense of humor, and what should have been a brief call turned into a long conversation. When Charles hung up, he was determined to meet "Ollie."

Charles had once predicted that he would marry a redheaded girl who could play the piano. Although Ollie's hair was brown, she was a pianist. He began dropping by her house to try out new gadgets and listen to her play. He even installed a telephone beside her piano so she could entertain the party line.

Eye ailments had caused Charles to drop out of Ohio State University, but with Ollie's support he returned for mechanical and electrical engineering degrees. They married in 1905, shortly after he was hired by the National Cash Register Company in Dayton. Honeymooning in Detroit, they rode in an automobile for the first time after Charles fixed the grateful owner's ignition system and helped him crank up the engine.

Back in Dayton, Ollie handled all their bookkeeping and finances once she realized that Charles was oblivious to such matters. "She was the general manager," Charles said later. "A perfect supplement to an absent-minded inventor." He focused on other things, such as inventing the first electrical cash register, illuminating indicators, and adding machines for N.C.R. After three years Ollie suggested that he quit his job and work independently, saying they could manage on the money she had saved.

Eventually Charles sold his company, Delco Labs, which made automobile starters, batteries, and spark plugs, to the United Motor Company. When it became General Motors under his friend, Alfred Sloan, "Ket" had amassed so much money that they endowed the Sloan-Kettering Institute for Cancer Research in New York City.

## ROBINSON JEFFERS AND UNA CALL KUSTER

*"Dearest-in-the-universe"*

ROBIN AND UNA MET IN 1905 when they were students at the University of Southern California. He was eighteen, filled with the shy intensity of the poet he would become, and she was twenty, self-assured . . . and married. Men were easily attracted to the petite young woman with thick chestnut hair. Like Robin, Una devoured books. They talked endlessly about literature, philosophy, and music.

Robin's parents tried diverting him by taking him to Europe, where he studied at the University of Zurich. Returning to USC, he studied medicine for three years—to become not a doctor but a better poet, he said. Next he took courses in forestry in Seattle. Everything interested Robin, but he couldn't forget Una.

In 1912 his grandfather left him a small legacy. In Los Angeles, Robin saw Una driving in an open car as he was crossing the street. They stared at each other and smiled. Soon afterward they began corresponding and meeting in secret.

"I need you so much," he wrote. "There's no living—no delight or adventure—nothing but a bad blank—until we're together—for good." The following year Una's husband agreed to a divorce, and she and Robin married.

"She gave me eyes, she gave me ears and she arranged my life," Robin wrote, quoting Wordsworth. Una would be Robin's inspiration, amanuensis, and audience.

Impending war in Europe discouraged them from going abroad, so they headed instead for the Sur coast of California, a region that would inspire many of his poems. "When . . . we looked down through the pines and sea-fog on Carmel Bay, it was evident that we had come without knowing it to our inevitable place," he recollected. He built Tor House on Point Sur, overlooking the ocean, and they stayed there for the rest of their lives.

## DIETRICH BUXTEHUDE AND ANNA MARGARETHA TUNDER

*A perfect fit*

ANNA'S FATHER, FRANZ, WAS THE organist at St. Mary's, the most prestigious church in Lübeck, Germany. When he died in 1667, auditions were held for a replacement. Dietrich was thirty and had already established a reputation as a fine organist and composer in Denmark.

Young men in seventeenth-century Europe frequently married the daughters or widows of their predecessors—Dietrich's brother, Peter, married the widow of the town barber and took over his business. But Herr Tunder hadn't made such an arrangement with Dietrich; if he had, there would have been no need for auditions. Consequently, St. Mary's got the best organist and *werkmeister,* and Dietrich and Anna married because they were in love.

They probably met in spring, 1668, when he arrived in Lübeck. As the twenty-one-year-old daughter of a musician, Anna knew well the responsibilities involved at St. Mary's. Her older sister had married the church cantor, so Anna's betrothal to Dietrich that summer ensured that church "business" remained happily within the family. She and Dietrich were married at St. Mary's, of course, and celebrated at a friend's home across the street. Like all citizens of Lübeck, their wedding was controlled by strict sumptuary laws that dictated the number of guests, the kinds of refreshments, the bride's trousseau, and the value of the newly married couple's wedding gifts.

Dietrich and Anna were given second-floor apartments in St. Mary's Werkhaus, on the south side of the church yard and only a short walk from the bustling marketplace. For the remainder of what would be a long and fruitful life, Dietrich and Anna lived in Lübeck, where his fame as a composer and performer continued to grow. Years later the young Johann Sebastian Bach would tramp two hundred miles just to meet Dietrich and listen to his sacred music.

## HERMAN MELVILLE AND ELIZABETH SHAW

### *"tears of the happy"*

ON THE MORNING OF HIS wedding day in 1847, Herman found a four-leaf clover. Through all the years of his marriage to "Lizzie," he never stopped believing that the sweet, plentiful, and useful plant was the perfect symbol of their love.

They married at Boston's New South Church three days after his twenty-eighth birthday. After honeymooning in New Hampshire and Canada, they settled at 103 Fourth Avenue in New York City. Lizzie's father, Judge Lemuel Shaw, the chief justice of the Massachusetts Supreme Court, had once been a classmate of Herman's late father. Lemuel paid for the newlyweds' home, and Herman dedicated *Typee* to him because of his many kindnesses.

By 1850 Herman and Lizzie had moved to Arrowhead, in Pittsfield, Massachusetts, where he wrote his greatest novel, *Moby-Dick*. "We breakfast at 8 o'clock," she wrote her parents. "Then Herman goes for a walk and I fly up to put his room to rights, so that he can sit down to his desk immediately on his return. Then I bid him goodbye, with many charges to be an industrious boy and not upset the inkstand." Later Herman would read his latest pages aloud to Lizzie, who copied his final drafts.

Occasionally Herman picked a bunch of clover and laid it on their maplewood mantel for Lizzie. Once, the clover was dampened by melting snow, and she called the droplets "tears of the happy." After forty-four years of marriage, Herman dedicated his book of poems, *Weeds and Wildings,* to Lizzie with these words: "I yearly remind you of the coincidence in my chancing on such a specimen by the wayside on the early forenoon of the fourth day of a certain bridal month, now four years more than four times ten years ago."

## ALFRED SISLEY AND MARIE LESCOUEZEC

*"Madame Sisley" at last*

TWO DAYS BEFORE ALFRED AND Marie married in Cardiff, Wales, in 1897, they signed documents confirming that he was the father of their two children. This was no surprise to family and friends, however. It occurred thirty years after he and Marie began living together. Their "irregular liaison" started in Paris in 1866. Alfred's wealthy English parents had sent him to France nine years earlier to study business. Instead, he became friends with Renoir, Monet, Bazille, and other early Impressionists. He studied art, set up a studio, and painted country landscapes and village streets. At twenty-six, he was good-looking and serious, with a short dark beard and a pipe in his mouth.

Marie came from a very poor family in the village of Meurthe-et-Moselle and was five years older than Alfred. Frequently she posed for some of the painters, while learning to become a florist. Renoir said that Marie had "a lovely little face . . . a very sensitive nature and was exceedingly well-bred." Since Alfred rarely painted figures, she is only an indistinct form in the landscape of his "Lady with a Parasol."

Alfred's parents disliked Marie and stopped sending money to him during the Franco-Prussian War, when his father's health and financial situation deteriorated. Alfred and Marie lived in villages outside Paris, and he began painting more steadily, now that art was his only means of income. "The Lesson" is one of the few pictures he made of their children.

In the summer of 1897 one of Alfred's patrons sent him to Wales for inspiration. Marie came, too, for they had planned, at last, to marry. After their civil wedding, they stayed at the Osborne Hotel on the Welsh coast near Langland Bay, walking along the beaches and gazing at the rocky cliffs. Alfred immortalized everything in what became his last great series of paintings.

## WILLIAM S. GILBERT AND LUCY BLOIS TURNER

*"Oh, happy day, with joyous glee,*
*We will away and married be!"*
—THE PIRATES OF PENZANCE

"W.S." PROPOSED TO LUCY SHORTLY after his play *Dulcamara, or the Little Duck and the Great Quack* opened in London in December 1866. The play, a farcical parody of Donizetti's *L'Elisir d'Amore*, was so silly that even W.S. eventually called it "nonsense," but it gave the thirty-year-old playwright a taste of success and the courage to contemplate marriage.

"Kitten" was the seventeen-year-old blue-eyed and blond daughter of an Indian Army officer when she married W.S. at St. Mary Abbot's church in Kensington in 1867. W.S. was always thinking up new plots and jotting down lyrics—even on their honeymoon in France. Kitten didn't mind; she was sweet-tempered, tactful, and devoted, and although W.S. was easily exasperated, his rages were directed at sloppy stagehands and ill-prepared actors, not his "darling" wife.

They bought a large house at 24, The Boltons, in South Kensington and enjoyed hosting parties for neighborhood children. They also lavished lots of attention on their pets. When a stout woman reporter commented that his dogs seemed to like her, W.S. couldn't resist saying, "Why not? It's rare that they see a bone with so much meat on it."

W.S. admitted that his musical knowledge was limited to two tunes—"One is 'God Save the Queen,' the other isn't." By 1870 he had teamed up with the young composer Arthur Sullivan, whose music was as delightful, playful, and humorous as W.S.'s words. Their hits included *The Pirates of Penzance, Iolanthe, The Mikado,* and *The Yeomen of the Guard.*

Gilbert and Sullivan enjoyed a lifelong satisfying partnership, almost as perfect as W.S.'s marriage to Kit.

## BILL HANNA AND VIOLET WOGATZKE

*"wedded best friends"*

JUST LIKE THE CARTOON COUPLE Fred and Betty Flintstone, the Hannas have been together for a long, long time. They met in Los Angeles in 1935, when Bill was working for the producers of Looney Tunes and Merrie Melodies. He double-dated with a coworker who'd been seeing Vi's twin sister. At twenty-two, both girls were brown-haired and diminutive, but Bill quickly sensed that Vi was "a distinct and unique individual in her own right," he wrote years later in *A Cast of Friends.*

Like him, she'd been living on her own for a while and had a warm and supportive family. Bill was twenty-five and had never known anyone like Violet. Good marriages, like peaceful childhoods, are the best foundations for a happy life, he believed. He was sure he could recreate the secure and loving homelife of his youth with Vi.

They were married in 1936 at Immaculate Conception Church in Los Angeles and took a two-week honeymoon at Lake Tahoe. After they moved into an apartment on Olympic Boulevard, Bill was offered the terrific opportunity of working in MGM's cartoon studio . . . and he grabbed it! This new position led to another "marriage made in heaven" when Bill met Joe Barbera. Although the fast-talking, street-smart New Yorker's personality was nothing like low-key, outdoor-loving Bill's, their work together was brilliant, from Tom and Jerry, the cat and mouse stars of more than 100 hilarious cartoons, to Huckleberry Hound, Yogi Bear, and, of course, the Stone Age cavemen and women of Bedrock, USA.

Bill considers himself "lucky," although his family and career have had their share of heartaches. To him, "prosperity" has meant working in an industry he adores, having wonderful kids, and living with a woman he calls "pretty much . . . the same girl I first met back in 1935."

## GEORGE WESTINGHOUSE AND MARGUERITE WALKER

*The seat beside her wasn't taken*

ALTHOUGH GEORGE HAD NOT YET invented the air brake for railways, it was only fitting that he met the girl of his dreams on a passenger train in 1867. While traveling from New York City to Albany, he and Marguerite bumped into each other as their car lurched forward. She was deeply absorbed in *The Scarlet Letter* and hadn't noticed the twenty-year-old man sitting beside her, although he was enchanted with her.

They began chatting about her book and the beautiful Hudson River outside, while stealing glances at each other. George also talked about some of his ideas, and pretty soon Marguerite realized that listening to him was more fascinating than Mr. Hawthorne's story. After serving briefly in the Civil War, George had come home to Schenectady full of ideas for practical inventions. He'd always been a bit of a daydreamer and had dropped out of college to work in his father's machine shop. Already George had obtained a patent for a rotary engine, invented when he was fifteen years old.

Before Marguerite disembarked, she and George exchanged addresses. They started corresponding immediately, and he began shuttling between their homes in Schenectady and Roxbury, New York. Three weeks later they were engaged.

They married in Roxbury and lived with George's parents until they could afford their own home. George's first major success was creating a single system of railroad brakes, powered by compressed air, that drastically reduced the number of train wrecks. One of his customers was the railroad magnate Commodore Vanderbilt.

Within four years George and Marguerite had moved to Pittsburgh where he established the Westinghouse Air Brake company. He also invented electrically operated brakes for subway cars, turbine engines, and shock absorbers for automobiles, and helped harness Niagara Falls for hydroelectric power.

## ANNE MARBURY AND WILLIAM HUTCHINSON

*He always loved her*

ANNE AND WILL MARRIED IN 1612, long before she was banished from the Massachusetts Bay Colony because of her religious beliefs. They had grown up in Alford, England, overlooking the North Sea, where Will's father owned a dry goods business and her father was an outspoken, rebellious clergyman who was banned periodically from preaching.

Will was tall and thin, with freckles and a friendly smile. Five years older than Anne, he began noticing the self-assured young girl by the time she was thirteen. Sometimes Will's father gave him spare bolts of cloth for the Marburys. Anne never forgot sweet Will, even after the Marburys moved to London a year later.

Francis Marbury was given his own parsonage at the Church of St. Martin's in the Vintry, and it seemed as if bleak times were finally over. Anne heard many religious discussions in her home and spoke her mind, which few women did. "There was nothing but the great mingle-mangle of religion" in England at that time, she wrote later. Everything—astronomy, philosophy, the arts, even literature—had religious overtones.

Sadly, her father died, and the family made plans to vacate the rectory. One afternoon Will appeared in the doorway, offering his condolences and help with the packing. What he wanted most was to convince the grief-stricken Anne to marry him, and with his gentle, loving ways he succeeded.

They married three weeks after Anne's twenty-first birthday and returned to Alford. Will took over his father's business, and soon he and Anne were raising the first of their fourteen children. Twenty-two years later Reverend John Cotton, the fervent leader of their church in St. Botolph's, convinced his flock of separatists to emigrate to America. In 1634 the Hutchinsons boarded the *Griffen* and sailed for Massachusetts.

## MOSS HART AND KITTY CARLISLE

*"Moss was the most wonderful thing
that ever happened to me"*

AFTER ATTENDING PRIVATE SCHOOLS IN Europe in the 1920s, Kitty, who was from New Orleans, made her society debut in Rome. Her mother had hoped that her bright, charming daughter would capture a prince or other aristocrat, but after two disappointing "seasons," she encouraged her to find a career instead. She was glad when Kitty chose the theater and confident that she could succeed in musical comedy. Her mother also predicted a fairy-tale ending: one day Kitty would marry a man who also was part of the theater.

Back in the states, Kitty performed in Broadway musicals and then went to Hollywood, where she sang and acted in musical comedies and played the ingenue in the Marx Brothers' *A Night at the Opera*. Her romance with Moss didn't begin until late 1945, when they met at a party following a rally for World War II war bonds.

He was a tall, dark-haired, Bronx-born, forty-one-year-old, Pulitzer Prize–winning playwright and director who wrote the books for many plays with Irving Berlin, Cole Porter, and George S. Kaufman. By the time Moss met Kitty, he was writing independently. One day he would direct *My Fair Lady* and *Camelot*.

They married eight months later in New Hope, Pennsylvania, and spent their honeymoon performing in a road company production of *The Man Who Came to Dinner,* which Moss had written with Kaufman. Afterwards they settled in New York City. Moss wrote the screenplays *Gentleman's Agreement* and *A Star Is Born,* and Kitty became a panelist on TV quiz shows such as *To Tell the Truth*. She continued performing and singing, and in 1976 she became chief arts administrator of New York State.

## JAMES MCNEILL WHISTLER AND BEATRICE GODWIN

*"Trixie is my luck"*

"JIMMIE" LOOKED OVER HIS SHOULDER nervously when he married "Trixie," half expecting Maud, his former model and mistress, to show up at the parish church of St. Mary Abbot's, Kensington. But only a few friends knew about his wedding plans in 1888; everyone else read about it the next day. "The Butterfly is captive at last," reported the London *Times,* referring to the painter's distinctive signature and trademark.

Mrs. Godwin was the thirty-two-year-old widow of the architect who had designed Jimmie's house in Chelsea. In 1884 she posed for his full-length portrait "Harmony in Red: Lamplight." Standing before a warm red background, Trixie radiates exuberance and pride. Her large figure is wrapped in a red cape, and she tilts her head and smiles confidently. Two years later she and Jimmie became romantically involved, after her husband's death.

They might have continued as lovers indefinitely if close friends hadn't persuaded them to tie the knot and helped out with the arrangements. When Jimmie and Trixie arrived at the fashionable church, she was wearing a blue gown and hat and he—ever the dandy—was dressed in a tight-fitting frock coat, yellow gloves, and new hat. "After the ceremony," the best man recalled, "we adjourned to Whistler's studio, where he had prepared a banquet. The banquet was on the table, but there were no chairs. So we sat on packing cases." Café Royal catered the food and Buzzard's supplied the tiered wedding cake, ordered by Trixie's sister Ethel. Jimmie thought it was too ugly to eat and refused to sit near it.

The honeymooners went to France for three months, and Jimmie painted five small paintings and etched more than thirty copper-plates. With Trixie, his life was relaxed as well as fulfilling. Before her, there had been many mistresses, but Trixie was the only woman Jimmie ever loved.

## LORENZO DA PONTE AND ANN GRAHL

*His "bella inglesina"*

AFTER YEARS OF COUNTLESS AMOROUS adventures, Lorenzo married "Nancy" in 1792. It was the forty-three-year-old Venetian librettist's first and only marriage, but life with his "beautiful, fresh and adorable bride" would bring him forty-six years of happiness.

He had left Italy ten years before, after cavorting in escapades with his friend Casanova. Jealous husbands and religious oppression bore down on Lorenzo as he headed for Vienna, where he became Emperor Joseph II's court poet and the brilliant librettist for Mozart's operas *The Marriage of Figaro, Don Giovanni,* and *Così Fan Tutte.* But in 1791 Mozart's death and more romantic dalliances caused Lorenzo to pack his bags again.

In Trieste, a friend asked Lorenzo to make arrangements for him to marry a wealthy young woman, but the girl's father canceled everything when he sensed that the absent suitor was only interested in winning her large dowry. Nancy and Lorenzo were greatly relieved, for she had been giving him French lessons and—in between vocabulary exercises and verb conjugations—they had fallen in love.

"My joy," Lorenzo wrote later in his memoirs, "was so great . . . that neither of us could say a word for the . . . rest of the evening." They were married soon afterward, "and with the courage, or to be more exact, with the temerity of a young blade of twenty," he took Nancy from Trieste after the wedding festivities. "That evening, we reached Leibach, where we stopped for the night, and . . . Amor and Hymen taught me to dry the tears of a tender girl who was leaving parents and friends, perhaps forever, to be mine."

Lorenzo wrote additional librettos as well as poetry and translations. Eventually he and Nancy came to New York, where they helped introduce Italian opera to the United States and he became Columbia College's first professor of Italian language and literature.

## PETER STUYVESANT AND JUDITH BAYARD

*"Old Silver Leg's" sweet love*

PETER SAILED HOME TO HOLLAND in 1645 for rest and recuperation after his right leg was shattered by a Portuguese cannonball on the Caribbean island of St. Maarten. The brave Dutch soldier and governor of Curaçao had encouraged his men to keep fighting for twenty-eight days until at last they retreated. Although Peter ended up losing his leg, the tragedy brought him a wife.

He moved in with his married sister Anna Bayard and her family in Alphen, not far from Leiden where Peter was fitted for a wooden leg. A plain, ordinary one wouldn't do: the war hero's peg leg sported wide bands of silver. Soon "Old Silver Leg" was hobbling around the Bayards' house, enjoying the special attentions of Anna's sister-in-law Judith. She was fascinated by Peter's stories about his exploits, and he was deeply touched by her kind assistance. He also loved hearing her play for him on the Bayards' spinet piano.

They married that summer at the Walloon church in Breda, where Judith's late father had been the minister. On top of Judith's head was a small jeweled crown, worn by every bride in her family for generations. On Christmas Day, 1646, she and Peter voyaged to the New World, where the Dutch West India Company had asked him to be director-general of the Nieuw Netherland colony. They stopped for a few months in Curaçao and arrived in Nieuw Amsterdam harbor the following May, shortly before their first son was born.

The company gave them farmland, which they called "Stuyvesant's Bouwerie," roughly from 5th to 17th streets and from the East River to Park Avenue in today's New York City. They also built a fine house farther downtown, near what is now Whitehall Street. Flower and vegetable gardens were laid out in neat rows and patterns, behind the "Great House," long considered the grandest residence in Manhattan.

## DANIEL BOONE AND REBECCA BRYAN

*"my little girl"*

ACCORDING TO THE FAMOUS AMERICAN frontiersman, a man needed three things to be happy—"a good gun, a good horse and a good wife." Years after Daniel married Rebecca in 1756, he told their ten kids that their courtship began on the day he decided to "try her temper."

Daniel and Rebecca sat together under a tree while she sorted fresh-picked cherries and he fiddled absentmindedly with his knife. He began tossing his knife into the dirt, point first. One time he aimed for the edge of Rebecca's white cambric apron, just to see if she'd get angry. When Rebecca didn't complain, he knew she was the girl for him.

Daniel was twenty-one and Rebecca was seventeen when they married in a triple wedding ceremony with two other couples from the Boone and Bryan extended families. They probably celebrated afterwards at a wedding party held in their first home, a cabin on the Boone family property. Quilts, linens, furniture, and other gifts were displayed, as well-wishers drank toasts of rum, cider, and whisky. Following a popular tradition, wedding attendants escorted the bride and groom upstairs to bed, tucked them in under the covers, and merrily went back downstairs. There everyone sang and danced loudly, making bawdy jokes about "thumping good luck" for the newlyweds and occasionally sending up trays of food.

Soon Daniel was blazing trails in the Appalachian mountains, carving his initials into trees and marking the spots where "D Boon cilled A BAR." He and Rebecca preferred living in the backwoods, away from the growing numbers of settlers. Although Daniel was a hunter, he also was a Quaker, opposed to war and usually sympathetic to Native Americans. When he discovered a "hunter's paradise" in Kentucky in the late 1760s, he and Rebecca headed west through the Cumberland Gap.

## JACK LEMMON AND FELICIA FARR

### *His "Farfel"*

FELICIA AND JACK MARRIED IN Paris in 1962 while he was filming *Irma la Douce.* He'd been a successful actor ever since his Broadway debut nine years earlier. But in 1956, a year after he won an Oscar for his role as Ensign Pulver in *Mister Roberts,* Jack's first marriage ended. He and Felicia met on a movie set a few months later, and he was immediately captivated by the beautiful actress. "I took one look at her and—that was it!" he recalled afterward. Jack was smitten but reluctant to get involved. So was Felicia, whose first marriage had also ended in divorce.

Occasionally they'd have tempestuous battles, although neither one doubted the other's love. Once, after Felicia refused to open her front door for Jack, he pounded on it so hard that his fist smashed through the plywood panel. Eventually she framed the splintered piece and gave it to him as an anniversary gift.

After six years Jack finally proposed on the telephone from Paris, and Felicia flew there from Los Angeles. At their wedding, he wore a dark suit and she wore a sleeveless lace dress with long white gloves. Her hair was swept up in a French knot and covered with a finely dotted veil.

They were married by the mayor and then drove off in a friend's white Rolls-Royce, dragging ridiculously oversized two-gallon cans behind them. That morning Jack had performed in a scene requiring him to jump into the Seine River. Unfortunately, the unsuspecting bridegroom swallowed some polluted water and had an upset stomach throughout his honeymoon!

Felicia appeared in films, including *Kiss Me Stupid* in 1964 and *Kotch,* which starred their good friend Walter Matthau and which Jack directed. Occasionally she and Jack have acted together. In 1986 they appeared in Blake Edwards's comedy *That's Life,* along with Blake's wife, Julie Andrews, and children from both families.

## MARY JESSAMYN WEST AND HARRY MCPHERSON

*"I love thee"*

UNDULATING SAGEBRUSH COLORED THE SOFT brown hills of Yorba Linda, California, when Jessamyn and "Max" married in a Quaker ceremony at the Friends Church in 1923. Thirty years later the region gained fame as the hometown of Jessamyn's distant cousin Richard Milhous Nixon, for whom she used to baby-sit.

Jessamyn and Max met at Whittier College and were engaged by the end of her freshman year. Their first home was in Hemet, where Max's parents had a fruit orchard. He finished his Ph.D. in education, and Jessamyn taught in a one-room schoolhouse. Max encouraged her to earn a Ph.D. in English literature, although it meant spending the summer studying at Oxford University in England. Few young women in the 1920s left their husbands to cross the United States alone and go to England, but Max knew that Jessamyn could handle whatever happened.

Jessamyn was twenty-nine when she contracted a dangerous form of tuberculosis shortly before she took her oral examinations at University of California, Berkeley. For the next two years, she lived in a sanitarium until her mother and Max brought her home, having been told by doctors that she would probably die. Steadfastly, they took care of Jessamyn. During her long recuperation, her mother, Grace, told her stories about her forebears. Jessamyn recalled, "Grace knew . . . the limbo in which I lived. . . . Since I had no life of my own . . . she gave me her own life . . . as a Quaker girl on a farm in southern Indiana at the turn of the century."

Convalescing, Jessamyn began to write, adapting her mother's tales into poems and stories. With Max's encouragement, her work was submitted to publishers. *The Friendly Persuasion* brought Jessamyn literary acclaim in 1945 and was eventually made into a motion picture.

## HELEN HAYES AND CHARLES MACARTHUR

*Peanuts and emeralds*

IN 1924, AT A COCKTAIL party in a New York City art studio, Irving Berlin was playing his love song "Always" on the piano while George Gershwin hovered nearby, waiting for his chance to tickle the ivories. Helen had come with the playwright Marc Connelly, who explained that their hostess, a commercial artist, wanted lots of people milling about and posing, as if in a stage set, for a magazine cover she was producing.

Helen was twenty-four, with silky light brown hair and a magnificent smile. She rarely socialized and was dazzled by all the celebrities she saw. When a very handsome fellow approached her and asked, "Want a peanut?," she nodded, entranced, and he poured several peanuts into her hand. Then he smiled and said, "I wish they were emeralds."

The fellow was Charlie. Helen's mother and friends warned her about him; he was known as a drinker, a cad, and "bad news." Sooner or later he'd leave her, just as he'd walked out on his wife two years before. Until that night Helen's life had been devoted to stage performances. Her mother, who was her agent, also feared that a romantic involvement with a separated man could end Helen's career. But Charlie became the love of Helen's life. "It is a miracle that he rescued me from the corner of that studio and from the shadows of an endless childhood," she wrote in *Helen Hayes: On Reflection*. They married in 1928, soon after his divorce was finalized. That same year Charlie and Ben Hecht's hit play *The Front Page* opened on Broadway.

Years later Charlie returned from a trip to India, dumped a small bag of emeralds in Helen's lap, and told her, "I wish they were peanuts!"

## WILLIAM BLAKE AND CATHERINE BOUCHER

*"when she speaks, the voice of Heaven I hear"*

CATHERINE INSPIRED, ASSISTED, AND MODELED for William, whose mystical poems and engravings still mesmerize art lovers today.

> *Abstinence sows sand all over*
> *The ruddy limbs and flaming hair,*
> *But Desire Gratified*
> *Plants fruits of life and beauty there.*

She sketched William's "ruddy limbs and flaming hair," capturing his strong features and intense expression. He immortalized his "Sweet Shadow of Delight" in a picture of a lovely young woman sitting by the edge of their bed.

They met in 1781 after he'd been rejected by another girl. William roamed London aimlessly, stopping by the Boucher home to visit Catherine's father, a market gardener. He wasn't there, but his daughter was. She listened sympathetically to William's sad tale. "I pity you deeply," she said. "You do?" he replied. "Then I love you."

He was twenty-four and she was twenty when they married a year later, at St. Mary's, the parish church in Battersea. Catherine was dark-haired and spirited, but like most young women of her class, she was illiterate and could make only a cross under William's name on the marriage register.

Their first home was at 23 Green Street, Leicester Fields. William taught Catherine to read and write and explained the secrets of engraving, bookbinding, and the coloring of prints. She also began drawing and painting. They produced magnificently illustrated volumes, such as *Songs of Innocence, Songs of Experience, Jerusalem,* and William's principal prose work, *The Marriage of Heaven and Hell.* Later, commissions arrived for illustrations of hymn books, poems, songs, and stories. "My Wife has undertaken to Print," William wrote a friend, "which She does to admiration. . . . In short I have Got everything . . . under my thumb."

## DAVY CROCKETT AND POLLY FINDLAY

*"a sweetheart for me"*

IN DAVY'S AUTOBIOGRAPHY, THE LEGENDARY backwoodsman remembered meeting "one of the prettiest little girls . . . I had ever seen" at a Tennessee reaping party in 1806. A few weeks later he went to Polly's house, but finding her with another man, he "began to think I was barking up the wrong tree."

"Her mother was deeply enlisted for my rival and I had to fight against her influence as well as his. But the girl herself was the prize I was fighting for, and . . . she welcomed me."

One night they accidentally met in the woods. Polly "had been traveling all day and was mighty tired; and I would have taken her up and toated her, if it hadn't been that I wanted her just where I could see her all the time, for I thought she looked sweeter than sugar, and by this time I loved her almost well enough to eat her."

They decided to marry, but Polly's mother "appeared to be mighty wrathy and when I broached the subject she looked at me as savage as a meat axe." Fortunately, Mr. Findlay was friendlier and said his wife just needed time to get used to the idea. Davy declared he would return in a week with a horse for Polly, "and she must be ready to go."

When he arrived, Polly's father begged them to get married at their house, saying her mother had come to accept their plans. Davy agreed, located the parson, "and got married in a short time, for I was afraid to wait long, for fear of another defeat. . . .

"Having gotten my wife, I thought I was completely made up and needed nothing more in the whole world. But I soon found out this was a mistake—for now having a wife, I wanted everything else . . . !"

*Date approximate.

## ENRICO CARUSO AND DOROTHY BENJAMIN

*"Credi all' amore . . . tu sei amato"*
*("Believe in love . . . you are loved")*
—ANDREA CHENIER

WHEN THE WORLD-ACCLAIMED OPERATIC TENOR encountered Dorothy at a party in Manhattan in 1918, "We both knew from that moment that our lives would be united," she wrote many years later.

They had met once before, at a gathering held in Enrico's honor. Dorothy had been accompanied by her family's housekeeper, a young Italian woman who hoped to become a professional singer. Enrico drove them home afterwards, and when Dorothy realized she had left her gloves behind, he graciously gave her his own pair as a replacement.

Enrico was twenty years older than twenty-five-year-old Dorothy, whose stodgy, critical father called her a spinster. Mr. Benjamin, a wealthy and prominent lawyer and editor, viewed entertainers with disdain. Although Enrico had been a dinner guest several times, Mr. Benjamin considered him a lowborn foreigner and hot-blooded "public singer." It didn't take long, however, for Enrico and Dorothy to declare their love and decide to marry.

At first Dorothy's father declared that he would never approve such a union; then he demanded that Enrico pay *him* half a million dollars for the privilege of marrying his daughter! Dorothy was outraged. She stormed out of their house and went to Enrico's hotel. The next morning they married at New York City's Marble Collegiate Church.

"I did not want my daughter to marry riches or a voice or an orator, just a man," Mr. Benjamin asserted. "However, she is a mature woman and Caruso is forty-five. Therefore, the match cannot be ascribed to the ardor of youth," he added snidely. Secretly, he adopted the housekeeper and left her everything in his will. He never forgave Dorothy, but the years she spent with Enrico were the best part of her life.

## JAMES GARFIELD RANDALL AND RUTH PAINTER

*Shared passions for life, and history*

RUTH'S FATHER, A HISTORY PROFESSOR at Roanoke College in Virginia, began inviting Jim to dinner in 1915. One day "Dr. Randall" would become a well-known and respected Civil War historian and biographer of Lincoln, but then he was simply a brilliant young professor. Ruth was Dr. Painter's bright and beautiful daughter and had not yet realized her talent for writing biographies of famous American women. Since the sudden death of Jim's first wife, he had concentrated exclusively on teaching and research—until Ruth, full of youthful optimism and enthusiasm, brought joy to his heart again.

Friends and relatives decorated the College Church in Salem, Virginia, with white flowers and tall white candles when Ruth and Jim married in 1917. Baked inside their wedding cake were a miniature silver thimble, symbolizing the "spinster," a silver button for the "bachelor," and a tiny silver heart for a happy marriage.

"Jim and I had all the ancient good-luck signs with us on our wedding day, bright sunshine, a cricket chirping on the hearth of the parlor that evening, and I myself got the little silver heart in my piece of cake. I still have it," Ruth said in her autobiography.

Within three years she and Jim moved to the land of Lincoln, where he became a history professor at the University of Illinois in Urbana. Ruth helped with Jim's research and manuscript editing, and before long she was writing, too.

In 1947, when President Lincoln's private papers were finally made available to academicians, Jim and Ruth took the next train to Washington, D.C., and pored over documents at the Library of Congress. His reputation as a Lincoln scholar soared, and Ruth wrote acclaimed biographies of Mary Lincoln, Elizabeth Custer, and other wives of famous men.

## ULYSSES S. GRANT AND JULIA DENT

*"Remember I shall cling to you"*

"CAPTAIN GRANT WAS AS COOL under the fire of the clergyman's questions as he had been under the batteries of the Mexican artillery," said Emma Dent after her sister's 1848 wedding. Julia had just married the twenty-six-year-old officer on a hot and rainy summer night in her parents' St. Louis, Missouri, town house.

Candles shaped like stars lighted the twenty-two-year-old bride's way as she descended the narrow staircase in a white watered silk gown with a tulle veil and a "corsage bouquet" of white Cape jessamine flowers. Her three bridesmaids also wore white. "Lyss's" three groomsmen wore their army dress uniforms; seventeen years later, two of them would surrender to General Grant at Appomattox when the Civil War ended.

Lyss and Julia spent their wedding night in the Dents' home. The next day friends followed a southern tradition by throwing bouquets of flowers at the newlyweds when they set off by boat to visit Lyss's family in Ohio. "He asked me to sing to him, something sweet and low, and I did," said Julia. "I do not remember any of the passengers on that trip. It was like a dream to me."

She was the pint-sized sister of one of his West Point classmates when they met. Lyss began visiting frequently, and one spring day after a rainstorm, he and Julia went riding in an open carriage and stopped before a bridge over a swollen ravine. "Now, if anything happens, remember I shall cling to you," she told him. Lyss smiled and nodded, and when they reached the other side, he proposed. They married soon after he returned from the Mexican wars.

Fifty years later the president's wife recalled their early days together in St. Louis—"They were not dark but bright and charming, as it was always sunshine when he was near." She still had his wedding gift, a daguerreotype picture of himself, which she kept in a locket on a velvet wrist strap.

## LEWIS HINE AND SARA ANN RICH

*Working together, "armed" with a camera*

LEWIS FIRST BEGAN TAKING PHOTOGRAPHS in New York City in 1903, the year before he came home to Oshkosh, Wisconsin, and married his sweetheart, Sara. Like him, she was a schoolteacher. Lewis taught natural studies and geography at the Ethical Culture School in Manhattan where the principal, Frank Manny, convinced him that photography could be a powerful way to teach children about the world.

Lewis and Sara settled in Yonkers, north of the city, and he started taking pictures of classroom activities. After school he and Frank rode the subway downtown and photographed immigrants arriving at Ellis Island. Although more than ten million people emigrated to the United States during the first decade of the twentieth century, "foreigners" were rarely considered worthwhile subjects for photography. But Lewis's camera eloquently captured the fear, exhaustion, and exhilaration of newly arrived immigrants in the noisy and chaotic inspection halls.

By 1907 social welfare agencies were hiring him to photograph oppressive working conditions in coal mines and factories in cities such as Pittsburgh. Sara supported his decision to quit teaching, although it meant giving up a steady income.

For the next ten years Lewis was a staff photographer for the National Child Labor Committee's ongoing campaign to raise public awareness about the evils of child labor. He and Sara traveled from Maine to Texas, documenting children working in mills, factories, canneries, and sweatshops. He took the pictures while Sara took notes and recorded important data.

Sometimes Lewis's camera had to be smuggled inside, and interviews were conducted surreptitiously. The information they gathered wasn't written down until after they left a building, before the bosses realized what was going on. The unsettling and graphic results played a valuable role in developing legislative reforms to eliminate child labor.

## ANTONIO STRADIVARI AND ANTONIA MARIA ZAMBELLI

*Making music as well as love*

ANTONIA WAS THIRTY-SIX YEARS OLD, with the wide hips, small waist, slender neck, and curved shoulders of a magnificent violin. Why wouldn't Antonio notice her in the town of Cremona, Italy? In 1699 the widowed violin maker was fifty-five, with grown sons and a successful business. And yet . . . Antonia's full skirt swirled and skimmed the cobblestoned street as she chatted briefly with a neighbor, then hurried off around a corner.

Some men said that all women were the same—like all violins. But Antonio knew that each one was unique. A violin's superiority was determined by specifics—the thickness of the wood, the height of the bridge, the arch of the back, the slope of the belly. What music could be brought forth from a fine violin . . . or a woman?

Back in his workshop, Antonio sat at his bench, surrounded by wedges of maple and pine, sandpaper, chisels, clamps, planes, varnishes, saws, glue pots, and other vital pieces with which he painstakingly built his creations. He would marry again, he decided, as soon as he could convince the lovely Antonia.

They were wed that summer at the parish church of San Donato. Antonio's output had always been remarkable, even during his first wife's illness, but the violins he made during the years he spent with Antonia were even more astonishing. The name Stradivari would in time become synonymous with all fine violins. Antonio's richly beautiful, wine-brown, orange-red, or golden wood creations—instruments that one's fingers ached to touch—would be given proper names, such as the "Lafont," the "Castelbarco," the "Ward," and the "Russian," after the fortunate few who played them. Paganini, Heifetz, Zimbalist, and other great musicians would draw magnificent music from Antonio's violins for many years to come.

## LAURA INGALLS AND ALMANZO WILDER

*The sound of sleigh bells*

THE TV CHARACTER LAURA GOT married on the popular show *Little House on the Prairie*, but the real Laura wrote about it first in *These Happy Golden Years* and *The First Four Years*, sequels to her series of fictionalized memoirs that began with *Little House in the Big Woods*.

The Ingalls family came west in a covered wagon and settled in DeSmet, South Dakota. "Manly" was ten years older than Laura, and he and his brother had already established a homestead nearby. Sleigh bells signaled Manly's arrival when he drove Laura to and from a settlement twelve miles away during the time she held a temporary job as a teacher. Fierce winter weather and the distance required her to board with another family, so the homesick fifteen-year-old was deeply touched to see Manly outside her schoolhouse on Friday afternoons, waiting to take her home for the weekend.

Afterward Laura returned to school in DeSmet, but Manly continued calling for her on Sundays. Two years later, in 1885, they exchanged their first kiss when he offered her a garnet and pearl ring and proposed marriage. Joyfully, Laura accepted, as long as the word "obey" was omitted from her vows, because she didn't think she could obey anyone "against my better judgment."

"And so on Thursday, the 25th of August, at 10 o'clock in the morning the quick-stepping brown horses and the buggy with the shining top flashed around the corner at Pierson's livery barn . . . and drew up at the door."

In her finest dress, which was black cashmere, Laura rode with Manly to the preacher's, got married, and returned to her parents' home for a celebration dinner. She and Manly moved into a two-room gray frame house he had built. Within ten years they had settled on Rocky Ridge Farm in Mansfield, Missouri, where Laura wrote about farm and country life.

## TIZIANO VECELLIO AND CECILIA OF CADORE

### *"Marriage—Italian Style"*

SOMETIME IN THE EARLY 1520s "Titian," who was about thirty-five years old and already known as a great Venetian painter and portraitist, returned to his hometown, Cadore, an Alpine village in northern Italy. There he met Cecilia, the exquisitely beautiful daughter of the town barber. Titian sketched her, wooed her, and won her. In Venice she became his housekeeper and mistress and bore him two sons, Pompanio and Orazio.

In 1525 Cecilia became gravely ill. While no one knows for sure if she was really dying, everyone believed she was on her deathbed. Maybe she and Titian should marry, if only to legitimize the children? But the artist was reluctant; like most men, he was content with the way things were.

Cecilia knew her lover well: Didn't the two love goddesses he painted in his "Sacred and Profane Love" symbolize his visions of womankind? Their flesh was erotic, soft, and touchable, but it was the idealized Venus who represented eternal and divine love to Titian, not the well-dressed wife beside her. True, he also immortalized Cecilia in his magnificent "Madonna and the Rabbit"; how tenderly she looks at the young child. That man knew the joys of fatherhood and what it meant to be a loving parent.

Cecilia could barely lift her head from her pillow. If she couldn't live as Mrs. Vecellio, perhaps at least she could die that way. Marry me, she beseeched Titian, gasping. Reluctantly, he acquiesced. A priest was summoned, and the wedding was held in the bedchamber immediately.

Soon afterward the new bride recovered. The bridegroom, to his surprise, was sincerely overjoyed. Years later, when Cecilia really died, Titian mourned her deeply and never married again.

*Date approximate.

## HENRY LOUIS MENCKEN AND SARA HAARDT

*"I have the one perfect husband"*

ALTHOUGH "H.L.," THE CIGAR-CHOMPING, HARD-BOILED writer, was known for his satirical wit, biting criticism, and combative journalism, he was always sweetly tender with Sara. When they met in 1923, he had already written widely about American society and the "booboisie," lambasting bigotry and hypocrisy and condemning blue laws, puritanism, and temperance crusades. Few literary figures of the Jazz Age and the Roaring Twenties were as influential as the Baltimore *Sun*'s H.L. Mencken.

He was forty-two when he guest-lectured about writing at Baltimore's Goucher College, and Sara was a young instructor who accompanied him to lunch. H.L. was attracted by her dry wit, literary knowledge, elegance, and beauty. He began taking her out for dinner and escorting her to literary soirees, but almost seven years passed before the famous bachelor decided to tie the knot.

One problem was Sara's health. Within a year she was fighting tuberculosis and was in and out of sanitariums. When she improved, she quit teaching and became a freelance writer. H.L. gladly provided practical advice, and soon Sara's stories and sketches were appearing in *Vanity Fair, Century,* and other popular magazines. By the time she and H.L. married in 1930, Sara had established her own literary reputation and was working on screenplays and novels.

Years earlier, H.L. had poked fun at marriage, but now he concluded, "I am a firm believer in monogamy. . . . It is comfortable, laudable and sanitary." He and Sara were married in Baltimore's St. Stephen the Martyr Church. After honeymooning in Canada, they moved into a third-floor apartment at 704 Cathedral Street. Sara had decorated it tastefully with Victorian furniture and artwork, but she didn't blink when her new husband impishly "enhanced" the new dining room wallpaper with cartoon figures of Mutt and Jeff and Krazy Kat, cut from the Sunday funnies.

## JOHN HANCOCK AND DOROTHY QUINCY

*"I am yours forever"*

" 'TIS SAID THAT JOHN HANCOCK courts Dolly Quincy" wrote a local wag in Braintree, Massachusetts. But when King George III's troops marched into Lexington and Concord in April 1775, wedding plans were postponed as the groom-to-be, an outspoken patriot, fled to Philadelphia. Fortunately, his good friend Paul Revere had been out all night warning everybody that the British were coming, enabling John to skip town and join the Continental Congress, where he was made president.

Dolly remained in her parents' home, fretting about John. The parlor walls had been freshly covered with blue paper decorated with cupids and hearts for a wedding ceremony put off indefinitely. John pined for his "dear Dolly" and begged her to at least "write me often" and send "long letters." He sent her caps, stockings, thread, a summer cloak, and a white kid fan from Paris, which she would carry at their nuptials.

The British blockade of Boston prevented John from returning, so in late summer Dolly married him at the Burr mansion in Fairfield, Connecticut. John was thirty-eight, wealthy and good-looking. Dolly was blond and beautiful, and ten years younger. The festivities were simple, due to wartime shortages and the unsettling times. A few days later bride and bridegroom rode by coach over dusty rutted roads to Philadelphia, where the congress reopened in September. The following spring, when John signed the Declaration of Independence, his name was the largest—so King George could read it without his spectacles!

John Adams, Thomas Jefferson, and Benjamin Franklin often visited the Hancocks. Adams was particularly impressed by Dolly. "Among a hundred men at this house, she lives and behaves with modesty, decency, dignity and discretion," he wrote. By 1780 the Hancocks had resettled on Beacon Hill in Boston. John was elected governor of Massachusetts (and would be reelected nine times).

## GIUSEPPE VERDI AND GIUSEPPINA STREPPONI

*"Carissima"*

"NOT EVERYBODY CAN WRITE *AIDA*, but somebody has to pack and unpack the trunks," said "Peppina." The great soprano did much more than that during her life with Giuseppe, but she often underplayed her position in light of his greater genius.

In 1840, after Giuseppe's first wife died, the twenty-seven-year-old composer doubted that he could ever write operas again. But when he read the libretto for *Nabucco*, he was deeply moved. "La Strepponi," already an internationally known prima donna, said if he composed the music, she would sing the leading role of Abigaille. Her enthusiasm was inspirational. *Nabucco* became Giuseppe's first major success, premiering at Milan's La Scala in March 1842, and performed fifty-seven times that year, more than any other production.

Peppina's voice began failing a few years later and she retired from the stage, but she and Giuseppe remained true collaborators. She had a wonderful ear and was a kind but firm critic. She helped him shape many arias, including "Sempre libera" from *La Traviata*. Another magnificent joint effort was the adaptation of the score of *Jerusalem* in 1847. They worked together, taking turns writing lines alternately:

Peppina: "Angel from Heaven! . . . May I die in the arms of a husband!"

Giuseppe: "Let me die with you! My death will be . . ."

Peppina: ". . . sweet!"

They became lovers soon afterward, eventually settling in Sant' Agata in northern Italy. In 1859 they were married in a brief ceremony in the village of Collonges-sous-Salève near the French and Swiss border. Only their coachman and the village bell ringer witnessed the legalization of a union that lasted, altogether, more than fifty years. Back in Sant' Agata, the local band played selections from Verdi operas as grown men and women cried "Viva Verdi!" and wept with happiness.

"*Mio caro Verdi . . .*" Peppina said. "Without you I am a body without a soul."

## ELIZABETH STEVENSON AND WILLIAM GASKELL

*"my bonny wee bride"*

ELIZABETH WAS TWENTY-ONE WHEN SHE met William, an assistant minister in Manchester, England. He was struck by the dark-haired, intelligent, and vivacious young woman. They both enjoyed nature walks, poetry, music, and art and became engaged within a few months. William was twenty-five and would become a devoted husband who applauded his wife's eventual success as a poet, novelist, and biographer. During their engagement he told his sister, "You can't imagine how lonely I feel without her. . . . I am now writing with her rings on my fingers . . . with her likeness lying before me."

They married in 1832 at the parish church in Knutsford, where Elizabeth had grown up. Friends followed a medieval wedding tradition called "well-dressing" by strewing red sand on the street and enhancing it with flower patterns made with white sand poured from funnels. They also recited:

> . . . *Long may they live*
> *Happy may they be,*
> *And blest with a numerous*
> *Pro-ge-ny!*

Elizabeth and William honeymooned in Ffestiniog in north Wales while his sister fixed up their house at 14 Dover Street in Manchester. They moved in on Elizabeth's twenty-second birthday, September 29.

William was not only a clergyman but a professor of English history and literature. He and Elizabeth held literary gatherings for his students, encouraging them to write freely on whatever subjects pleased them.

Elizabeth gave birth to six children and performed social work with William in Manchester's sooty slums. Together, they wrote the poem, "Sketches Among the Poor." As "Mrs. Gaskell," she made her literary debut with *Mary Barton* in 1848. Two years later, chapters of her novel *Cranford* appeared in Charles Dickens's magazine, *Household Words*. After her friend Charlotte Brontë died in 1855, Elizabeth wrote her definitive biography.

## JIM JORDAN AND MARIAN DRISCOLL

### *Fibber McGee & Molly*

FOR ALMOST THIRTY YEARS, MILLIONS of Americans tuned in their radios Tuesday nights at 9:30 and howled with laughter as Fibber, an outrageous but lovable prevaricator, was once again caught in a lie by his long-suffering wife, Molly, who ended up proclaiming, " 'Taint funny, McGee!" She didn't put her ladylike foot down often, but Fibber always jumped when she did. That's probably why their make-believe marriage lasted at "79 Wistful Vista."

"Fibber was a bum," Jim said years later. "He never worked and was constantly taking advantage of his friends. That was the mystery of the show: how he managed to keep any friends at all. But he was likable . . . in the same way that Archie Bunker is."

Jim and Marian were teenagers in the St. John's Church choir in Peoria, Illinois, when they met. Even then Jim hammed up his performances, while Marian, who intended to become a music teacher, took her singing more seriously. Five days after they married in 1918, Jim left on an army troop train for Georgia and France, returning the following July. For the next six years he and Marian worked at odd jobs and sang in churches and lodges and on vaudeville stages. A major break came on a 1931 show called *The Smackouts*. Jim played a talkative but ineffectual grocer "smack out of everything" except long-winded, unbelievable stories.

The Jordans became "Fibber McGee and Molly" in 1935. Marian also portrayed other characters, including Teeny, the exasperating neighbor child whose whiny "Why, mister, why, mister?" drove Fibber to tears, and the sorrowful Mrs. Wearybottom, who spoke in monotonous run-on sentences. Every week Fibber horrified Molly by trotting down the hall to his famous overstuffed closet. When he opened it, everything—old shoes, tin cans, dumbbells, books, and more—tumbled out, prompting him to say, "Gotta straighten out that closet one of these days."

SIGMUND FREUD AND MARTHA BERNAYS

*September 13, 1886*

"One is very crazy when one is in love."

## BENJAMIN FRANKLIN AND DEBORAH READ

*"Keep your eyes wide open before marriage,
half shut afterwards"*

"BEING CALLED ONE MORNING TO Breakfast, I found it in a China Bowl with a Spoon of Silver. They had been bought for me without my knowledge by my Wife, and had cost her the enormous sum of three and twenty shillings, for which she had no Excuse or Apology to make, but that she thought *her* husband deserv'd a Silver Spoon and China Bowl as well as any of his Neighbors," wrote Ben in his *Autobiography*.

The future inventor, statesman, and ambassador was munching on a roll when he first spotted Deborah in Philadelphia, shortly after he arrived from his home-town, Boston. He rented a room in her parents' home, "made some Courtship," and proposed the following year, when he and Deborah were both eighteen. Un-fortunately, her mother discouraged them. Ben was going to England soon; why not wait until he returned?

While he was gone, Deborah married a cad who already had a wife and who eventually fled to the West Indies to escape creditors. When Ben came back, Deb-orah had been abandoned by her "husband" *and* her mother! This time, Ben "took her to wife 1 September 1730."

They lived above his Market Street print shop, where Deborah assisted Ben and also ran their book and stationery shop next door. Her fear of ships and ocean travel prevented her from sailing to Europe with him, but she managed their busi-ness affairs whenever he went away. Ben's first publishing success was *Poor Richard's Almanack,* filled with recipes, weather forecasts, lunar charts, and the homespun wisdom readers still appreciate today. Deborah gasped when he flew kites in thun-derstorms until he explained that he was learning about electricity and promptly invented lightning rods. He also invented bifocals, established the first lending library, and founded Philadelphia's first volunteer fire department.

## BENJAMIN WEST AND ELIZABETH SHEWELL

*Devoted to his art, and to Betsy*

SHORTLY BEFORE BEN MARRIED "BETSY" in 1764, the twenty-five-year-old artist painted "The Choice of Hercules," depicting the Greek hero standing between a demure figure of Virtue and a seductive, voluptuous Vice. Classical themes were popular in eighteenth-century England, where Ben had come to study art.

Back home in Philadelphia, Betsy's well-to-do parents were glad when the poor artist left town and went to Europe. No art schools or museums existed in colonial America at that time; even good art supplies were difficult to find. Ben and Betsy knew that he needed to study the old masters and develop his talents. He had saved every penny he could for his trip and was assisted also by a rich merchant who admired him.

In a few years the English were calling Ben "the American Raphael." Fame and financial success were his; all he needed was Betsy—would she marry him in London? Yes, she wrote, even if her family objected.

Family legends recount that Betsy's older brother locked his twenty-two-year-old sister in her room when he learned about her plans, but one of Betsy's maids smuggled in a rope ladder. When Betsy found out that Ben's father and her cousin Matthew were sailing to England, she threw the ladder out of her bedroom window, climbed down, and ran off to join them.

She married Ben at the church of St. Martin-in-the-Fields, and they settled down on Castle Street in Leicester Square, London. Eventually Ben became president of the Royal Academy of Art and was known as the "father of American art." Betsy kept a detailed diary of life in late eighteenth-century London. Even fifty years later, she could look back and say her husband "never had a fault."

## SIR EDMUND HILLARY AND LOUISE ROSE

*"Really, life is too good to be true"*

LOUISE HAD A PRETTY GOOD idea of what she was getting into when she married Edmund in 1953. The tall, good-looking thirty-four-year-old mountaineer had climbed to "the roof of the world"—Mount Everest's peak in the Himalayas—and had just been knighted by Queen Elizabeth for his achievement.

Louise's father was president of the New Zealand Alpine Club, and she and Edmund had known each other for years. The eleven-year age gap between them had prevented them from becoming romantically involved previously. Now that Louise was almost twenty-three and studying the violin at the Sydney, Australia, Conservatory of Music, Edmund decided to see her on his way home to New Zealand.

He wasted no time admitting his true feelings. He proposed forthwith and asked her to go with him to England, where he'd agreed to give some lectures. "Somewhat in a daze she consented and I was overjoyed," he wrote in his autobiography. Then the fearless adventurer, who'd taken more risks in a few years than most people take in a lifetime, added, "It certainly proved the most sensible action I have ever taken."

The wedding was held in New Zealand on Louise's birthday. Afterward she and Edmund flew to London, with stopovers in Australia, Java, Singapore, and other exotic places. Louise's "bubbling enthusiasm" thrilled Edmund and charmed well-wishers and reporters along the way. She wrote their parents, "I'm really not sure if I'm dreaming or not. . . ."

Edmund went on other expeditions, including a 1958 "Race to the Pole" in Antarctica, and supported many humanitarian causes for the people of Nepal. He and Louise trekked through the Himalayan mountains together, hiking along hillside paths bordered by orchids, magnolias, and wildflowers, and he felt the wonder of seeing familiar sights "through her delighted eyes."

## WILLIAM LLOYD GARRISON AND HELEN BENSON

*"I have opened my heart to you"*

LLOYD MET HELEN IN 1833, when the well-known abolitionist spoke against slavery at an African church in Providence, Rhode Island. It was easy to spot the few white faces in the audience, and Lloyd's eyes fell on "a plump and rosy creature with blue eyes and fair brown hair." Helen's brother George introduced her to the "great Garrison" afterward. A few days later Lloyd left for a speaking tour in England and didn't begin courting Helen for almost a year.

He wasn't the first abolitionist in America, but he was the first to campaign for slaves' "immediate and complete emancipation." Lloyd's weekly periodical, *The Liberator*, was wildly controversial. At times he was arrested, attacked, and dragged through streets with a rope around his neck, but nothing weakened his resolve.

Regarding Helen, however, Lloyd was timid and shy. Lacking the courage to propose in person, he sent her a letter instead. "However strong might have been your attachment for me, I would never have revealed it to you had you not first offered yourself to me," she said after they became engaged.

He was twenty-nine and she was twenty-three when they married in her father's house in Brooklyn, Connecticut. After a brief, simple wedding reception honoring Lloyd's requests for "no extravagances" or "showy" food, the new couple moved to Roxbury, a suburb of Boston.

They called their home Freedom's Cottage and took in boarders to help pay the rent. Two days later Lloyd wrote, "I can hardly realize as yet, that I am married, although I have one of the best wives in the world." Although Lloyd traveled often, he helped with the housework whenever he was home. "If there is anything I am fitted for it is to tend babies," he said. Eventually they had seven children, cared for by equally devoted parents.

## FRITZ KAHLENBERG AND INGEBORG WALLHEIMER

*Love in perilous times*

SHE WAS TALL, SLENDER, AND radiantly beautiful. In her early twenties, Ingeborg was several years younger than Fritz, whose bright blue eyes and light-hearted manner belied the strain of being a Jew hiding in wartime Amsterdam. He and Ingeborg met in the Dutch Underground, a resistance group of valiant men and women who dedicated their lives to ending the Nazi reign of terror by setting bombs, transporting munitions, forging documents, and delivering clandestine messages. Anyone caught was either killed or sent to a slave labor camp.

Fritz never stayed for long in his attic hideout at 36 Michelangelo Street or in other relatively safe havens throughout the region. Determined to let the world know what was happening, he recruited a group of photographers called the "Hidden Camera," who secretly took pictures—at great personal risk—of military movements, the persecution and deportation of thousands of Jews, resistance bombings and German reprisals, the brutally cold "Hunger Winter" of 1944–1945, and finally, liberation by the Allies.

Fritz taught Ingeborg how to operate a camera, which she carried inside her shoulder bag. As if rummaging for something, she would press the lens against a tiny hole cut in the leather and snap pictures of events in the streets. She also transported weapons to resistance fighters by pushing baby carriages loaded with Sten guns under the blankets. When the war ended, she and Fritz were honored by the United States government and General Eisenhower for "gallant service" in assisting the Allied defense.

In 1946 they were married in a civil ceremony in Amsterdam, followed by a reception at the Wallheimers' home. The celebrants danced to popular American tunes such as "Begin the Beguine," played on the family's record player. Subsequently Fritz and Ingeborg sailed to New York, where they produced many documentary and travel films.

## THOMAS WOOLNER AND ALICE GERTRUDE WAUGH

*"Love comes divinely, gladdening mortal life"*

"TO MY WIFE, ALICE GERTRUDE, I offer this vision of the past," wrote Thomas in *Pygmalion*. Seventeen years after they married in 1864, he composed his book-length poem about the mythical Greek sculptor who fell in love with his beautiful statue of a woman, which subsequently came to life. A sculptor as well as a poet, it was only fitting that Thomas should be attracted to the legend. Thirty-one years later George Bernard Shaw wrote a play about it; *My Fair Lady* was based upon it, too.

Like other Pre-Raphaelite artists of his generation, Thomas chose uplifting themes for his work. He was thinking of his new bride when he wrote "Beautiful Lady" six months after their wedding:

> *"I love my Lady; she is very fair . . .*
> *How beautiful she is! A glorious gem,*
> *She shines above the summer diadem*
> *Of flowers!"*

He and Alice were married at St. James's Church, Paddington, and honeymooned on the British island of Guernsey. After traveling through Dartmouth, Exeter, and Salisbury, they settled at 29, Welbeck Street in London's Cavendish Square and stayed there for the rest of their lives.

England's poet laureate Alfred, Lord Tennyson, and his wife, Emily, the Carlyles, Edward Lear, and other talented English friends sent gifts and good wishes to the happy couple. Thomas immortalized them and other writers, statesmen, and monarchs in busts and statues. His statue of John Stuart Mill is on the Thames embankment, and his bronze statue of Captain Cook overlooks Sydney harbor in Australia. Occasionally Alice posed for Thomas. He missed her terribly whenever she left Welbeck Street and proclaimed "the house has received its soul again" when she came home.

## ALLAN PINKERTON AND JOAN CARFRAE

### *"We Never Sleep"*

JOAN KNEW THAT ALLAN WAS a quick-thinking, intelligent man, but she never expected that he'd become a master detective. Yet nothing was ever simple. The day after their 1842 wedding in Glasgow, the twenty-three-year-olds fled to the United States. If they'd stayed in Scotland, Allan would have been thrown in jail.

They had met five years before, at a meeting of Chartist supporters campaigning for wage increases and better conditions for British workingmen. Allan was impressed by the pretty brown-haired girl. Most young women—even those who worked in factories, as Joan did—didn't think much about justice and the rights of others, especially if it meant risking their own jobs. He offered to escort Joan home; from then on they were inseparable. But when massive Chartist demonstrations brought a wave of police arrests, Allan and Joan left.

They settled near Chicago, where he found work as a barrel maker. His workshop became a "station" for runaway slaves on the Underground Railroad when he and Joan joined the Abolitionist crusade.

Allan became a detective almost by accident. One day he discovered the hideout for counterfeiters on a deserted island in the Fox River, west of Chicago. When he showed some bogus bills to the sheriff, a posse was organized to arrest the band. Local merchants called Allan a hero, encouraging him to do more detective work. In 1846 he was Kane County deputy sheriff, and four years later he established the first private detective agency in the world. The Pinkerton Detective Agency broke up robber gangs run by Jesse James, the Wild Bunch, and the Younger brothers. Allan never quit until he caught the "bad guys," inspiring Joan to suggest the agency's motto: "We Never Sleep."

During the Civil War, Allan directed counterespionage activities for President Lincoln and helped organize the nation's first Secret Service bureau.

*Date approximate.

## KING GEORGE III OF ENGLAND AND
## PRINCESS CHARLOTTE OF MECKLENBURG

*"Ich will!"*

"YOU'RE GOING TO BE QUEEN of England," Charlotte's mother said in 1761 when George's formal proposal of marriage arrived. Two months later the German princess was on a ship bound for Great Britain.

George, who was twenty-three and would rule for sixty years, had a fair amount of latitude in choosing a wife. Charlotte was seventeen, plain-looking but healthy, with a dignified presence and charm. Until she learned to speak English, she and George conversed in French and German. Marriage plans were delayed when the king came down with chicken pox, but Charlotte sent him a lock of her hair to soothe him. She curtsied before George when at last they met, but he promptly picked her up and hugged her affectionately. After the royal family met her, George made sure that they dined alone. Then everyone got all dressed up and walked to the Chapel Royal, across the road from the palace.

It had been a very hot day, and the heat lasted into the evening. At 10:00 P.M. Charlotte, wearing a purple velvet cape trimmed with ermine and a silver wedding gown enhanced by diamonds, stood under a domed canopy until the king came down the aisle to claim her. "Courage, Princess, courage," whispered George's brother William, who noticed she was trembling. The Archbishop of Canterbury conducted the ceremony, and Charlotte confirmed her vows with "Ich will." Two weeks later she was crowned in Westminster Abbey.

Although history remembers George primarily for losing the American colonies, he was a loving husband and father to twelve surviving children. He and Charlotte liked being home with their kids, giving them a somewhat boring, traditional life. She devoted her spare energies to charitable causes, especially the welfare of British women and children. He didn't discuss affairs of state with her . . . but he might have done better if he had!

## RICHARD STEELE AND MARY SCURLOCK

### *"Yr Obedient Husband"*

DICK MET "MOLLY" IN LONDON at his first wife's funeral in 1706. He had been married for only two years, and it was fairly common knowledge that he'd married the elderly widow primarily for the property she held in Barbados. One day the thirty-five-year-old English dramatist and essayist would be immortalized with Joseph Addison for their periodicals, the *Tatler* and the *Spectator,* but now all Dick could think about was beautiful Molly.

At the Kit-Cat club and other coffeehouses he frequented, Dick described the twenty-eight-year-old Welshwoman to friends such as writer Jonathan Swift. Dick nicknamed her "Prue" and "Molly" and pursued her intensively, although she did little to encourage him. Before long he was proposing marriage and declaring in ardent letters that he was "tenderly, passionately, faithfully thine." He asked Molly's widowed mother to intercede, after overstating his assets and minimizing his debts. Maybe Dick was erratic, extravagant, and impulsive; he also was brilliant and adoring. If only Molly's "fair lips" would say yes, giving him "in one monosyllable more than all the eloquence in the world could express."

At last, on September 8, 1707, they secured a marriage license. Dick was ecstatic: "Methinks I could write a volume to you; but all the language on earth would fail in saying how much and with what disinterested passion I am ever yours."

In truth, no records exist of a wedding ceremony. For some reason the marriage was kept secret, but a month later Dick and Molly moved into a house on London's Bury Street, "third door, right hand, turning out to Jermyn St." Molly saved hundreds of Richard's letters and eventually donated them to the British Museum.

To Dick, September 9 would always be the day "in which you gave me your hand and heart."

## RICHARD STRAUSS AND PAULINE DE AHNA

*"my Pauksl"*

"IN WEIMAR I WON MY beloved Pauline" wrote the German composer in his *Recollections and Reflections.* The magnificent singer "had followed me as a pupil and was . . . an excellent Pamina, Elvira, Elsa, Elisabeth and Evchen and even had the pluck to sing Fidelio and Isolde."

They had known each other for seven years when they announced their engagement to a stunned group of musicians in May 1894. While rehearsing Richard's opera *Guntram,* Pauline made a mistake and began arguing with him. At first only angry words flew between the stage and Richard's podium. Then she hurled the musical score, which struck him on the head. Pauline stormed off to her dressing room, and Richard followed, furious. The door slammed shut and their loud arguing continued. Then . . . silence. A few musicians tiptoed to Pauline's door and knocked on it timidly. Richard opened it, smiling broadly. "I have just become engaged to Fräulein de Ahna," he proclaimed.

Richard's parents thought the high-strung diva was unsuitable for their genius son. This saddened him greatly, but he was resolute. He told his parents that he and Pauline would see them as little as possible "so long as the woman whom after much deliberation I have chosen as my wife, and whom in spite of her faults I love and admire, irritates you and embitters your life."

Richard's wedding gift to Pauline was a group of German lieder, or songs—"Cacilie," "Secret Invitation," and "Tomorrow"—which he gave her soon after their wedding. She was thirty-one and he was thirty years old. Already he had completed his famous *Till Eulenspiegel,* based upon Flemish legends of an endearing prankster and folk hero. The years ahead would be filled with symphonic poems, songs, and operas he would compose, including *Salomé* and *Der Rosenkavalier.* Even after Pauline retired from opera singing, she continued to be Richard's greatest admirer and the "model interpreter" of his songs.

## AGATHA MILLER CHRISTIE AND MAX MALLOWAN

*Second spring*

THE FAMOUS ENGLISH WRITER OF mystery and detective novels met Max at a Middle Eastern archaeological site in 1930. He was an Oxford classical scholar and the twenty-four-year-old assistant to the project leader at Ur, an ancient settlement not far from Baghdad. Agatha was forty and depressed after a recent divorce.

They took long car trips to visit sites. Nothing fazed Agatha—not flea bites, nor the brutally hot weather, nor car trouble that left them in the Arabian desert without water or shelter. Their Bedouin driver set off on foot to seek help, leaving them alone overnight. By the time they returned to the main base, Max had fallen in love.

Agatha liked Max a lot, but marriage was out of the question. Once burned was bad enough; besides, the "very unsuitable" difference in their ages surely would doom any permanent relationship. Fortunately, Max pursued her. After a romantic trip back to London on the *Orient Express,* Agatha concluded (as she wrote in her autobiography) that "nothing in the world would be as delightful as being married to him."

Slipping away from family and friends, she and Max were married in the chapel of St. Columba's Church in Edinburgh, Scotland. Two days later they crossed the English Channel by boat and took the *Orient Express* to Venice for a honeymoon before continuing to Greece and back to Ur.

In their frequent travels, Agatha helped Max by cataloguing and photographing finds he uncovered. He assisted her with archaeological information for some of her stories, such as *Murder on the Orient Express* and *Murder in Mesopotamia.* Years later Max summed up everything by saying, "After being stuck in the sand . . . we never looked back." Neither could have "guessed that the short journey to Baghdad would lead to a longer union . . . destined to last the best part of fifty years."

## JOHN F. KENNEDY AND JACQUELINE BOUVIER

*"What I want more than anything
else in the world is to be married to him"*

THEY BOTH WERE INCREDIBLY GOOD-LOOKING and driven to succeed. John's family was wealthier, but Jackie was classy and refined. She was an accomplished equestrian; he was allergic to horses. He loved touch football; she quit soon after she broke her ankle. Outgoing on the surface, deep down John was as insular and private as Jackie was.

They met at a Georgetown dinner party in May 1951. She was a twenty-one-year-old George Washington University senior, and the Massachusetts congressman was thirty-three. "I leaned across the asparagus and asked her for a date," John recalled later. They didn't get serious until the following winter, when Jackie was a cub reporter for the *Washington Times-Herald* and John's Senate race had begun.

Jackie's mother and stepfather, the Auchinclosses, wanted a small, dignified wedding, but the Kennedys insisted that the senator they hoped would be president one day be married in a grand, elaborate affair. Parties began a week before. On the day of the 1953 wedding, thousands of people stood outside St. Mary's Church in Newport, Rhode Island. John's brother, Robert, was the best man, and Jackie's sister, Lee, was her matron of honor.

The wedding day was not entirely blissful. Jackie's stepfather escorted her down the aisle because her mother made sure that her alcoholic father didn't show up at the ceremony and embarrass everybody. The Auchinclosses threw a party for twelve hundred guests at Hammersmith Farm, their country estate. At nightfall, the newlyweds flew to New York to spend their wedding night at the Waldorf-Astoria Hotel. Honeymooning in a private villa in Acapulco, John caught a nine-foot-long sailfish, which was mounted and displayed on his Senate office wall; later it hung in the White House.

## SIGMUND FREUD AND MARTHA BERNAYS

*"One is very crazy when one is in love"*

SOMETHING WAS DIFFERENT WHEN SIGMUND came home from work in April 1882. Usually the twenty-six-year-old medical doctor raced to his room without stopping to chat with family guests in the dining room, but he was struck by the sight of an attractive young woman with long dark hair and large expressive eyes. Martha was tall, slim, and twenty-one, with an air of self-assurance. Like Eve in the garden of Eden, she was also peeling an apple!

Love-struck, Sigmund began sending red roses to Martha and calling her "Princess." In late May they took their first walk together. They exchanged books, and she baked cakes for him to "dissect." Holding hands under his parents' table, they considered themselves unofficially engaged.

That summer, Martha's family moved from Vienna to Wandsbek, a Hamburg suburb, possibly to keep the young couple apart since marriage would have to wait until Sigmund's practice was established. In December, he bought Martha a garnet engagement ring. Until they married in 1886, he wrote more than nine hundred letters to his "precious darling," discussing his growing interest in patients suffering from symptoms with no known physical causes.

They were married in civil and religious ceremonies in Wandsbek and honeymooned for two weeks on the Baltic coast. Back in Vienna, Martha spent her small dowry to furnish their apartment and borrowed chairs from the porter who lived in the basement. Sigmund hung a sign by their doorway stating that he specialized in nervous diseases.

Two years later he wrote a friend, "We live pretty happily in steadily increasing unassumingness. When we hear the baby laugh we imagine it is the loveliest thing that can happen to us." By 1891 they had moved to a more spacious apartment at Berggasse 19, and they stayed there for the next forty-seven years.

## RALPH WALDO EMERSON AND LYDIA JACKSON

*"Give all to love; obey thy heart"*

SHORTLY BEFORE WALDO MARRIED "LYDIAN" in 1835, the transcendentalist writer bought a spacious, square white house in Concord, Massachusetts. Their new home had an ample garden and a Doric portico and wasn't far from Walden Pond, where Waldo often walked.

At one of his lectures, he had "gazed with great delight upon the beautiful face until he caught the maiden's eye." She was enthralled by Waldo's powerful ideas. His first wife had died after a brief marriage, but Lydian restored his enthusiasm for life. Their courtship consisted largely of letters and Waldo's hurried trips to her home in Plymouth. Once she looked up into his intense blue eyes and asked if he thought her conversation was uninteresting. "Uninteresting?" he laughed gently. "It is heaven."

His marriage proposal was so stilted, she said she would accept only if he came to her "with a joyful heart" and convinced her that he loved her. Like Waldo, Lydia was thirty-two years old, an intellectual and a poet. She added an *n* to her name because he thought that "Lydian Emerson" sounded more harmonious.

They married at her home, Winslow House, at 7:30 in the evening. Waldo arrived after a rainstorm, and the autumnal sun brightened what had been a dreary day. The following morning they drove to Concord. Lydian planted seeds and bulbs from her Plymouth garden. They also cultivated roses and a small fruit orchard. Waldo often worked in the garden after breakfast, turning the soil and gathering his thoughts. On gusty spring days he placed their aeolian harp by an open window. Sweet breezes strummed the harp strings lightly, soothing everyone indoors and out.

That year Waldo worked on his poem about the Revolutionary battle of Concord, which included the now famous words, "Here once the embattled farmer stood, And fired the shot heard round the world."

## JAMES MADISON AND DOLLEY PAYNE TODD

*"this day I give my Hand to the Man*
*who of all others I most admire"*

MUCH AS THE FUTURE PRESIDENT hated sea travel, Dolley was the real reason he didn't sail to France with James Monroe in late spring, 1794. His former Princeton classmate Aaron Burr had introduced him to the twenty-six-year-old blue-eyed, black-haired, pink-cheeked young widow and mother in Philadelphia. James couldn't stop thinking about her. At forty-three, he had been reluctant to marry since being jilted ten years before. He certainly kept busy—working on the Bill of Rights' creation and ratification, determining the roles of the president, forming an independent national judiciary, and other significant matters . . . but recently he'd been feeling lonely.

Most probably he proposed to Dolley in a letter, although none survives to confirm this. We do know that she became ill, possibly with malaria. He went to Montpelier, his family's estate in Virginia, and attended to a sick houseguest. Weeks passed, and James didn't hear from Dolley. He'd shared his feelings with her cousins, however, who wrote Dolley that "he thinks so much of you in the day that he has Lost his Tongue, at Night he Dreams of you & Starts in his Sleep a Calling on you to relieve his Flame for he Burns to such an excess that he will be shortly consumed & he hopes that your Heart will be callous to every other swain but himself."

At last Dolley sent James a letter, accepting his proposal. They married at Harewood in the Shenandoah Valley, the plantation home of Dolley's sister Lucy and her husband, George Steptoe Washington. James wore a low-cut waistcoat with a lace jabot at the neck and gave Dolley a necklace of medallions depicting scenes of Roman history. During the boisterous wedding supper, bridesmaids snipped off his lace ruffles to save as souvenirs.

### PAUL KLEE AND LILY STUMPF

*"Dearest beloved heart"*

PAUL AND LILY HAD BEEN in love for eight years when they married in 1906. Her parents had opposed the match, doubting that the young Swiss artist could ever support a family. But nothing weakened Lily's devotion. When she first met Paul, he was a nineteen-year-old student from Berne who came to Munich to study music, literature, and art. "It is not my task to reproduce appearances," he wrote, after he had decided to concentrate on painting. "For that there is the photographic plate. . . . I want to reach the heart."

Lily was twenty-two, an accomplished pianist and music teacher, when Paul called on her father, a medical doctor. Dr. Stumpf discouraged his daughter from seeing Paul, at first gently, then adamantly. Lily protested; she and Paul were kindred spirits, passionately in love with books, music, and each other. At last she announced that they intended to marry. Paul begged Dr. Stumpf to accept their decision. Finally, he did, "though he asks sardonically what we plan to live on."

The answer was simple: Lily would work so Paul could paint. Their son, Felix, remembered, "In the little flat in Munich, my mother . . . gave music lessons from morning to night and her husband . . . had to see to the chores and look after the baby. The kitchen was his room; there his pictures and drawings saw the light. . . ."

Afternoons, Paul took Felix to a park where the son played and the father painted. Much of Paul's work was fanciful and witty; he was inspired by primitive art and children's drawings, as well as Cubism and Surrealism. Thanks in part to Lily's willingness to work full-time in an era when few wives did, within four years of their marriage Paul's first exhibition was held and his career was launched. Fanciful paintings such as "Twittering Machine," a pen-and-ink drawing tinted with watercolor, and "At the Mountain of the Bull," in watercolor and oil, influenced other artists of the twentieth century.

## WILLIAM ABBOTT AND BETTY SMITH

*His first partner*

ABBOTT AND COSTELLO BECAME A team years after "Bud" Abbott found his most lovable partner. The son of a circus advance man and a bareback rider, Bud grew up in show business and was treasurer of Washington, D.C.'s, National Theater when Betty caught his eye in 1918. The pert seventeen-year-old dancer from Buffalo, New York, had changed her name from Jenny Mae Pratt when she left home and joined an acrobatic act. She was working at the National when a well-heeled fan took the cast for a Sunday cruise on the Potomac. Suddenly, one of the performers foolishly dived into the water. The current was treacherous, and while everyone stood on the deck wondering what to do, Bud jumped in and rescued the hysterical girl. Betty was "hooked" too; nineteen-year-old Bud was a hero.

A week later they drove to Alexandria, Virginia, after the midnight show, got married, and were back in time for the matinee. When the show closed, they developed their own comedy skits, with Bud playing the straight man unaware that Betty was getting laughs behind his back.

Eventually Bud began performing with other comics, too. In 1936 he and Betty had dinner with Lou Costello and his wife at Reuben's, a New York City deli. When Lou's straight man became ill, Bud stepped in as the perfect replacement. They found success first on the burlesque and vaudeville stages, then on radio shows, on Broadway, and in feature films.

Betty was happy to watch the new comedy team take off. She and Bud moved to Hollywood where they held parties for hundreds of people under huge circus tents. After thirty-two years of marriage, they renewed their wedding vows in a traditional Jewish ceremony—a tribute to Bud's mother, who never lost faith in her son or her daughter-in-law.

## SIR ARTHUR CONAN DOYLE AND JEAN LECKIE

*"Elementary," said Arthur*

"MY HONEYMOON BEGAN ON THE day I was wed, and will continue right through eternity," said the father of the modern detective story and creator of Sherlock Holmes years after he married Jean in 1907. They had met ten years before, when she was twenty-four and the burly writer with a walrus moustache was thirty-eight and married. Sadly, his wife, Louise, was gravely ill, and the strain of caring for an invalid was almost unbearable for Arthur.

Jean was warm and adoring, with hazel green eyes, dark blond hair, and an untroubled acceptance that Arthur would never leave Louise or hurt her deliberately. They fell in love quickly, but for a long time only Arthur's mother, "the Ma'am," knew about it, and she approved as well. When at last Louise died, Arthur waited a year to marry Jean.

A few close friends and relatives attended the quiet ceremony at London's St. Margaret's, Westminster. Arthur, wearing a frock coat, white waistcoat, and a white gardenia in his lapel, looked "supremely happy," said a reporter. Jean wore a white silk gown appliquéd with Spanish lace and pearls over silver tissue. Arthur recited his vows "in a clear, fervent voice, but the bride's replies were barely audible."

The reception was livelier; writers, including Bram Stoker and James M. Barrie, and 250 other guests watched Arthur carry his new bride up the Hotel Metropole's red-carpeted stairs so she wouldn't get entangled in her train. They honeymooned on the Continent, traveling as far as Constantinople.

Settling down at Windlesham, a country estate in Sussex, Arthur wrote more Sherlock Holmes stories, as well as plays, adventure novels, and treatises on spiritualism. Jean said, "Whenever I heard my husband's dear voice in the distance, or he came into a room, something radiant seemed to enter and permeate the atmosphere."

## ELIZABETH BARRETT AND ROBERT BROWNING

*"How do I love thee? Let me count the ways"*

ONE OF THE WORLD'S MOST romantic love stories began in January 1845, when Robert sent Elizabeth a note: "I love your verses with all my heart, dear Miss Barrett."

She was almost thirty-nine, a fragile recluse in her widowed father's house at 50 Wimpole Street, London. Robert was thirty-three, a handsome bachelor who'd already written "My Last Duchess," "The Pied Piper of Hamelin," and other poems and plays. Five months passed before they actually met, but a lively correspondence between the two poets began immediately. Because of Robert, "the face of all the world is changed," wrote Elizabeth in *Sonnets from the Portuguese.*

What weighed upon the two lovers most heavily was Edward Barrett's tyrannical demand that none of his children ever leave home or marry. He was "as immovable as stone," said Elizabeth. But nothing would deter her from seeing Robert. Not only did he bring passion into her life, he gave her the strength and will to venture outside for short walks and carriage rides.

On September 12, 1846, Elizabeth slipped out of the house and married Robert in St. Marylebone Church. The wedding ring was put on and quickly removed before the bride and groom left by separate doors. Trembling, Elizabeth returned home and composed a farewell letter to her "dearest Papa," to be delivered after she and Robert had gone. Robert could not bear to call on "Miss Barrett" at her house when she was, in fact, Mrs. Browning. Letters flew back and forth, until Elizabeth wrote, "By tomorrow at this time, I shall have *you* only, to love me— my beloved!"

On September 19, "a delicious day," said Robert, they boarded a train for Southampton, then the ferry to France, where they honeymooned in Paris before continuing on to Florence, Italy. To Elizabeth, they were "living as in a dream . . . loving and being loved better every day."

*Date their marriage truly began.

## LEWIS LATIMER AND MARY WILSON

### *"My Venus shall be ebony"*

BY THE TIME LEWIS AND Mary met in the early 1870s, the future inventor had been a draftsman for over five years. The son of fugitive slaves granted freedom in Massachusetts, Lewis had served in the Union navy when he was sixteen and subsequently found employment at a patent law firm in Boston. Mary was from Fall River, and she encouraged Lewis to learn as much as possible at work. Although Lewis could be shy about expressing his growing love for Mary, he wrote about it easily:

> *Let others boast of maidens fair,*
> *Of eyes blue and golden hair,*
> *My heart, like needle ever true,*
> *Turns to the maid of ebon hue.*

They married two weeks after his twenty-fifth birthday and settled in Boston. Within a year Lewis and a partner had secured their first patent, for a railroad car "water closet." Alexander Graham Bell also asked Lewis to use his self-taught draftsman's skills to make the necessary patent application drawings of his new "telephone." Bell would remain eternally grateful; thanks to Lewis's speed and competence, their submission was filed only hours before another inventor's.

In the 1880's, after Lewis formulated a way to make inexpensive long-lasting carbon filaments for lightbulbs while working for one of Thomas Edison's competitors, the great man convinced him to join his organization. In later years Lewis volunteered at Manhattan's Henry Street Settlement House, helping new immigrants learn English and mechanical drawing. Unfortunately, most of Lewis's achievements were not fully recognized during his lifetime. Mary remained his most loyal admirer and the inspiration for his greatest poetry:

> *O'er marble Venus let them rage.*
> *Who set the fashions of the Age.*
> *Each to his taste; but as for me*
> *My Venus shall be ebony.*

## MAUD POWELL AND H. GODFREY TURNER

*A deep love of music and each other*

FOR MAUD, BECOMING AN INTERNATIONALLY acclaimed woman violinist in the late nineteenth century had required many sacrifices, including giving up an ordinary childhood to "train train train," forgoing activities that might damage her hands—and not wasting time with suitors. Opportunities to play professionally were limited; sitting beside men in orchestras was "improper," and women were considered too delicate for the rigors of rehearsals and performances. But Maud, whose Uncle John had explored the Grand Canyon and whose Aunt Emma was the first woman to climb Pikes Peak, had abundant grit and talent. By the time she was thirty-five, she had performed for European kings and queens as well as countless people in small towns across the United States.

Maud was thirty-six and performing in London when she met "Sunny," the genial forty-four-year-old English manager of John Philip Sousa's band. Sunny knew a lot about music and had a wonderful knack for making Maud laugh. After the tour concluded Maud returned to America, and soon afterward he proposed. Sunny understood Maud's life as a performer and promised to be a true companion and lover.

They were married in 1904 at a farm near Pawling, New York. "Madame" Powell, as she would be known professionally, always wore her gold wedding ring on her right hand, keeping her left hand as agile as possible. She and Sunny built a home by the water in Great Neck, Long Island, and called their boat *Fiddle-Dee-Dee*. Sunny managed Maud's career, accompanied her on tours, and wrote advertisements proclaiming that Maud had "the Arm of a Man, the Heart of a Woman and the Head of an Artist." She was the first instrumentalist to record for RCA Victor, and her recordings became worldwide best-sellers. In 1989 three compact disc recordings of her music were reissued by the Maud Powell Foundation, based in Arlington, Virginia.

## BARRY MORRIS GOLDWATER AND MARGARET JOHNSON

*"There wasn't any escape" from his persistent proposal*

THE TALL, BLUE-EYED FUTURE SENATOR from Arizona proposed to "Peggy" in a telephone booth on New Year's Eve, 1933. He had been visiting her in her hometown of Muncie, Indiana, and "was running out of money and out of patience," he wrote in his autobiography. "For the umpteenth time I asked her to marry me. She said yes."

They first met three years before, when Peggy and her mother were shopping in Goldwaters department store in Phoenix, Arizona. Barry was a $15-a-week junior clerk who thought Peggy was very pretty, with a good sense of humor and a delightful laugh. Unfortunately, the petite blue-eyed brunette wasn't impressed with him or his "hick town." She dropped by again the following year, and Barry went back east to see her. He proposed in person, by letter, and over the telephone, but nothing—not even his gift of a caged lovebird—worked until that night in the phone booth.

Once Peggy accepted, Barry wanted to get married immediately, but first she and her mother took a four-month cruise around the world, which they had been planning for a long time. Fearing that Peggy might fall for another guy in a shipboard romance, Barry sent lots of letters that greeted her at every port. When at last she arrived in New York harbor, he gave her his grandmother Sarah's wedding ring from 1854.

They married in Muncie in 1934 and settled in Arizona, which Peggy grew to love and where she and Barry began studying and collecting American Indian art. Even after he was elected to the Senate, ran for president, and became known as a leader of conservatism in America, for Barry nothing ever compared with the night that Peggy said yes.

## PAUL REVERE AND RACHEL WALKER

*"the Fair One that is nearest my Heart"*

RACHEL MARRIED PAUL IN BOSTON in 1773, two years before he took his "midnight ride" warning everyone that "the British are coming!" The previous spring Paul chanced to see Rachel outside his gold and silversmith shop. She knew that Paul's wife had died recently and offered to walk home with him and visit his little children. They took such a liking to the cheerful young woman that Paul began courting her. On the back of a bill for "mending a spoon," he composed a riddle spelling out Rachel's name:

> *Take ¾ of a pain that makes traitors confess (**RAC**k)*
> *With 3 parts of a place which the wicked don't bless ((**HEL**l)*
> *Join 4/7 of an exercise which shopkeepers use (**WALK**ing)*
> *Add what bad men do when they good actions refuse (**ER**r)*
> *These 4 added together with great care and art*
> *Will point out the Fair One that is nearest my Heart.*

Two months after Paul and Rachel married, colonists disguised as Indians boarded English ships and threw more than three hundred chests of tea into Boston harbor to protest taxation without representation. It's likely that Paul was one of the "Indians"; he'd been active in the growing revolutionary movement. As a messenger for the Committee of Public Safety, he carried news about the tea party all the way to New York and Philadelphia.

Whenever he rode off, his "dear Girl" managed his business and their home. Like Paul, Rachel was energetic and feisty. Their marriage would be filled with love and devotion. In 1775, when British soldiers pursued him on his famous ride, Rachel sent him money and a letter warning him not to "attempt coming into this towne again." She closed by saying "adieu my Love" and eventually met him in Charlestown with his "little lambs," their children.

## HEINRICH SCHLIEMANN AND SOPHIA ENGASTROMENOS

*"She loves me as a Greek, with passion, and I love her no less."*

HEINRICH FIRST SAW SOPHIA'S FACE in a photograph. Her eyes were intelligent and her beauty was flawless; she also spoke classical Greek. A few years earlier the forty-seven-year-old self-made German millionaire and linguist had retired from business to fulfill his childhood dream—locating the ancient city of Troy. After completing his doctorate in archaeology and ending a very unhappy marriage, Heinrich went to Greece to find his own "Helen of Troy."

Seventeen-year-old Sophia was everything he wanted. At first she accepted Heinrich's proposal simply because her parents told her to marry the wealthy man. This made Heinrich furious. What did *she* want? If a life filled with archaeological discovery and adventure wasn't enough, he wanted nothing more to do with her. Sophia apologized profusely; of course she wanted him! In 1869 they married in the tiny candlelit church of St. Meletios in Athens, near her parents' home. The festivities lasted until 1:00 A.M., when Heinrich and Sophia sailed away on a ship aptly named *Aphrodite.*

Heinrich was generous, brilliant, and passionate. Although he could be high-strung and demanding, Sophia's gaiety softened him. She understood his determination to prove the basis for the legends of the *Odyssey* and *Iliad,* and in 1873 they uncovered extraordinary treasures in Turkey, near what would be identified subsequently as King Priam's palace. Sophia evaded the local police by wrapping a dazzling array of gold, silver, and copper helmets, goblets, vases, diadems, and jewelry in an enormous red shawl and smuggling them out of the country. Years later Heinrich told her, "I can never celebrate our marriage enough, for you have always been my beloved wife and at the same time my comrade . . . by Zeus! I will marry you again in the next world!"

## HELEN GURLEY AND DAVID BROWN

*"The difference between David and me and some other people with ideas is that we sit down and do it."*

THREE YEARS AFTER HELEN MARRIED David in 1959, her book *Sex and the Single Girl* became a best-seller and "how-to guide" for unmarried women in the new sexually permissive era. When they met in Los Angeles, Helen was a thirty-six-year-old copywriter and the highest paid woman in advertising on the West Coast. David was a journalist and motion picture producer who'd been married and divorced twice. Much as he liked the "brown-eyed, smart" and "very sexy" woman who was financially independent because of her own hard work, he was not in a hurry to tie the knot again.

Helen waited more than a year before she brought up the subject. As she says in his book *Let Me Entertain You,* "I tendered my ultimatum . . . it was time for marriage and I wanted *him.*" When that didn't work, she told him she wasn't going to see him anymore. A few days later he proposed.

One of the first things David did after he married Helen was to encourage her to write a book based on her experiences as a single working woman. David even suggested the dynamite title. In 1965 Helen became editor-in-chief of seventy-nine-year-old *Cosmopolitan* magazine and turned it into an upbeat, splashy publication aimed at showing single women (and married women who "thought single") how to get as much as they possibly could out of life. She also created the first male centerfold.

David produced successful films such as *Jaws, The Sting, The Verdict,* and *Cocoon* and also worked in publishing. But the best thing he ever did was marry Helen: "Stick a pin in me and she jumps," he has said. "If someone appears to hurt me she cries out."

## ARTHUR EVANS AND MARGARET FREEMAN

*"the find of a lifetime"*

ARTHUR HAD BEEN WORKING AT an archaeological site at Ragusa (now Dubrovnik) when war broke out in the Balkans in 1877 and the dig was disbanded. The twenty-six-year-old English writer sent war dispatches to London papers but had not yet determined his life's work—uncovering the ancient civilization of Crete, including King Minos' palace at Knossos—when he met the English historian Edward Freeman and his twenty-nine-year-old daughter.

Although Miss Freeman was dressed demurely in a tight-waisted dress, white gloves, and a large hat, Arthur saw that she was lively, well educated, and an excellent listener. She found the thickset, dark-complexioned man bright and energetic, poking the air with his walking stick, "Prodger," to stress his points of view.

Arthur followed the Freemans back to England, brimming with stories about life in the magnificent coastal region of Ragusa and fantasizing about taking Margaret back one day. It wasn't hard to convince her. In 1878 they married in Nash Mills, his birthplace, and sailed for Casa San Lazzaro, their home by the Adriatic Sea. Margaret learned the local Serbian language and soon was playing music on a rented piano. Arthur brought relief supplies to dispossessed families and continued writing dispatches about the war in Bosnia and Herzegovina for the next three years. But the Austrians, who had become embroiled in the battle, accused Arthur of spying and threw him into Ragusa's ancient prison. He languished there for six weeks until Margaret convinced the police that Arthur's maps were of only prehistoric sites. The men visiting their house, she explained, carried ancient coins, pottery shards, and other archaeological finds, not ammunition or arms.

After Arthur was freed, he and Margaret returned to England. Subsequently they set off for Greece, where treks to ancient ruins fired their dreams to uncover an ancient world.

*Date approximate.

## HUME CRONYN AND JESSICA TANDY

*"The odds were impossible . . ."*

BEFORE HUME WAS INTRODUCED TO Jessica backstage after her 1940 performance in A. J. Cronin's *Jupiter Laughs,* he stepped outside during intermission and watched her—still wearing her costume—leap into a taxi. That year she had brought her daughter Susan with her to New York, leaving behind her husband, actor Jack Hawkins, and their shaky marriage. Every night Jessica raced back to her hotel to check on Susan . . . and always returned in time for the next act.

Hume was divorced and briefly engaged to someone else before he realized that he loved the petite, blue-eyed actress. Jessica had a much harder time making up her mind. Hume courted her with lavish dinners and drives in his snappy Buick roadster. He also had the lead role in a dismal flop called *Mr. Big.*

He wasn't having luck with Jessica, either. "I had asked her to marry me so many times that I had almost lost count," he wrote in *A Terrible Liar.* "Her unequivocal nos lasted for about eighteen months," but in summer, 1942, she went to Reno, Nevada, for a divorce and married Hume in Los Angeles, after he completed filming *Shadow of a Doubt* for Alfred Hitchcock.

Jessica wore a pink and gray suit at their wedding, held in a gardenia-filled chapel of the Beverly Vista Community Church and followed by a garden party behind Romanoff's restaurant. Hume was thirty-one and his next project was Hitchcock's masterpiece, *Lifeboat.* Jessica was thirty-three and had just signed a five-year film contract. Within two years they played a husband and wife in *The Seventh Cross,* a wartime thriller.

"You are the music to which my world is set" were the words Hume had inscribed inside Jess's wedding ring. They were husband and wife, actors, costars, and parents. And they would be very happy.

## ERNEST H. SHEPARD AND FLORENCE CHAPLIN

### *"Kip" and "Pie"*

IN 1899 IT WASN'T EASY for men and women to get to know each other at London's Royal Academy School of Art, because their classes and lunchtimes were held separately. But Ernest and Florence kept running into each other at Roberson's Art Supplies in Camden Town and Lyons tea shop across the street from school. Florence, whose grandfather had founded *Punch* magazine, was twenty-four, three years older than Ernest. He found her cleverness and talent greatly appealing.

"Oh my girl," he wrote after they admitted their love. "If I could hold your hand I shouldn't be so troubled and worried about money and things, the same old worry you know, that I shan't get rid of till I *do* something!" By 1902 he had sold his first oil painting and was selling cartoons and drawings to newspapers and magazines. The following year Ernest was commissioned to do a painting for Morden College Chapel, and Florence worked on a mural for Guy's Hospital. Realizing that at last they could manage financially, they bought a double bed and Worcester china dinnerware and were married in 1904.

Ernest remembered his own childhood well and had the knack of seeing things from a child's point of view. His favorite works were the illustrations he drew in the 1920's for A. A. Milne's stories about Christopher Robin and Winnie-the-Pooh and for Kenneth Grahame's *The Wind in the Willows.*

The Shepards settled in tiny Arden Cottage at Shamley Green in Surrey and called each other by their childhood nicknames, "Kip" and "Pie." After their son and daughter were born, they moved to Red Cottage, a larger house, where they continued sketching and painting. Kip used the real Christopher Robin's stuffed toys as models for the animals in Milne's books, but Winnie-the-Pooh was fashioned after "Growler," the chubby bear belonging to Kip's own son, Graham.

## HENRY LOUIS GEHRIG AND ELEANOR TWITCHELL

### *"My Luke"*

THE NEW YORK YANKEES' STAR first baseman may have been an "Iron Horse" on the playing field, but alone with women, Lou was shy and reticent. He and Eleanor had been dating for six years, but he still struggled to find the right words. Finally Eleanor asked, Do you want to propose to me? Yes, he answered, blushing and relieved. Well, I accept! she answered. That afternoon he hit a home run at the stadium!

Lou's mother didn't like his fiancée, but Mrs. Gehrig didn't think any girl was good enough for her boy. She also thought that baseball was "a bunch of nonsense," although she'd grown to accept it. But Lou was only thirty years old. Why did he need to get married? Didn't Mama always take good care of him? If you get married, I won't be at your wedding, she threatened.

So she wasn't invited. Instead, Lou and Eleanor married suddenly on the last day of the 1933 baseball season, in what Eleanor jokingly called the "classiest wedding ever held in Westchester County." Workmen were fixing up their new apartment at 5 Circuit Road, New Rochelle, when the mayor arrived with the marriage license and a motorcycle caravan of cops.

After the short ceremony and a champagne toast to the "coatless groom" and his "besmudged bride," the police escorted Eleanor and Lou to Yankee Stadium. Although he didn't hit any home runs that day, at least he made no errors in the field.

Six years later on Lou Gehrig Day, he said, "When you have a wife who has been a tower of strength and shown more courage than you ever dreamed existed, that's the finest I know." Referring to his serious illness, he added, "I might have had a bad break, but I have an awful lot to live for."

## P. G. WODEHOUSE AND ETHEL NEWTON ROWLEY

### *"Plummie" and his "Bunny"*

PELHAM GRENVILLE, KNOWN AS "PLUM," married Ethel at New York City's Little Church Around the Corner less than two months after they met in 1914. Although the thirty-two-year-old British writer's stories were humorous and lighthearted, he was woefully inexperienced socially and longed to be married. Plum fell for Ethel right away: she was twenty-nine and long-legged, with a delightful zest for life. She also was a widow with a young daughter named Leonora, whom Plum adored and nicknamed "Snorkles."

Like one of the bumbling characters in his comic novels, Plum's proposal of marriage was slightly calamitous. He had a nasty cold, which kept Ethel at arm's length, and when it was time to utter those magic words, "Will you marry me?," Plum began sneezing uncontrollably. Even their wedding ceremony was "marred" when the minister arrived late, apologetic but also jubilant. Sorry I was detained, he said, but I've just made a pile of money in the stock market!

The next day Plum and Ethel headed for the Long Island seashore, where they had spent much of their courtship that summer riding the waves and lying on the beach. In November they moved into an apartment at 375 Central Park West.

"It was an awfully curious thing how everything altered just after we married," Plum said later. Ethel, who was gregarious and social, took charge of his affairs while he concentrated on writing. Besides magazine stories and play adaptations, he also wrote song lyrics for Irving Berlin, Jerome Kern, Cole Porter, and George Gershwin. Eventually Plum wrote more than one hundred novels about lovable characters with zany names like Bingo, Oofy, Pongo, Stiffy, Nobby, and Mugsy. Most famous was Bertie Wooster, a befuddled aristocrat who was invariably rescued from disaster by his levelheaded "gentleman's gentleman," the valet Jeeves.

Plum and Ethel also kept many housepets and established an animal shelter on Long Island.

# OCTOBER

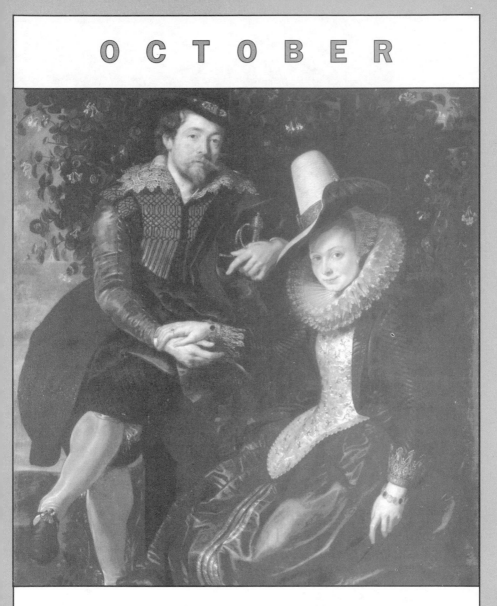

## PETER PAUL RUBENS AND ISABELLA BRANT
*October 3, 1609*

He painted them clasping hands in a bower of honeysuckle, symbols of fidelity and love.

## WILLIAM JENNINGS BRYAN AND MARIE BAIRD

### *"Won, 1880. One, 1884"*

A YEAR BEFORE "MAMIE" MARRIED Will in 1884, the lawyer and future Populist drafted a document certifying that "I . . . do love Marie E. Baird better than . . . any one else in the world . . . I always will love her, will be good to her and contribute as largely as possible to her happiness and usefulness."

They met when Will and other Illinois College men attended a tea hosted by the women's division. The men called the place "Jail for Angels" because they were so strictly watched, but Will managed to chat with Mamie. A year later, when the principal realized that Miss Baird was being courted, he escorted her to the next train home. Right after her train departed from the station, Will, who'd stowed away in the baggage car, sat down beside her and proposed.

They waited four years to marry, until Will was earning more than $500 a year. Just before the wedding, he confessed he'd been rehearsing " 'with all my worldly goods I thee endow' so as to make it duly impressive. If you dare laugh when I say that, I won't kiss you when he tells me to salute my bride."

After honeymooning in St. Louis, the Bryans lived in Illinois. Mamie took care of their home, began raising their children, and studied law under Will's instruction. They moved to Nebraska, where she was admitted to the bar in 1888 and Will was elected to Congress two years later. Subsequently he became a journalist and editor-in-chief of the Omaha *World-Herald.* At thirty-six, he was the Democratic party's presidential nominee; he lost to McKinley, but his fame and influence were ensured.

In some ways Will was ahead of his time, advocating women's suffrage and the regulation of banks and railroads in an era when robber barons were making fortunes. Will and Mamie never forgot the plight of ordinary people.

### JOHN CONSTABLE AND MARIA BICKNELL

*"Nothing that could happen in this world can ever change or abate my love for you"*

MARIA'S GRANDFATHER, THE WEALTHY CHURCH rector of East Bergholt in Sussex, England, threatened to disinherit her if she married that no-account landscape painter in 1809. Since Grandpa controlled all the money in the family, everyone was afraid of him. John's mother gave Grandpa one of John's drawings of his church, hoping to appease him. Instead, he handed John a few coins, saying, "Buy some little article by which you may be reminded of me, when I am no more." But like so many mean-spirited human beings, Grandpa lived on and on.

The Constables' flour mill barely supported the family, let alone a wife for John. He might have made a good living painting portraits, which were popular at that time, instead of the landscapes he preferred. He painted the Constable gardens and mill many times and would also paint Salisbury Cathedral, Hampstead Heath, and other favorite places.

John was not prepared to give up Maria. "Flatford Mill" was accepted by the Royal Academy, and his paintings began to sell. "Be assured we have only to consider our union as an event that must happen, and we shall yet be happy," he wrote Maria.

John's parents died by 1816, leaving their son a small inheritance. Soon afterwards he married Maria at St. Martin-in-the-Fields Church in London—without her grandfather's consent. Friends lent their country house in Dorset for a honeymoon, and John created a series of paintings of Weymouth Bay nearby. One day his pictures would be hung in London's National Gallery and in the Victoria and Albert Museum.

P.S. Grandpa died a few years later, and that's when they discovered he wasn't very rich, after all—but he had managed to intimidate everybody just the same.

## PETER PAUL RUBENS AND ISABELLA BRANT

*A glorious picture of marital love*

PETER PAUL MET ISABELLA AT his brother's wedding in Antwerp in spring, 1609. The thirty-one-year-old Flemish baroque painter was struck by the radiant beauty of his new sister-in-law's nineteen-year-old niece. Isabella's father, Jan, was a wealthy and cultured public servant with a strong knowledge of ancient history. Over the years he became very close to Peter Paul, who adored his Isabella.

She was "an excellent companion, whom one could love—indeed had to love with good reason," wrote Peter Paul. Isabella had "no capricious moods . . . but was all goodness and honesty." She wore a jeweled white satin gown when they married that fall in Antwerp's Abbey of St. Michael. Soon afterward he immortalized the occasion with a meticulously painted double portrait of them seated in a bower of honeysuckle and flowers—popular symbols of love and fidelity. Isabella sits beside her husband, who crosses his legs nonchalantly and leans on a jeweled sword hilt. Her hand rests gently on top of his, and the hem of her crimson gown delicately brushes his shoe. Their clothing is elegant, and they look at us confidently, as if to say, we are pleased with each other and with our lives.

At first they lived with Isabella's father, who provided Peter Paul with a studio large enough for him to paint fifteen-foot-high religious triptychs. He usually painted ample-bodied women with golden hair, but Isabella, by contrast, was slim and dark, with an oval face and pointed chin. She often posed for his Madonnas, and later their children modeled for their father, too.

Fortunately, Peter Paul was well paid for his art, enabling him to design and build a gracious home with classical lines and an Italianate garden filled with trees and flowers. It still stands in Antwerp and can be seen in the backgrounds of many of his pictures.

# OCTOBER 4

## WILLIAM WORDSWORTH AND MARY HUTCHINSON

*"the blessed time of early love"*

"ON MONDAY, 4TH OCTOBER, 1802, my brother William was married to Mary Hutchinson," wrote Dorothy Wordsworth in her journal. That morning she sat by her window, watching William and Mary walk toward Brompton church. Dorothy and William had been extremely close, and although she couldn't bear to witness his wedding, in time she welcomed her sister-in-law into the family fold.

The wedding day was low-keyed, in deference to Dorothy's dejection. The bride and groom received few gifts and thought their friends didn't believe the marriage would last. Dorothy's uncle Henry called William a "vagabond" because he lacked a regular profession, but years later he admitted he had read some of William's poems and thought they were very good.

Mary was sunny, tender, and devoted to William, who called her "a Phantom of delight." Like the Wordsworths, Mary had been orphaned at a young age, and she grew up in her grandparents' care. Now she and Will were each thirty-two, and he had already written remarkable poems, including "Lines Composed a Few Miles Above Tintern Abbey" and "Lucy Gray." Shortly before the nuptials, he wrote "A Farewell" to Dove Cottage, saying "A Gentle Maid . . . Will come to you . . . And love the blessed life that we lead here."

Their marriage lasted forty-eight years. On the rare times that Mary and William were separated, she wrote impassioned notes to "my best beloved, my soul," professing that "every nerve is full of thee." He confessed, "I love thee so deeply and tenderly and constantly . . . that I scarcely can bring my pen to write of anything else." Much of Will's best work, including completion of *The Prelude*, was written after his marriage. Eventually he became poet laureate of England.

## GOWER CHAMPION AND MARJORIE BELCHER

*May I have this dance?*

GOWER SAT BEHIND MARGE IN junior high school in Los Angeles, but the future dance team didn't fall in love until after he returned from coast guard service during World War II. They had met in the ballet school run by Marge's father, Ernest Belcher, soon after Gower and his divorced mother, a dressmaker, came to California from Illinois. Mr. Belcher's star pupils included Shirley Temple, Gwen Verdon, and Cyd Charisse; one day Marge and Gower would also bring fame to his school.

At sixteen, Marge had been Walt Disney's model for the heroine in *Snow White and the Seven Dwarfs*. She also danced in a frilly tutu for cartoonists, in a role later performed by an animated hippo in *Fantasia*. She was fresh-faced, bubbly, and skilled in everything from ballet to tap. As Marjorie Bell, she appeared in the 1939 film *The Story of Vernon and Irene Castle*, not knowing that within ten years she and Gower would become as famous as the Castles had been earlier in the century.

After winning an amateur dance contest, Gower had quit high school and danced in clubs and in bit parts in Hollywood films. Following his coast guard tour of duty, the team of Gower and Bell was born. They both were twenty-six when they married in 1947, soon after Gower's performance in the film *Till the Clouds Roll By*, His mother made all their costumes, including those worn at their smash-hit debut at the Waldorf-Astoria Hotel's Persian Room in New York City. MGM Studios signed the Champions to a film contract, beginning with *Mr. Music* and *Show Boat*. Later they appeared on television variety shows and in a situation comedy, *The Marge and Gower Champion Show*. Gower excelled as a choreographer and director, and Marge also appeared in dramatic roles.

## GLENN MILLER AND HELEN BURGER

### *"In the Mood"*

"TO GLENN, THE MEANEST MAN in the world," Helen wrote on the photograph she gave him in 1926 after he quit the University of Colorado. Glenn had been in dance bands on campus, coming up with incredibly fresh sounds by playing popular tunes in new ways. It was pretty remarkable, especially since he'd failed a first-year course in harmony!

Besides music, Glenn also loved Helen, the serious, soft-spoken young woman he'd met in class. Someday, he promised, they'd get married, but right now he was taking his trombone and heading for California. After two years of long-distance phone calls, letters, and brief reunions, Helen started giving up hope. Perhaps her parents were right and Glenn was "unstable," like most musicians. Had he ever really proposed? She began dating other boys.

Glenn was working on the East Coast in 1928 when he heard that Helen was "practically engaged" to someone else. He sent her a telegram immediately, begging her to take a train to New York and marry him right away. Fortunately, she consented!

They married in a small ceremony and settled into a modest apartment at 30–60 29th Street in Astoria, Queens, with their pet bull terrier, Pops. Home was just a short subway ride from the Manhattan clubs and recording studios where Glenn was a freelance trombonist and arranger. He and Helen managed well financially, but she encouraged him to form his own band, even if it meant giving up a regular paycheck. Blending saxophones and clarinets, the Glenn Miller Orchestra developed unique musical renditions. "Moonlight Serenade" became their theme song. Other smash hits included "In the Mood," "Tuxedo Junction," and "Little Brown Jug." During World War II Glenn formed the U.S. Air Force Band to entertain troops in Europe.

## JOHN ALDEN AND PRISCILLA MULLENS

*A triumph of romantic love*

"IN THE OLD COLONY DAYS, in Plymouth the land of the Pilgrims" begins Longfellow's famous poem, "The Courtship of Miles Standish." Poetic license accounts for some of the details, but the story of a young man who is sent to propose marriage for his older friend and ends up winning the girl himself is charming and believable.

A brutally cold first winter killed many Pilgrims in Plymouth, including Priscilla's family. By the spring of 1621, the colony was quite small, and the nineteen-year-old maiden was living with another family. She was known for her skill at the spinning wheel, and that's where John usually found her when he came calling. He was blond, blue-eyed, and about twenty-two. They had met on the *Mayflower*, where John maintained the ship's water and beer barrels. The ship's Captain Standish was thirty-five and considered middle-aged. Soon after his wife died, he asked John to woo Priscilla for him, prompting her to pose that legendary question: "Why don't you speak for yourself, John?"

Poor John was torn between his loyalty to Miles and his passion for Priscilla! Miles had spoken before John had the chance. But Priscilla's remark startled him, and "Into the open air John Alden, perplexed and bewildered,/Rushed like a man insane, and wandered alone by the seaside." Only after he had made his peace with Miles did John ask Priscilla for her hand.

They were married in a civil ceremony performed by William Bradford, governor of the colony. That summer John and other colonists had built a common house, storerooms, and plank houses with thatched roofs, including a commodious one for himself and Priscilla. Subsequently Miles married, too. Later the two families lived near each other in Duxbury, which they founded, and much later the Aldens' daughter Sarah married the captain's son Alexander.

*Date approximate.

## OSWALD NELSON AND HARRIET HILLIARD

*"The Adventures of Ozzie and Harriet"*

OZZIE PROPOSED TO HARRIET IN the backseat of a sedan in 1935 as they drove across Texas with other members of his dance band. They had met three years earlier when Ozzie was searching for a female vocalist. Harriet—formerly Peggy Lou Snyder, a Des Moines beauty queen—was a specialty dancer and mistress of ceremonies in a restaurant, and "it took me about thirty seconds to decide that she was the girl I was looking for," he wrote in *Ozzie*.

Harriet had "a beautiful face, a fantastic figure, and a wealth of talent and experience." She and Ozzie quickly developed a breezy style, singing boy-girl duets and making lighthearted banter. As they incorporated personal remarks and routines into their performances, Ozzie added extra lyrics to popular songs.

They married at Ozzie's parents' home in Hackensack, New Jersey, in 1935 but didn't take a honeymoon for four years. Right after the wedding Harriet left for Hollywood and a singing role in *Follow the Fleet*. Soon after she returned to New York, she became pregnant with their older son, David.

The Nelsons moved to Hollywood in 1941, after Eric ("Ricky") was born, and kept on working in films. When comedian Red Skelton canceled his radio show to join the army in 1944, *The Adventures of Ozzie and Harriet*—about an average American family—went on the air on October 8, their ninth anniversary. Ozzie wrote most of the scripts, which generally dealt with problems and complications (usually caused and made worse by Ozzie) and resolutions (usually worked out by Harriet). He was forty and she was thirty-five when they started, but they were billed as "America's Favorite Young Couple." Although "1847 Rogers Road" was a fictitious address, the Nelsons' own white clapboard, green-shuttered colonial house in the Hollywood Hills was shown at the start of every show.

## PATRICK HENRY AND DOROTHEA DANDRIDGE

*An eager bridegroom*

BY THE TIME "DOLLY" MARRIED Patrick in 1777, the bold Revolutionary War statesman and orator had already brandished his ivory letter opener in Richmond, Virginia, and staunchly proclaimed, "I know not what course others may take, but as for me, give me liberty, or give me death!"

She was an old friend's daughter and Martha Washington's cousin. Patrick proposed that summer after the Virginia Assembly had adjourned. He spent the next months in special meetings and racing back and forth to Hanover County to see Dolly. Perhaps the forty-one-year-old widowed governor of Virginia feared that his twenty-one-year-old bride-to-be would change her mind. (Hadn't Patrick talked to her of liberty?) The dashing naval war hero John Paul Jones had also been a suitor.

Most couples published church banns announcing their impending nuptials for three consecutive Sundays and then got married. Some paid two pounds for a marriage license and married within days. That's what Patrick wanted: He left Williamsburg on October 7 and rode nearly one hundred miles over bad roads to the Dandridge estate in upper Hanover to marry Dolly two days later.

Marriage to a governor meant a spirited but dignified wedding reception with hearty toasts and glorious feasting. For Patrick, it also meant allying his cause with aristocratic families in favor of the Revolution. After the festivities he and Dolly and children from his first marriage drove to their home in the Governor's Palace at Williamsburg.

"P.H. was perhaps the best husband in the world," wrote his sister Jane's husband, because "it is said that he never took any important step without consulting Dolly." Years later, when Patrick's daughter Anne was about to be married, he told her that "matrimonial happiness does not depend upon wealth . . . but in minds properly tempered and united."

## EDWARD, THE BLACK PRINCE, AND JOAN OF KENT

*"My dearest and truest sweetheart"*

EVER SINCE EDWARD'S BIRTH, HIS parents King Edward III and Queen Philippa had been talking about choosing an appropriate wife for him. Why not a French princess, or the Count of Flanders's daughter? Edward paid little attention to these discussions, preferring to put on his shiny black armor and throw himself into jousting tournaments and military battles. For years he barely noticed "little Jeanette," his fair-haired, sweet-faced second cousin who fluttered about the fourteenth-century court in ermine robes and silk dresses, bringing a smile to everyone's face.

Joan was sociable and merry and soon married off to Sir John Holland. When he died, she was left with vast property holdings and a handsome pension. Many suitors came calling on the thirty-two-year-old widow, who still had a joyful disposition as well as a comely figure.

At thirty, the Black Prince was more handsome, dignified, and courageous than ever, but he was beginning to feel discontented and dejected. He'd played a decisive role at the battle of Poitiers in France, and yet . . . it wasn't enough.

At court, he spoke to Joan about her suitors' proposals. Tears filled her eyes. "I desire none of them," she said. Her heart was already bound to the most chivalrous knight on earth, someone—alas!—whom she could never tell. Edward put his arms around his cousin's shoulders, urging her to confess, who was this knight? Perhaps, if Edward had not been affected by her tears and womanly grace, he never would have heard . . .

They married at Windsor in 1361, overriding his parents' concerns that the match was somewhat unsuitable. Edward became a devoted husband, and Joan never wavered in her love for him. Two years later he was named Prince of Aquitaine and they moved to the south of France.

## WILLIAM JEFFERSON CLINTON AND HILLARY RODHAM

*"I loved being with her"*

BILL AND HILLARY WERE MARRIED in 1975 by a minister named Nixon, just a year after she worked on the House Judiciary Committee's impeachment inquiry of President Nixon. The Clintons had met four years before at Yale Law School. Bill first saw Hillary in class, and she noticed him in the lounge. He spotted her again in the library. Usually Bill was easygoing and loquacious, but all he did was stare. Finally Hillary walked up to him and said, If we're going to keep looking at each other, I ought to introduce myself. Bill was so stunned, he couldn't remember his own name! "That's exactly how we met," he's said. "And we've been together ever since."

After Hillary left Washington, she taught at the University of Arkansas Law School and ran a legal aid clinic. Bill practiced law and taught at the law school, too, but his goal was running for state office. The following year he began campaigning for state attorney general.

In summer, 1975, Hillary went home to Illinois, trying to sort out her feelings for Bill. He met her plane when she returned to Fayetteville in August and drove her into town. En route they passed a small brick cottage that she'd admired on California Street. Bill said that he'd bought it and furnished it . . . right down to flowered sheets on an antique bed. "So you're going to have to marry me!" he asserted, laughing.

After years of wanting no one else, that was all it took to convince Hillary. She and Bill were married in their own living room and celebrated with hundreds of friends and relatives at an Arkansas state senator's home. The bride wore a Victorian-style cream-colored wedding dress she had bought the day before.

Three years later Bill became the nation's youngest governor since the Depression. And that was just the beginning!

## LOUIS ARMSTRONG AND LUCILLE WILSON

*"My house is filled with happiness"*

AFTER THREE FAILED MARRIAGES, THE forty-year-old jazz trumpeter and singer finally found someone who was *good* for him: "It was love at first sight with Lucille because of the color of her skin," said the New Orleans–born musician. "When she danced at the Cotton Club she was the darkest in the company." His band had begun a six-month stint, and "Satchmo" couldn't take his eyes off twenty-four-year-old Lucille.

Even then he'd mop his overheated brow with a white handkerchief as he blasted away at his trumpet, rousing the black and white nightclub crowd into a joyful frenzy. Louis dated Lucille a few times, although she discouraged him; getting involved with a married man always meant trouble.

So he got a divorce and convinced her to marry him in 1942. The following year, when Louis was on the road, Lucille purchased a modest house on 107th Street in Corona, Queens, New York, and told Louis about it on the telephone. Hotels were perfectly fine places to live, he said; he didn't need a home.

When he arrived, he told his cabdriver to wait outside while he checked out the place. But in a few minutes Louis was beaming, and he invited the cabbie to join them for dinner! Once again Lucille had Louis's best interests at heart. Most of the time she stayed out of his professional life, although she traveled with him whenever possible. In 1950 they had a private audience with Pope Pius XII, who asked Louis if they had any children. "No, your Holiness," Louis answered. "But we keep on tryin'!"

In 1947 Louis began performing with other jazz all-stars and developed a new group of fans among the younger, postwar generation. The popularity of his 1964 gravel-voiced rendition of "Hello, Dolly!" has outlasted many Beatles hits.

## HARRY ELLIS DICKSON AND JANE GOLDBERG

*"my anchor, my protector, my nurturer, my life"*

HARRY AND JANE'S 1935 WEDDING ceremony lasted less than three minutes, causing the groom's mother to wonder, were they "really married?" They'd asked Rabbi Stephen Wise, who had officiated in his study at New York's Free Synagogue, to "make it as short as possible," and that's exactly what he did.

It didn't take the future violinist of the Boston Symphony Orchestra much longer than that to fall in love with Jane four years before, after he arrived in Berlin to study music. His teachers at Boston's New England Conservatory of Music had warned the twenty-three-year-old musician not to get romantically involved. Concentrate on your violin, they told him.

But Harry met Jane at a party and was immediately "smitten," he wrote years later in *Beating Time: A Musician's Memoir*. Jane was American, but she'd lived abroad for so long that her German and French surpassed her English. She was nineteen and a social worker at a home for retarded children outside Berlin. She and Harry attended concerts, the theater, and the opera, and he serenaded Jane privately with sweet melodies on his violin.

In 1933 they returned to America when the Nazis took over Germany. Harry supervised orchestras for the WPA in Boston. Jane worked for an orphanage in New York. When she visited Harry in Boston, he proposed in Franklin Park. After their very quick wedding they settled in Boston, where Harry soon began his lifelong association with the Boston Symphony Orchestra, also becoming assistant conductor of the Boston Pops.

Twenty years later Harry and Jane returned to Berlin and visited his former German landlady. Frau Tils wasn't surprised that they were married; she'd known from the beginning that they were meant for each other.

## BEATRIX POTTER AND WILLIAM HEELIS

### *"My Willie"*

SHORTLY BEFORE BEATRIX MARRIED WILLIAM in 1913, the well-known children's book author wrote *The Tale of Pigling Bland*. It was her only love story, charming and somewhat autobiographical, about a pig who's locked up with another pig named Pigwig. When the two pigs escape, they race "over the hills and far away," hand in hand and in love.

The forty-seven-year-old writer knew about restrictions: All her life, her parents had limited her freedom. Beatrix taught herself to draw, paint, and write stories. When she was forty, with the proceeds from sales of *The Tale of Peter Rabbit*, she bought herself a seventeenth-century cottage and working farm in England's Lake District.

As Beatrix's wealth increased, she asked William, a slightly younger country lawyer, to find more properties for her. He was fascinated by the London writer who loved the north country as much as the "natives," and he corresponded with Beatrix regularly. But when they became engaged in 1912, her parents objected strongly. Her brother Bertram was rarely home these days. If Beatrix married, who would take care of them in their declining years?

Bertram confessed that he had been married secretly for the past seven years, which explained his frequent (and long) absences. If his sister wanted to marry, no one should stop her! That winter Beatrix became very ill and was bedridden for weeks. Gradually her parents' feelings changed, and as Beatrix wrote about Pigling Bland, she also began planning her wedding in the fall.

She and William married at St. Mary Abbot's church, Kensington, and settled down at Castle Farm, one of her country properties, where they raised prizewinning sheep. Although Beatrix insisted that Pigling Bland and "the portrait of two pigs arm and arm—looking at the sunrise—is not a portrait of me and Mr. Heelis," it's clear that their love inspired her delightful tale.

## GERALD R. FORD AND ELIZABETH BLOOMER

*"standing by my side, as she always has"*

"WE CAN'T GET MARRIED UNTIL next fall and I can't tell you why," "Jerry" told "Betty" when he proposed in February 1948. The thirty-five-year-old Michigan lawyer had decided to run for Congress but had promised the local Republican party that he wouldn't announce his candidacy until June.

Right from the beginning, Betty always trusted Jerry. Unlike her first husband, Jerry was unaffected, honest, and sincere. Years later, when he became the thirty-eighth president, his forthright nature helped to heal the nation after the Watergate scandals.

They were married at Grace Episcopal Church in Grand Rapids two weeks before election day. Betty wore a dark satin dress and carried a large bouquet of roses. Some guests remembered that the groom, who'd been totally distracted by the upcoming election, showed up wearing one black shoe and one brown one, but Jerry always insisted that his shoes had been the same color . . . until he stepped in mud outside the church door.

The honeymoon lasted only a few days and included political rallies. Jerry resumed his campaigning with Betty, who took time off from her job as a department store fashion coordinator. Although many midwesterners frowned on divorce, they still voted for Jerry and sent him to Washington.

In January 1977, right before Jerry's presidential term of office ended, he and Betty returned to the White House after attending a farewell party. The Marine Band members were there, so Jerry took his first lady's hand and asked for a last dance. They spun around the floor to the bittersweet tune, "Thanks for the Memory," as friends and supporters appeared on cue and began dancing around them. Betty "gave a gasp of surprise and then tears came to her eyes. . . . Seeing her so happy was one of the greatest joys of my life," Jerry recalled afterward.

## JOAN SUTHERLAND AND RICHARD BONYNGE

*"La Stupenda" and her "Svengali"*

BY THE TIME THE AUSTRALIAN-BORN musicians married in 1954, Richard was devoting himself to guiding Joan's career as a coloratura soprano. "It was clear that hers was the greater talent," the gifted pianist realized, and "helping her would be a full-time occupation."

They met as teenagers in Sydney, where he played the piano as she sang for the ladies of the Queen Victoria Club. Richard always loved opera, especially nineteenth-century bel canto operas, and Joan had a perfect set of vocal cords. She debuted at the Sydney Opera House in 1947 and came to London four years later. Richard, a student at the Royal Academy of Music, convinced Joan to try becoming a dramatic soprano instead of a contralto. Easy for you to say, she laughed. You make music with your fingers; I have to do it with my throat!

Joan's mother feared that her daughter's voice could be ruined, but she permitted Joan to work with Richard. He wouldn't accept payment, so they began inviting him to dinner. Soon he was at their flat daily, helping Joan prepare for her Covent Garden audition. He proposed after they decided he would move into their home. "This is silly," he told Joan. "You know your mother isn't going to like me living here like this. Why don't we get married?" They did, at a Methodist church on the following Saturday, although few people—including Joan's mother—knew until afterwards.

Joan, who was twenty-seven, carried red carnations and wore a red velvet dress with a large gray hat. Richard was twenty-four and wore a gray suit and a large bow tie. They celebrated afterward with champagne and homemade apple teacake. The groom's parents were thrilled, and even Joan's mother accepted the situation. She cabled, "You naughty children. Watch yourselves. Love, Mum."

## RUBE GOLDBERG AND IRMA SEEMAN

*"I'm the guy"*

IN 1915, WHEN IRMA MET Rube at a charity dinner at Delmonico's restaurant in Manhattan, his cartoons were syndicated in newspapers nationwide and he earned more than many corporation presidents. But that didn't impress Irma, whose wealthy father owned the White Rose Tea and Grocery Company. What mattered to the twenty-one-year-old Ethical Culture School graduate were Rube's good looks, self-confidence, and sweet nature. She also liked his animated film spoof, *The Boob Weekly*—"all the news that nobody wants to hear."

The thirty-two-year-old artist courted Irma in his cartoons. She symbolized beauty and charm, while he was just an ordinary guy, wooing his beloved dreamboat by strumming guitars underneath her window or performing other attention-getting tricks. Rube's best jokes were always about himself or other poor "boobs" struggling through life.

The night before their 1916 wedding, Rube went drinking with some friends and ended up in jail for disorderly conduct. He managed to convince the cops that he was getting married in the morning, and they released him just in time for the ceremony. It took a two-week trip to Jamaica to soothe his somewhat hysterical bride.

Irma's clothing, telephone conversations, and opinions inspired her artistic husband, as did married life and the birth of their two sons. Nagging, unattractive women in Rube's cartoons were now replaced by bright young flappers with interesting ideas. Children became precocious and highly entertaining, and Rube began supporting women's right to vote.

His humor was best expressed in a unique blend of cartoon and commentary. He worked alone, often in their West 75th Street town house, with Irma as his only critic. One day Rube's name would be in the dictionary to describe a contrivance that "by extremely complex roundabout means" (pulleys, ropes, dogs, revolvers, brooms, and you-name-its) achieves what could have been done simply.

## JOSEPH HAYNE RAINEY AND "MME. SUZETTE"

*Together . . . through the best and worst times*

"THE PREVAILING SPIRIT OF THE South is either to rule or ruin," said Joseph in 1872, two years after he became the first African-American congressman from South Carolina during the Reconstruction Era. Ten years earlier Joseph could have entered the Capitol only as a servant; now he was speaking on the floor of the House and would serve four consecutive terms. *All* Americans needed the federal government's protection from the Ku Klux Klan, he insisted, convincing his peers to enforce the 1866 Civil Rights Act and the Fourteenth Amendment.

Joseph's wife, Susan, beamed with pride. They'd been through so much since marrying in Philadelphia in 1859. She was an accomplished dressmaker from the West Indies who spoke French and called herself "Mme. Suzette." Joseph's slave parents had purchased their family's freedom in Georgetown, South Carolina, and provided him with an education. He was twenty-seven when he went "up north" and met and married Susan. That October, John Brown's raid on Harpers Ferry was on everyone's mind. No one knew when slavery would end, but at last it did seem possible.

Joseph and Susan settled in Charleston, where he became a barber. Three years later, when the Confederate army began drafting free black men, the Raineys fled on a blockade-running ship to Bermuda, which had abolished slavery. Joseph opened a barber shop on Tucker's Lane in St. George, offering services "executed in artistic style." As "Mme. Suzette, Dress and Cloak Maker," Susan introduced the latest fashions and quickly developed a fine clientele and reputation.

Joseph's shop became a meeting place for sailors bringing news about America's Civil War. After it ended in 1865, Joseph and Susan headed for home. With faith in government and political action, he ran for office and became an active proponent of civil rights legislation.

*Date approximate.

## FRANK GILBRETH AND LILLIAN MOLLER

*Cheaper by the Dozen*

WHEN LILLIAN MARRIED FRANK IN 1904, he said he wanted six sons and six daughters. She'd been working on her doctorate in psychology and wanted a career as well as motherhood. "How on earth" would that be possible? Don't worry, said her confident thirty-five-year-old husband. "We teach management, and we shall have to practice it."

He'd already invented a gravity mixer for cement and a moving scaffold that enabled bricklayers to work more productively. He and Lillian became known as "efficiency experts," establishing industrial engineering and management sciences. Their ideas also led to improved services for the disabled, and streamlined kitchens with labor-saving devices such as step-on trash cans and refrigerator door shelves.

They had met in 1903 at the Boston City Library. Lillian, who was twenty-five, had come from California with other young women and a chaperone on their way to Europe. Frank—the chaperone's cousin—showed them the sights, including M.I.T.'s Lowell Laboratory, which he had constructed ahead of deadline. The more the blue-eyed young man spoke about his time-and-motion studies, the more captivated Lillian became. He was at the dock in New York when her ship returned in the fall and escorted her to the theater—unchaperoned for the first time in her life. At Christmastime Frank came to California and proposed to Lillian on the Golden Gate Bridge.

They were married on a Wednesday (Lillian's mother's "lucky day") at her parents' Oakland home and traveled by train to Manhattan, after stopping at the St. Louis World's Fair. Later they moved to Montclair, New Jersey, with their growing brood. In 1948 two of their children wrote a book about their family, in which everyone participated in decisions and housekeeping, and kept track of work with charts and a follow-up system. There even was a "birthday gift buyer" whose job also included remembering when everyone's birthday occurred.

N.B. See November 27 for another October 19 story.

## BENJAMIN HARRISON AND CAROLINE LAVINIA SCOTT

*"A pious moonlight dude"*

BEN WAS SEVENTEEN IN 1850 when he fell in love with Carrie at Miami University of Ohio. As the grandson of the ninth president (and the future twenty-third President, with Carrie by his side), Ben took his schoolwork seriously and planned to become a lawyer.

Carrie's father ran the female academy affiliated with the all-men's college. He locked his school gates every evening until Carrie convinced him that get-togethers with the "men of Miami" might be a wholesome idea. Soon the good-natured young man with a sandy mustache began dropping by and taking Dr. Scott's brown-haired, outgoing daughter for buggy rides. They talked about music and art—her greatest passions—and attended a dancing party that her parents would have considered "scandalous" if they'd found out about it. Within a year the fellow whom his friends called the "pious moonlight dude" was secretly engaged to Carrie.

Ben studied law in Cincinnati after graduation, and Carrie taught music and sewing in Oxford. He missed her terribly and pestered the post office clerks daily to make sure he got all her letters. Love was a "mysterious disease," Ben said. The separation made Carrie sad and exhausted as well.

Dr. Scott married them in the family's front parlor on a cool autumn morning in 1853. Carrie wore a gray traveling dress, and Ben wore a black frock coat over a black satin vest. After the wedding breakfast they left for The Point, the Harrison family's home outside Cincinnati.

By 1854 they had settled in Indianapolis. Ben practiced law and allied himself with the Republican party's antislavery group. Less than a week after their wedding, Ben wrote that Carrie "is now sitting at the fire plying her needle. . . . Her presence and the consciousness that she is my wife . . . afford an infinitude of quiet happiness."

## SIR WALTER RALEGH AND ELIZABETH THROCKMORTON

*"sweet empress of my heart"*

WHEN QUEEN ELIZABETH FOUND OUT that her favorite knight—oh, Ralegh! her gallant and loyal (until this!) captain of the Guard—had secretly married one of her ladies-in-waiting in 1591, she imprisoned them in the Tower of London.

The Virgin Queen was proud and vain, and almost twenty years older than Walter. He was about twenty-nine, six feet tall, intelligent, bold, and muscular when he caught the queen's eye ten years earlier by placing his cloak over a muddy path to protect her royal feet. She rewarded him with a new wardrobe, honors, and extensive privileges. He became her Oracle and Wit, as well as a naval hero, New World explorer, statesman, historian, and poet.

Walter's platonic verses to his queen were read frequently at court, but now he was penning private lines filled with sexual allusions and passionate descriptions of "wanton kisses," "violet breath and lips of jelly"—for "Bess." Their romance had been fraught with danger from the beginning. At twenty-seven, blue-eyed, blond Bess was no empty-headed maiden but an accomplished, witty, and graceful woman who'd been serving the queen for years and was currently her maid of honor. Bess and Walter saw each other often, but usually under Elizabeth's watchful eyes. Hadn't they sworn their allegiance to their queen? She thought they loved her! Instead, they had been bribing guards and sneaking away to make love.

They bore the consequences of their love bravely. After Bess became pregnant, she and Walter were married in a secret ceremony in autumn. Wagging tongues at court may have given them away, but Elizabeth didn't react publicly until late spring, after Bess's son was born. Enraged and deeply hurt, she locked up her traitorous servants. Several months later she released them. Walter and Bess fled to his estate at Sherborne in Dorset, for what would be their happiest days together.

*Date approximate.

## CESAR CHAVEZ AND HELEN FABELA

*Valiente y constante, for each other and La Causa*

THE FUTURE LEADER OF MIGRANT farmworkers was fifteen when he met Helen at an ice cream shop in Delano, California, in 1942. Cesar had endured another backbreaking day picking crops in the San Joaquin Valley with other Mexican-American migrant laborers when he noticed a girl with flowers in her hair. Helen was fourteen and worked after school in a grocery store. She thought Cesar was handsome, although his dark eyes seemed sad. Ever since his family lost their Yuma, Arizona, farm and became migrant workers, he had attended dozens of different schools. Now Cesar had quit school altogether. He married Helen in Delano in 1948 after he returned from service in the navy.

Their first "home" was a one-room shack without running water or heat in a migrant labor camp. They left, going wherever work could be found picking crops. They tried sharecropping but couldn't make a living. For a while they lived in *Sal Si Puedes* ("Escape if You Can"), a San Jose barrio, but work was scarce and sporadic. By the time three of their eight children were born, Cesar had become a grassroots union organizer. Later he said, "If you're outraged at conditions, then you can't possibly be free or happy until you devote all your time to changing them."

In 1962 the National Farm Workers Association was established to help members find decent work and housing. Helen kept the books and managed the credit union. The association grew over the next eight years, organizing nonviolent strikes, marches, and consumer boycotts of grapes. Cesar fasted for "*La Causa*," and Helen was arrested on picket lines. In 1970 contracts were signed with the biggest producers of California table grapes, setting fair wages, mandating increases and picking bonuses, and health insurance for workers, and prohibiting the use of many pesticides.

## SARAH JOSEPHA BUELL AND DAVID HALE

*"unbroken happiness"*

IN 1813 MOST SINGLE MEN in Newport, New Hampshire, kept their distance from the local schoolteacher, Sarah Buell, who always wanted to talk about philosophy and literature. Someday she would become the first woman editor of *Godey's Ladies' Magazine*, but at twenty-four, Sarah was well on her way to becoming a spinster until she met David, a brilliant young attorney from a neighboring village who'd recently hung up his shingle in town.

David started dropping by the Rising Sun Tavern, owned by Sarah's father, who introduced him to his daughter. Soon David and Sarah were exchanging books and spending all their free time together. With David's encouragement, Sarah also wrote poetry and stories.

The day before her twenty-fifth birthday, Sarah married David in her father's tavern, and they moved into a white frame house facing the village green. "We commenced, soon after our marriage, a system of study and reading . . . from 8 o'clock until 10—two hours in twenty-four. How I enjoyed those hours!" she wrote. They studied French, natural sciences, the classics, and writing, for David had "that combination of intellectual and moral powers which make the perfectly balanced mind. . . . To me, the period of our union was one of unbroken happiness."

Five years later Sarah was dying from consumption when David bundled her into their gig, took her for an extended ride through the mountains, and cured her with plenty of fresh air and wild grapes. Sarah ate grapes for the rest of her long life; like her beloved David, the fruit gave her strength to achieve more than most women of her day. She became an abolitionist, reformer, and champion of women's rights, and in 1863 she convinced President Lincoln to establish "a national day of Thanksgiving."

Not everything Sarah wrote was high-minded and serious; "Mary Had a Little Lamb" was composed simply for her children's amusement.

## ALICE THOMPSON AND WILFRID MEYNELL

*"My sweet sweet Wilfrid"*

ALICE WAS A WELL-KNOWN AND respected poet in Victorian England by the time she was twenty-eight. Soon after returning from a holiday in Tuscany, she met Wilfrid, a literary critic and journalist, at an afternoon party in London. He'd just read *Preludes,* Alice's first published volume of poetry, and lauded her particularly for "The Garden":

> *Come, my own,*
> *Into thy garden; thine be happy hours*
> *Among my fairest thoughts, my tallest flowers. . . ."*

Wilfrid was fascinated by Alice. They began exchanging sonnets as well as lengthy letters in which she stated, "I should like never to receive any kisses but those I shall never part with." They became engaged on New Year's Day, 1877, and were married the following fall by the bishop of Nottingham, an old friend.

While rearing eight children, Alice continued writing essays and poetry and working with Wilfrid on the two periodicals he edited, *Merry England* and the *Weekly Register.* They labored tirelessly together in satisfying comradeship as editors, authors (often using pen names), and proofreaders, and still managed to give time to humanitarian causes, especially women's suffrage.

Years later, their children would recall how hectic Thursday—deadline day—always was in their home at Palace Court, London. Hectic? Perhaps, but also filled with the keen sense of purpose and fulfillment.

"To W.M.," Alice wrote, dedicating her poem "At Night." One stanza reads:

> *Oh, which are they that come through sweetest light*
> *Of all these homing birds?*
> *Which with the straightest and the swiftest flight?*
> *Your words to me, your words!*

---

*Date approximate.

## JOHN ADAMS AND ABIGAIL SMITH

### *"Lysander and Diana"*

THE FUTURE PRESIDENT WAS A twenty-seven-year-old stocky, fair-haired, struggling lawyer when Mary Smith's fiancé brought him along to Weymouth parsonage, south of Boston. Reverend Smith's middle daughter, Abigail, was clever and petite, with an oval face and luminous, wide-spaced eyes. She lacked John's college education, but she had read all the books in her father's extensive library and enjoyed discussing everything with the brilliant Harvard graduate.

She and John were terrific letter-writers, adopting pen names from ancient history and mythology, as many young people did in colonial America. Abigail was "Diana," "spreading Light and Beauty and Glory all around her," said John. He called himself "Lysander," after the great Spartan admiral and statesman. Within a year they were talking about marriage, with John declaring that he was "ready to *have you* at any Time."

Shortly before their wedding in 1764, John predicted that their life together would be long and happy. He wrote, "You shall polish and refine my sentiments of Life and Manners, banish all the unsocial and ill natured Particles in my Composition, and form me to that happy Temper, that can reconcile a quick Discernment with a perfect Candor."

That summer Abigail purchased a white challis wedding gown embroidered with tiny red flowers. She was almost twenty and John was twenty-nine when they were married by her father in the Weymouth meeting house. A lively reception followed, at which the men smoked, drank, and shared indelicate wedding-night stories while the women sat in another room, gossiping and giving the new bride advice.

John and Abigail moved into an old saltbox cottage on ten acres of land across the way from his widowed mother's home in Braintree, now Quincy. John set up his law office in the front room so he could be close to Abigail all day long.

## NOAH WEBSTER AND REBECCA GREENLEAF

*wed'ding (wed'ing) n.—nuptial ceremony,*
*nuptial festivities, marriage*

NOAH DIDN'T HESITATE TO GO to Philadelphia when Ben Franklin invited him in 1787. *Webster's Spelling Book* was the first publication devoted to language of the new United States, and both men were highly pleased. "Becca," a wealthy Boston merchant's daughter, met Noah at a holiday party and was impressed by his intelligence and drive. The "walking question mark" (his nickname at Yale) was fascinated by words; they were his strongest passion . . . besides Becca.

Shortly before she went home that summer, Noah confessed his growing love in a letter: "*Without you* the world is all alike to me; and *with you* any part will be agreeable. . . . You must go, and I must be separated from all that is dear to me."

He worked hard, writing pamphlets and giving lectures in support of the recently completed Constitution of the United States. Marriage would have to wait for the struggling writer whose income was sparse and erratic. "I sometimes go to dances and other parties, where I see ladies," he wrote, "but there is not a Becca Greenleaf among them: no such tenderness, such delicacy, such sentiment, such unaffected goodness."

If his future brother-in-law hadn't lent Noah money in 1789, he could not have afforded to marry Becca. She was twenty-three and he was thirty-one when they married in her parents' home. Fifteen years later Becca encouraged Noah to devote himself full-time to linguistics and lexicography, even though it meant financial risk. In his upstairs study overlooking the future site of Amherst College, which he subsequently helped establish, Noah worked at a wide semicircular table piled high with reference books, grammars and small dictionaries, and a bowl of fruit and nuts, refilled regularly by Becca. Three years later he completed his *Compendious Dictionary of the English Language*.

## EDWARD R. MURROW AND JANET BREWSTER

*"Love and luck"*

"YOUR SON EDWARD JOYFULLY ANNOUNCES the acceptance of Miss Janet Huntington Brewster of a personal permanent fellowship, providing board, room and tuition, from next summer till death do us part," Ed wrote in 1933. The twenty-five-year-old future radio news commentator and analyst knew just the right words to please his parents. They were very happy, especially since Janet's photo implied that she didn't "look like a flapper."

They'd met in New Orleans at a convention of student activists. Ed was twenty-four and Janet two years younger. Afterward they corresponded regularly. He was glad that his blond "Hunka" (so nicknamed because Janet was part-Swedish) also cared about social and political issues. By the time they were engaged, Ed was working for an educational exchange program for students that set up international debates among scholars and also helped displaced German-Jewish scientists and academic refugees come to the States.

With the impassioned honesty and moral tone that infused his radio broadcasts through the London blitz and other World War II crises, he wrote Janet, "Above all else, there must be nothing cheap and nothing small in our lives. They must burn with a clear bright light."

An Episcopal minister married them at the Brewsters' Middletown, Connecticut, home. They honeymooned by driving to the West Coast and parts of Mexico. A year later they moved to London, where Ed managed Columbia Broadcasting's European news bureau. Hiring such correspondents as William L. Shirer and Eric Sevareid, he collected information that became invaluable once war was declared and Ed broadcast eyewitness accounts from London. Janet assisted him by reporting on such matters as the evacuation of British children. She also headed the Bundles for Britain relief program.

## ÉDOUARD MANET AND SUZANNE LEENHOFF

*"Ma cherie Suzanne"*

"MANET HAS JUST ANNOUNCED THE most unexpected news," said his poet-friend Charles Baudelaire in 1863. "He's leaving this evening for Holland, from which he will bring back *his wife!* . . . It seems that this wife is not only beautiful but very good and also a very talented musician." She also had been Édouard's mistress for the past twelve years.

The thirty-one-year-old painter knew how to keep a secret. Édouard first met the fair, blue-eyed Dutch pianist thirteen years earlier, when his parents hired her to teach music to their three sons. It was the teacher, not her sonatas, who captivated Édouard. "Maman" figured out very quickly what was going on, but no one ever told "Papa," who would have been horrified by his son's indiscretion.

Papa died in 1862, leaving Édouard enough money to paint and support a family, which was particularly important because one of the wedding guests was eleven-year-old Léon-Édouard Koëlla, known as Suzanne's younger brother but probably their son. Léon appeared in many of his father's paintings, including "Reading," in which he reads to his mother in their Paris apartment.

Although Édouard couldn't bear scandals in his private life, he was perfectly comfortable with them in his art. The year he and Suzanne married, his painting "Olympia" was accepted by the Salon, a welcome surprise after the rejection of his magnificent and equally sensational "Luncheon on the Grass" two years earlier. In "Olympia," a blatantly nude young woman reclines on a bed, wearing nothing but a flower in her hair, a bracelet, a black velvet ribbon around her neck, and one silk slipper. The painting was extremely realistic, causing many Parisians to call it immoral.

Suzanne worshiped Édouard and deeply respected his work. His devotion was equally strong. "I kiss you as much as I love you," he wrote long after their love affair began.

## THOMAS ASSHETON SMITH AND MATILDA WEBBER

*"Tally-ho, Matilda!"*

MATILDA AND TOM MET AT a fox hunt, which wasn't surprising since all he ever did was ride with his hounds. Away from his horses and stables, Tom cared little for what he wore, but in his bright red riding coat, black hat, and boots, the immensely wealthy sportsman and squire of a huge Hampshire estate looked particularly spiffy.

Matilda was from Binfield Lodge in Berkshire. She loved the hunt almost as much as Tom. They decided to marry in late October 1827, when the hunting season began. From then on, they hosted lavish get-togethers for foxhunting friends, including the Duke of Wellington. After eating beef pasties, hashed mutton, and other breakfast delights, riders mounted their horses and prepared to take off in pursuit of "Reynard."

The first half of the nineteenth century were the "golden years" of foxhunting, before the rise of wire fences and railways that cut across open fields. By the time Tom married Matilda, he was known as a great leaper, guiding his horse over the hedges at full gallop. He also had earned the title Master of the Hounds.

Matilda and Tom remodeled and expanded the stables at his estate, Tedworth, to accommodate more than fifty horses. They built airy and spacious kennels for one hundred hounds, including Tarquin, Trimbush, Trimmer, and Tomboy, who could always be counted on to bring home the fox's head. A glass-enclosed conservatory that was 315 feet long, 40 feet wide, and high enough for birds to fly indoors was also constructed on the grounds, so Tom and Matilda could ride in the winter! He kept riding at least four times a week into his eighties, sometimes putting his head into a bucket of water if he began to procrastinate.

They were lucky, he told Matilda. Life was good, and it was "Thank God for everything!"

## FEDERICO FELLINI AND GIULIETTA MASINA

*"Fefe" and his "Ciccina"*

THE FUTURE FILM DIRECTOR AND his favorite leading lady met in Rome during the harrowing days of World War II. "Fefe" was a twenty-three-year-old radio and film scriptwriter whose military records had been destroyed in a bombing, enabling him to avoid conscription and usually elude German occupation troops. "Ciccina" was twenty-two, a university student, actress, and pantomimist.

A few years earlier Fefe's sketches about a married couple named Cico and Pallina had formed the basis for a humorous radio series. When plans developed to turn it into a film, he decided to meet the actress currently playing Pallina.

Introducing himself to her on the telephone, he said, "I am fed up with life, but before I die I would like to see what my heroine looks like." Ciccina hoped he was kidding but agreed to have lunch, rather than "risk having a corpse on my conscience."

The young couple found a tiny haven of peace and romance in each other's arms amid wartime bombings and destruction. They were married in 1943 by a monsignor living next door to Ciccina's aunt on the Via Lutezia. Within a week Fefe escaped capture when he and other Italians were rounded up by the Germans near the Spanish Steps. In a scene as heart-stopping as those he would write and direct, Fefe hopped off the transport truck and boldly embraced a German officer as if they were long-lost friends—before disappearing into an ancient alley.

After the war Fefe and Roberto Rossellini used stolen Nazi cameras to film *Open City,* a powerful antifascist story. More extraordinary films followed, including the Oscar-winning *La Strada,* starring Ciccina as Gelsomina, *La Dolce Vita, 8½,* and *Amarcord.* "When you marry in your early twenties, you grow up together," Fefe said, adding, "Giulietta has told me a few times . . . that I didn't grow up at all."

## WILL DURANT AND IDA KAUFMAN

*"My dear sweet terrible beloved"*

THE FUTURE AUTHORS OF THE award-winning *The Story of Civilization* and other "biographies of mankind" met and fell in love in 1912, when twenty-six-year-old Will taught English at a progressive school in Manhattan and Ida was his teenaged student. He had recently quit the Catholic seminary and "seemed more a poet than a teacher," said Ida, a precocious Ukrainian Jewish immigrant enthralled by Will's passions for Whitman and Shakespeare. She was bursting with opinions and questions. As she recalled later in their *Dual Autobiography,* although Will was older, he was very naive, "and here I was, close at hand, crazy with life and energy, and physically in full bloom."

Will quit teaching but continued seeing Ida, after convincing Mrs. Kaufman that he was trustworthy. The young couple spent long afternoons holding hands and sitting in the park. Finally Will said he had to get away to think. He rode 150 miles to Albany on a bicycle, traded it in for a canoe, and paddled back to New York City on the Hudson River. It was storming when Will arrived. Exhausted and wet, he stumbled into the Kaufmans' apartment and fell asleep at Ida's feet. "When he awoke," she recalled, "we quietly assumed that we were pledged to each other forever."

Swinging her roller skates over one shoulder, Ida met Will at City Hall and married him in 1913. Afterward she tried teaching Will how to skate, but he said it was more difficult than reading Plato. Ida's mother, who ran a newsstand near Grand Central Station, encouraged them to live with her until they could manage financially. Ida continued her schooling, and Will, who lectured to help support his "Ariel" and their family, won a scholarship to pursue graduate studies at Columbia University.

# NOVEMBER

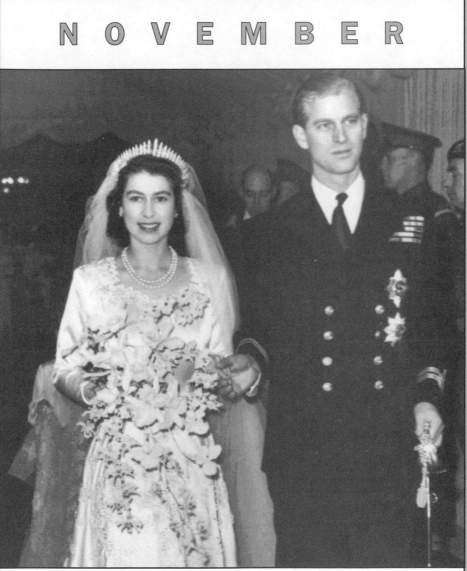

## PRINCESS ELIZABETH OF THE UNITED KINGDOM
## AND PHILIP, DUKE OF EDINBURGH

*November 20, 1947*

In their first unposed picture together, "Elizabeth Alexandra Mary Windsor" and
"Lieutenant Philip Mountbatten" exit Westminster Abbey.

## AGNES SURRIAGE AND
## SIR CHARLES HENRY FRANKLAND

### *Local girl makes good*

PULLING YOUR LOVER OUT OF earthquake rubble may not be the only way to get him to marry you but it worked for Agnes in 1755.

Initially she captured the baron's heart with a soulful glance. In the summer of 1742 "Harry," the twenty-six-year-old British collector of customs at the port of Boston, dropped by Marblehead's Fountain Inn, where Agnes was scrubbing the tavern floor. She was sixteen and winsome, with long black ringlets, but her dress was skimpy and her feet were bare. Harry was enthralled and offered to buy shoes for Agnes. He also convinced her impoverished parents to let him take their fair daughter to Boston and pay for her education.

After a few years she probably became his mistress, and they moved to a grand house in Hopkinton. Agnes's sweet devotion suited Harry's sensitive and scholarly nature perfectly. They loved each other dearly but knew that his aristocratic family would never approve of a marriage.

A decade later they sailed to England and then on to Lisbon, Portugal. On the morning of November 1, 1755, an earthquake rocked the city. Thousands of people, including Harry, were buried in ruins. Agnes searched for him frantically and finally extricated him from piles of masonry and debris. Possibly Harry had been struck in the head by a large rock, because the traumatic event shocked him to his senses. They *would* marry, he declared, regardless of his family's objections!

Thankfully, his parents also came to *their* senses; Agnes, who had saved their precious son, became their beloved daughter-in-law. Back in Boston, Lord Frankland and his new lady moved into a mansion on Garden Court Street in the north end of town and became leaders of Boston society. Subsequently they returned to Lisbon, where he served as the British consul-general.

*Date approximate.

## MILTON ABORN AND MARJORIE PRESSER

*Love for light opera, and each other*

EVEN BEFORE MARJORIE FELL IN love with Milton, she was charmed by the lanky, dark-haired young man's recitations of lines from great plays and renditions of popular songs, especially those by Gilbert and Sullivan. Whatever Milton was doing, he'd also be warbling, humming, or singing a tune. His days as a traveling salesman were over, he told her in 1892. He'd been starstruck by musical theater.

Soon after Milton arrived in Boston with his sample case, he headed for the theater district, naively hoping his talents and enthusiasm would get him a role in some production. When no one offered him a part, he boldly organized his own company and put on Andrian's *The Mascot*. An up-and-coming theatrical manager named B. F. Keith was so impressed that he hired Milton as a comedian and stage manager for his vaudeville shows. Milton also stepped in to sing melodies by Victor Herbert and other popular composers and convinced Keith to do condensed versions of popular operettas.

Milton and Marjorie were married in Boston later that year, shortly before they came to New York. There Milton and his brother founded the Aborn Light Opera Company, offering light opera at affordable prices. They produced operas "for those who love it and not for those who come to compare clothes," Milton said, making a not-so-subtle jab at Metropolitan Opera-goers more interested in those people sitting in the "diamond horseshoe" than in what was happening on stage.

For years the Aborns were the only ones keeping standard light opera alive. If one of the soloists failed to show up, Milton stepped in on short notice to perform, loving every minute. Milton and Marjorie lived on West 57th Street, not far from Broadway. Marjorie attended all his shows, applauding her husband as well as his productions.

## ELIZABETH HARMAN AND FRANK PAKENHAM, 7TH EARL OF LONGFORD

*"the literary Longfords"*

YEARS AFTER FRANK AND ELIZABETH married in 1931, she was gathering material for her biography of Queen Victoria and smiled when she came across a sweet note the young monarch sent her beloved Albert the night before their 1840 wedding. How similar that message was to one that Frank had written right before *their* wedding: "My darling, Just a line to say that I love you . . . Your loving loving Frank."

They'd met at Oxford in 1927 when she was a philosophy and classics student and he was a young don. Theirs would be a life intimately connected to English power, politics, and literature. Elizabeth wrote biographies of British rulers, books such as *Jameson's Raid* about a settlers' revolt in nineteenth-century South Africa, and a two-volume biography of Lord Wellington, who had married a family ancestor.

Frank served in English government as lord-in-waiting to King George VI, first lord of the Admiralty, and leader of the House of Lords. He also was a publisher and a respected writer, concentrating on religious and biographical books. Their large family would be called "the literary Longfords" because five children (including Antonia Fraser and Rachel Billington) and other relatives also became writers, especially in the area of British history.

Their wedding day began "in a whirlwind of flying autumn leaves and white tulle," Elizabeth wrote in her memoir, *The Pebbled Shore*. She wore a cream satin dress decorated with love knots and a wreath of orange blossoms. Her twelve bridesmaids wore white satin dresses under jewel-toned velvet jackets. They arrived somewhat late at St. Margaret's church in London, which was just as well, since Frank got there only moments before the ceremony—he and his best man had gone "next door" to Westminster Abbey by mistake and only realized their error because so few people were there!

## BETSY GRISCOM AND JOHN ROSS

*Always rebels*

MRS. GRISCOM DEFINITELY HAD MIXED feelings when her twenty-year-old daughter ran off and married John Ross in 1773. You never could stop Betsy from doing what she wanted. John was a nice enough young man but . . . he wasn't a Quaker. If that didn't bother Betsy, it certainly upset her parents.

On the other hand, John adored Betsy, and he *was* an upholsterer. They'd always have a nice steady income. Betsy was an excellent needleworker—look at her beautiful quilts and samplers. Like John, she had apprenticed with Mr. Webster after school, and together they could make anything—draperies, coverlets, swags, flounces, gimp, and the occasional flag. Not too much call for flags these days, what with a war brewing against England. But you never knew. One day they might become popular again. . . .

Why were my parents upset when I married John? thought Betsy, stitching fabric in their Arch Street shop in Philadelphia. If they didn't want me to meet non-Quakers, they shouldn't have sent me to the public school on 4th Street.

By the time Betsy was forbidden to see John, they were too much in love to stop. If they couldn't meet openly in town, they could always take walks in the woods or sit on the banks of the Schuylkill River. It was cold that November night when John rowed their small open boat across the Delaware River and they dashed to Hugg's Tavern in New Jersey. A justice of the peace married them in front of the fireplace, and John kissed his new bride passionately before they headed back to Philadelphia.

For the next two years he worked beside her until he enlisted to fight in the Revolution. And then one day George Washington and a few compatriots came asking Mrs. Ross to sew something really special—a new flag for their cause.

## JAMES ALFRED WIGHT AND JOAN CATHERINE DANBURY

*A marriage filled with all things bright and beautiful*

"AS I CRAWLED INTO BED ... it occurred to me ... that there are few pleasures in this world to compare with snuggling up to a nice woman when you are half frozen," James wrote in *All Things Bright and Beautiful,* but his wife wasn't the least bit upset. If not for Joan's prodding, "James Herriot" never would have written anything. They married in 1941 on the same day the twenty-five-year-old veterinarian joined a Yorkshire, England, practice. He and Joan moved into an apartment above the ivy-covered Georgian office building. The daughter of a local farmer, she wasn't surprised to spend their honeymoon testing cows for tuberculosis.

James kept a daily journal about the animals he tended and also recounted tales of his experiences to friends and family at the dinner table. Pausing at the conclusion of a particularly exhilarating story, James often said that one day he would write a book. Usually Joan nodded sweetly as if to say, Of course you will, dear. But after twenty-five years, she'd had enough. "Who are you kidding?" she asked. "Vets of fifty don't write first books!"

That was all he had to hear. He bought a typewriter and taught himself how to use it. He wrote stories, sent them to publishers, and got them back, rejected. He read books on how to write and read good literature with a critical eye. Still working seven days a week, sometimes all night long, James finally completed *If Only They Could Talk* and sold it only after Joan convinced him to ignore the rejections and keep submitting it.

"The thing that had changed everything was the tranquil basis of my home life," James wrote. He called Joan "Helen" in his books and said her "presence was a warm infinity, a measureless peace."

## BERNARD MALAMUD AND ANN DE CHIARA

*"Too many are afraid to take their chances with love"*

"NOT LONG AFTER PEARL HARBOR, while I was teaching at night and writing . . . I met a warm, pretty young woman at a party," said Bern years after he met Ann in 1942. The twenty-eight-year-old Brooklyn-born writer had been working at various jobs. What mattered most was having time to write. He taught evening classes to immigrants in Flatbush, Brooklyn, and started seeing Ann, who lived in Manhattan. They began going out on weekends and writing each other during the week. Ann's letters were bright and clever, revealing a deep sensitivity for literature.

He'd thought about marriage but feared it would hurt his career, especially since he wasn't sure he would succeed. Besides, could a wife ever understand what was going on in his head? And could she manage their family when he needed to work?

Ann could, he realized. After they married in 1945, "she enticed me across the bridge into Manhattan," where they settled down in Greenwich Village. Bern wrote articles and short stories and taught at a high school in Harlem. He also began reading African-American history and fiction, which later inspired him to write his novel *The Tenants.* Ann worked, too, until their first child was born.

Four years later they headed west. Bern began teaching English composition at Oregon State College and wrote primarily about Jewish-American life in New York. He also completed *The Natural,* an allegorical novel about baseball. Bern revised his work repeatedly—sometimes more than a dozen times—and Ann typed new drafts from his handwritten copy. The rewards would be great: a lifetime of powerful novels and short stories and awards, including the Pulitzer Prize and National Book Award.

## CHARLES DANA GIBSON AND IRENE LANGHORNE

*His very own "Gibson girl"*

IRENE'S LONG SATIN GOWN SWISHED seductively as she crossed the floor at Delmonico's restaurant and approached Charles's table in 1894. The talented young illustrator, who was dining with two friends, felt the perfumed presence of the blue-eyed blonde as she passed by. One of his companions, who'd met Irene previously, jumped up to say hello and returned to the table, saying, What luck, I'm giving a tea tomorrow and she's agreed to stop by.

Irene knew quite well who "C. D. Gibson" was—his delightful and sophisticated magazine illustrations and cartoons had captivated her during her finishing school year in New York. And everybody knew his "Gibson Girl," the epitome of decorum, charm, and good breeding whose fame would continue until World War I. Many women claimed to be her model, but actually she was an idealized composite of many well-bred young ladies Charles knew . . . until he met Irene, who became the "real thing" for him.

She was one of four gorgeous and spirited Langhorne girls from Richmond, Virginia. Charles was transfixed; now his sketchbooks were filled with lovers picnicking or standing in the pouring rain, gazing adoringly into each other's eyes. When Irene went home, Charles wrote to her constantly and visited her as well. Then he sent her a picture of his Gibson Girl, pensively wondering, "Yes or no?"

They were married in St. Paul's church in Richmond in 1895 before a crowd of New Yorkers and local friends and relations so exuberant that they knocked over an elaborate canopy hanging above the church door.

Wherever the Gibsons went on their European honeymoon, their fame and love were so apparent that people stared. This inspired Charles to sketch "The Wedding Journey," in which newlyweds sitting at their breakfast table notice a pair of eyes in their morning eggs.

## PHINEAS TAYLOR BARNUM AND CHARITY HALLETT

*"the most wondrous woman I have ever seen"*

"I DO NOT APPROVE OF early marriage," "P.T." said fifty years after he married "Chairy" in 1829. "But, although I was little more than nineteen years old when I was married . . . if I had waited twenty years longer I could not have found another woman so well suited to my disposition and so admirable and valuable in every character as a wife, a mother and a friend."

The future circus impresario was a store clerk in northwestern Connecticut when he was asked to accompany a young lady back home to Bethel. She'd just purchased a new bonnet, and the weather looked particularly ominous. "I assented," he said, "and was introduced to Chairy Hallett, a fair, rosy-cheeked buxom girl with beautiful white teeth."

She hoped someday to travel. He said that New York City was bustling with energy and excitement; someday he would take her there. P.T.'s enthusiasm was irresistible. Chairy laughed easily and made quick comebacks to his jokes. They became engaged in the summer of 1829 but kept it a secret because their parents disapproved. In November, P.T. and Chairy skipped off to New York City and were married in her uncle's parlor on Orchard Street.

They moved into a boardinghouse in Bethel, and P.T. pursued a variety of enterprises, including operating a fancy goods store, selling lottery tickets, running for office, and publishing a newspaper—which brought him sixty days in jail on a libel conviction. Everything he did was done boldly, with the same cocky spirit that marked his future career of turning the circus into the greatest show on earth. Even his book *Struggles and Triumphs of P. T. Barnum* became one of the best-known autobiographies of its time.

## ANNA MARY ROBERTSON AND THOMAS SALMON MOSES

*"we were a team"*

"GRANDMA MOSES" WAS AN OLD lady when she began painting, but she'd been artistic and creative all her life. Ever since she married Tom in 1887, Anna had found time in between her household and farm chores to make a quilt, sew doll clothes, or stitch something fancy out of wool.

She was a twenty-six-year-old "spinster" when she met her tall, blue-eyed husband-to-be. They both worked as hired hands for a farmer in upstate New York. Thomas was a decent, industrious man, which meant a lot to Anna. "In those days, many of the boys were chicken thieves!" she wrote in *Grandma Moses: My Life's History*. They were married in the minister's home in Hoosick Falls, a town she later memorialized in many of her paintings. Thomas put on his only suit, and Anna wore a dark green dress with a high collar and black high-buttoned shoes. With her intuitive sense of color, she stuck a bright pink feather in her dark green hat.

For the first time in her life she traveled more than twelve miles from home when they boarded a train heading south to work on a North Carolina horse farm. They changed their minds in Virginia, however, after falling in love with land in the Shenandoah Valley. Eighteen years later they resettled on a farm in Eagle Bridge, New York, not far from the Vermont border. Anna ran out of wallpaper while decorating the parlor, so she painted a large picture on the firescreen to help beautify the room.

Partners in everything, she and Thomas took care of each other: "I believed, when we started out, that we were a team and I had to do as much as my husband did, not like some girls, they sit down, and then somebody has to throw sugar at them."

## LOUIS JACQUES DAGUERRE AND LOUISE GEORGINA SMITH

*Worth a thousand words*

AT A PARIS SOIREE IN 1809, Louis sipped his wine and wondered who was speaking French with such a delightful foreign accent. Turning around, the twenty-two-year-old scene painter saw a sweet-faced young woman chatting with several men. Louise was nineteen and lived in Paris with her English parents. Her smooth dark hair was parted neatly above her creamy white forehead, and soft ringlets dangled saucily over her ears. Wonderful cheekbones, Louis observed, thinking he'd like to sketch her merry expression. One day he would develop a new process for fixing images on paper, but now he could do only what artists had always done—paint the attractive mademoiselle's portrait.

He married Louise the following year at the Reformed Church of Paris. Louis was charming and talented, with boundless energy and perseverance. Sometimes he showed up at parties walking on his hands! He loved to dance and occasionally got small parts performing in crowd scenes at the opera house.

Using the camera obscura, an artists' device dating from the Renaissance, Louis painted tiny three-dimensional scenes in dioramas, as well as 360-degree panoramic spectacles of battlefields and exotic places. By 1824 he was studying lenses and other optical equipment, figuring out how to transfer pictures seen in the camera obscura onto translucent glass. Other inventors and chemists were also thinking of ways to fix images from the camera obscura. By the 1830s Louis's process was successful! The ancient dream of preserving how people and places actually looked at a specific moment in time had been attained. "Daguerreotypes" weren't better than fine paintings, but everyone agreed they were definitely more "real."

Of course, no photographs were taken at Louis and Louise's wedding, but ever since his great invention was popularized, virtually all brides and grooms have commemorated their special day by smiling for the camera . . . and saying "cheese!"

## KING HENRY I OF ENGLAND AND PRINCESS EDYTHA

### *"Lion of Justice" and "Maud"*

NO SOONER DID HENRY BECOME King of England in 1100 than he decided to marry a Saxon princess. As William the Conqueror's youngest son, the good-looking thirty-two-year-old monarch had been expected to "marry well," but he chose Edytha because he really loved her. Besides, intermarriage between Normans and Saxons would help appease the locals.

The golden-haired daughter of the late King Malcolm of Scotland was one of the few remaining descendants of the exalted King Alfred. Others had sought Edytha's slim white hand, but none lured her away from the convent where she'd grown up—until Henry. Besides being handsome, he also read Latin, saying that "an unlettered king is no better than a donkey with a crown."

Many nobles opposed the union, pressuring the abbess to declare that the princess had already taken her religious vows. Forthwith, the archbishop questioned Edytha in order to decide if she should return to the convent or become queen of England instead. (Some choice!) Edytha claimed that she wore her veil primarily to discourage unworthy suitors and—she paused, glancing toward her antagonists—to preserve her virginity against violent Normans! Thankfully, the archbishop believed her and decreed that she and Henry could be married right away.

The ceremony was held in the grand stone chapel of Westminster. Edytha changed her name to Matilda (her late mother-in-law's name) and became known as "Good Queen Maud." After many years wearing dark colors and a nun's black hood, now Maud favored blues, reds, and greens in her dress and in the royal apartments. She also started a trend by unbraiding her long hair and wearing it loose over her shoulders. Above all, her fairness and intelligence were admired, and everyone recognized the positive influence she exerted on Henry, who repudiated the absolute rule of his older brother Rufus and paved the way for the Magna Carta of 1215.

## JULIE ANDREWS AND BLAKE EDWARDS

*"Life is tremendous fun with him"*

"I'D HATE TO BE MARY POPPINS," Blake has said, describing Julie's public image—a blend of the perky, wholesome characters she's played—as a tremendous burden. But the Oklahoma-born film writer, director, and producer is comfortable with "Blackie," the nickname Julie gave him. It pretty much sums up his dark sense of humor and his devilish zeal and creativity.

He was forty and almost divorced when they met in 1963 at a Hollywood party thrown by Peter Sellers, star of Blake's comedy *A Shot in the Dark*. Afterward they ran into each other occasionally. Blake thought that Julie was pristine and proper, like her on-screen image. But at twenty-seven, she was feistier than she seemed and would divorce her first husband a few years later. With her glorious singing voice, she'd been the toast of Broadway in *My Fair Lady*. But *Camelot,* which opened in December 1960, would be her last play for a long time. She took her young daughter and moved to Hollywood to make films and, eventually, fall in love with Blake.

They were married in a small private ceremony in 1969 at one o'clock in the afternoon beside a waterfall in their Beverly Hills garden. Life centered on their new family, which included his and her children as well as two adopted Vietnamese daughters.

In 1995 Blake produced a musical stage version of their 1982 smash-hit film, *Victor/Victoria*. Julie returned to Broadway after an absence of more than thirty years and gave a showstopping performance time after time.

## E. B. WHITE AND KATHARINE SERGEANT ANGELL

*"Dear Katharine (very dear . . . )"*

"ARE YOU ELWYN BROOKS WHITE?" Katharine asked "Andy" in *The New Yorker* magazine's reception area in 1926. She was happy to meet the twenty-six-year-old author of the fine prose pieces she'd been editing regularly. One day he'd also write children's classics, such as *Stuart Little*. Katharine was gracious, intelligent, and seven years older, and he deeply appreciated her kind manner, which made him feel at ease. Years later Andy couldn't remember exactly when he fell in love with Katharine, although he was "half in love with her for a long time." Unfortunately, she had two children and was married to someone else. It took a few years for her unhappy marriage to end and for Katharine and Andy to reach what he called "the most beautiful decision" in his entire life.

Things fell into place quite suddenly in 1929. After getting a marriage license at City Hall in Manhattan, they ate lunch in a midtown speakeasy and drove fifty miles north to Bedford Village, accompanied only by Katharine's Scottish terrier, Daisy. Unable to find a justice of the peace, they convinced a Presbyterian minister to marry them in his church (while Daisy got into a fight with his dog!). They were back in the city by dinnertime and returned to work the following day. Less than two weeks later a short trip out of town inspired Andy to write "Natural History." Not only is his poem about the silken, spidery threads connecting him to Katharine, but it presages his children's book *Charlotte's Web*.

Katharine stayed on at *The New Yorker*. Eventually she and Andy bought a farmhouse in Maine where they lived, wrote, and edited many books, including *The Subtreasury of American Humor* in 1940.

## MERCY OTIS AND JAMES WARREN

*"the best friend of my heart"*

SIXTEEN-YEAR-OLD MERCY COULDN'T WAIT TO attend her brother's Harvard graduation in 1744. Although she didn't have his formal schooling, the young girl from Barnstable, Massachusetts, had read every book he owned and had no trouble keeping up with the college-educated men. At a commencement day picnic, Mercy began talking with James Warren, a sandy-haired junior from Plymouth. Thus began a rich intellectual relationship that lasted the rest of their lives. Like his friend John Adams, James actually preferred women with bright minds and scholarly abilities.

Ten years later Colonel Otis gave away his eldest daughter in a small wedding ceremony in Barnstable. Mercy and James stayed for a few days, and she wore a richly embroidered second-day dress at extended festivities. Then they headed north to his farmhouse by the Eel River in Plymouth, twenty-five miles away. They rearranged his bookshelves, mixing her books with his, and added many more volumes to an ever-growing library.

Later, as a housewife and mother of five sons, it would have been easy for the only woman in the house to suppress her own creativity and channel all her energies into family life, but Mercy wrote poetry, plays, and commentaries. After her satirical poem about the Boston Tea Party appeared in the Boston *Gazette*, John Adams praised her cleverness and humor. Like John and Abigail, Mercy and James were deeply committed to the Patriots' cause. They spoke out in favor of independence long before many members of the Continental Congress were bold enough to do so.

Even after many years of marriage, Mercy could write to her beloved John, "I take up my pen, which as the needle to the pole, immediately directs itself toward you, the powerful magnet, the center of my early wishes and the star which attracts my attention."

## HERNANDO DE SOTO AND ISABELLA DE BOBADILLA

*"I will wait for you all my life, darling"*

WHEN HERNANDO WAS A LITTLE muchacho, Isabella's wealthy, powerful father, Don Pedrarias, had taken the future conquistador into his home, educated him, and let him play with his own children. By 1536 Hernando had returned from Peru with Pizarro and was worth more than four million dollars. He was thirty-six, athletic and handsome, with brooding dark eyes, a well-trimmed black beard, and a reputation for bravery and tenacity. Isabella was six years younger, a passionate senorita so trustworthy and intelligent that one day he would appoint her acting governor of Cuba.

For years they had suppressed their love, fearing the don's fury if his favorite daughter became romantically involved with someone "beneath" her class. Secretly, Hernando carried one of Isabella's handkerchiefs and wore her small gold cross under his armor. He knew that Don Pedrarias had arranged for the murder of his explorer son-in-law, Vasco Balboa, husband of Isabella's sister Maria.

Fortunately, the don died, and Isabella's mother, Doña Isabel, gladly made the arrangements for a sumptuous wedding. Isabel and Hernando were married at the Bobadilla family chapel in Valladolid, Spain, the day after Doña Isabel deeded a large ranch in Panama to Hernando as part of her daughter's dowry. Although the groom rarely wore elaborate clothing, it's likely that he dressed like all the wedding guests, who were decked out in decorative armor, velvet and taffeta suits, scented gloves, satin leggings, colored leather boots, and plenty of heavy gold rings, buckles, and neck chains.

The newlyweds stole away to Segovia and wandered blissfully around Roman aqueducts and Moorish castles. Hernando loved making love to Isabella night after night and taking long walks with her in the gardens of their mansion in Seville . . . but after a few years he yearned to go exploring again. Within five years, he was the first European to see the Mississippi River.

## GOODMAN ACE AND JANE EPSTEIN

*A pair of "Ragged Individualists"*

BY THE TIME *MR. ACE AND JANE* began broadcasting in 1948, radio listeners already knew they could expect nonstop hilarity from the zany couple who'd been making them laugh for more than twenty years. The petite, hazel-eyed blond first met her tall, sandy-haired husband-to-be in Kansas City, where "Goody's" dry wit enlivened the high school newspaper and helped him get a job on the Kansas City *Post*. He changed his last name to Ace from Aiskowitz around the time he married Jane in 1922 and also began doing short stints on the radio.

*Easy Aces,* their most famous show, evolved about seven years later when Goody's station director frantically signaled him to stay on the air. Performers for the next program hadn't shown up; could Goody fill in the time? Not missing a beat, he introduced the audience to "my roommate," Jane. They started ad-libbing about a gruesome local murder that had occurred recently, during an argument over a bridge game. "Would you care to shoot a game of bridge, dear?" Jane asked casually. Their banter was quick and punchy. Delighted listeners begged the producers to keep the entertaining duo on the show. Eventually it became a clever and urbane sitcom about a New York City advertising man and his wife, and was a nationwide success for the next fifteen years. The two stars moved to New York, where they kept writing most of the scripts and were on the air two or three nights a week.

Goody also wrote comedy routines for other hit shows, and Jane kept coming up with hilarious malapropisms. "I've been working my head to the bone," she often said wearily. Many of her expressions, such as "Time wounds all heels" and "You could have knocked me down with a feather," are classic one-liners even today.

## LYNDON BAINES JOHNSON AND CLAUDIA ALTA TAYLOR

*"I'm ambitious, proud . . . and very madly in love with you"*

"WELL, HONEY, YOU'VE BROUGHT HOME a lot of boys, but this time I think you've brought home a man" said "Lady Bird's" father when he met Lyndon in 1934. As secretary for a Texas congressman, the twenty-six-year-old "man" from Johnson City, outside Austin, was making frequent trips back and forth to Washington, D.C. He was "tall and gangling," Lady Bird recalled years later, and he "talked quite incessantly."

Lyndon pursued the shy, twenty-two-year-old small-town girl from East Texas relentlessly, although his enormous energy and drive almost overwhelmed her. "It was like finding yourself in the middle of a whirlwind," she said. Two months after they met, the even-tempered young woman who would later be called "the knot of the family" decided to take the plunge with her strong-minded suitor. Bird and Lyndon were married on a Saturday night in St. Mark's Episcopal Church in San Antonio. Friends attended, but no family members were present. The groom forgot to get a ring and asked a friend to buy one at Sears, Roebuck right before the ceremony.

In their haste to leave for a honeymoon in Mexico, the newlyweds neglected to take their marriage certificate. Twenty years later a friend who worked in the San Antonio courthouse discovered the document and gave it to the Johnsons. When LBJ became president, he made his friend the postmaster of San Antonio.

A month after their wedding Bird and Lyndon moved to an apartment on Kalorama Road in Washington. Two years later he was elected to Congress. Long before he became president, the future first lady ran her husband's office whenever he was away, lobbied for his causes, and escorted visiting constituents around town with her unqualified grace and charm.

## PETER MARK ROGET AND MARY TAYLOR HOBSON

### *"My ever precious friend, my darling husband"*

ALTHOUGH PETER'S GREATEST FAME WOULD be achieved with his *Thesaurus of English Words and Phrases,* he didn't write the enduring reference book until he was seventy-one years old, long after he married Mary in 1824. They met in Liverpool, where she was a wealthy cotton merchant's only daughter. Almost twenty-nine, Mary was well educated, idealistic, warm, and self-confident—which suited the highly respected physician, scientist, and educator. Now forty-five, Peter had become a doctor of medicine at the age of nineteen and devoted his life to his work, his ailing mother, and his spinster sister.

Like many tall, thin men, Peter was somewhat stooped, but his mind was brilliant. Even if Mary didn't understand everything he talked about, she was a wonderful listener with a keen grasp of his work.

Their wedding in the parish church of St. Philip, Liverpool, was followed by a glorious reception hosted by Mary's parents. She and Peter left for his London home immediately and found stacks of congratulatory notes and gifts waiting on the marble-topped hall table. Mary began keeping a daybook of their life at 39 Bernard Street. Fondly, she described afternoons visiting sick patients together and "R" promising to teach her algebra in the evening, or reading a book aloud to him while he made sketches of optical illusions. He contributed many scientific articles to journals and the *Encyclopaedia Britannica.*

Peter spent too much time doing research to earn a great deal of money. A few years after their marriage, Mary told her twin brother about the pangs of jealousy she had felt for the clothes and lifestyle of a wealthy woman they both knew . . . until the woman's rich but boring husband appeared. Then "I looked at my best of husbands by my side," Mary said affectionately, "and all my envy vanished."

## JACK LONDON AND CLARA CHARMIAN KITTREDGE

*His ideal "mate-woman"*

JACK MARRIED CHARMIAN IN 1905, the day after his divorce from his first wife was final. His novel *The Call of the Wild* had been published the previous year; at twenty-nine he was one of America's best-known young writers. When word leaked out about the quick ceremony arranged by Jack's publisher, William Randolph Hearst, reporters surrounded the couple at Chicago's Hotel Victoria, asking them if their marriage was legal.

"If my marriage is not legal in Illinois, I shall remarry my wife in every state of the union!" Jack contended. Charmian hated all the publicity, but she had "Jack adorable—my perfect bridegroom and lover, at last." She was thirty-five and had been his mistress for two years. She was prim . . . and rebellious, ladylike . . . and lustful. Jack exulted in their "wonderful physiological affinity, that makes the feel of our flesh good and a joy." Earlier that year Charmian had typed and edited his adventure-love story *The Sea-Wolf* while he covered the Russo-Japanese war as a newspaper correspondent. He had modeled the plucky character Maude Brewster after Charmian, a pattern he followed in many of his works.

Charmian was Jack's comrade in adventure—unafraid to ride a horse astride, wield a pistol, and sail around the world on the *Snark* with her "mate man." Later she would keep journals of their ventures to the South Seas, and eventually she would become Jack's biographer. He loved her deeply for the rest of his life and penned these precious words to her:

> *Sometimes I just want to get on top of Sonoma Mountain*
> *to shout to the world about you and me.*
>
> *Arms ever round and around.*
>
> *Mate Man.*

## PRINCESS ELIZABETH OF THE UNITED KINGDOM
## AND PHILIP, DUKE OF EDINBURGH

*Quite the royal wedding*

TWO HOURS BEFORE ELIZABETH AND Philip were married at Westminster Abbey in 1947, her diamond tiara frame snapped and was sent out for emergency repairs. Then her white orchid bouquet disappeared, until a maid remembered it had been stuck in a porter's icebox for safekeeping. And at the last minute, two pearl necklaces—wedding gifts from her parents—were retrieved from St. James's Palace. They had been on display with more than three thousand other gifts, including five hundred cans of pineapple from Australia and a loincloth spun and made by Mahatma Gandhi himself!

The future queen and her prince consort had met shortly before World War II. "Lilibet" was thirteen and immediately attracted to her good-looking eighteen-year-old third cousin who had been exiled to Paris with other members of the Greek royal family. Philip served in the Royal Navy and corresponded with Lilibet until the war ended. The day before the wedding, he was created Duke of Edinburgh. Although it's been said that he, with ancestors going back to Charlemagne, had more "blue blood" than Elizabeth, she definitely had more money.

Elizabeth was granted extra ration coupons for her white satin wedding gown covered with crystal stars and roses made of pearls. Philip's widowed mother, who had become a nun, took off her black habit and wore a lace dress for the occasion. After the ceremony, crowds showered the bride and groom with rose petals as they rode off in their coach. The weather was a bit chilly, so they snuggled beneath small rugs and tucked their feet under hot-water bottles and one of Elizabeth's corgi dogs on the floor.

Within six years she became the queen of England, causing Philip to chuckle when someone asked him if he was a male chauvinist. "I'd find it a bit difficult, in my position, wouldn't I?" he replied.

## PEARL ZANE GREY AND LINA ELISE ROTH

*"the most adorable and wonderful of women"*

ON A LAZY SUMMER AFTERNOON in 1900, Zane kissed the girl he called "Dolly" on the banks of New Jersey's Delaware River. The twenty-eight-year-old dentist had been canoeing with his younger brother, Romer, when they paddled by three girls sitting on the shore and flirted with them.

Dolly was seventeen and a college student in Manhattan; Zane lived there, too, not far from his office at 100 West 74th Street. He wrote when he could and dreamed of giving up dentistry entirely. He told Dolly that his happiest times at the University of Pennsylvania had been spent playing baseball and reading adventure novels. Soon she was dropping by his office and helping to proofread Zane's manuscripts.

"A Day on the Delaware," about fishing, was his first published piece in 1902. Slowly, Zane's success and confidence grew. With Dolly's approval and support, he quit dentistry when they married in 1905 and moved to a cottage in Lackawaxen, Pennsylvania. Six weeks later they took a honeymoon trip to California by train, stopping at the Grand Canyon and other western sights.

Back east, Zane sold more articles about fishing as well as "wild west" stories combining situations of brutal violence with romantic interludes. He continued making trips with Dolly or by himself, gathering material for stories and finding peace in the vast open spaces. "I need this wild life, this freedom, and I'll come back to love you to death," he wrote Dolly while traveling to a ranch in Arizona.

*Riders of the Purple Sage* was a 1912 best-seller that popularized the western frontier. The Greys moved to California, and eventually Zane wrote more than eighty books and hundreds of stories. Many were adapted as motion pictures. Dolly negotiated all his sales and always got top dollar for them.

## THOMAS CRAPO AND JOANNA STYFF

*His "plucky sailor"*

THOMAS HAD SAILED ALL OVER the world by the time he married Joanna in 1872, but she became his best "mate" and probably the first woman to cross the Atlantic in a small boat.

When they met in Marseilles, Thomas was thirty; Joanna was eighteen and full of youthful enthusiasm for adventure. After they were married on board ship, he brought her home to Massachusetts. Within a few months they returned to the sea on cargo ships, enduring ice storms, heavy winds, gales, and fog. Thomas dreamed about winning fame and perhaps fortune by sailing solo from the United States to England.

He commissioned the construction of the *New Bedford*, a two-masted dory that was 19'7" long, 6'2" wide, and 30" deep. Too small to carry a chronometer, it would be steered by dead reckoning. But Joanna "was all anxiety about my intended trip," he said, and she insisted "that if I went she should go too."

When they set sail in May, 1877, the docks were filled with cheering crowds. *The New York Times* predicted failure because "when nature placed men's offices in towns and their homes in the suburbs she made provision for temporary separations which are absolutely necessary" for married couples. Instead, "the little boat skimmed over the surface of the water like a duck" and "the welcome voice of my partner" soothed Thomas's ears. With barely enough room to sit or lie down, he and Joanna took turns sleeping and steering their dory.

They pushed on for twenty-three days, through storms, sunshine, and near-collisions with sperm whales puffing vapor through their blowholes "like steam from the spout of a teakettle." When they reached England, Thomas's steering hand was temporarily paralyzed and Joanna was feverishly ill. Crowds surrounded them, and women reached out to touch Joanna. She was the "lion of the hour," said Thomas. Even Queen Victoria was impressed!

## CLARE BOOTHE AND HENRY ROBINSON LUCE

*Passionate about writing, work, and each other*

"HARRY" AND CLARE'S 1935 MARRIAGE in Old Greenwich, Connecticut, brought together two strongly competitive and ambitious people. She was a thirty-two-year-old divorced writer and editor whose 1936 play about husband-snatching, *The Women,* was called the most brilliant social satire of its time. Harry was thirty-seven, married, and worth millions, having established *Time* and *Fortune* magazines. With Clare's help he would create the photo-magazine *Life,* as well as *Sports Illustrated.*

They'd met briefly a few times, but Clare finally got Harry's attention at a party honoring Cole Porter at the Waldorf-Astoria's Starlight Roof. Since Harry had snubbed her before, that night she decided to be brazen and outspoken. Steering him aside, Clare spoke boldly and directly, and to her surprise . . . he liked it!

At the evening's end they rode down in an elevator together, and Harry blurted out, "Do you know that you are the great love of my life?" He showed up at her home three days later, suggesting that they spend the next year getting to know each other. They'd get married if she fell in love with him, too.

Somewhat astonished, Clare didn't reply right away. Instead, she took a lengthy cruise with a girlfriend. When Clare returned, she saw a lot of Harry. She was intelligent, outgoing, and gorgeous; he was hardworking, gruff, and serious, but also fascinating, brilliant, and intense. The following spring he told his wife he wanted a divorce.

After honeymooning in Cuba, the Luces returned to New York. Harry was probably the most innovative publisher of his time, and Clare was his equally talented spouse. In the early 1940s she became a Europe-based correspondent and wrote news stories about conditions there as war approached. Clare was elected to Congress from Connecticut in 1943 and later became an ambassador to Italy and Brazil.

## WILLIAM HARVEY, M.D., AND ELIZABETH BROWNE

*"A blessing goes with a marriage for love"*

EVEN BEFORE WILLIAM FIGURED OUT how blood circulated through human bodies, looking at Elizabeth made his heart beat faster! A month before their 1604 marriage he was admitted to the London College of Physicians, enabling him to practice medicine and lecture on anatomy and surgery.

William was twenty-six when he married Dr. Lancelot Browne's twenty-four-year-old daughter at the Church of St. Sepulchre in London. Brides didn't start tossing their bouquets until the following century, but William and Elizabeth's friends probably indulged in another popular custom—flinging a stocking at them. First they escorted them to the bridal chamber and tucked them into bed. Then friends sat down at the foot of the bed and took turns tossing a stocking over their shoulders at the bride and groom. A hit meant that lucky person would soon be married.

"My wife had an excellent and well-instructed parrot, which was long her delight . . . and so tame that it wandered about freely all over the house," William wrote years later. The bird, a "splendid talker," sat on a perch near their dinner table and "conversed" with them while they sipped hot coffee, a new beverage from Turkey. Female parrots rarely spoke or sang, so they believed the parrot was a male until it died and a postmortem revealed an unfertilized egg inside its oviduct. The parrot's death saddened the Harveys, but it taught William not to trust his own opinions until they could be proved.

Dissections also helped William understand the inner workings of the heart and its system of valves. Until he presented his discoveries, most people thought that blood ebbed and flowed through the body like the tides of the ocean. Instead, William explained, the heart is a muscle that moves blood along by squeezing and relaxing.

## WILL ROGERS AND BETTY BLAKE

*"The day I roped Betty, I did the star performance of my life"*

"MY DEAR BETTY . . . I AM not 'smoothe' like boys you have for sweethearts. But I know you have not one that will think any more of you than I do," Will wrote Betty before she married him in 1908. "I am yours with love," he concluded, and remained a devoted husband even after he became America's "Poet Lariat," philosopher-cowboy star, and folk hero.

He met Betty in Oologah, Oklahoma, where she was visiting her sister. Although he was sweet on Betty right away, Will also wanted to be a trick rope performer. She went home to Arkansas and he went into vaudeville, but he kept in touch, sending letters, books, sheet music, and other gifts until she finally agreed to marry him.

A Congregational minister in Rogers, Arkansas, performed the short ceremony in the Blakes' home. Afterward Will and Betty boarded a train for New York City, stopping in St. Louis to celebrate Thanksgiving.

Throughout the 1920s and 30s, Will was the widely quoted, beloved conscience of America, telling hard truths about political and social issues with an easy grin and low-keyed charm and humility. One-quarter Cherokee Indian, he liked pointing out, "My ancestors didn't come over on the *Mayflower*—they met the boat!" In the *Ziegfeld Follies*, he'd start swinging his lariat and saying, "Well, I only know what I read in the papers." With a bemused look on his face, he'd talk about the news and chew gum while roping inanimate objects, small animals, and an occasional member of the audience. "Swingin' a rope's all right," he'd kid. "If your neck ain't in it."

Will laughed when folks said he ought to run for President, but eventually his statue was placed in the U.S. Capitol building.

## GEORG VON TRAPP AND MARIA AUGUSTA KUTSCHERA

### *"God's Will Hath No Why"*

FANS OF *THE SOUND OF MUSIC* will never forget the touching love story of Georg, the wealthy Austrian baron, and Maria, the twenty-two-year-old religious novice hired to tutor his seven children. After Georg's wife's death, the decorated World War I submarine commander moved with his family to a villa near Salzburg. A kind but formal housekeeper presided over everyone and expected Maria to keep her high spirits under control. Besides, it was whispered, the baron was "practically engaged" to Princess Yvonne, another believer in rigid standards of behavior—for example, children were never welcome at weddings.

The baron was polite, but Maria sensed great sadness beneath his pleasant manner. "Dear Lord, send him a good wife who will be a good mother to his dear children, and let him be happy from now on," she prayed. Little did she know that *she* would be that wife.

Maria's exuberance was impossible to suppress, and at last the baron realized that she, not Princess Yvonne, had brought joy back to his heart. With the children's help, he proposed. After the reverend mother convinced the novice that turning away from the convent didn't mean turning away from God, Maria accepted Georg.

They married in 1927 in the church of the convent where Maria had been sequestered. Her stepsons escorted her down the aisle, and Georg walked with his older daughters. Within ten years he lost his fortune, and the entire Trapp family began singing folk songs, carols, and religious and secular music at festivals and concerts.

They emigrated to the United States shortly after the Nazis invaded Austria. After World War II the Trapps organized an Austrian relief program and a music camp and lodge in Stowe, Vermont. They performed for many years, until the children's marriages and separate careers made it impossible.

## JOHN CHARLES FRÉMONT AND JESSIE ANN BENTON

*Married life began the day Dad found out about it*

WHEN THOMAS HART BENTON, THE fiery senator from Missouri, learned that his seventeen-year-old daughter had secretly married a penniless explorer, he was furious. Lieutenant Frémont was a twenty-eight-year-old nonentity whom the senator had tried to get rid of by sending him out west to explore government territories. It made no difference that his daughter adored the army lieutenant, who was as romantic and impetuous as she.

On October 19, 1841, Jessie slipped away from her parents' Washington, D.C., home. After a short wedding ceremony performed by one of the few clergymen in town not afraid of Senator Benton, the bride and groom parted. More than a month passed before they walked into her father's study and announced the big news. Benton exploded, sent Jessie to her room, and told John to leave the house and never come back. But Jessie wouldn't budge. She clutched John's hand and quoted Ruth in the Bible—"Whither thou goest, I will go. . . ."

Hearing his beloved daughter's heartfelt words, the thunderstruck senator calmed down and asked his wife to prepare a suite of rooms upstairs for the newlyweds. If Jessie was going to stand by her husband, her father was going to stand by her.

On November 27, he placed an announcement in the papers stating that Jessie Ann Benton had married John Charles Frémont. Usually the groom's name is listed first, said the editor. "Damn it, sir!" Benton retorted. "John Frémont did not marry my daughter; she married him!"

Eventually John surveyed most of the territories between the Mississippi River and the Pacific Ocean, became the first senator from California, and was elected governor of Arizona. Jessie wrote books and articles and turned John's notes about routes to Oregon into useful reports and invaluable guides for pioneers heading west.

*Date of their public announcement.

### HENRY FIELDING AND CHARLOTTE CRADOCK

*"the most excellent of women"*

"HER HAIR, WHICH WAS BLACK, was . . . luxuriant. . . . Her black eyes had a lustre in them, which all her softness could not extinguish. . . . Her cheeks were of the oval kind; and in her right she had a dimple, which the least smile discovered. . . . Her complexion had rather more of the lily than of the rose; but when exercise or modesty increased her natural colour, no vermilion could equal it. . . . Her neck was long and finely turned; and here . . . I might justly say, the highest beauties of the famous *Venus de Medicis* were outdone."

Like Henry's literary heroines—Sophie Western in *Tom Jones* and Amelia Booth in *Amelia*—Charlotte was spirited, beautiful, loyal, and affectionate. Henry fell in love with her in Salisbury, where his family was residing. He'd been born in Glastonbury, Somerset, and usually spent the winters in London writing poetry, plays, and dramatic criticism.

For many years Henry, who became one of the first English novelists, had a hard time making ends meet. He ate and drank too much and was often in debt, spending most of his money as soon as he earned it. But basically Henry was an honest man who enjoyed heaping contempt on hypocrisy, sham, and meanness through his writings. He also was passionate, bright, and bursting with an enthusiasm for life. At twenty-seven, he was mad about Charlotte, and she couldn't resist him.

They married in 1734 in St. Mary's, a small Norman church at Charlcombe, near Bath, and left for London and the theatrical season. Their first home was in Buckingham Street, just off the Strand. Charlotte's mother had died recently, and her small legacy helped them weather the unpredictable income of Henry's undependable profession. For him, Charlotte would always be the "one from whom I draw all the solid comfort of my life."

## THEODOR SEUSS GEISEL AND HELEN PALMER

*She had the right idea!*

MILLIONS OF CHILDREN SHOULD BE glad the future "Dr. Seuss" listened to Helen when they were at Oxford University together. The former editor-in-chief of Dartmouth's humor magazine intended to acquire a Ph.D. in English—until Helen noticed his doodlings. A Wellesley College graduate with a keen eye and hearty enthusiasm for life, she advised him to become not a professor but an artist. That was an amazing suggestion, especially since Ted's high school art teacher told him he'd never learn to draw. Within a year he had thrown in his "doctoral towel" and headed for Europe. Helen completed her master's degree and met her mother on the Continent. They traveled with Ted for a while before sailing back to the states, where Helen taught school in New Jersey and waited for his return.

He was twenty-three and Helen was twenty-eight when they exchanged wedding vows in her mother's Brooklyn apartment in 1927, four months after *The Saturday Evening Post* purchased Ted's first cartoon. Wedding cake and punch were followed by a rowdy champagne supper hosted by his father in a nearby speakeasy.

The newlyweds moved into a walk-up apartment at 319 West 18th Street in New York City. Ted's cartoons caught the eye of an ad executive, who hired him to draw ugly insects for their pesticide campaign, "Quick, Henry! The Flit!" For the next seventeen years, Ted's artwork appeared on billboards and in periodicals, but when he sold *And to Think That I Saw It on Mulberry Street* in 1937 (after twenty-seven rejections), his life's work really began.

He called himself "Dr.," poking fun at the degree he never earned, and used his mother's maiden name, planning to save his real name for more serious work! Helen wrote books and often assisted Ted with story ideas. They created documentary films during World War II and won two Academy Awards.

## LUCILLE BALL AND DESIDERIO ARNAZ Y DE ACHA III

*He loved Lucy!*

ON A BRIGHT FALL MORNING in 1940 Lucy and Desi drove from Manhattan to Greenwich, Connecticut, and got married. The ceremony was brief, because Desi's band was performing five times a day in New York.

They'd met earlier that year on the movie set of *Too Many Girls* and fallen like a ton of bricks for each other. The future famous redhead was a blonde with gorgeous blue eyes. At twenty-nine Lucille had already been in quite a few movies. Twenty-three-year-old Desi was a Hollywood newcomer repeating his Broadway role of a Cuban football player. She nicknamed him "Dizzy" and he called her "Lucy." Their romance was passionate and tempestuous. Seven months later he convinced her to marry him.

All the jewelry stores were closed, so they bought a ring at Woolworth's and were married by a justice of the peace in the Byram River Beagle Country Club. Standing before a blazing fireplace, the newlyweds kissed their marriage license as well as each other, then raced to New York. "We were back at the Roxy a few hours later," Lucy always remembered. "The audience yelled and screamed. It was terrific."

They stayed at the Hotel Pierre until the band's engagement ended and then took a train back to Hollywood. Their first home, a ranch in the San Fernando Valley, was called Desilu, the same name they gave the production company they established in 1950. In 1951 *I Love Lucy* began, shortly after their daughter Lucie was born.

For a while they had wondered if they would ever have children. Desi's mother declared that the reason they were childless was because they had not been married in a Catholic church. To appease her, Lucy and Desi married again—in a religious ceremony with Mama as Lucy's matron of honor—and guess what? At the age of forty, Lucy became pregnant!

# DECEMBER

## GEORGIA O'KEEFFE AND ALFRED STIEGLITZ
*December 11, 1924*

At Lake George, N.Y., circa 1938–a rare picture of the two artists together.

## WILLIAM SHAKESPEARE AND ANNE HATHAWAY

*"such as I am, all true lovers are"*

WILL FELL IN LOVE WITH Anne in 1582, when he was eighteen and she was twenty-six. Ardent yearnings sent the precocious lad back and forth between his home in Stratford-upon-Avon to hers in nearby Shottery and eventually produced the timeless result—Anne became pregnant. They made plans to marry, but Will was still considered a minor who needed his parents' consent. The young couple's news would not have shocked their families or the local folk, who knew about many similar unions. A special marriage license was granted by the local bishop on November 27 or 28, and the banns were called immediately, before Advent. It's likely that the ceremony was performed on December 1.

"William Shagspere" and "Anne hathwey" were married at a church in Temple Grafton, a small village near Shottery, and lived for a while with Will's parents on Henley Street. Susannah Shakespeare was born the next May, and twins followed three years later. Will probably worked with his father, a glover, until London's theaters and Elizabethan court life drew him to the big city more and more. He loved his family deeply, and although he spent a great deal of time acting and writing plays in London, he came back to Stratford whenever he could.

Perhaps, when he married Anne, he told her what King Henry V would one day declare to Katherine of Valois in Will's play *Henry V*. Marry me, he asks, and as time goes by, I shall try to become a better and better husband:

> *The elder I wax, the better I shall appear . . . thou hast me, if thou hast me, at the worst; and thou shalt wear me, if thou wear me, better and better.*

## THEODORE ROOSEVELT AND EDITH CAROW

*"tender, gentle . . . and always loving"*

EDITH WAS STARTLED WHEN TEDDY showed up for their wedding in Hanover Square, London, wearing bright orange gloves, a gift from his best man. But since thick fog blanketed St. George's Church as well as the entire city, this made it much easier to spot the twenty-eight-year-old bridegroom.

In 1886, four days after the future president lost New York City's mayoralty election, he sailed for England to marry Edith. Six years had passed since his first wife died after a brief marriage. Edith had hoped to win back the love Teddy had shown her during their childhood years. She'd loved him all her life, ever since she and his sisters called him "Teedie" and they played together in his family's Manhattan townhouse.

For almost two years Teddy had grieved for Alice and kept busy reading Tolstoy's novels, writing a biography of Senator Thomas Hart Benton, hunting wild game, and cattle farming in the Dakota Badlands. He had avoided seeing Edith until he encountered her one day in his sister's house. Edith noticed that Teedie had grown a droopy reddish-brown mustache, but he still had the same toothy grin and exuberant blue eyes behind his round spectacles. She was still slender yet shapely, with a poise and graciousness that would serve her well through the White House years. He proposed a month later, but they agreed to wait another year before marrying.

Few people attended the wedding ceremony, but news leaked out back home. After a four-month honeymoon on the Continent, the newlyweds returned to a rousing welcome. In the spring they moved to Sagamore Hill on Long Island's Oyster Bay and had a blissful time, with Teddy steering their "jolly rowboat" through channels and coves as Edith read to him from the works of Browning, Matthew Arnold, and Thackeray.

## JOHANN SEBASTIAN BACH AND
## ANNA MAGDALENA WÜLKEN

*"meine Frau liebste"*

JOHANN WAS FORTUNATE AND FLATTERED when his patron, the German Prince Leopold of Cöthen, permitted him to marry Anna in Bach's own home in 1721. The prince, who controlled everything, also helped him procure Rhine wine at a discount for the nuptial celebration. The thirty-six-year-old composer had recently completed his Brandenburg Concertos and had been widowed for the past eighteen months. Now he was marrying a woman sixteen years his junior, with whom he would form one of the most significant partnerships in the history of musical composition.

Anna Magdalena, a court trumpeter's daughter, was an accomplished soprano whom Johann probably had met during one of her guest appearances at Cöthen, where he was the musical director. Like her serious, stocky husband, she was a brilliant musician. Their passion for each other was intense; over the next nineteen years she bore him thirteen children, and several became eminent musicians.

They remained in Cöthen for a year and then moved to Leipzig, where Johann became musical director and teacher at St. Thomas's church and school. Knowing he had not been the town fathers' first choice for the position, Johann composed a new cantata every week—an incredible feat, as most composers would have been worn out producing just one a month.

Anna Magdalena copied all of Johann's scores, in between housework, childbirth, and child care. She probably wrote some music as well. Manuscripts of their music notebooks still exist, and in some cases it's impossible to tell who composed what. Whether or not Johann wrote the following poem in Anna Magdalena's notebook, it echoes his adoration and love for his *"Frau liebste"* (most beloved wife):

> *Oh, how my heart with joy is filled*
> *To see your beauty blooming,*
> *Till all my soul with music's thrilled*
> *My heart with joy overflowing.*

## JEAN-AUGUSTE-DOMINIQUE INGRES
## AND MADELEINE CHAPELLE

*"My excellent wife"*

"HE'S A PAINTER. NOT A house painter, but a great history painter, a great talent," Madeleine wrote to her sister shortly before she married Jean-Auguste in 1813. Furthermore, he didn't drink, gamble, or stay out late and was known as a kind and decent man.

Trusting to luck and optimism, Madeleine left her home and millinery business in Gueret, France, and set off for Rome to meet her intended husband. They had been corresponding for several months, ever since her cousin suggested they might suit each other. As a way of introduction, Jean-Auguste sent her a small self-portrait he had sketched.

The thirty-three-year-old French artist, who would become known for painting luminous skin tones in exquisite portraits and sensuous nudes, had been living in Italy for seven years. Work was going well, but he ached for a wife and family. He had been engaged twice before but had broken off with women he believed would not respect his devotion to art.

Madeleine met him by Nero's tomb. He saw her first as she descended from a coach. She was slim and small-boned, with a round face and eyes he would immortalize over and over again.

"I have joined my fate to an excellent wife who makes me perpetually happy," Jean-Auguste wrote after they were married at the church of San Martino in Rome. Madeleine became an adoring helpmate, model, business manager, and protector. Knowing how much ugly sights upset her husband, at times she would cover his eyes with her shawl and lead him past beggars through the streets of Rome.

"My private life makes for an unrivaled happiness," he told friends. With Madeleine, it always was that way.

## DAVID BEN-GURION AND PAULINE MUNWEIS

*"I want only two things—Eretz Israel and you"*

FEW BRIDES WOULD BE HAPPY to hear what David told "Paula" shortly before their 1917 marriage: Leave America and come with me to a small, impoverished country without electricity, gas, or automobiles. Thirty years later he became a founder and the first prime minister of the state of Israel.

Paula, a Russian immigrant from Minsk, sensed that he would become a great man. They had met the previous year at the home of a Manhattan doctor. Paula was his cheerful, outgoing nurse, more anarchist than Zionist. The thirty-one-year-old curly-haired activist from Plonsk, Poland, impressed her, and she offered to help him do research for a book.

Their life together would be hard, dedicated to David's stalwart commitment to the establishment of Israel. Right after they were married at City Hall in Manhattan, Paula returned to work and David went to a committee meeting. He also placed an announcement in a Yiddish newspaper, stating that they were married on 20 Kislev 5678, according to the Hebrew calendar.

They moved into an apartment at 531 Bedford Avenue in Brooklyn, and Paula began her lifelong habit of taking care of David. After three months he wrote, "I feel as if I were in love with you for the first time." Usually the foundation of Israel was foremost in his thoughts, but there were moments when all he wanted was "to give myself up to your arms, and forget everything but you."

Five months later he joined the Jewish Legionnaires, fighting alongside the British in Palestine and wresting control from the Turks by the end of World War I. "Be strong in body and spirit," David wrote Paula, now pregnant. A great future was in store for the man often called the "George Washington of Israel" and his wife.

### PETER PAUL RUBENS AND HELENA FOURMENT

*"At home, very contented"*

"I HAVE MADE UP MY mind to marry again . . . and have taken a young wife of honest but middle-class family . . . one who would not blush to see me take my brushes in hand," wrote Peter Paul in 1630. After his first wife died in 1626, one of the greatest painters of his century left Antwerp and wandered throughout Europe to escape loneliness and despair. Returning home, the fifty-two-year-old Flemish artist designed the "Life of Achilles" for tapestry merchant Daniel Fourment and became enchanted with his youngest daughter.

Helena was dreamy-eyed, blond . . . and sixteen. When they married in the Church of St. Jacques, Peter Paul bestowed strings of pearls, diamond earrings, gold chains with diamonds, and a large diamond ring on his beautiful bride. Like many young spouses in "May-December" marriages, she instilled joy, vitality, and passion into her husband's life and work. The art he produced during their years together is considered his most mature and remarkable.

He painted her often, beginning with a wedding portrait of Helena in a sumptuous gown with a sprig of myrtle—the flower of Venus—in her hair. Next was a scene depicting Peter Paul escorting Helena toward an ornate pavilion in their garden. Wearing a yellow and black gown and a large straw hat decorated with tulips, she is clearly the focus of the picture. Her stepson Nicolaas follows along and watches an elderly servant feed two peacocks symbolizing Juno, the goddess of marriage.

Helena enjoyed posing for Peter Paul; she wore plumed hats, regal gowns, quaint caps, Old Testament robes, loose negligees, and stiff satin dresses. In "Little Fur" she is naked except for a skimpy fur wrap. It's a very personal picture, possibly begun when he surprised her getting dressed one day. It was also the only painting left specifically to Helena in his will.

## ROBERT PENN WARREN AND ELEANOR CLARK

*"the happening that is you"*

WHEN ELEANOR AND "RED" FELL in love in the spring of 1944, each had been unhappily married. At a party thrown by another writer, Katherine Anne Porter, the Kentucky-born thirty-nine-year-old author of the Pulitzer Prize–winning novel *All the King's Men* was immediately attracted to Eleanor. She was thirty and working for the Office of Strategic Services in Washington. After the war she became particularly well-known for her essays, book reviews, and literary works, including *Rome and a Villa*.

Red kept writing superb fiction, but now he found he could no longer compose good poetry. After he married Eleanor in 1952, however, they traveled in Italy, and he "felt freer" than ever and developed "a whole new sense of poetry." Within two years Red had completed *Promises: Poems,* which he dedicated to their two young children and which won him his second Pulitzer Prize, as well as other awards.

Usually he and Eleanor worked apart at their seventeenth-century converted barn in Fairfield, Connecticut. Most days they began at 9:00 A.M. and wrote for about five hours. Usually Eleanor typed her material, and Red wrote in longhand. The family cat liked snoozing beside Eleanor; their dog stayed with his master.

Most of Red's stories were based in the South and projected strong feelings of time and place. Eleanor was descended from New England forebears, and he kidded her, saying, "My wife's a Yankee girl, she's as Yankee as they get, they don't get any Yankier." Although she only worked part-time while raising their children, *The Oysters of Locmariaquer* won her the National Book Award. In later years Red read great works of literature aloud to Eleanor in the evenings, and they knew that for them, being writers was the best kind of life.

## JOHN DONNE AND ANNE MORE

*"Thou art the best of me"*

IN 1601, WHEN ANNE'S FATHER learned that she had secretly married Lord Egerton's poet and secretary, he practically dragged his daughter home, insisted that John be fired, and then had him imprisoned. All this for love—but it was worth it. One day John would become an Anglican priest and dean of St. Paul's, but now his love for Anne inspired him to write wonderfully sensual and romantic poetry.

After expeditions to the Azores and Cádiz, John had entered the service of the Lord Keeper of the Great Seal of London and subsequently met his seventeen-year-old niece. No one sensed the fiery passion beneath the very proper conversations Anne and John exchanged publicly. At night he slipped upstairs to her bedroom, where she welcomed him with warm embraces and sweet whispers of delight. Their clandestine trysts were perilous—how long, they wondered, before her powerful father discovered what was going on?

> *Though he hath oft sworn, that he would remove*
> *Thy beauty's beauty, and food of our love,*
> *Hope of his goods, if I with thee were seen,*
> *Yet close and secret, as our souls, we have been.*

A few weeks before Christmas the lovers—eighteen and twenty-seven years old—found a sympathetic clergyman who married them. Anne's father flew into a rage, declaring that not only had John violated civil and canon law by marrying a minor without her parents' consent, but she had married *beneath* her class!

John's imprisonment was brief, but he never found steady employment again. Faced with public humiliation, he retreated into poetry more and more. Relatives, friends, and patrons helped support the Donnes for a while. By 1605 they managed to procure a small house in Mitcham.

> *Only our love hath no decay;*
> *This no tomorrow hath, nor yesterday . . .*

*Date approximate.

IN 1948,
telegram becau
to propose!" Ruby

In 1946, the tale.
Ruby, who'd grown up i
a twenty-two-year-old Hunte
Ossie was twenty-seven and fro
served in World War II and then g
about a wounded African-American soic
returns home. The play had a very short run,
together. They also appeared together in *Anna Lucasta.*

They married during a break from rehearsals for *Smile of*
opened on Broadway a month later. Subsequently they staged a benem
aid African-American victims of racial prejudice. Over the years Ossie and R
fought hard for civil rights and never accepted stereotypical roles that insulted
African Americans. "I have a rule," Ossie said. "Never to sell more of myself than
I can buy back before the sun goes down."

The 1959 production of *Raisin in the Sun* was one of many times they performed together. In 1961 they starred in his own Broadway play *Purlie Victorious,* about an African-American minister who wants to build a church where blacks and whites can pray together.

The play was a major hit, enabling Ossie and Ruby to become more outspoken champions of social justice. As Purlie (and, indirectly, Ossie and Ruby) said, being black was "a thing of beauty: a joy; a strength; a secret cup of gladness . . ."

n a ski week-
ne noticed was
t have to look way
ed and divorced twice,
-looking, easy-going, and
ated frequently, even though
g involved with a divorcée with
led Ruth "my little skiing accident"

wish refugees who had lost many relatives in the
e to the United States in 1941 and joined the army. Ruth
ars in a Swiss orphanage and then emigrated to Israel, where she
independence. She came to the states in the late 1950s. By the time she
Fred she had earned a master's degree in sociology from the New School for
Social Research.

Not above using "feminine wiles" to win her new beau, Ruth invited Fred for dinner, even though she barely knew how to boil water. The meal was superb, thanks to a talented friend who did all the cooking! The day before the wedding Fred's parents came to Ruth's apartment and won her heart by not criticizing her casual housekeeping style.

Ruth and Fred were married at the Windermere Hotel on the Upper West Side of Manhattan and honeymooned in Pennsylvania's Pocono Mountains. Nine years later she earned her doctorate in family counseling at Columbia and began helping other people enjoy "good sex."

## GEORGIA O'KEEFFE AND ALFRED STIEGLITZ

*"Oh Georgia—we are a team!"*

"AT LAST, A WOMAN ON paper!" said Alfred the first time he saw Georgia's drawings in 1916. Her friend had secretly shown them to the well-known photographer at "291," his Fifth Avenue art gallery in Manhattan. At fifty-two, Alfred was a major figure in photographic art, prophet of the machine age, guide, teacher, and discoverer of new genius. Although he was married, the most passionate relationship of his life had just begun.

He hung up Georgia's drawings and was shocked when she insisted that he take them down. Most young artists were awe-struck before the great Stieglitz, but here was twenty-nine-year-old Georgia, arguing with him! At last she let him become her exhibitor and promotor . . . and then her trusted friend and lover. Even Alfred's letters were inspiring, "like fine cold water when you are terribly thirsty."

They were an eye-catching couple, Alfred in his black loden cape that set off his bright white hair and Georgia in a white blouse and black skirt, with her jet-black hair pulled back tightly. He liked the bustling city, but Georgia preferred being by herself. He loved her angular, exotic features and photographed her many times. Alfred left his wife, but it took years to get a divorce.

At last, on a cold, foggy day in 1924, he and Georgia took a ferry to Cliffside Park, New Jersey, and were married at the home of John Marin, a close friend and painter. For a while they lived in a Manhattan skyscraper named the Shelton, which inspired some of Alfred's photographs and Georgia's paintings, such as "The Shelton with Sunspots."

Alfred continued to promote her work and guide her career. She became an internationally known abstract artist whose paintings of greatly enlarged flowers and desert scenes are mesmerizing, erotic, and mystical.

## RICHARD HENRY STODDARD AND ELIZABETH DREW BARSTOW

*"That sweet sweet love of thine!"*

RICHARD AND ELIZABETH MADE THEIR ways to New York City independently and met one summer evening in 1851 at the home of mutual friends. But as Richard recalled fifty years later, "nothing remarkable happened. It never does when it is expected to. . . . I was a penniless young man of about 25, good-looking, it was thought, with a knack for writing verses, but ill-dressed, careless in my personal appearance, and with no manners to speak of. She was . . . about the same age . . . handsome . . . and had been accustomed to be tenderly cared for all her life. The only thing we shared in common was a love of books."

Even so, Elizabeth invited Richard to her parents' house in Massachusetts for the Independence Day holiday. They "read and talked and walked and rode together" constantly. The following December they went to Manhattan's Church of the Good Shepherd, where the pastor "found it easier to marry the poet than to praise his verses." Five years later Richard wrote:

> *The bridal flower you gave me,*      *Then this may fade and wither,*
> *The rose so pure and white—*        *No longer kissed by me,*
> *I press it to my lips, dear,*          *For these, my burning kisses,*
> *With tears of soft delight. . . .*      *Will then be showered on thee!*

The Stoddards settled in lower Manhattan and devoted themselves to their young sons and literature. After a volume of Richard's poems was well received, Nathaniel Hawthorne helped him find work as customs inspector at the port of New York; the job offered a good living and gave the Stoddards time to write. But their works would not be as significant as the literary salons they hosted at their home at 329 East 15th Street. Richard and Elizabeth offered erudite criticism and influenced great writers such as William Cullen Bryant, Longfellow, Lowell, and Melville.

*Date approximate.

## MARGARET HILDA ROBERTS AND DENIS THATCHER

*"I was just lucky with Denis. Absolutely marvelous!"*

ENGLAND'S FUTURE PRIME MINISTER DIDN'T wear white at her 1951 wedding because the groom had been married before. Twenty-five years passed before the facts were publicly admitted, but that's why Margaret came down the aisle of Wesley's Chapel in East London in a bright blue floor-length velvet gown and matching hat and ostrich feather. Wedding guests stared, but no one realized that the bride's outfit—which, incidentally, was the Tories' official color—was copied after a dress worn by the eighteenth-century duchess of Devonshire and immortalized in a painting by Sir Joshua Reynolds. Afterward Margaret, ever practical, turned her wedding gown into a dinner dress.

She and "D" had met almost three years earlier when he drove her back to London after a political party meeting in the country. D was good-looking, thirty-three, and the director of his family's paint and chemical business, but twenty-three-year-old Margaret's passions were only for politics. Years later he recalled that she was "beautiful, very kind and thoughtful. Who could meet Margaret without being completely slain by her personality and intellectual brilliance?"

She had been a research chemist before they married, but D's substantial income now enabled Margaret to study law and become a barrister. Queen Elizabeth's recent succession to the throne increased Margaret's determination to advance as much as any man. She was a tax lawyer and the mother of twins when she entered the House of Commons in 1959.

Twenty years later she became prime minister and served for eleven and a half years. Along the way, D was always there to help Margaret. At times she was called the Iron Lady, but he remained her constant friend, sometimes the only one whom she could definitely trust. "He's not my second fiddle," Margaret said. "He's first fiddle in his own orchestra. In fact, he's his own conductor."

## ALEXANDER HAMILTON AND ELIZABETH SCHUYLER

*"Beloved by you, I can struggle
with every embarrassment of fortune"*

IN 1780 GEORGE WASHINGTON'S WARTIME aide-de-camp, Colonel Hamilton, married the girl of his dreams in the sumptuous drawing room of her parents' Albany, New York, mansion. "Betsey" was the only one of four Schuyler daughters who gave her parents the chance to throw a wedding; all the others eloped!

The good-looking twenty-three-year-old soldier from St. Croix lacked wealth and social position and was probably illegitimate, but Philip Schuyler was sufficiently impressed by Alexander's financial acumen. Schuyler's respect for his son-in-law continued growing, especially when Alexander refused any monetary help at times when his family's finances were strained.

"I love you more and more every hour," he wrote Betsey a few months before their wedding. "You not only employ my mind all day, but you intrude on my sleep. I meet you in every dream."

White candles encircled by holly branches highlighted Betsey's face on her wedding day. Standing before the minister, she wore her grandmother's lace veil over her own fashionable white wig and glanced at the expectant groom in a black velvet coat, white silk stockings, and breeches. Alexander's glittering rhinestone shoe buckles were a gift from his friend the Marquis de Lafayette.

A year later Alexander led his troops in the Revolution's last battle at Yorktown. Then he galloped home to Albany and the waiting arms of his pregnant wife. They moved to a house at 57 Wall Street in New York City, next door to his law office. Betsey was Alexander's secretary and assisted him with his speeches. He promoted various causes, including the abolition of slavery and restructuring the economy. "It is impossible to be happier than I am in a wife," he wrote years later. Nothing ever dimmed the future secretary of the Treasury's devotion to his Betsey.

## FRÉDÉRIC AUGUSTE BARTHOLDI
## AND JEANNE-ÉMILIE BAHEUX DE PUYSIEUX

*Jeanne-Émilie, ma chérie*

JEANNE-ÉMILIE POSED FOR THE body of the Statue of Liberty, which Frédéric designed and constructed during the 1870s and 80s, but Miss Liberty's dour face is most probably modeled after the sculptor's long-suffering mother.

The forty-year-old bachelor spotted his wife-to-be after a wedding outside Paris in 1873. The first things Frédéric noticed were Jeanne-Émilie's elegance, poise, and graceful arms. He'd been looking for a model who would willingly stand for hours with one arm upraised . . .

Frédéric lived with his widowed mother, who discouraged him from thinking about marriage. He was crushed when he found out Jeanne-Émilie was only a dressmaker's assistant; Maman would never sanction such a relationship! After all, he'd been commissioned to create a huge monument representing freedom and independence, to be given by France to the United States.

Jeanne-Émilie moved to Paris, found a job, and posed for Frédéric. She watched his supple fingers transform clay into a four-inch model of a well-proportioned, dignified Roman woman in classical attire. It didn't take long before she and Frédéric fell in love, but they agreed to put off marriage until Maman got used to the idea.

In 1876 Frédéric was in New York City studying Bedloe's Island, where his copper and steel statue would be placed, when he convinced Jeanne-Émilie to come to America and marry him at last. The ceremony was held at the Newport, Rhode Island, home of painter John LaFarge, and celebrations lasted until New Year's Day. The new bride loved everything about America, including popcorn made by the fireplace.

Jeanne-Émilie stood proudly beside Frédéric ten years later when "Liberty Enlightening the World" was unveiled in New York harbor. His monumental work still welcomes countless travelers and immigrants.

## SHIRLEY TEMPLE AND CHARLES BLACK

*His sweetheart, as well as America's*

BY THE TIME SHIRLEY WAS twenty-one, the world's most famous child actress had earned $10,000 a week during the Great Depression, had rescued a major film studio from bankruptcy, and was treated like royalty everywhere she went. She also had ended a sorrowful four-year marriage and was the mother of a young daughter.

On vacation in Hawaii a few months before her twenty-second birthday in 1950, Shirley met a "tall, deeply tanned" man "with a brilliant smile and thick black hair." As she recalled in her autobiography, *Child Star,* Charlie was thirty and knew very little about her. He also disliked name-dropping, causing Shirley to conclude, "Either he knew no one of importance or had no desire to impress me"— until a few weeks later, when he gave her his World War II military silver star.

The press spied on the lovers relentlessly and announced their engagement before they had decided it themselves. Once she and Charlie realized it was futile to deny it, they made plans to get married before the year was over. Their families were the only guests at the wedding at Charlie's parents' home in Monterey, California. He and Shirley exchanged their vows before a fireplace decorated with Christmas boughs at 4:30 in the afternoon. The officiating judge said he'd never seen a happier couple.

He may have been right. Shirley could have become one of those "has-been" actresses who suffer through a series of unhappy marriages. Instead, she had found a dependable and devoted husband who encouraged her to pursue other careers besides acting. Eventually she became involved in worthy civic and political causes. Later on she became a delegate to the United Nations and ambassador to Ghana and Czechoslovakia.

## EBENEZER BUTTERICK AND ELLEN AUGUSTA POLLARD

*Necessity—and Yankee cleverness—
were the "mothers" of their invention*

THE DAY THAT ELLEN THREW down her chalk and scissors and told Eben she was tired of creating patterns every time she made new pieces of clothing, they started thinking of a way to standardize patterns so they could be used over and over again.

They had met in Sterling, Massachusetts, when Ellen began working at Eben's tailor shop. Right away she knew that he was enterprising and smart, and he realized that she would be a valuable business assistant. She was nineteen and he was twenty-four when they married in 1850. Ellen continued helping out even after their children were born, and Eben listened when she said there probably were lots of mothers who'd like patterns from which to make their family's clothing.

Until then, worn-out shirts, dresses, and suits were usually taken apart and used as models for new ones. It was a time-consuming activity, and patterns always had to be adjusted for size changes, especially in growing children. Furthermore, unless a dressmaker was particularly talented, styles rarely changed and the same old fashions were duplicated over and over again.

The first patterns Eben and Ellen made were for boys' shirts and were cut from sturdy cardboard. Using their own children and nephews as models, they devised a system of standardized paper patterns in a variety of sizes. Everyone in the family—aunts, uncles, and cousins—pitched in when the Buttericks moved to Fitchburg in 1863 and began marketing tissue paper patterns in batches of one hundred, assembled and folded by hand. But making a lot of money wasn't the only important thing in Eben and Ellen's lives. Eventually the thriving Butterick Company also published magazines like *The Delineator,* which focused on serious issues such as women's suffrage and aid to orphans and other dependent children.

## PETER COOPER AND SARAH BEDELL

*"my nearest, and best earthly friend"*

ONE OF NINETEENTH-CENTURY NEW YORK'S most revered inventors, manufacturers, and philanthropists, Peter started out a poor man who, with the support of "Sally, the guiding star of my life," succeeded in virtually everything he pursued. Their most enduring monument would be Cooper Union for the Advancement of Science and Art, established in the 1850s.

He and Sally met in 1813 and were married in her father's home in Hempstead, Long Island, where Peter worked briefly in the textile trade. Sally operated looms and spinning wheels and was the perfect wife for an up-and-coming businessman. They were a prudent couple, never buying anything they couldn't pay for in cash. Soon Peter invented a simple but effective lawn mower and a self-rocking cradle operated by a pendulum and equipped with a small cloth that fluttered and "kept the flies off the little one."

They opened a grocery store in Manhattan a few years later, opposite the eventual location of Cooper Union. Sarah rose every morning at 3:00 A.M. to bake what Peter called "the best bread in New York," and she also created recipes for the calf's-foot jelly he manufactured. Subsequently Peter established an iron works in New Jersey, where he built the Tom Thumb steam engine for the Baltimore & Ohio Railroad and perfected iron strong enough to fireproof buildings.

As the Coopers' wealth increased, Peter and Sarah helped many relatives find jobs and manage through hard times. As a city alderman Peter advocated paid police and fire departments, an improved water supply system for the city, and better public schools. Cooper Union provided free lectures and courses in art and engineering to working-class people. Women were particularly encouraged to attend and develop marketable skills, so they would not have to marry "bad husbands."

## ROBERT FROST AND ELINOR WHITE

### *Kindred spirits*

WHEN ELINOR SUBMITTED SOME OF her poems to Rob, chief editor of their high school's literary magazine in Lawrence, Massachusetts, in 1892, she already knew he was brilliant. He was impressed by Elinor's beauty and intellect and would eventually recall their encounters in his poem "Meeting and Passing." They were covaledictorians at graduation, when they exchanged rings and became secretly engaged. Rob was mad about Elinor and wanted to marry, but she insisted on going to St. Lawrence University first. He headed for Dartmouth, but he longed for Elinor and found schoolwork uninspiring.

After a few months he came home to write poetry and work in a mill. He also taught Latin at his mother's private school and wrote to Elinor, begging her to return. She told Rob she would marry him if he could earn enough money to support them, but "we *must* not be a burden to either of our families." Grief-stricken and frustrated, he recovered slightly when one of his poems was published in a national magazine.

His first publication in book form was *Twilight,* a leather-bound volume of five poems printed privately, at Rob's own expense. Only two copies were produced; he kept one and gave the other to Elinor. At last she understood Rob's incredible need to write poetry. Completing her education in three years, she began teaching at his mother's school. Evenings, Elinor read every poem he wrote.

In 1895 they were married by a Swedenborgian minister and friend in one of the empty schoolrooms during the winter vacation, returning to their teaching jobs in January. They struggled financially for years, during which time Rob was a schoolteacher, journalist, and farmer. It wasn't until 1915 that he began to be known as one of America's best-loved poets.

## SANDRA DAY AND JOHN JAY O'CONNOR III

*"We liked each other immediately"*

MORE THAN THIRTY YEARS BEFORE Sandra became the first female justice of the Supreme Court, she was working on the law review at Stanford University Law School when she ran into another student editor at the library. John was from San Francisco, two months older than Sandra and a member of the class one year behind her.

Very few women attended law schools in 1951, and he was immediately taken with the blond young woman with hazel eyes. She laughed easily at his funny stories, and they chatted together often. Pretty soon they began dating steadily. After their romance blossomed, Sandra brought him home to the Lazy B, her parents' 155,000-acre ranch in southeastern Arizona. "We like John," said her father. "But I've seen better cowboys!"

Sandra was twenty-two when she graduated third in her class in June 1952, and married John the following December in her parents' living room. After a spirited reception for two hundred wedding guests in a new barn, the newlyweds flew to Acapulco for their honeymoon. Then they came back to Stanford, and John completed his final year. Sandra looked for a job at a private law firm, but all she was offered was the position of legal secretary! Not willing to settle, she found work in the public sector as deputy attorney of San Mateo County in California.

A year later John was drafted. They went to Germany, where he served as an army lawyer. She worked, too, as a civilian lawyer for U.S. forces in Frankfurt. For the next three years the O'Connors traveled around Europe and skied in the Austrian Alps. When they returned to the states, they began practicing law in Arizona and stayed there until President Reagan invited Sandra to Washington, D.C., in 1981.

## CAPTAIN JAMES COOK AND ELIZABETH BATTS

*A winter solstice wedding*

MARRYING A SEA CAPTAIN AND explorer, Elizabeth knew that James would be away a great deal. But she gave him the best gifts any wife could offer: peace of mind that things would be all right at home and assurances that she was proud of him. Most important, she always loved him—on dark nights when thick fog crept over London and stars lit the southern skies above the Pacific, and on endlessly long days when sweet birds chirped and flowers bloomed gloriously in elegant English gardens, but men at sea saw nothing but more sea. Like most seafarers' wives, she never slept well on stormy nights. Elizabeth would lie awake, twisting the ring she always wore, which contained a lock of James's hair.

They met in 1762, soon after he came back from North America, where he'd been mapping safe channels in the St. Lawrence River. James was thirty-four and considered the best navigator and surveyor in the Royal Navy. Elizabeth was twenty-one and had been visiting relatives in Shadwell, a popular sailors' neighborhood near the Thames where James had found lodgings.

They fell in love quickly, and after two months they bundled up in warm cloaks and high boots and walked across open fields to St. Margaret's Church in Barking, where a minister married them. They remained in Shadwell until James sailed off to survey Newfoundland. He returned the following November, and they settled into a three-story brick house at 88 Mile End Road in a suburb east of London.

Over the years their house was filled with furniture, maps, and curiosities that James brought back from his voyages. In fragile wooden ships he crossed the Antarctic Circle, rounded the Cape of Good Hope and the Horn, and explored New Zealand, Australia, Hawaii, Tahiti, and other parts of Polynesia.

## BERTHE MORISOT AND EUGÈNE MANET

*"the most cherished woman in the world"*

THE SPRING BEFORE BERTHE MARRIED Eugène in 1874, the first Impressionist exhibition was condemned by the established art world for being too revolutionary. Few people liked Impressionism, and fewer were interested in paintings by a woman. But Berthe, who had studied with Corot, couldn't stop searching for something new in art, any more than Degas, Monet, Renoir, or Eugène's brother Édouard could. These close friends influenced and posed for each other and even purchased each other's work to stay afloat financially.

Eugène painted, too, but he lacked the others' talents and dedication. He had a fine critical eye, however, and was impressed by Berthe's work. Light and shadow were brilliantly balanced, and her feathery brushstrokes and unblended hues created sweet harmonies of spirit and color. She wanted marriage and children—but not if it meant giving up her work. This he understood and always respected. When a newspaper reviewer called the Impressionists "lunatics," Eugène almost challenged him to a duel. Finally one afternoon, as he and Berthe painted by the water's edge in Normandy, he confessed his love and proposed.

She was thirty-three years old and he was forty when they married in Passy, a Paris suburb. Eugène described himself as a "man of property" in the church registry, for in truth he lived off family money and had no clear profession. But Berthe was content and told her brother, "I have found an honest and excellent man, who I think loves me sincerely."

Édouard painted a charming, whimsical portrait of Berthe relaxing in a chair and covering her face with a fan. Although it's hard to see her long dark hair and intense green eyes, a gold ring is prominently displayed on her finger. Eventually Eugène worked in civil service and wrote a novel, and Berthe continued painting her glorious pictures.

## MICKEY MANTLE AND MERLYN JOHNSON

*"We were best friends"*

MARRYING MERLYN WAS MUTT MANTLE'S idea almost as much as it was Mickey's. Mutt thought his bashful, country-bred son needed the stabilizing influence and love of his devoted hometown girlfriend once he became a major league ball player.

They'd been dating since Mickey returned to Oklahoma after playing for the New York Yankees' farm team. Before long he and the high school majorette were going steady. Being with the cute brunette was distracting for an eighteen-year-old boy: one cold night they raced to a movie theater so fast, Mickey forgot to turn off the engine of his '47 Chevy. Hours later they had to find a policeman to pry open one of the car windows.

They got engaged at Christmastime the following year, when they passed a jewelry store on their way to the movies (again!) and saw a quarter-carat diamond engagement ring that cost Mickey a month's salary. It was money well spent on the woman who stuck by him through good years and bad ones, eighteen in the limelight of Yankee stardom and professional baseball and other times facing the tough, sobering realities of illness and tragedy.

Mickey didn't want a church wedding, so in 1951, after his first season as a full-fledged Yankee, he and Merlyn were married by a minister in the Johnsons' Picher, Oklahoma, living room. With no aisle to walk down, Merlyn came out of the bedroom and Mickey came out of the bathroom. He wore a dark suit, and she wore a pearl-trimmed champagne silk dress and a green hat.

After a wedding cake and punch celebration beside the Christmas tree, they spent their wedding night in a nearby motel and then drove to Arkansas with recently married friends. Within two years Mickey had replaced Joe DiMaggio as starting center fielder.

## WALTER SCOTT AND CHARLOTTE CARPENTER

*"Dear dear Charlotte, how I adore you!"*

"I HOPE THE RING IS wide enough. . . . I dare say I shall blunder putting it on," Walter fretted to Charlotte in 1797. She had the jitters, too, and begged Walter to make sure that she didn't see his judgmental parents the night before the wedding. Nervously she reminded him, "I shall be yours *for ever*; does not that sound awful?"

"Did you ever know a man go mad with joy?" replied the future author of *Ivanhoe, Rob Roy, Lady of the Lake,* and other tales of Scottish history, romance, and chivalry. He'd been in love before and was deeply hurt when the young lady jilted him for someone else. Then, at the age of twenty-six, Walter spotted Charlotte on horseback near Carlisle, on the English border of Scotland. She was French-born and twenty-seven, with large dark eyes and jet-black hair. That night they both attended a dance, and he escorted her in to dinner afterwards. "I admire of all things your laughing Philosophy," he told her, for Charlotte was good-natured, lively, and confident of Walter's abilities. He immortalized her years later in the character of Julia in his popular novel *Guy Mannering.*

Walter slipped Charlotte's wedding ring on her finger without a mishap when they married on Christmas Eve in Carlisle Cathedral and subsequently settled into a thatched cottage outside Edinburgh. He practiced law but felt the pull of poetry more and more. Two years later he was appointed sheriff deputy of Selkirkshire and began writing for publication. Popular lines from his works include "a miss is as good as a mile," "as old as the hills," and "Tell that to the marines—the sailors won't believe it."

Their financial life was not always easy, but neither one ever forgot Walter's fervent prediction when they met: "When care comes we will laugh it away, or if the load is too heavy we will sit down and share it between us till it becomes almost as light as pleasure itself."

## FLAVIUS PETRUS SABBATIUS JUSTINIANUS AND THEODORA

*His "gift from God"*

NO ONE KNOWS THE EXACT day in 524 that Justinian, heir to the throne of Byzantium, married Theodora, a comic actress and exotic dancer, but it seems fitting to imagine that this famous couple of early Christianity was married on Christmas Day.

He was Emperor Justin's forty-year-old nephew, and she was the twenty-five-year-old daughter of the bear-keeper at the Hippodrome. Theodora had long dark lashes, a voluptuous figure, a lusty sense of humor, and great intelligence. Justinian loved her to distraction and gave her plenty of money, property, power, and independence—things few married women of her time ever had. That's because he wanted Theodora as his colleague as well as his consort.

For a few years she had been his mistress because he couldn't legally marry someone so far beneath his rank. But in 524 he managed to have the law changed and married his "sweetest charmer" forthwith. The Emperor Justin uttered no complaints; he himself had loved and wed a former courtesan. Theodora even managed to charm the bishops, who were impressed by her theological knowledge and convictions.

She could be resolute and ruthless, compassionate and charitable. She established hospitals for the poor, set up refuges for homeless girls, and opened an unused palace on the Bosporus for poor and abused women. If not for her, Justinian probably would have lost his throne seven years later during the Nika riots between hostile factions of government.

As emperor, Justinian was the political and spiritual leader of Byzantium. With his "revered wife's" help he brought 200-year-old Constantinople to its economic and cultural heights and strove to restore the empire of ancient Rome. Today, in the church of San Vitale in Ravenna, Italy, Justinian and Theodora still stand in all their glory, peering down through time from golden mosaics crafted and installed almost 1,500 years ago.

*Date approximate.

## JAMES RUSSELL LOWELL AND MARIA WHITE

*"happy as two mortals can be"*

*The snow had begun in the gloaming,*
*And busily all the night*
*Had been heaping field and highway*
*With a silence deep and white.*

JAMES WROTE "THE FIRST SNOWFALL" FIVE years after he married Maria in 1844. Their wedding day in Massachusetts was much like the poem. Horses pulled sleighs through the deep snow as friends and family gathered in the parlor of the Whites' Watertown home. The poet Henry Wadsworth Longfellow came with his wife, Fanny, who wondered why Maria's dress was exceedingly plain.

If Fanny had known Maria better, she would have realized that the twenty-three-year-old poetess cared little for worldly possessions. She and James had postponed their marriage until they could manage on their own, but even now the struggling twenty-five-year-old lawyer had few clients. Deep down, he yearned to quit the law and devote his life to writing lines like "And what is so rare as a day in June?" With Maria's blessing and support, that would be possible after all.

They met when he was a Harvard student and she was the serenely beautiful sister of a classmate. Maria, a descendant of the martyred religious leader Anne Hutchinson, encouraged James to cultivate lofty ideals. She was an ardent abolitionist whose poem "Africa" would be called her greatest achievement. James also wrote antislavery tracts and essays; *The Biglow Papers* is a satirical denunciation of the Mexican Wars. For a short time he and a friend published a literary magazine with stories and poems by Poe, Hawthorne, and Elizabeth Barrett Browning.

The Lowells gave away money to needy friends and strangers, even when they had little to spare. But nothing ever spoiled the happiness James knew with his "glorious girl." With her he had found "the perfect joy of loving and being loved."

## FREDERICK PHILIPSE AND MARGARET HARDENBROOK

*The "Prince of Traders" and "Margaret the Commercial"*

MANY DUTCH-BORN WIVES IN COLONIAL America were shrewd businesswomen, but Margaret was particularly talented. When she and Frederick married in 1662, she was a wealthy and beautiful young widow who maintained her late husband's company, shipping furs to Holland in exchange for Dutch products sold in Nieuw Amsterdam. Undaunted by ocean travel, she often accompanied the pelts on her own fleet of ships to the Netherlands, which eliminated the need for profit-cutting middlemen.

Like Margaret, Frederick loved commerce, as well as investing in real estate. He was an architect-carpenter for the Dutch West India Company when he first arrived in the New World, but soon he was making a small fortune speculating in wampum, used for trade with the Indians. He also dealt in Indian coats, horses, grain, liquors, feather pillows, furs, and other staples.

Nothing topped sitting with Margaret in front of his large open fireplace, sipping mulled cider and talking about futures, commodities, and other business affairs. Frederick couldn't believe his good fortune: Here was a well-educated woman who could share her husband's responsibilities as he enlarged his overseas trade. Margaret liked this ambitious man who didn't object to his wife using her maiden name in her commercial enterprises.

They married in December, probably right before New Year's Day when family members and friends usually visited each other. No doubt the church deacons joined in the wedding festivities and collected well-wishers' donations to help those who were less fortunate. In time Frederick became one of the founders of the city of Yonkers and built a fine manor house on highlands overlooking the Hudson River. By 1674 he was the wealthiest citizen of the city of New York.

*Date approximate.

## JOHN STEINBECK AND ELAINE ANDERSON SCOTT

*The third time was a charm*

"BEING MARRIED TO ME IS a very hard thing," the internationally acclaimed author wrote Elaine in 1949. *The Grapes of Wrath* and *Of Mice and Men* had inspired countless readers to protest social injustices, but now it was John who was sad and depressed. His second wife had taken their two young sons away and divorced him, after admitting that she had never really loved him. Not only that, his best friend had just died.

He was forty-seven-years-old, exhausted creatively and tapped out financially. While struggling to write the filmscript for *Viva Zapata!*, he met Elaine, who became his salvation. She was thirty-five and Texas-born and had worked on Broadway in casting and stage management. Her marriage to actor Zachary Scott was virtually over; she, too, was searching for a peaceful, loving attachment.

Soon after Elaine's divorce was final in 1950, she and John were married at his publisher's home in New York and spent their wedding night at the St. Regis Hotel. After a week-long honeymoon in Bermuda, John was back at work at their Manhattan brownstone at 206 East 72nd Street. Within two years he had completed another masterpiece, recalling the story of Cain and Abel and man's ancient struggles with good and evil. When Elaine read the manuscript and realized its biblical tone, she suggested the title: *East of Eden,* from Genesis.

In 1962 John was awarded the Nobel Prize for Literature. He and Elaine first heard the news at their summer cottage in Sag Harbor, New York. She was so flustered, she put the bacon she was frying into the refrigerator! A few years later, for her birthday, John placed a stepping-stone on the grass and inscribed these words in the wet cement:" *"Ladye, I take recorde of God, in thee I have myn erthly joye."*

## JOHN NICHOLAS RINGLING AND MABLE BURTON

*Lovers of art, and each other*

"THE CIRCUS KING" WAS THIRTY-NINE before he decided to settle down and marry, and thirty-year-old Mable was smart enough not to try and change him. Like the circus he and his brothers founded in 1884, John was bursting with physical power and energy. His arms were as thick as a wrestler's, and his voice was very deep. But like many large men, John spoke softly and maintained an air of dignity and decorum. If the self-made businessman smoked too many cigars and was occasionally egotistical and imperious, so be it. Mable adored her big bear of a husband, and by accepting his imperfections, she won his steadfast adoration.

They probably met in Atlantic City, New Jersey, where the attractive, diminutive young woman was living and working after coming east from a small town in Ohio named Moons. Whatever attracted the intensely private couple to each other, they kept it to themselves.

They were married in the Hoboken city clerk's office in 1905. A few days later they sailed to Europe, where they looked at new circus acts and visited many cathedrals and museums. The trip sparked John and Mable's interest in art and culture, which eventually developed into a lifelong love. They studied art between the circus seasons and began purchasing works at auctions.

By 1911 John and Mable were spending their winters in Sarasota, Florida. Ten years later construction began of Ca'd'Zan ("house of John"), a grand waterfront mansion built in the style of a Venetian palazzo. In an outrageous gesture of fun, they commissioned life-size bas-relief panels of themselves dressed (actually *un*-dressed) like Adam and Eve! Much of the artwork that enhanced the palazzo was later displayed in the John and Mable Ringling Museum of Art, which they built on the grounds beside their home.

## JOHN PHILIP SOUSA AND
## JANE VAN MIDDLESWORTH BELLIS

*"When you change your name to mine . . ."*

ON FEBRUARY 22, 1879, AMERICA'S future "March King" was rehearsing the Philadelphia Church Choir in Gilbert and Sullivan's *H.M.S. Pinafore* when he noticed "a remarkably pretty girl with the loveliest complexion I had ever seen." "Jennie" sang in the chorus, but they had never met. Today, however, was her birthday—just like President Washington, she pointed out—and when rehearsals ended, her colleagues congratulated her and introduced her to the conductor.

She was just sixteen, and he was twenty-five years old. When Philip looked into her eyes under "a cloud of chestnut hair," bells rang, cymbals clashed, and every musical metaphor he could imagine popped into his head! Although Jennie's singing abilities were limited, he managed to keep a spot for her in the choir.

They became engaged the following fall, after Philip convinced her father that he had $150 in the bank and could afford to hire a cook. More important, Mr. Bellis had faith in Philip. He was always humming something and drumming his fingers on the table. He had composed the "International Congress" fantasy for Offenbach's orchestra three years before. Now he was working on operettas, orchestral pieces, and songs. He wrote "When you change your name to mine . . ." shortly before he and Jennie were married by a Baptist minister at the Bellises' home. Within a year Philip became the youngest leader of the United States Marine Corps Band and took it (and Jennie) on tour through the United States and Europe.

Eventually Philip composed more than one hundred stirring marches, including "Semper Fidelis," which became the Marines' official march, and "The Stars and Stripes Forever," his most famous work and his personal favorite. Philip liked to stand up while composing, often beside the big square piano in the living room. Jennie always sat nearby, handing him fresh quill pens.

## ROY ROGERS AND DALE EVANS

*"King of the Cowboys" and "Queen of the West"*

BACKSTAGE AT A CHICAGO RODEO show in October 1947, Roy asked Dale what she was doing New Year's Eve. Since they both were sitting on horseback, she thought this was a funny time to pose such a question. Then, using his well-known cowboy charm, Roy took a ruby ring out of his pocket and put it on Dale's finger. "Why don't we get married?" he asked his stunned costar. The lights dimmed in the arena, and they rode out into the spotlight. "Yes," she whispered, right before they sang the National Anthem to a crowd of cheering spectators who had no idea what had happened.

When they did find out, they went wild. The famous yodeling cowboy and western hero had gone and married that cute gal who did so much singing and riding with him. It would be a marriage made in heaven—and in the barn. Even their horses, Trigger and Buttermilk, got along.

One of the first times Roy and Dale met was on the movie set of *The Cowboy and the Senorita*. She hadn't been on a horse since childhood and gratefully accepted Roy's riding tips and advice. After two failed marriages, she wasn't looking for romance, but when Roy's wife died suddenly, Dale helped him work through his sadness. The former Leonard Slye and Frances Smith were married at a friend's Oklahoma ranch during a snowstorm that delayed the minister for hours. Instead of a ten-gallon hat and chaps, Roy donned a real suit. Dale wore a powder blue dress and carried roses.

Since horse years are usually counted every New Year's Day, it's not surprising that the following morning the quintessential cowboy told his bride they'd already been married one whole year.

*"YIPPEE-EYE-O-KI-AY!"*

# BIBLIOGRAPHY

MORE THAN TWO THOUSAND BOOKS, magazine and newspaper articles, corporate archives, and historical societies were consulted for this book. I was assisted also by knowledgeable people and archivists at the Anheuser-Busch Company, St. Louis, MO; the Butterick Company, Inc., New York, NY; the family of Fritz and Ingeborg W. Kahlenberg; the Historical Society of Martha's Vineyard, MA; the John and Mable Ringling Museum of Art, Sarasota, FL; Mr. Henry Z. Steinway of Steinway & Sons, New York, NY; the Sterling Historical Society, Sterling, MA; and the Richard Tucker Foundation, New York, NY.

Staff personnel at the following libraries were particularly helpful: the British Library, London; the Frick Art Reference Library, New York, NY; Greenwich Library, Greenwich, CT; Manhattanville College Library, Purchase, NY; Library of the Metropolitan Museum of Art, New York, NY; New York Public Library system, especially the Performing Arts branch, New York, NY; Purchase College Library of the State University of New York, Purchase, NY; Sarah Lawrence College Library, Bronxville, NY; Scarsdale Public Library, Scarsdale, NY; White Plains Public Library, White Plains, NY.

Space limitations and the vastness of my topic prevent me from including a complete bibliography. The following list provides sources I relied on most heavily. In many cases similar information appeared in more than one book; my apologies to any biographers or historians whose works I have inadvertently omitted.

## REFERENCE WORKS

*Current Biography.* New York: H. H. Wilson, 1940. Published monthly and bound annually ever since.

*Dictionary of American Biography.* New York: Scribner, 1929. Additional volumes have been added by decade.

*Dictionary of Literary Biography.* Detroit: Gale Research, 1970's and subsequent editions.

*Dictionary of National Biography* ed. Sir Leslie Stephen and Sir Sidney Lee. London: Oxford University Press, 1882. The most complete source of British biographical material; subsequent editions and volumes have been added.

*Europa Dictionary of British Women*, ed. Crawford, Hayter, Hughes, Prochaska, Stafford & Vallance. Detroit: Gale Research, 1983. Sketches of famous and relatively obscure women.

*European Authors 1000–1900: A Biographical Dictionary of European Literature*, ed. Stanley J. Kunitz and Vineta Colby. New York: H. H. Wilson, 1967.

Hart, James D. *The Oxford Companion to American Literature*, 4th ed. New York: Oxford University Press, 1965.

Harvey, Paul. *The Oxford Companion to English Literature*, 4th ed., revised by Dorothy Eagle. New York: Oxford at Clarendon Press, 1967.

*Junior Book of Authors*, ed. Stanley J. Kunitz and Howard Haycroft. New York: H. H. Wilson, 1934 and subsequent editions.

Katz, Ephraim. *The Film Encyclopedia*. New York: Thomas Y. Crowell, 1979.

*Larousse Dictionary of Painters*. New York: Larousse, 1981.

*Major Authors and Illustrators for Children and Young Adults*. Detroit: Gale Research, 1989, 1993.

*National Encyclopedia of American Biography*. New York: J. T. White Company, 1893 with subsequent editions.

*Notable American Women 1607–1950*, ed. Edward T. Jones. 3 volumes. Cambridge, MA: Belknap Press of Harvard University, 1971. Sketches of famous and quite obscure American women.

*Twentieth Century Authors: A Biographical Dictionary*, ed. Stanley J. Kunitz and Howard Haycroft. New York: H. H. Wilson, 1942.

## BOOKS AND ARTICLES

Adams, Ansel. *Autobiography*. Boston: Little Brown, 1985.

Adams, Brian. *La Stupenda: A Biography of Joan Sutherland*. Victoria, Australia: Hutchinson, 1980.

Adams, Russell. *King Gillette*. Boston: Little Brown, 1978.

Adler, Kathleen, and Tamar Garb (eds.). *The Correspondence of Berthe Morisot*. London: Camden, 1989.

Albornoz, Miguel. *Hernando de Soto, Knight of the Americas*. New York: Franklin Watts, 1986.

Allen, Steve. *Hi-Ho Steverino!* Fort Lee, NJ: Barricade Books, 1992.

———. *Mark It and Strike It: An Autobiography*. New York: Holt, Rinehart & Winston, 1960.

Alpert, Hollis. *Fellini: A Life*. New York: Atheneum, 1986.

Anderson, Ronald, and Anne Koval. *James McNeill Whistler: Beyond the Myth*. New York: Carroll & Graf, 1994.

Anthony, Edward. *O Rare Don Marquis*. Garden City, NY: Doubleday, 1962.

Anthony, Katharine. *First Lady of the Revolution*. Garden City, NY: Doubleday, 1958.

Ashe, Arthur, and Neil Amdur. *Arthur Ashe: Off the Court*. New York: New American Library, 1981.

Ashe, Arthur, and Arthur Rampersand. *Days of Grace: A Memoir*. New York: Knopf, 1992.

Bacall, Lauren. *Lauren Bacall By Myself*. New York: Knopf, 1979.

Baker, Russell. *The Good Times*. New York: William Morrow, 1989.

———. *Growing Up*. New York: Plume, New American Library, 1982.

Baldwin, Neil. *Edison: Inventing the Century*. New York: Hyperion, 1995.

Barnum, P. T. *Struggles and Triumphs of P. T. Barnum by Himself*. London: MacGibbon & Kee, Fitzroy Edition, 1967.

Battestin, Martin C. *Henry Fielding: A Life*. New York: Routledge, 1989.

Bedell, Madelon. *The Alcotts: Biography of a Family*. New York: Clarkson N. Potter, 1980.

Bell, Ian. *Dreams of Exile: Robert Louis Stevenson*. New York: Henry Holt, 1992.

Benny, Joan, and Jack Benny. *Sunday Nights at Seven: The Jack Benny Story*. New York: Warner, 1991.

Bentley, Judith. *Justice Sandra Day O'Connor*. New York: Julian Messner, 1983.

Bergreen, Laurence. *As Thousands Cheer: The Life of Irving Berlin*. New York: Viking, 1990.

Bernstein, Burton. *Thurber: A Biography*. New York: Dodd, Mead, 1975.

Berthoud, Roger. *The Life of Henry Moore*. New York: Dutton, 1987.

Bettman, Otto. *Johann Sebastian Bach as His World Knew Him*. New York: Birch Lane, 1995.

Black, Hugo, Jr. *My Father, Hugo Black: A Remembrance*. New York: Random House, 1975.

Black, Shirley Temple. *Child Star*. New York: McGraw-Hill, 1988.

Blythe, Cheryl, and Susan Sackett. *Say Goodnight, Gracie!* New York: Dutton, 1986.

Bode, Carl. *Mencken*. Carbondale, IL: Southern Illinois University Press, 1969.

Boller, Paul F., Jr. *Presidential Wives: An Anecdotal History*. New York: Oxford University Press, 1988.

Borsch-Supan, Helmut. *Caspar David Friedrich*. New York: George Braziller, 1974.

Brady, Kathleen. *Lucille: The Life of Lucille Ball*. New York: Hyperion, 1994.

Branson, Ruth. *The Life and Many Deaths of Harry Houdini*. New York: Random House, 1992.

Brochu, Jim. *Lucy in the Afternoon*. New York: William Morrow, 1990.

Brown, David. *Let Me Entertain You*. New York: William Morrow, 1990.

Burns, George. *Gracie: A Love Story*. New York: Putnam, 1988.

Caesar, Sid, with Bill Davidson. *Where Have I Been? An Autobiography*. New York: Crown, 1982.

Cantor, Eddie. *My Life Is in Your Hands*. New York: Curtis, 1928.

Carner, Mosco. *Alban Berg: The Man and His Work*. London: Duckworth, 1975.

Carney, Raymond. *American Dreaming: The Films of John Cassavetes and the American Experience*. Berkeley, CA: University of California Press, 1985.

Carroll, David. *The Taj Mahal: India Under the Moguls*. New York: Newsweek Wonders of Man Series, 1972.

Carter, Rosalynn. *First Lady from Plains*. Boston: Houghton Mifflin, 1984.

Castle, Irene, as told to Bob and Wanda Duncan. *Castles in the Air*. Garden City, NY: Doubleday, 1958.

Cate, Curtis. *Antoine de Saint-Exupery: His Life and Times*. New York: Putnam, 1970.

Chagall, Marc (trans. Elizabeth Abbott). *My Life*. Scranton, PA: Haddon Craftsmen, 1960.

Chandler, Charlotte. *I Fellini*. New York: Random House, 1995.

Chaplin, Charles. *My Autobiography*. New York: Simon & Schuster, 1964.

Cheuse, Alan, and Nicholas Delbanco (eds.). *Talking Horse: Bernard Malamud on Life and Work*. New York: Columbia University Press, 1996.

Cole, Michael. *John Glenn*. Springfield, NJ: Enslow, 1993.

Colum, Mary. *Life and the Dream*. Garden City, NY: Doubleday, 1947.

Cook, Bruce. *Dalton Trumbo*. New York: Scribner, 1977.

Cook, Don. *Charles de Gaulle: A Biography*. New York: Putnam, 1983.

Cott, Nancy F. (ed.). *Woman Making History: Mary Ritter Beard Through Her Letters*. New Haven, CT: Yale University Press, 1991.

Courthion, Pierre. *Georges Rouault*. New York: Harry N. Abrams, 1962.

Crapo, Captain Thomas. *Strange but True: The Life and Adventures of Captain Thomas Crapo & Wife*. New Bedford, MA: Thomas Crapo, 1893.

Crawford, Deborah. *Four Women in a Violent Time*. New York: Crown, 1970.

Crockett, David. *The Autobiography of David Crockett*. New York: Scribner, 1923.

Cronyn, Hume. *A Terrible Liar: A Memoir*. New York: William Morrow, 1991.

Dallek, Robert. *Lone Star Rising: Lyndon Johnson and His Times, 1908–1960*. New York: Oxford University Press, 1993.

Darlington, Beth (ed.). *The Love Letters of William and Mary Wordsworth*. Ithaca, NY: Cornell University Press, 1981.

Daugherty, Sonia. *Ten Brave Women*. Philadelphia: Lippincott, 1953.

Davis, Linda. *Onward & Upward: A Biography of Katharine S. White*. New York: Harper & Row, 1987.

Desmond, Adrian J., and James Moore. *Charles Darwin: The Life of a Tormented Evolutionist*. New York: Warner, 1991.

Dickson, Harry Ellis. *Beating Time: A Musician's Memoir*. Boston: Northeastern University Press, 1995.

Doring, Ernest H. *How Many Strads?* Chicago: William Lewis, 1945.

Drake, James A. *Richard Tucker*. New York: Dutton, 1984.

du Maurier, Daphne. *Enchanted Cornwall: Her Pictorial Memoir*. New York: Viking Penguin, 1989.

Dunaway, David. *How Can I Keep From Singing: Pete Seeger*. New York: McGraw-Hill, 1981.

Duncan, David Ewing. *Hernando de Soto*. New York: Crown, 1996.

Dunning, John. *Tune In Yesterday: The Ultimate Encyclopedia of Old-time Radio, 1925–1976*. Englewood Cliffs, NJ: Prentice-Hall, 1976.

Durant, Will and Ariel. *A Dual Autobiography*. New York: Simon & Schuster, 1977.

Eaton, Quaintance. *Sutherland & Bonynge, An Intimate Biography*. New York: Dodd, Mead, 1987.

Eaves, T. C. Duncan, and Ben D. Kimpel. *Samuel Richardson, A Biography*. New York: Oxford University at Clarendon Press, 1971.

Edwards, Anne. *Early Reagan: The Rise to Power*. New York: William Morrow, 1987.

Edwards, Lee. *Goldwater: The Man Who Made a Revolution*. Washington, DC: Regnery, 1995.

Eells, George. *Robert Mitchum: A Biography*. New York: Franklin Watts, 1984.

Ellmann, Richard (ed.). *Selected Joyce Letters*. New York: Viking Compass, 1975.

Englund, Steven. *Grace of Monaco*. New York: Doubleday, 1984.

Falkner, David. *The Last Hero: The Life of Mickey Mantle*. New York: Simon & Schuster, 1995.

Falkof, Lucille. *Helen Gurley Brown: The Queen of Cosmopolitan*. New York: Garrett Educational, Wizards of Business Series, 1992.

Fitz Lyon, April. *Lorenzo da Ponte, A Biography of Mozart's Librettist*. New York: Riverrun, 1982.

Fonteyn, Margot. *Fonteyn: Autobiography*. New York: Knopf, 1976.

Forbes, Esther. *Paul Revere and the World He Lived in*. Boston: Houghton Mifflin, 1942.

Ford, Gerald R. *A Time to Heal*. New York: Harper & Row, 1979.

Fordin, Hugh. *Getting to Know Him: A Biography of Oscar Hammerstein II*. New York: Random House, 1977.

Franklin, Benjamin. *Autobiography of Benjamin Franklin*. New York: Harper & Bros, 1956.

Fraser, Antonia (ed.). *Love Letters*. New York: Knopf, 1977.

Freedman, Russell. *Jules Verne: Portrait of a Prophet*. New York: Holiday House, 1965.

Freud, Ernst (ed.). *The Letters of Sigmund Freud.* London: McGraw-Hill, 1960.

Funke, Lewis. *The Curtain Rises: The Story of Ossie Davis.* New York: The New York Times Company and Grosset & Dunlap, 1971.

Gehrig, Eleanor, with Joseph Durso. *My Luke and I.* New York: Crowell, 1976.

Geison, Gerald. *The Private Life of Louis Pasteur.* Princeton, NJ: Princeton University Press, 1995.

Gerin, Winifred. *Elizabeth Gaskell: A Biography.* New York: Oxford University at Clarendon Press, 1976.

Gill, Gillian. *Agatha Christie: The Woman and Her Mysteries.* New York: Free Press, 1990.

Goldman, Albert. *Elvis.* New York: McGraw-Hill, 1981.

Goldwater, Barry. *With No Apologies: The Personal and Political Memoirs of United States Senator Barry Goldwater.* New York: William Morrow, 1979.

Gonzales, Doreen. *Madeleine L'Engle, Author of A Wrinkle in Time.* New York: Dillon, 1991.

Gordon, Lyndall. *Charlotte Brontë.* New York: W. W. Norton, 1994.

Greenfield, Howard. *Caruso.* New York: Putnam, 1983.

————. *F. Scott Fitzgerald.* New York: Crown, 1994.

Gresham, William L. *Houdini: The Man Who Walked Through Walls.* New York: Henry Holt, 1959.

Gridley, Marion E. *American Indian Women.* New York: Hawthorn, 1974.

Griswold Del Castillo, Richard, and Richard A. Garcia. *Cesar Chavez: A Triumph of Spirit.* Norman, OK: University of Oklahoma Press, 1995.

Gruber, Frank. *Zane Grey.* New York: World, 1970.

Guinness, Sir Alec. *Blessings in Disguise.* New York: Knopf, 1986.

Hanna, Bill, and Tom Ito. *A Cast of Friends.* Dallas: Taylor, 1996.

Harris, Michael D. *Always on Sunday: Ed Sullivan, An Inside View.* New York: Meredith, 1968.

Hart, Kitty Carlisle. *Kitty: An Autobiography.* New York: Doubleday, 1988.

Hayes, Helen. *Helen Hayes: On Reflection.* New York: M. Evans, 1968.

Heckscher, August. *Woodrow Wilson, A Biography.* New York: Scribner, 1991.

Henry, Arthur, and Alfred Hill. *Antonio Stradivari: His Life and Work.* New York: Dover, 1963.

Hermann, Dorothy. *A Gift for Life: Anne Morrow Lindbergh.* New York: Ticknor & Fields, 1993.

Hersey, John. *Antonietta.* New York: Vintage Books, 1991.

Herzstein, Robert. *Henry Robinson Luce: A Political Portrait of the Man Who Created the American Century.* New York: Scribner, 1994.

Higonnet, Anne. *Berthe Morisot*. New York: Harper & Row, 1990.

Hillary, Sir Edmund. *Nothing Venture, Nothing Win*. New York: Coward, McCann & Geoghegan, 1975.

Hobson, Fred. *Mencken: A Life*. New York: Random House, 1994.

Hodges, Sheila. *Lorenzo da Ponte: The Life and Times of Mozart's Librettist*. London: Granada, 1985.

Holmes, Charles S. *The Clocks of Columbus: The Literary Career of James Thurber*. New York: Atheneum, 1972.

Horowitz, Sylvia L. *The Find of a Lifetime: Sir Arthur Evans and the Discovery of Knossos*. New York: Viking, 1981.

Hotchner, A. E. *Sophia: Living and Loving—Her Own Story*. New York: William Morrow, 1979.

Howard, Leon. *Herman Melville: A Biography*. Los Angeles: University of California Press, 1951.

Hubbard, Elbert. *The Story of the Steinways*. East Aurora, NY: Roycrofters, 1939.

Hyams, Joe. *Bogart & Bacall: A Love Story*. New York: David McKay, 1975.

Jellison, Charles A. *Ethan Allen, Frontier Rebel*. Taftsville, VT: Countryman, 1969.

Johnson, Osa Leighty. *I Married Adventure*. New York: Lippincott, 1940.

Kaplan, Daile. *Lewis Hine in Europe: The Lost Photographs*. New York: Abbeville, 1988.

Kendrick, Alexander. *Prime Time: The Life of Edward R. Murrow*. Boston: Little Brown, 1969.

Klee, Felix. *Paul Klee*. New York: George Braziller, 1962.

Klein, Mina, and H. Arthur Klein. *Käthe Kollwitz: A Life in Art*. New York: Holt, Rinehart & Winston, 1972.

Kollwitz, Hans (ed.). *The Diary and Letters of Käthe Kollwitz*. Evanston, IL: Northwestern University Press, 1988.

LaCouture, Jean. *DeGaulle, The Rebel 1890–1944*. New York: Norton, 1990.

Latham, Frank B. *A Century of Serving Customers, 1872–1972: The Story of Montgomery Ward*. Chicago: Montgomery Ward, 1972.

Laver, James. *Whistler*. New York: J. J. Little & Ives, Cosmopolitan Book Co., 1930.

L'Engle, Madeleine. *Two-Part Invention: The Story of a Marriage*. New York: Farrar, Straus, & Giroux, 1988.

Lengyel, Emil. *All Her Paths Were Peace*. New York: Thomas Nelson, 1975.

Levy, Jacques. *Cesar Chavez: Autobiography of La Causa*. New York: W. W. Norton, 1975.

Lindbergh, Anne Morrow. *Hour of Gold, Hour of Lead: 1929–1932*. New York: Harcourt Brace Jovanovich, 1973.

Longford, Elizabeth. *The Pebbled Shore: The Memoirs of Elizabeth Longford.* New York: Knopf, 1986.

Magarshack, David. *Chekhov: A Life.* London: Faber & Faber, 1952.

Mallowan, Max. *Memoirs.* New York: Dodd, Mead, 1977.

Manfull, Helen. *Additional Dialogue: Letters of Dalton Trumbo.* New York: M. Evans, 1970.

Mantle, Mickey, with Herb Gluck. *The Mick.* Garden City, NY: Doubleday, 1985.

Maraniss, David. *First in His Class: A Biography of Bill Clinton.* New York: Simon & Schuster, 1995.

Marek, George. *Gentle Genius: The Story of Felix Mendelssohn.* New York: Funk & Wagnalls, 1972.

Markus, Julia. *Dared & Done: The Marriage of Elizabeth Barrett and Robert Browning.* New York: Knopf, 1995.

Martin, Mary. *My Heart Belongs.* New York: William Morrow, 1976.

Mazlish, Bruce, and Edwin Diamond. *Jimmy Carter: An Interpretive Biography.* New York: Simon & Schuster, 1979.

McAdoo, Eleanor Wilson (ed.). *The Priceless Gift: The Love Letters of Woodrow Wilson & Ellen Axson Wilson.* New York: McGraw-Hill, 1962.

McCabe, John. *Charlie Chaplin.* Garden City, NY: Doubleday, 1978.

McCullough, David. *Truman.* New York: Simon & Schuster, 1992.

Mee, Charles L. *Rembrandt's Portrait: A Biography.* New York: Simon & Schuster, 1988.

Mellon, James. *Nathaniel Hawthorne in His Time.* Boston: Houghton Mifflin, 1980.

Milford, Nancy. *Zelda: A Biography.* New York: Harper Perennial, 1992.

Miller, Edwin Haviland. *Melville: A Biography.* New York: George Braziller, 1975.

————. *Salem Is My Dwelling Place: A Life of Nathaniel Hawthorne.* Iowa City: University of Iowa Press, 1991.

Milton, Joyce. *Loss of Eden: A Biography of Charles and Anne Morrow Lindbergh.* New York: HarperCollins, 1993.

Morgan, Judith and Neil. *Dr. Seuss & Mr. Geisel: A Biography.* New York: Random House, 1995.

Moses, Grandma. *Grandma Moses: My Life's History.* New York: Harper & Bros., 1952.

Moutoussamy-Ashe, Jeanne. *Daddy and Me: A Photo Story of Arthur Ashe and his daughter, Camera.* New York: Knopf, 1993.

Nelson, Ozzie. *Ozzie.* Englewood Cliffs, NJ: Prentice-Hall, 1973.

Niven, Penelope. *Carl Sandburg: A Biography.* New York: Scribner, 1991.

Norman, Winifred Latimer, and Lily Patterson. *Lewis Latimer.* New York: Chelsea House, Black Americans of Achievement, 1994.

Oakley, Meredith. *On The Make: The Rise of Bill Clinton*. Washington, D.C.: Regnery, 1994.

Oates, Stephen. *Let the Trumpet Sound: The Life of Martin Luther King*. New York: Harper & Row, 1982.

Ogden, Chris. *Maggie: An Intimate Portrait of a Woman in Power*. New York: Simon & Schuster, 1990.

Okada, Amina, and M. C. Joshi. *Taj Mahal*. New York: Abbeville, 1993.

Packwood, Cyril Outerbridge. *Detour—Bermuda, Destination—US House of Representatives: The life of Joseph Rainey*. Bermuda: Baxter's, 1977.

Paper, Lewis J. *Brandeis*. Englewood Cliffs, NJ: Prentice-Hall, 1983.

Parini, Jay. *John Steinbeck: A Biography*. New York: Henry Holt, 1995.

Payne, Darwin. *Owen Wister: Chronicler of the West, Gentleman of the East*. Dallas: Southern Methodist University Press, 1985.

Payne, Robert. *The Gold of Troy*. New York: Funk & Wagnalls, 1959.

Pearson, Hesketh. *Sir Walter Scott: His Life and Personality*. New York: Harper & Bros., 1954.

Persico, Joseph E. *Edward R. Murrow: An American Original*. New York: McGraw-Hill, 1988.

Pfalum, Rosalynd. *Grand Obsession: Marie Curie and Her World*. New York: Doubleday, 1989.

Phillips-Matz, Mary Jane. *Verdi: A Biography*. London and New York: Oxford University Press, 1993.

Presley, Priscilla Beaulieu, with Sandra Harmon. *Elvis & Me*. New York: Putnam, 1985.

Radcliffe, Donnie. *Hillary Rodham Clinton: A First Lady for Our Time*. New York: Warner, 1993.

Randall, Ruth P. *I Ruth: Autobiography of a Marriage*. Boston: Little Brown, 1968.

Robinson, Roxana. *Georgia O'Keeffe: A Life*. New York: Harper & Row, 1989.

Rogers, Pat. *Henry Fielding*. New York: Scribner, 1979.

Rogers, William Garland. *Carl Sandburg, Yes*. New York: Harcourt Brace Jovanovich, 1970.

Rosenblum, Naomi. *A World History of Photography*. New York: Abbeville, 1984.

Ross, Ishbel. *Silhouette in Diamonds: The Life of Mrs. Potter Palmer*. New York: Harper, 1960.

Sandburg, Maxine Sylvia. *The Life and Career of Adolphus Busch*. Austin, TX: University of Texas Press, 1951.

Saxon, A. H. *The Life & Art of Andrew Ducrow and the Romantic Age of the English Circus*. Hamden, CT: Archon, 1978.

Schiff, Stacy. *Saint-Exupéry: A Biography*. New York: Knopf, 1994.

Schonberg, Harold C. *The Lives of the Great Composers*. New York: W. W. Norton, 1970.

Seaman, Barbara. *Lovely Me: The Life of Jacqueline Susann*. New York: William Morrow, 1987.

Shaffer, Karen, and Neva Greenwood. *Maud Powell, Pioneer American Violinist*. Ames, IA: Iowa State University Press, 1988.

Sheed, Wilfrid. *Clare Boothe Luce*. New York: Dutton, 1982.

Shivers, Alfred S. *Jessamyn West*. New York: Twayne, 1972.

Singer, Mark. "Goody." *The New Yorker*, Vol LIII, #7, April 4, 1977, p. 64 ff.

Smith, Cynthia. *What Has She Got?* New York: Donald Fine, 1991.

Smith, Linnell Nash. *Loving Letters from Ogden Nash: A Family Album*. Boston: Little Brown, 1990.

Snyder, Kerala J. *Dietrich Buxtehude, Organist in Lubeck*. New York: Schirmer, 1987.

Spada, James. *Grace: The Secret Lives of a Princess*. New York: Doubleday, 1987.

Spivey, Richard L. *Maria*. Flagstaff, AZ: Northland Press, 1989.

Spoto, Donald. *Lenya*. Boston: Little Brown, 1989.

Stasz, Clarice. *American Dreamers: Charmian & Jack London*. New York: St. Martins, 1988.

Steinbeck, Elaine, and Robert Wallstein (eds.). *Steinbeck: A Life in Letters*. New York: Viking, 1995.

Stern, Jane, and Michael Stern. *Happy Trails: Our Life Story by Roy Rogers & Dale Evans*. New York: Simon & Schuster, 1994.

Stone, Irving. *Clarence Darrow for the Defense*. Garden City, NY: Doubleday, 1969.

Strauss, Richard. *Recollections & Reflections*. London: Boosey & Hawkes, 1949.

Swindell, Larry. *Charles Boyer: The Reluctant Lover*. Garden City, NY: Doubleday, 1983.

Taylor, Judy, et al. *Beatrix Potter: The Artist and Her World*. London: F. Warne and National Trust of London, 1987.

Teveth, Shabbtai. *Ben-Gurion: The Burning Ground 1896–1948*. Boston: Houghton Mifflin, 1987.

Thomas, Bob. *Bud & Lou: The Abbott and Costello Story*. Philadelphia: Lippincott, 1971.

Thomas, Danny. *Make Room for Danny*. New York: Putnam, 1991.

Thompson, Lawrence. *Robert Frost: The Early Years*. New York: Holt Rinehart & Winston, 1966.

Thurber, Helen, and Edward Weeks (eds.). *Selected Letters of James Thurber*. Boston: Atlantic Monthly Press of Little Brown, 1980.

Thwaite, Ann. *A. A. Milne: The Man Behind Winnie the Pooh*. New York: Random House, 1990.

Tierney, Kevin. *Darrow, A Biography*. New York: Crowell, 1979.

Traeger, Jorg (ed.). *Caspar David Friedrich*. New York: Rizzoli, 1976.

Trapp, Maria Augusta. *The Story of the Trapp Family Singers*. Philadelphia: Lippincott, 1949.

Truman, Margaret. *Bess W. Truman*. New York: Macmillan, 1986.

Turnbull, Andrew. *Scott Fitzgerald*. New York: Scribner, 1962.

Vestal, Bud. *Jerry Ford, Up Close*. New York: Coward, McCann & Geoghegan, 1974.

von Gelder, Lawrence. "Fritz and Ingeborg Kahlenberg, Dutch Wartime Photographers." Obituary in the *New York Times*, October 23, 1996.

Wagenknecht, Edward. *James Russell Lowell*. New York: Oxford University Press, 1971.

Waife-Goldberg, Marie. *My Father, Sholom Aleichem*. New York: Simon & Schuster, 1968.

Walker, Frank. *The Man Verdi*. New York: Knopf, 1962.

Wallace, Irving, and Amy Wallace. *The Two: A Biography*. New York: Simon & Schuster, 1978.

Watkins, Floyd, and John Hiers (eds.). *Robert Penn Warren: Talking*. New York: Random House, 1980.

Wayne, Jane Ellen. *Gable's Women*. Englewood Cliffs, NJ: Prentice-Hall, 1987.

Wechsberg, Joseph. *Verdi*. New York: Putnam, 1974.

Weinberg, Arthur and Lila. *Clarence Darrow: A Sentimental Rebel*. New York: Atheneum, 1987.

Welk, Lawrence, with Bernice McGeehan. *Wunnerful, Wunnerful! The Autobiography of Lawrence Welk*. Englewood Cliffs, NJ: Prentice-Hall, 1971.

West, Jessamyn. *The Woman Said Yes: Memoirs*. New York: Harcourt Brace Jovanovich, 1976.

Westheimer, Ruth, and Ben Yagoda. *All in a Lifetime: An Autobiography*. New York: Warner, 1987.

Westman, Paul. *John Glenn: Around the World in 90 Minutes*. Minneapolis: Dillon, 1980.

White, Christopher. *Peter Paul Rubens*. New Haven, CT: Yale University Press, 1987.

Widener, Don. *Lemmon: A Biography*. New York: Macmillan, 1975.

Wilder, Laura Ingalls. *The First Four Years*. New York: Harper & Row, 1971.

Williams, Charles. *The Last Great Frenchman: A Life of General de Gaulle*. New York: John Wiley, 1993.

Williams, Chester. *Gable*. New York: Fleet Press, 1968.

Williams, John Hoyt. *Sam Houston: A Biography of the Father of Texas*. New York: Simon & Schuster, 1993.

Willis, Resa. *Mark & Livy: The Love Story of Mark Twain and the Woman Who Almost Tamed Him.* New York: Atheneum, 1992.

Windeler, Robert. *Julie Andrews: A Biography.* New York: St. Martins, 1983.

Wyeth, Betsy (ed.). *The Wyeths.* Boston: Gambit, 1971.

Young, Hugo. *The Iron Lady: A Biography of Margaret Thatcher.* New York: Farrar, Straus & Giroux, 1989.

Youngman, Henny. *Take My Life, Please!* New York: William Morrow, 1991.

Zee, Donald. *Sophia.* New York: David McKay, 1975.

Zolotow, Maurice. *Stagestruck: The Romance of Alfred Lunt and Lynn Fontanne.* New York: Harcourt Brace & World, 1964.

NOVEMBER: Photograph of Princess Elizabeth and Philip, Duke of Edinburgh, exiting Westminster Abbey. Provided by UPI/Corbis-Bettmann.

DECEMBER: Photograph of Georgia O'Keeffe and Alfred Stieglitz, taken by Josephine B. Marks, as published in *Stieglitz: A Memoir/Biography*, by Sue Davidson Lowe. Farrar, Straus & Giroux, 1983. By permission of Sue Davidson Lowe.

# I N D E X

DELANCEY, Susan—January 1
DENT, Julia—August 22
DICKSON, Harry Ellis—October 13
DIGBY, Sir Kenelm—January 13
DISNEY, Walt—July 13
DONCIEUX, Camille—June 26
DONNE, John—December 8
DOSTOYEVSKY, Fyodor—
    February 15
DOUD, Mary Geneva—July 1
DOYLE, Sir Arthur Conan—
    September 18
DRISCOLL, Marian—August 31
DUCKWORTH, Alice Hammond—
    March 21
DUCKWORTH, Julia Prinsep—
    March 26
DUCROW, Andrew—May 24
DUDLEY, Anne—March 24
DUFFUS, Susan—February 4
DU MAURIER, Daphne—July 19
DURANT, Will—October 31
DWIGHT, Sarah—March 1
DYKE, Elizabeth—March 25
EARHART, Amelia—February 7
EASTMAN, Linda—March 12
EDISON, Thomas Alva—February 24
EDWARD, Duke of Windsor—June 3
EDWARD III, King of England—
    January 24
EDWARD, THE BLACK PRINCE—
    October 10
EDWARD THE CONFESSOR—
    January 23
EDWARDS, Blake—November 12
EDYTHA, Princess—November 11
EIFFEL, Gustave—July 8

EISENHOWER, Dwight David—July 1
ELDRIDGE, Florence—May 30
ELIZABETH of Bavaria—April 24
ELIZABETH, Princess of England—
    February 13
ELIZABETH, Princess of the United
    Kingdom—November 20
ELSTON, Susan Arnold—May 6
EMERSON, Ralph Waldo—
    September 14
EMMA of Normandy—July 30
ENGASTROMENOS, Sophia—
    September 24
EPSTEIN, Jane—November 16
EVANS, Arthur—September 26
EVANS, Dale—December 31
EVE—February 29
FABELA, Helen—October 22
FANSHAWE, Sir Richard—May 18
FARR, Felicia—August 15
FELLINI, Federico—October 30
FIELDING, Henry—November 28
FINCH, Heneage—May 31
FINCHER, Cleo Beth—March 13
FINDLAY, Polly—August 19
FISHER, Marie—February 28
FISHER, Orpheus—July 24
FITZGERALD, F. Scott—April 3
FOLSOM, Frances—June 2
FONTANNE, Lynn—May 26
FONTEYN, Margot—February 6
FOOTE, Irene—May 28
FORD, Gerald R.—October 15
FOSTER, Josephine—February 23
FOURMENT, Helena—December 6
FRAGONARD, Jean-Honoré—
    June 17

# Wedding Days of Family and Friends

COUPLES' NAMES

WEDDING DAY

_____     _____

_____     _____

_____     _____

_____     _____

_____     _____

_____     _____

_____     _____

_____     _____

_____     _____

_____     _____

_____     _____

_____     _____

_____     _____

_____     _____

_____     _____

_____     _____

# Wedding Days of Family and Friends

COUPLES' NAMES                                          WEDDING DAY

_____          _____

_____          _____

_____          _____

_____          _____

_____          _____

_____          _____

_____          _____

_____          _____

_____          _____

_____          _____

_____          _____

_____          _____

_____          _____

_____          _____

_____          _____

# Wedding Days of Family and Friends

COUPLES' NAMES                                    WEDDING DAY

_____    _____

_____    _____

_____    _____

_____    _____

_____    _____

_____    _____

_____    _____

_____    _____

_____    _____

_____    _____

_____    _____

_____    _____

_____    _____

_____    _____

_____    _____

_____    _____

DEAR READER:

Can you suggest other "great couples in history"?
Susan J. Gordon would love to hear from you.

Write to her c/o William Morrow and Company, Inc.
1350 Avenue of the Americas
New York, N.Y. 10019

Provide as much of the following information as possible
regarding each couple:

- Husband's name

- Husband's birth date

- Wife's maiden name and former name(s)
  (if previously married)

- Wife's birth date

- Couple's wedding date and place

- Couple's nationalities

- Where the couple lived

- Couple's achievements
  (what did they do that makes you admire them?)

- Sources of your information